D1879465

DALITS IN EARLY BUDDHISM

DALITS IN EARLY BUDDHISM

Paramanshi Jaideva

KALPAZ PUBLICATIONS
Delhi–110 052

DALITS IN EARLY BUDDHISM

(Dalit, History, Buddhism)

Rs. 890

© Paramanshi Jaideva

ISBN: 81-7835-122-6

All rights reserved. No part of this book may be reproduced in any manner without written permission

Published in 2002 in India by
Kalpaz Publications
C–30, Satyawati Nagar
Delhi–110 052
E-mail: kalpaz@hotmail.com

Lasertypesetting at: Varsha Graphics, Delhi
Printed at: Chawla Offset

Contents

Preface

The rules and regulations governing social life and individual conduct differed according to the orders in society, only the four 'varnas' being taken into account by the law-givers. The origin of these four classes in most of the later works with slight variations and interpretative additions. The pre-eminence of the Brahmin had secured him numerous social privileges. According to Gantama, all varnas must serve their superiors; which meant that the Brahmin, as the most superior among the varnas, was entitled to the services of the others.

The theme has been weaved into ten comprehensive chapters, along with a bibliography have deep bearing on ancient caste system, socio-economic position of Sudras in the society, the effectiveness of Brahmanism and Buddhism in the life of Sudras, the general concept of untouchability before the advent of Buddhism, untouchable as mentioned and elaborated in the Pali text and the plan, programme, efforts and the success achieved by Buddhist religion in connection with the abolition of untouchability. The last Chapter on evaluation and conclusion deal with the liberalising influence of the Buddhist revolt and of Vaishnava compassion leading the Brahmins to devise ways and means of assuring spiritual betterment to the Sudra in the Brahminic ways of rites and sacraments. It is evident that the performance of the Brahminic rites and sacraments by a large section of the people had a selfish interest for the Brahmin, which he could not have entirely lost sight off. In fact the religious rites and sacraments required the services of a Brahmin. If the Sudras wanted to perform the Brahmanic rites and sacraments. They would invariably have to requisition the services of a Brahmin.

The present study analyses the general beliefs of the Buddha who unquestionably was a great social reformer for all human beings and that his efforts for the emancipation of women and lower castes created a sort of social revolution in Indian society.

The occupational classification led to the ideal theory of castes which earmarked certain duties as the authorised modes of gaining livelihood and were generally peculiar to each caste and ordinarily forbidden to the others. The Brahmin must subsist on teaching and officiating as priest at the sacrifice of the castes that were entitled to offer such religious worship and by accepting gifts. The Kshatriya was to live by administration and the profession of arms. Similarly, agriculture, trade and pastorial pursuits were to the exploited by the Vaisya, while the one occupation prescribed for the Sudra was service of the other castes. The idea then an impure person imparts pollution by his touch and even by his near approach to a member of the first three castes finds definite expression in the law-texts of this period.

Paramanshi Jaideva

Acknowledgements

I am greatly indebted to Dr. Jaideva Mishra (Reader, Deptt. of A.I.H. and Archaeology, Patna University, Patna) for his kind supervision and valuable guidance in completion of this research work. His inspiration to me for selection of research topics and also research work during the period of given times came into existence with more extended patience in scene of analyzing and conceptual thought relating to position of the Sudras as revealed through the Pali texts.

I am thankful to Dr. B.P. Roy, Head of Department, A.I.H. and Archaeology, Patna University, whose initial concept concerned with given research work that has been undertaken into account for completion of research during the period of research work.

I cannot forget the versatile teachers such as Dr. A.K. Singh and others, Deptt. of A.I.H. and Archaeology, Patna University, for their inspiring attitude.

I am very much obliged to my dearest husband Dr. Sanjay Paswan, M.P., whose cooperation might be accounted for completing such research work.

I am very much indebted to my father-in-law Sri Mahabir Ram and mother-in-law Smt. Krishna Devi, for their encouraging attitude during the completion of the present research work.

I am also very much thankful to my parents Sri Rajeshwar Prasad and Smt. Pushpa Prasad for their inspiration.

I also thank my brother-in-law Dr. Yogendra Prasad, for his cooperation. In addition, I cannot forget love and affection of my niece Miss Rachna Ranjan.

Paramanshi Jaideva

1

Ancient Caste System

The present chapter reveals the introductory idea on division of caste system during the ancient period. In the Rigveda, the earliest literature of the first period, three classes of society are very frequently mentioned, and named Brahma, Kshatra, and Viś. The first two represented broadly the two professions of the poet-priest and the warrior-chief. The third division was apparently a group comprising all the common people. It is only in one of the later hymns, the celebrated Purushasūkta, that a reference has been made to four orders of society as emanating from the sacrifice of the Primeval Being. The names of those four orders are given there as Brāhmana, Rājanya, Vaiśya, and Sūdra, who are said to have come respectively from the mouth, the arms, the thighs, and the feet of the Creator. The particular limbs associated with these divisions and the order in which they are mentioned probably indicate their status in the society of the time, though no such interpretation is directly given in the hymn.

The origin of these four classes is repeated in most of the later works with slight variations and interpretative additions. The Taittirīya Saṁhitā, for example, ascribes the origins of the four classes to the four limbs of the Creator and adds an explanation. The Brahmins are declared to be the chief because they were created from the mouth, punning on the word "mukha" ("mouth" and "chief"). The Rājanyas are vigorous because they were created from vigour. The Vaiśyas are meant to be eaten, referring to their liability to excessive taxation, because they were created from the stomach, the receptacle of food. The Śūdra, because he was created from the feet, is to be the transporter of others and to subsist by the feet. In this particular account of the creation not only is the origin of the classes interpreted theologically, but also a divine justification is sought to be given to their functions and status. The creation-theory is further amplified here to account for certain other features of these social classes. God is said to have created certain deities simultaneously with these classes. The Vaiśya class, the commoners, must have been naturally very large, and this account explains that social fact by a reference to the simultaneous creation of Viśvadevas, all and sundry deities, whose number is considerable. We are told that no deities were created along with the Śūdra and hence he is disqualified for sacrifice. Here again, the social regulation which forbade a Śūdra to offer sacrifice is explained as an incidental consequence of the creation.[1]

The fact that the four classes are described as of divine origin, although in a later hymn, must be taken as a sufficient indication that they were of long duration and very well-defined, even though the exact demarcation of their functions, the regulations guiding their interrelations, and the extent of their flexibility may not be referred to in the main body of the Rigvedic literature, which is avowedly of a liturgical nature.

The Śátapatha Brāhmana lays down different sizes of the funeral mound for the four classes. The terms of address are also different, varying in the degree of politeness. In the "Human Sacrifice" the representatives of these orders are dedicated to different deities. A passage in the Aitareya Brahmana warns a Kṣhatriya to avoid certain mistakes in the sacrificial ritual. If he commits a particular mistake, it goes on to say, "one like a Brahmin shall be born in his line who in the second or third generation from his has the power of becoming a Brahmin, and likes to live as a Brahmin." Similarly for two other mistakes he shall have a Vaiśya-like Ren and a Sūdra-like son capable of becoming a full-fledged Vaiśya or Sūdra in two or three generations. It is clear, that though the classes had come to be almost stereotyped by the end of the Vedic period, it was not altogether impossible for an upward or downward change to occur in a particular family in two or three generations.[2]

The third order in society, namely the Vaiśya, figures singularly little in Vedic literature. The Aitareya Brāhmana describes him as a tributary to another, "to be lived upon by another," and "to be suppressed at will." Representing the common people, both the composition and the functions of this class are shadowy. According to the Taittirīya Saṁhitā, the greatest ambition of a Vaiśya was to be the "Grāmanī" or the village headman. "The son of a Vaiśya woman is never anointed a king," so says the Śatapatha Brāhmana.[3] Though, in comparison to the higher classes, the Vaiśyas' position was rather insignificant, yet the class was definitely marked off from the Sūdras.

The name of the fourth class, the Śūdra, occurs only once in the Rigveda. It seems the class represented domestic servants, approximating very nearly to the position of slaves. The Śūdra is described as "the servant of another," "to be expelled at will," and "to be slain at will." The Pānchavimśa Brāhmana defines this position still more precisely when it declares that the Śūdra, even if he be prosperous, cannot but be a servant of another, washing his superior's feet being his main business. Yet according to the same work some of the king's ministers were Śūdras. The milk to be used for fire-oblation was not allowed to be milked by a Śūdra. He was not to be addressed by a person consecrated for a sacrifice. He is declared to be unfit for sacrifice and not allowed even to be present in the hall where the sacrifice was being offered. The Śátapatha Brāhmana goes to the length of declaring that the Śūdra is untruth itself.[4] Illicit connection between an Ārya male and a Śūdra female is mentioned, and the uneasiness felt by the Śūdra husband whose wife is a mistress of an Ārya is also hinted at.[5] In this connection we may mention that Vasishtha quotes a Brāhmana text to the effect that a woman of the black race, meaning the Śūdra people, was meant only for enjoyment and not for furtherance of any higher motives.[6]

In the Rigveda a marked distinction was drawn between the Ārya and the Dāsa. In the later Vedic literature this demarcation tends to be drawn between the Ārya and the Śūdra, who is being described as of dark colour. As if to preserve the memory of this change, as a part of sacrificial rites a mock fight between an Ārya and Śūdra, in which the former necessarily wins, is prescribed. This change is perhaps due to the increasing association between the Aryan people and the Indian aborigines resulting in illicit unions not only between Ārya males and Śūdra females but also between Śūdra men and Ārya women.

Besides the four orders are mentioned in the Rigveda, occupations like blacksmith, leather-worker, barber, physician, goldsmith, merchant, and chariot-builder. We do not know which of these occupations were comprised in any of the four orders, nor can we say that each of them constituted a separate class. We know for certain that status of the Rāthakāra—the chariot-builder—was high enough to preclude his being classified with the Śūdras. The formulae for placing the sacrificial fire include one for the Rāthakāra, indicating his high status even in religious matters.

A great consolidation of the position of the Brahmin class, while the degradation of the Śūdras comes out in marked contrast to the growing superiority of the Brahmins. The discomfiture of the Kṣhatriya is complete, and the Vaiśyas, at least the general mass, have progressively approximated to the Śūdras. The first indication of the appreciation of the Brahmin's position is to be found in the implication underlying the sacred law that in strictness its dictates are meant primarily for the Brahmin. Vasishtha quotes some Vedic texts to inculcate the view that a Brahmin is born with three debts, viz., to the Gods, to the manes, and to the sages. The discharge of these debts was to be achieved through sacrifices, progeny, and Vedic studies. These are fulfilled through the life of a student and of a householder. According to the philosophy of life current in this period, these debts should have been common to the Kṣhatriya and the Vaiśya, yet it is only the Brahmin that is singled out as pre-eminently the one *varṇa* on whom the discharge of these debts was incumbent. The three lower castes are ordered to live according to the teachings of the Brahmin, who shall declare their duties, while the king is exhorted to regulate their conduct accordingly.[7]

The importance of sacrifices and ritualism had been growing and with it the prestige of the priest. The privilege of officiating at sacrificial sessions and other religious rites was exclusively preserved as a divinely appointed and hereditary function of the Brahmins. As the monopolist of ritual procedure, the Brahmin naturally became important. In another way also, he gained in respect because he fulfilled a very fundamental function in the general philosophy of life of these times. As the *Mahābhārata* has it, "sacrifice sustains both the manes and the gods,"[8] and the Brahmin alone could ensure the proper performance of sacrifices. He was further represented as very beneficial to the political head of the society. Vasishṭha quotes a Vedic text, declaring that the king obtains the sixth part of the merit which Brahmins accumulate by means of their sacrifices and good work.[9] Gifts had been praised since the Vedic times, and in the literature of this period, they were enjoined as a moral duty, the performance of which brought merit to the giver. "He who, places on the skin of a black antelope, sesamum, gold, honey, and butter, gives it to a Brahmin overcomes all sin."[10] Āpastamba declares that a king, who without prejudice to his servants gives land and money to deserving Brahmins, gains endless heavenly worlds. The Brahmin alone could rightfully accept the gifts. As a channel of easy acquisition of merit he thus gained added importance. "The offering made through the mouth of a Brahmin, which is neither split nor causes pain (to sentient creature) nor assails him (who makes it), is far more excellent than an *agnihotra*."[11] All these circumstances and growing unintelligibility of the scriptural language conspired to make the Brahmin almost a god on earth. The pre-eminence of the Brahmin was so great that the *Mahābhārata* declared that really speaking there was only one "varṇa", viz., the Brahmin and the other varṇas were merely its modifications.[12] Though Gautama quotes the Vedic texts which declare that the Kṣhatriya assisted by the Brahmin prosper, and that the union of the two alone upholds the moral order, yet he lays down that when a king and a Brahmin pass along the same road, the road belongs to the Brahmin and not to the king.[13] Vasishṭha declares that the Brahmin's King is Soma.[14] The *Mahābhārata* goes even further, and emphasizes the subordinate position of the Kṣhatriya, whose only support is pronounced to be the Brahmin. It explains away earthly sovereignty of the Kṣhatriya by a social analogy. Just as a widow takes to her deceased husband's brother, so has the earth resorted to the Kṣhatriya in default of the Brahmin. Between a hundred year old Kṣhatriya and a ten year old Brahmin the latter is said to be like the father.[15] And this was present in a society where age was the greatest consideration for respect.[16] The superiority of a child-Brahmin over an aged Kṣhatriya is also supported by Āpastamba.[17] It is thus clear that the union of the Brahmin and the Kṣhatriya that was advocated by Gautama must be understood to mean not an alliance between two equals but a tacit domination of the former over the latter.

This pre-eminence of the Brahmin had secured him many social privileges. According to Gautama, all varṇas must serve their superiors,[18] which meant that the Brahmin, as the most superior among the varṇas, was entitled to the services of the others. Naturally the Brahmin recognized no teacher who was not a member of his varṇa. It was only in times of distress that he was allowed to study under a non-Brahmin teacher, whom he surpassed in venerability on the completion of his studies.[19] This was against the general notions of respectability according to which the teacher must always be venerated by his pupils. The Brahmin might follow no gainful activity, yet as long as he continued the study of the Vedas, he was said to have fulfilled his purpose.[20] The Brahmin was exempt from the usual taxes.[21] If a Brahmin, who followed his lawful occupations, found a treasure, he had not to hand it over to the king.[22] Both the person and the property of the Brahmin were absolutely inviolate. Stealing the gold of a Brahmin and killing a Brahmin were regarded as heinous sins *(Mahāpātaka)*.[23] Raising one's hand or weapon in anger against a Brahmin, actually striking him, causing blood to flow from his body, unintentionally killing him, and wilfully murdering him were offences in the ascending order of their heinousness.[24] Wilful murder of a Brahmin was, of course, inexpiable. The Brahmin was exempt from corporal punishment.[25] The estate of heirless persons of the Kṣhatriya, Vaiśya and Śūdra varṇas went to the king, who had to distribute it among learned Brahmins, while the estate of an heirless Brahmin belonged directly to them.[26] The property of a Brahmin is described as the worst poison destroying him who takes it.[27] On the other hand, in order to defray the expenses of a marriage or of a religious rite, he may take the money of a Śūdra by fraud or by force. He may take the same with the property of those members of the other varṇas who neglect their religious duties.[28] Even to accuse a Brahmin of crime that he might have committed is a sin.[29] He must not be forced to be a witness at the instance of a non-Brahmin unless he is already mentioned in the plaint.[30] Even as regards the highly lauded and essential duty of a householder, viz., hospitality, the Brahmin has his privileges. He need not treat a non-Brahmin as his guest unless he comes on the occasion of a sacrifice.[31]

Though the various privileges of the Brahmin are sanctioned by the lawgivers, they insist from time to time that the Brahmin shall keep to the moral discipline of his class and conscientiously perform the duties laid down for him. They declare that a Brahmin who deviates from this path is equal to a Śūdra and as such there can be no harm in neglecting him.[32]

The statement that God created the Śūdra to be the slave of all is repeated and he is given the name "pādaja" (born from the feet). He is to be supported, to be fed, to be clothed with the remnants and castaways of food and raiment by the three varṇas.[33] He is contrasted with the Ārya, who, though younger than he, must be respected by him by rising from his seat.[34] Whereas in the Vedic period, as we have seen, the Dāsa was described as the black race, in this period the Śūdra is given that appellation.[35] Vasishṭha relegates him to the burial ground. The Veda must not be recited in his presence, no advice must be given to him, nor the remnants of the offerings to the gods. Holy law must not be expounded to him, nor must he be asked to perform a penance.[36] He shall use the old shoes, discarded garments, etc., of the members of the other varṇas, and eat the leavings of their food.[37] So great was the feeling against the Śūdra performing a sacrifice that Gautama exhorted a person to cast off his father if he either sacrificed with the money given by a Śūdra or officiated at his sacrifice.[38]

The philosophy of caste takes the sting off the institution and thus skilfully stereotypes it. During the later ages, therefore, this theory of caste has been rightly harped upon. The differences between the Śūdra theory of caste, detailed above, and this theory is significant. The Brahmin authors of the Śūdra promised salvation to the Śūdra only through the intermediary of births in higher castes. In plain words it was tantamount to asking him to wait till doomsday. The mark of inferiority was permanently impressed on him, and his low status was declared by implication to render it impossible for him to work out his salvation in his own person. The concession granted testifies only to the liberalism of the writers on Dharma. The *Gita,* on the other hand, disarams opposition on more counts than one. First, it tries to provide a rationale for the original division into four Varṇas. Secondly, it unequivocally asserts the virtual equality of these divisions as far as the value of their distinct work and their inherent capacity for working out individual salvation are concerned.

Stratification Among the Four Varnas

The post-Vedic period testifies to the rigid stratification and internal solidarity of the four varṇas. Each group was recognized as distinct, almost complete in itself, for its social life. Among the laws that were valid, provided they did not contradict the sacred precepts, are those of castes. Cultivators, traders, moneylenders, and artisans have authority to lay down rules for their respective classes.[39] It may be inferred that many of the sub-divisions within each varṇa—and undoubtedly by now there must have existed in each varṇa numerous sub-divisions—had rules of their own for their internal management. The word 'jāti' is applied by the great grammarian Patanjali to such ethnic groups as the Ābhîras, whom he declares, to be other 'jāti' than the Śūdra. By implication the Śūdras too were a 'jāti'. 'Varṇa' and 'jāti' would thus appear to be an interchangeable term. It is clear that other groups than the four traditional ones were not only in existence but had come to be recognized as 'jāti'.[40]

The four castes were even supposed to be distinguished by their origin and particular sacraments.[41] When officers were chosen from all castes, their positions were to be so adjusted as not to disturb the caste-order of precedence.[42] A number of major and minor offences are also enumerated as leading to loss of caste.[43] Social intercourse, eating, and intermarriage seem to have been the visible marks of an individual's assimilation in his group.[44] Clearly these groups and sub-divisions must have had each its own internal organization to carry out effectively the avoidance of social intercourse, eating and intermarriage with their defaulting members. Adherence to prescribed duties was neither wholly left to the sweet will of the individual, nor was it only to be enforced by the group. It was the duty of the king to see that the prescribed duties were performed by the proper individuals. If a man always neglected his prescribed duty and did what was forbidden, his property, with the exception of what was required for food and raiment, would be attached till he reformed his ways.[45]

Entitlement to the Practice of Dharma

The rules and regulations governing social life and individual conduct differed according to the orders in society, only the four 'varṇas' being taken into account by the law-givers. Others, like the mixed castes and outcastes, are mentioned, but their status in the eye of law and morals is not clearly defined. Even the Dharma was apportioned according to 'varṇa' The Brahmin was entitled to the practice of the whole of it, the Kṣhatriya to three-fourths of it, the Vaiśya to half, and the Śūdra only to a quarter.[46] A Brahmin was to be initiated in his eighth year, a Kṣhatriya in the eleventh, and a Vaiś ya in the twelfth.[47] A student while begging for alms, must use different formulae varying with his caste.[48] Of the eight forms of marriage only specific ones are enjoined for each caste. Where water is drunk for purification it must reach the heart, the throat, and the interior of the mouth in the case of the first three orders respectively. In case of the Śūdra it need touch only the extremity of the lips.[49] The higher the caste the shorter was the period of impurity to be observed at birth and death.[50] If a man of a lower varṇa carried the corpse of one of a higher caste or vice versa, the period of impurity was determined by the caste of the deceased. The higher castes had their cremation-grounds in different localities from those of the lower castes.[51] While asking a guest about his health, the terms to be used, according to the caste of the guest, were "Kuśala" in the case of a Brahmin, "anāmaya" in the case of a Kṣhatriya, and "ārogya" in respect of a Vaiśya and a Śūdra. A Brahmin must feed his Kṣhatriya guest after his Brahmin guests have had their meals. Other guests were to be fed together with one's servants.[52] In certain cases where a woman's husband had emigrated, the period of waiting prescribed for her varied according to her caste, being the shortest for a Śūdra and the longest for a Brahmin female.[53]

Offence and Crime

Baudhāyana allows a sane man of any of the four castes to be a competent witness in a legal proceeding.[54] Vasishṭha's opinion is less decided. He observes: "Srotriyas, men of unblemished form, of good character, men who are holy and love truth (are fit to be) witnesses. Or (men of) any (caste) may give evidence regarding (men of) any (other castes). Let him make women witnesses regarding women; for the twice-born men, twice-born men of the same caste (shall be witnesses), and good Śūdras for Śūdras and men of low birth for low caste men."[55] If a Śūdra committed theft, he had to pay back eight times the value of the property stolen. In the case of a Vaiśya thief, the penalty was doubled. A Kṣhatriya had to pay twice as much as a Vaiśya and a Brahmin four times. If a learned man committed theft, the punishment was very much increased.[56] A man committing adultery with a woman of his caste had to undergo a certain penance.[57] Adultery with a woman of a higher caste entailed punishment, the severity of which increased with the caste-status of the woman violated.[58] It seems that illicit intercourse with females of lower castes by males of higher castes was not regarded in the nature of a serious offence. Only adultery with a low-caste woman was condemned as a heinous crime, the punishment for which was either banishment or degradation to the caste of the woman.[59] If a Brahmin killed a Brahmin, he was to be banished from the kingdom with the mark of a headless trunk branded on his forehead; but if a man of any of the other three castes committed the same offence, the punishment was death and confiscation of all his property. For slaying a Kṣhatriya, a Vaiśya and a Śūdra the fine was a thousand, hundred, and ten cows respectively with a bull for the expiation of the sin in each case.[60] Even in the matter of taxation there seems to have been much inequality on the basis of caste. From Buddhist literature we gather that both the Kṣhatriyas and the Brahmins, though they owned the greater portion of the land, were free from taxes.[61]

Non-Acceptance of Food Offered

The Śūdra generally was regarded as so low that his food might not be accepted by the Brahmin. There is one exception to this attitude of the lawgivers, and that is the permission given by Āpastamba for food being prepared by a Śūdra under the guidance of the higher varṇas.[62] As suggestion for above this relaxation of the usual rule which must have been necessitated by the special conditions of South India from which Āpastamba hailed. The same author lays down very strict rules in the matter of acceptance of food by a Brahmin student, who has completed his studies but has not yet entered the life of a householder. In his opinion such a person shall not eat in the houses of people belonging to the three lower castes. He quotes, but evidently does not approve of, the view that he may take food offered by persons of the two castes, next in order, who follow the prescribed rules.[63] Baudhāyana exhorts such a person to beg for only uncooked food from the members of the first three caste and from the carpenters,[64] (Lit. chariot-makers). He enjoins a Brahmin to eschew Śūdra's food. A Brahmin observing this rule is said to be the worthiest object of gifts. If the injunction is broken, dreadful consequences will follow both for the recalcitrant individual as well as for his progeny. Recitation of the Veda or offering of sacrifices cannot obliterate the evil effects of such action. A person who dies with a Śūdra's food in his stomach will be born again as a pig or a Śūdra. If after partaking of such food a Brahmin be so unwise as to have a conjugal intercourse, the offspring will belong to the Śūdra, and the Brahmin cannot ascend to heaven.[65] In another passage Vasishṭha gives a list of persons whose food must not be eaten. They are the outcast, the Śūdra, the physician, carpenter, the washerman, the cobbler, etc.[66] Gautama is more strict in his rule, and allows a Brahmin to eat the food, evidently cooked food, given only by such of the twice-born persons as are praised for the proper performance of their duties. But he differs from others in this that he recognises the claims of some people, who are of the Śūdra class, for special treatment. The food offered by a herdsman, a husbandman, an acquaintance of the family, a barber, or a servant may be accepted.[67] A Brahmin may also accept food at the hands of a trader who is not at the same time an artisan,[68] the latter's food being forbidden by Āpastamba to a Brahmin student returned home.[69] According to Gautama the food of a carpenter is also taboo to a Brahmin.[70]

Idea of Defilement and Pollution

The idea that certain persons defile, while others sanctify the company, if they sit down to a meal in one row, is present in the Sūdras.[71] In this idea may be discerned the origin of the later practice not to dine in the same row with people of other castes than one's own. Āpastamba enjoins a Brahmin student, who has returned home, not to eat sitting in the same row with unworthy people.[72]

The idea that an impure person imparts pollution by his touch and even by his near approach to a member of the first three castes finds definite expression in the law-texts of this period, generally with reference to the persons who are outcasted and even specifically in relation to a class of people called Chaṇḍālas. According to Gautama a man who is guilty of the crime of killing a Brahmin, must live outside the village, entering it only for alms. When he thus enters the village he must step out of the road on meeting a member of the first three castes and make the way clear for him.[73] On touching a Chaṇḍāla or one who has touched a Chaṇḍāla one must immediately bathe with one's clothes on.[74] If a Brahmin unintentionally eats the food or accepts the presents given by a Chaṇḍāla he is outcast. But if he does so knowingly he becomes equal to a Chaṇḍāla.[75] The position of the Chaṇḍālas must have been very degraded. A householder is exhorted to throw some food for them and the outcastes along with that for crows and dogs outside the house, after all the members of the household have taken their meals.[76] In marked contrast stands the practice of people about the 2nd century or even the 5th century BC For no less a careful student of linguistic usage than Patanjali, while explaining a rule in Panini's grammar, imparts us the valuable information that the Chaṇḍālas were considered to be a variety of Śūdras, not necessarily the last. That they were not outcast in the sense of having to live outside the limits of town or village is implied; and that they were outcast only as far as the use of their food-vessels by members of the twice-born orders was concerned is explicitly stated. They were the *'apapātra* Śūdras' or simply *'apapātras'*, a term later used by Manu, too, about the Chaṇḍālas. The vessels used by them for taking their food could not be cleansed by any process to make them fit for use by the twice-born. This definite and clearcut information supplied by the great grammarian writing in about 150 BC is impliedly corroborated by the clever administrator Kautilya a few centuries later. The latter forbids the Chaṇḍālas to follow the custom of the Sūdras. By implication one may conclude that the Chaṇḍālas were for sometimes at least following the customs of the Sūdras, because they were actually considered to be a variety of them.

Avoidance of Proximity and Association

Three of the Dharma Śūtra writers have used the term *'apapātra'*, but in such a manner as to imply that the people, designated are different from Śūdras and sometimes from the Chaṇḍālas. But almost always they are exhorted to be treated like dogs and outcasts.[77] Āpastamba regards it as an offence even to speak to or to look at a Chandala.[78] The outcastes are to live by themselves as a community, teaching each other and marrying among themselves. Association with them by pure men is prohibited on threat of ex-communication. By association is meant either by a matrimonial alliance, officiating at their sacrifice, or even touching them.[79] It seems that the ideas of pollution had progressed further than these examples lead us to believe. Continued use by the Śūdras of the water in a well rendered it unfit for religious purposes. This at least seems to be the opinion of Baudhāyana who says that a Brahmin, who marries a Śūdra wife and dwells in a village where only well-water is available, becomes equal to a Śūdra.[80] There are many stories in the Jātakas, illustrating the scrupulous avoidance of the proximity of persons belonging to a despised or even a very low caste. The fear of pollution was not entirely confined to the Brahmins, but sensitive females like the daughter of a merchant in the story showed it in an excessive degree. The impurity of a person could also be imparted to objects touched by him.[81] The Chaṇḍālas lived outside the town in a hamlet of their own, and it seems that the other low castes, mentioned together with them, like Pukkasa, Rāthakara, Niṣāda, did likewise.[82]

Occupational Classification

The ideal theory of castes laid down certain duties as common to all of them and some as specific to each. Out of these some were prescribed as the authorised modes of gaining livelihood, and were generally peculiar to each caste and ordinarily forbidden to the others. The Brahmin must subsist on teaching and officiating as priest at the sacrifices of the castes that were entitled to offer such religious worship and by accepting gifts. The Kṣhatriya was to live by administration and the profession of arms.

Agriculture, trade, and pastoral pursuits were to be exploited by the Vaiśya, while the one occupation prescribed for the Śūdra was service of the other castes.[83] In times of distress one might follow the occupation peculiar to the lower orders, but never that of the higher, and preferably the one prescribed for the caste next in status to one's own.[84] Gautama is more lenient than other lawgivers and allows a Brahmin to take to agriculture and trade as lawful occupations, provided he employs servants to carry on the actual business and does not do the work himself.[85] That the Brahmins engaged themselves in occupations other than the lawful ones, either out of necessity or even ordinary, is clear from the injunction not to entertain at a Śrāddha-dinner Brahmins who follow the profession of Kṣhatriyas, or live by trade or by handicrafts.[86] When a Brahmin practises trade he is enjoined to abstain from dealing in certain articles. If he engages in agriculture, he must not yoke to his plough bullocks whose noses are pierced, nor must he plough after breakfast.[87] A few occupations like that of the carpenter, the charioteer, and the bard are assigned to some of the mixed castes that are described as the result of misalliance between the four castes. It will be noticed that the theory of occupations as proper pursuits of specific castes does not accommodate the artisans. It is not that there were no artisans in the society that their status does not seem to have been definitised. Indeed, Gautama distinguishes the artisans from those who live by personal labour, the latter expression being understood by the commentator to denote labourers like carriers.[88] Nay, crafts were so much advanced that pure artisans, who did not deal in their handiworks, were distinguished from artisan-traders.[89] That even members of the Kṣhatriya caste did engage in agriculture and other pursuits, not proper for their class, is proved by the Kambojas and Saurāshtras, who, though they are described as corporation of warriors who lived by agriculture and trade as much as by the profession of arms.[90] In view of the latter degradation of the artisan it is to be noted that the Kṣhatriya already describes them as of naturally impure character.[91]

In the Buddhistic literature many of the occupations are represented as having been hereditary and some of the classes like that of the Brahmin and the Ganapati, the representative of the Vaiśya, had definitely come to be regarded as such rigid castes that, though their members followed other occupations than those customary for their classes, they remained the members of their castes.[92] The Jātakas mention villages each of which consisted wholly of the followers of one occupation. Thus, there were smiths' villages and potters, villages.[93] Some of the crafts are spoken of as low, e.g., that of the barber, who is also referred to as of inferior caste.[94] Though the Buddhistic evidence as regards the actual professions taken up by the contemporary Brahmins must be taken with some discount—it was but natural for the Buddhist writers to hold up to ridicule their opponents by depicting them as violators of their own precepts—yet it must be pointed out that the cultivating and cattle-rearing Brahmin is an oft-recurring figure in the Pāli texts and once even a Brahmin carpenter is mentioned.[95]

Though the orthodox theory of caste is started in terms of only the broad categories of occupations, yet there are enough indications that in daily life further distinctions based on specialisation were recognised. Traders and craftsmen are mentioned in specific correlation to their special merchandise and craft. Giving directions for laying out the plan of the environs of the royal palace within the fort, Kautilya enjoins the localisation of trades and crafts in various quarters; and in this connection he mentions, as separate groups, dealers in grain, purveyors of liquids, dealers in cooked rice, those who sell fish, manufacturers of cotton threads, workers in bamboo, workers in hides, makers of gloves, ironsmiths and artisans working in precious stones.[96] From the evidence of the Jātaka literature,[97] we may conclude that these specific occupations were hereditary in this period, though the Brahminic theory of castes referred only to the larger categories. The Jātakas further bear testimony to the then incipient practice of naming sub-divisions of artisans on the basis of differences in the methods employed in carrying on the craft. Thus, the fishermen who used nets and baskets were called "Kevattas" in contradistinction to "Bālisikas" who were angling fishermen.[98]

Social Degradation and Servitude

The Śūdra gets socially more degraded, though ways and means are discovered for his religious emancipation. In the latter connection, the later division into *"sat"* and *"asat"*—good and bad—Sūdras first makes its appearance. And the rules regarding social and moral life, evincing greater degradation of the class, must evidently have been devised for the use of the latter class, viz., the "asat" Śūdras. Servitude is proclaimed to be a permanent condition of a Śūdra, whether he be actually bought or not. A Śūdra must not acquire wealth, because thereby he causes pain to the Brahmins.

Commitment of Offence

Manu roundly declares that a Śūdra cannot commit an offence causing loss of his caste, so degraded was he.[99] Where some kinds of spirituous liquors are forbidden to the members of the twice-born castes, the Śūdra is left to himself.[100] Evidently the Śūdra was regarded beyond the pale of moral influence. The Brahmin did not even condescend to expect of him an adherence to his high moral precepts. A householder, when sipping water for personal purification, must not use it if brought by a Śūdra. A member of the first three castes must not travel in the company of Śūdras. It seems that the Śūdras were considered to impart some sort of defilement to objects like bed and seat by their touch.[101] According to Kautilya, a Śūdra calling himself a Brahmin shall have his eyes destroyed by poison or shall pay the heavy fine of eight hundred "paṇas". If he violates a Brahmin female he shall be burnt to death. If he intentionally reviles or criminally assaults a Brahmin the offending limb shall be cut.[102]

Performance of Rites and Sacraments

In the sphere of religion the tendency is to forbid to the Śūdra the use of the most efficacious formulae and rites on the one hand, and to exhort him to perform most of the daily rites and the obligatory sacraments prescribed for the other castes. The doctrine of salvation through the conscientious discharge of the duties proper to caste is; indeed, mentioned here and there. But evidently the Brahmin law-givers of this period did not feel fully satisfied with that method of salvation. They had come to posses too much faith in the efficacy of the rites and sacraments to allow them to be neglected even by the Śūdra. The liberalizing influence of the Buddhist revolt and of Vaishnava compassion led the Brahmins to devise ways and means of assuring spiritual betterment to the Śūdra in the Brahminic way of rites and sacraments. It must also be mentioned that the performance of the Brahminic rites and sacraments by a large section of the people had a selfish interest for the Brahmin, which he could not have entirely lost sight of. Rites and sacraments require the services of a Brahmin. The Śūdra caste—the largest section of the people—was the only one which was denied sacred knowledge. If the Śūdras wanted to perform the Brahminic rites and sacraments they would invariably have to requisition the services of a Brahmin. To allow the Śūdra the privilege of these sacred performances was thus to ensure a large clientele for the Brahmin. Yet neither the genuine desire to widen the scope of his religious regulations so as to make it possible for the lowly Śūdra to work for his spiritual uplift in the Brahminic way, nor the selfish motive of procuring mass clientele was strong enough for the Brahmin to override completely his supreme faith in the sanctity of his lore or his high regard for ceremonial purity. He began to make a distinction between the Śūdra who behaved properly according to the Brahmin's ideas, and the Sūdra who was slovenly enough not to come up to this standard of conduct—the *"sat"* and the *"asat"* Śūdra. Only the former class of Śūdras was allowed the privilege of the practice of rites and sacraments though without the use of the Vedic formulae.

Yājñavalkya opines that the usual sacraments are accompanied by the recital of mantras only in the case of the first three castes. The Śūdras, by implication, were to perform them without the use of Vedic formulae. They had to use the ordinary formula of *"namas"* (obeisance). They may offer in the same way the daily sacrifices on the domestic fire and also the annual offering to the manes.[103] According to the Śukraniti, a Śūdra, must perform all the sacred duties incumbent on him with the help of the *"namas"* formula, which is explained here in the terminology, usual in the next period, as the mantras given in the Puranas.[104] Atri, Laghusankha, and Likhita draw a distinction between the Śūdras and the other castes by enjoining the Śūdra to undertake only charitable and welfare works and to eschew the Vedic performances.[105] Manu is more rigorous in his refusal of the right of the Śūdra to fulfil the sacred law of the Āryas. But even he is prepared to make a concession in the case of those Śūdras who are desirous of gaining merit, and exhorts them to imitate the practices of the virtuous.[106] Yājñavalkya also seems to recognize the higher claims of those

Śūdras whose conduct is proper according to the Brahminic ideas.[107] Ushanas, Brhadyama, and Laghuvishnu classify the Śūdras into *sat* and *asat*. The most potent agent for personal purification that the Brahmins have thought of, viz., the liquid made up by the mixture of cow's milk, curds, ghee, urine, and dung is, however, considered so sacred a thing that if a Śūdra drinks it, he commits as heinous a sin as a Brahmin who drinks spirituous liquor.[109]

The approximation of the Vaiśya to the Śūdra, already noticed in the last period, is carried further in this. In the account of the creation of the four castes from the body of the Supreme Being, Manu groups the two castes together as being produced out of that half of the body, which is less sanctified than the other half, above the navel, from which the Brahmin and the Kṣhatriya are represented to have emerged.[110] While dealing with the question as to who should be treated as his guest by a Brahmin, Manu and Vishnu recommend that a Vaiśya and a Sūdra guest may be allowed to eat with one's servants, out of compassion.[111] Yajnavalkya prescribes for the Vaiśya the same period of death-impurity as the one he recommends for a good Śūdra.[112] We have seen that Brahmin could not generally accept food offered by a Śūdra, though he could eat what was given to him by a Vaiśya. Some writers of this period extend this privilege to the good Śūdras, thus putting them on a par with the Vaiśyas.[113] According to Kautilya the issue of a Vaiśya by a Śūdra wife is a Śūdra.[114]

Objective of the Present Study

The present study analyse the general believes of the Buddha, who was a great social reformer for all human beings, and that his efforts for the emancipation of women and lower castes created a sort of social revolution in society. In this study, the researcher would find out whether or not the Buddha was a social revolutionary. He will not only analyse his stand on the various social problems, but also compare his ideas with other contemporary thinkers and religious leaders, while comparing them with the ideas of the thinkers of the preceding age.

No important work related to the subject-matter of the present research has been done so far which can clearly inform about the role of Buddhist religion in eliminating untouchability. But the very first creation on the origin of untouchability is of Dr. B.R. Ambedkar, the famous politician as well as protagonist of the Scheduled Castes. He composed *Achhoot, Kaun aur Kaise?* 1948, in the form of complete scripture of his famous narrative-creation, *Shoodra Kaun?* 1946. In the former book, it is informed that untouchability originated as a consequence of the hatred of Brahminas for the followers of the Buddhist religion near about 400 B.C. But this famous book is related to the origin of untouchability only and its data indicates that the learned author has worked on the mentality committed to Buddhist religion. Besides, he has concentrated less on those historical complications as a result of which this intricate institution came into birth in 600 B.C. Consequently, the reasons of the origin of this organisation are highlighted by the mental mode.

The expansive investigation of the original history of the scheduled tribes has been conducted by Dr. Vivekannda Jha in his thesis, *"Early History of Untouchables in India, 1972"*, in which the social economical aspects are objectively investigated and evaluated but the political and cultural history of the scheduled tribes is neglected. Although a number of wrong resolutions related to the origin of untouchability are denied here and it is discussed on the reaction of *Buddhist* religion but in another context. The exhaustive evaluation of the efforts of *Buddhist* religion against untouchability is not done. Thus, in order to conduct on this basic subject, the different types of literature and scriptures between 600 B.C. to 200 B.C. have been adopted as the fundamental source. However for the expansive evaluation of the origin and the state of untouchability, the *Vedic* scriptures of 600 B.C. are taken as the fundamental basis.

Although the main subject-matter of this thesis is not the origin and the state of untouchability but for the aggregate explanation of the efforts of the *Buddhist* religion against untouchability, it is necessary to throw light on the cause of the origin of untouchability. Where we come to know of the historical background of the hatred expressed for the untouchables through the *vedic* scriptures and those subsequent to *Vedic* period, at the same time the resolution and the state of untouchability come to light by the holy scriptures as well as the holy writs.

We have the expansive details of the efforts of *Buddhist* religion against high-low and untouchability through the *Buddhist* as well as the *Jaina* scriptures of 600 B.C.-200 C. For the study of the religious, social and economical state of scheduled tribes, the *Brahmana* scriptures and *smritis* between 200 B.C.–400 B.C. are used. Generally, the accepted chronological order of these scriptures is adopted.

The *Vedic* scriptures, mainly, the text of the *Rigveda* and *Atharava Vedas* offer knowledge about *Aryan* enemies and by these texts only, the socio-economic, political and cultural condition of the *Asuras,* the Aryans, viz., *Das* and the *Dasyus,* the *Nag,* etc., and those subsequent to Aryans add to our knowledge. The Aryan-enemies belonged mainly to another race and culture and therefore the former and successive hatred and enemity for the later continued for decades. When the Aryans seized the power from their enemies due to their background of hatred, they reached the high standard of economic progress. They began to hate the labour. On the other hand, the Aryan born species defeated by the Aryans came to the front in the form of the Shudra tribes and they were engaged in the service of the ruler categories of the Brahmins, the Kshatriyas and the Vaisya tribes, and production work in the form of *shramik* class. Simultaneously, those Aryan species remaining free, had their natural growth stopped and were bound had to spend their lives in tribal economy as well as social-cultural community. As a result of their racial living standard, devotion for the work and the hatred of the Aryan ruler classes for the Brahmana-Vedic opposing culture, tribal people were declared to be untouchables. Their political power and property were seized by the ruler classes and they began to be employed in agriculture as well as the works of artisan associated with agriculture. As a result thereof, were bound to spend a pitiable life.

We arrive at the explanation of the reaction of the Buddhist religion against untouchability and caste-separation through the Buddhist scriptures, such as Deeghnikaya, Majjhimnikaya, Sanyuttnikaya, Dhammpad, Jaatakas etc. It seems from the deities entered in the Buddhist scriptures that the Buddhist religion continued its movement against untouchability and the feeling as well as the high-low from 600 B.C. till the decades, they put it on a main footing in this movement and presented philosophic, psychological and practical programme before the society. Although the Buddhist religion could not attack much on the fundamental causes of untouchability, yet the other aspects were managed quite logically and progressing root of the Aryan rulers was made limited to a great extent. An attempt has made to explain the efforts of Buddhist religion completely in the present study.

Apart from this, we come to know about the situation of the Scheduled Tribes through the Brahmana, the Buddhist scriptures and the smritis. Many significant details are achieved in this connection through the Brahmana scriptures like *Manusmriti, Naradsmriti, etc.* and the *Buddhist* scriptures like *Milind-panhon, Sardhampundarik* etc. which inform about the political, social, economic and cultural life of the scheduled tribes. It seems very necessary for complete evaluation of the efforts of Buddhist religion that the detailed information about the status of the scheduled tribes be achieved and same is done in the present work.

For the complete evaluation of the origin of untouchability and its place in our society, the reaction of *Buddhist* religion against it and the mode of the movement and the historical role of *Buddhist* religion, the support is taken from the scriptures of many native and foreign authors, historians and investigators. For a clear explanation of the basic sources, complete ascertainment of this intricate social system and the tremendous perusal of the efforts of *Buddhist* religion, numerous examples from the appropriate scriptures are used at different places.

Notes and References

1. *A History of Ancient Sanskrit Literature* (Panini Office edition, 1912), p.106.
2. *Mahābhārata,* Śānti Parva, 39, 59.
3. Gautama, p. 231.
4. Āpastamba, pp.161-62.
5. Āpastamba, p.165; Gautama, p. 236.
6. Āpastamba, p.165; Vasishṭha, pp.109-10; Baudhāyāna, p. 233.
7. Gautama, p. 236.
8. Āpastamba, p.165.
9. Gautama, p. 237.

10. Baudhāyana, pp. 217, 243.
11. Baudhāyana, pp. 224, 313.
12. Gautama, p. 76.
13. Vasishṭha, p. 96.
14. Baudhāyana, p. 313; Āpastamba, p. 84.
15. Baudhāyana, p. 244.
16. Gautama, p. 236.
17. Gautama, pp.204-5; Baudhāyana, p. 239.
18. Gautama, p. 230.
19. *Mahābhārata*, Śānti Parva, 59, 38.
20. Āpastamba, p. 103.
21. Compare the allusion to Paijavana and other wealthy Śudras in the *Mahābhārata*.
22. loc. Cit. 1, 2, 72.
23. Gautama, p. 229.
24. JAOS, Vol. xiii, p. 82.
25. *Ibid.*, p. 83.
26. *Bhagavadgita*, ix, 32-33.
27. p. 89.
28. Gautama, pp. 204-05.
29. *Mahābhārata*, Śānti Parva, 48, 70.
30. p. 235.
31. pp. 102-03, 125.
32. *Mahābhārata*, Anuśāsana Parva, 4, 6.
33. *Mahābhārata*, Śānti Parva, 34, verses 31, 34, 36, 38, 59, 310.
34. Gautama, p. 206.
35. Āpastamba, p. 87; Vasishṭha, p. 96.
36. Vasishṭha, p. 95.
37. Gautama, p. 230.
38. *Ibid.*, p. 274.
39. Gautama, p. 234; also compare *Arthaśāstra*, (2), p. 203.
40. Vyākaranamahābhāshya, 1, 2, 72.
41. Vasishṭha, p. 25.
42. *JAOS*, Vol. xiii, p. 95.
43. Baudhāyana, pp. 217-18.
44. Cf. Āpastamba, p. 5.
45. Gautama, p. 238.
46. *Mahābhārata*, Śānti Parva, 34, 32-33.
47. Baudhāyana, p. 150.
48. Baudhāyana, p. 151; Vasishṭha, pp.56-58.
49. Baudhāyana, p. 167.

50. Vasishṭha, p. 29; Gautama, p. 246.
51. Gautama, p. 250; *Arthaśāstra*, (1), p. 56.
52. Gautama, pp. 204-05.
53. Vasishṭha, p. 92.
54. Baudhāyana, p. 204; Gautama, p. 243.
55. Vasishṭha, p. 82.
56. Gautama, p. 237.
57. Baudhāyana, p. 232; Āpastamba, p.165.
58. Vasishtha, pp.109-10; cf. *Arthaśāstra*, (2), p. 285.
59. *Arthaśāstra*, (2), p. 285.
60. Baudhāyana, pp. 201-02; Āpastamba, pp. 18-19; cf. *Arthaśāstra*, (2), p. 270.
61. Fick, p. 119.
62. Āpastamba, p. 103.
63. *Ibid.*, pp. 66-67.
64. p. 159.
65. Vasishṭha, p. 38.
66. *Ibid.*, p. 69.
67. Gautama, p. 262.
68. *Ibid.*, p. 263.
69. Āpastamba, p. 67.
70. Gautama, p. 264.
71. Vasishṭha, p.19.
72. Āpastamba, p. 61.
73. p. 280.
74. Gautama, p. 250; Baudhāyana, p. 171.
75. Baudhāyana, p. 235.
76. Vasishṭha, p. 50.
77. Vyakāranamahābhāshya, II, 4, 10; Āpastamba, I, 7, 21; I, 5, 16; II, 7, 17; Vasishṭha, XX, 16; Baudhāyana, I, 21, 15; II, 2, 13. N.B.R.G. Bhandarkar first drew attention to the important passage in Patanjali's Mahābhāshya in his Social History of India in 1901. He commented on it thus: "Patanjali mentions carpenters and blacksmiths as belonging to the Śūdra class. The lowest of them, the Caṇḍālas were in the same degraded condition as they are now" (Collected Works, Vol. II, p. 450). P.V. Kane in his History of Dharmaśāastra, Vol. II-pt. I (1941) observes: "Therefore it follows that Pānini and Patanjali included 'candalas', and 'mrtapas' among Śūdras" (p.168).
78. p. 103.
79. Baudhāyana, p. 220; Vasishṭha, p.5.
80. p. 244.
81. Fick, pp. 39, 43.

82. *Ibid.*, pp. 318, 323.
83. Vasishṭha, p.11; Gautama, pp. 224-30; Apasamba, pp.122-23.
84. Vasishṭha, p.12; Gautama, pp. 209, 211; Baudhāyana, pp. 225-40.
85. p.225.
86. Āpastamba, p.144; Gautama, p. 255.
87. Vasishṭha, pp.12-13; Baudhāyana, p.236.
88. Gautama, p.228.
89. *Ibid.*, p.263.
90. *Ibid.*, p.437.
91. *Ibid.*, p.221.
92. *Fick,* pp.180-81, 255, 276, 278.
93. *Ibid.*, p. 280.
94. *Ibid.*, pp. 327-30.
95. *Ibid.*, pp. 241, 246.
96. *Arthaśāstra,* (2), pp. 58-59.
97. Fick, pp. 276, 278-79.
98. *Ibid.*, p.302.
99. Manụ, viii, 413-14; x, 126.
100. Vishṇu, pp. 95-96.
101. Vishṇu, pp. 99, 198-99.
102. *Arthaśāstra,* (2), pp. 238, 275-76, 285.
103. *Yājñavalkya,* pp. 11, 86.
104. *Sukraniti,* p. 163.
105. Collection of Smritis, pp.11, 124, 182.
106. Manu, x, 126, 128.
107. *Yājñavalkya,* p.1165.
108. Collection of Smritis, pp. 48, 101, 122.
109. Vishnu, p.15; Collection of Smritis, p. 23.
110. Manu, i, 92.
111. Manu, iii, 112; Vishnu, p. 216.
112. *Yājñavalkya,* p.1165.
113. Collection of Smritis, p.122.
114. *Arthaśāstra,* (1). p. 164.

2

Brahminical Text in Respect of Shudras' Status

The present chapter reveals the positions of Śúdras in Brahminical Text. Research suggests that the Āryans on the Ganges, in the 'Middle Land' found themselves divided into three classes—first, the priests, or Brahmins; second, the warriors and king's companion, called in ancient times Kshatriyas, or the present day Rajputs; third, the husbandmen, or agricultural settlers, who retained the old name Vaisyas, from the root vis, which in the Vedic period had included the whole 'people'. These three classes gradually became separate castes; intermarriage between them was forbidden, and each kept more and more strictly to its hereditary employment. But they were all recognised as belonging to 'Twice-born' or Aryan race; they were all present at the great national sacrifices; and all worshipped the same Bright Gods.

Beneath them was a fourth or servile class, called Śúdras, the remnants of the vanquished aboriginal tribes whose lives had been spared. These were 'the slave-bands of black descent', the Dasas of the Veda. They were distinguished from their 'Twice-born' Aryan conquerors as being only 'once-born', and by many contemptuous epithets. They were not allowed to be present at the great national services, or at the feasts which followed them. They could never rise out of their servile condition; and to them was assigned the severest toil in the fields, and the hard and dirty work of the village community.

Of the four Indian castes, they had a tendency to increase. As the Aryan conquests spread, more aboriginal tribes were reduced to serfdom, as Śúdras. The warriors, or Kshatriyas, would constantly receive additions from wealthy or enterprising members of the cultivating class. When an expedition or migration went forth to subdue new territory, the whole colonists would for a time lead a military life, and their sons would probably all regard themselves as Kshatriyas. In ancient times, entire tribes, and at the present day the mass of the population throughout large tracts, thus claim to be of the warrior or Rajput caste. Moreover, the kings and fighting-men of aboriginal races who, without being conquered by the Aryans, entered into alliance with them, would probably assume for themselves the warrior or Kshatriya rank. We see this process going on in the present day among many of the aboriginal peoples. The Brahmins, in their turn, appear at first to have received into their body distinguished families of Kshatriya descent. In later times, too, we find that sections of aboriginal races were also 'manufactured' wholesale into Brahmins. Unmistakeable cases of such 'manufactures' or ethnical syncretisms are recorded; and besides the upper class agricultural Brahmins, there are throughout India many local castes of Brahmins, who followed the humble callings of fishermen, blacksmiths, ploughmen and potato-growers.

The Vaisya or cultivating caste did not tend, in this manner, to increase. No one felt ambitious to win his way into it, except perhaps the enslaved Śúdras, to whom any change of condition was forbidden. The Vaisyas themselves tended in early times to rise into the more honourable warrior class; and at a later period to be mingled with the labouring multitude of Śúdras, or with the castes of mixed descent. In many provinces they have now almost disappeared as a distinct caste. In ancient India, as at the present day, the three conspicuous castes were (1) the priests, (2) warriors of the Aryan birth, and (3) the Serf or Śúdras, the remnants of earlier races. The Śúdras had no rights; and, once conquered, they ceased to struggle against their fate. But a long contest raged between the priests and warriors for the chief place in the Aryan commonwealth.

Making investigation on Śúdras position under the feature of social-occupational groups *varnas* or what we designate today as castes, the fourth caste group were the Sudras and comprised the peasant farmer, the hunters and the fishermen. They were designated "once born" because they were not permitted to be initiated into spiritual life.

Divorced from the traditional caste groupings were the so-called outcastes, people who were scorned, isolated and forced to undergo a long list of social and economic disabilities because of their lowly origins. That means to say that the outcastes were not permitted to participate fully in Hindu life and had to exist on its fringes in the best way they could.

The *Varna* arrangement (caste system) has never been straight and unbending. Sometimes after the collapse of the Mauryan empire the four-fold caste system underwent a change to become more responsive to an increasingly complex society. As a result, far more complicated and elaborate system of sub-castes or *Jati* (literally, birth) evolved. The arrangement retained many of the basic features of the original caste system, but compartmentalised Hindus along much tighter, hereditary vertical lines.

Finding this trend, it may be remarked that in India, the *Jati* traditionally has been the primary social unit, the group within which marriages are arranged and dining normally takes place. Here the two words 'caste' and *Jati* come whose relationship has been analysed by Romila Thapar in conclusion with the sub-caste and has come to have more relevance for the day-to-day working of Hindu society than the main caste, but the *Varna* arrangement remained the overall theoretical framework (Romila Thapar, 1966:40)[1].

Rules Formulated in the Caste System

As the caste system evolved in India, Hindu leaders formulated innumerable rules, which prescribed inter-personal, inter-caste behaviour. The following might be considered as taboos warrant special consideration because they illustrated how highly stratified Hindu society became. A violation, even though unintentional and of a minor nature was sometime sufficient cause to banish the wrong-doer permanently from Hindu society.

1. Endogamy was rigidly observed. The caste into which a person was born determined the group from which a suitable

marriage partner could be selected. To marry outside one's designated *jati* was an act of defiance that resulted in the iconoclast's permanent banishment from his home, family, and friends.

2. Caste prescribed occupation. In a general fashion, each subcaste specified in one particular form of work. A son was expected to follow his father's work role; the son of a sweeper became a sweeper, a tin smith became a tinsmith, and so on. Hindu society made no provision for individual, social and occupational mobility, that is for a youngman to discontinue the sequential family-caste arrangement and turn to different trade or profession. On the other hand, it was possible for an entire caste to upgrade (or lower) itself over an extended period of time, generally through a joint dedication to such a goal.

3. Caste prohibition dealt with eating, drinking and other aspects of everyday social intercourse. A free co-mingling of diverse caste members either in private homes or public restaurants has never been sanctioned or expected to restrict their social life to people from the same group. Furthermore, each caste (but specially the upper castes) regulated what foods were acceptable, how and by whom they should be prepared, and of course, what had to be avoided and under what circumstances.

4. Regulation related to the collegial effects of the caste system. The members a group in many respects resembled a large family unit. In times of adversity when one of its members suffered some misfortune, the caste was expected to provide some assistance. Conversely, the caste leadership possessed the authority to drive from the caste anyone who violated its code of behaviour. Few punishments had such dire consequences as expulsion from one's traditional group. The offender was isolated from all members of his immediate family and friends. He was even barred from entering his home. No longer was he permitted to work his trade since he was denied acceptance by his former co-workers. All that a stigmatised, ostracized Hindu could do was to spend his remaining years in lonely disgrace and undergo punishment whenever it was stipulated for regaining caste purity.

Brahmanism (more accurately 'Vedism' or Vaidika, from Veda, the proper Indian term, less accurately 'Hinduism', a foreign word which means little more than 'Indianism'), and our treatment must be an impressionistic sketch by way of background.

The word Brahmin meant in the early Vedic period a sacred text, with an underlying sense of 'great' or 'excellence'. Later, in the time of the Pauravas, a Brahmin was personified as the Supreme Being or God Brahmin (Masculine, Nominative Brahmin), the original being out of whom the universe evolved. Sometimes this Brahmin is instead conceived more abstractly and philosophically as the impersonal absolute, with neuter gender, but nevertheless as having life (since the life of the whole universe emanated from it is sustained by it). From Brahmin is derived Brahmana, meaning a priest in possession of the sacred texts, or later a priest of God, which we anglicize as 'Brahman' (or 'Brahmin') and from which European writers have coined the derivative 'Brahminism'.

During the Ancient times the Vedic religion of the Aryans had consisted primarily in the worship of Gods, and the poetry and songs preserved in the Veda and forming its oldest component are mostly hymns of praise and supplication. The Gods were derived from the ancient Indo-European pantheon and represent on the one hand social abstractions and on the other natural phenomena. In the period of the Paurava codification, however, we are confronted with an entirely different religion, despite the continuing use of the old hymns. Offerings to the gods had long formed a part of the ancient religion, but these now became its centre, its essence. The ritual to which they had given rise became the 'science' of obtaining all good things and the gods fell into place as the servants of the ritual, necessary merely to receive the offerings. The desired good results of the ritual action were to come about not through any favour of the gods but directly as the mysterious effects of the action itself, success depending on the precision with which this had been performed. Henceforth, the really important and operative part of the Veda was the ritual part, interpreted as a set of injunctions governing correct performance.

The loss of practically all their independent significance by the gods had left the field of theology, cosmology and cosmogony open to new speculation, more sophisticated, more abstract, more systematic. It was here that the notion of the absolute or supreme being developed, the great Brahmin. Here also cosmogony gave birth to philosophy as a reasoned explanation of the origin and development of the universe. The earliest speculations of this kind appear already in some of the Vedic poetry and again entwined with explanations of the ritual in the ritual texts, but the latest part of the Veda consists of texts primarily devoted to this early philosophy (the Upanishads, or rather the five earliest among them, which alone are strictly canonical Veda and preserve the ideas of the Paurava period: Chandogya, Bṛhadāranyaka, Aitareya, Kauṣītaki and Taittīrya).

The poetry of the Aryans was antagonistic to the more original inhabitants of India and their civilisation, but during the Paurava period this old antagonism and even the fact of the conquest appears to have been practically forgotten. A considerable amount of intermixture of the conquering and conquered peoples had evidently taken place, indeed it has even been suggested[2] that the Brahmins, the hereditary priesthood among the presumed conquerors, were for the most part descended from the priests of non-Aryan peoples probably of the Indus civilization, who had managed to insinuate themselves into this favoured position in a spirit of compromise and in virtue of their superior education and intellectual skills. It is true that Brahmin genealogies are doubtful and in part un-Aryan looking, but unlikely that the more original Indians had succeeded in assimilating their conquerors to such a great extent in too early a period. There are few, though there certainly are some, ideas in the Vedic Canons which came into the traditions of the Aryans from outside instead of developing from within. Perhaps a significant element in the ritual, or in philosophical speculation, came from the Indus people, but there is little or no evidence to decide such questions. In Paurava texts outside the Vedic Canon, however, there is much that is generally thought to be of non-Aryan origin. It is clear (and is not affected by the problems of the chronology of the epic and the histories, ascribed to Paurava authors but much later in their extant forms) that there was a gradual synthesis of the Aryan and the more originally Indian traditions. This trend is characteristic for the history of Indian thought, which usually developed not by exclusion but by assimilation. The doctrines of alien traditions were not rejected but were suitably explained, so that they fitted into some grand scheme. At the same time they might be modified and reformed to produce an overall harmony.

The most prominent non-Aryan elements in the Brahmanism of the epic and the histories (Purāṇas) are the mythologies of the great Gods Viṣṇu (Vāsudeva) and Śiva and of the great Goddess Devi. These three were probably quite separate in origin, belonging to three different peoples in India. The Goddess as now known is often associated with either Viṣṇu or Śiva as a subordinate partner or consort, but these may be early synthesis. The mythology of Viṣṇu by itself seems to suggest a synthesis between several separate gods, who came to be regarded as manifestations of the same supreme being. As eventually incorporated into the histories these various conceptions of the godhead were brought into relation with Brahman or Brahmā in various ways, depending on which one of the four was held to be the really ultimate godhead and which was of subordinate manifestations. Their appearance in books of history was due to the fact that the latter began with narratives of the creation and evolution of the universe, therefore with theology.

Another probably non-Aryan element in the histories is the accounts of the origin and progress of civilization, including the election by the people of the first king and law-giver (to ensure the maintenance of principle in social relationships), and the legend of King Prthu, who levelled the Earth, developed agriculture and trade, and built cities and villages.

Among doctrines probably non-Aryan is that of the reincarnation or transmigration of the soul, which is barely mentioned in the latest part of the Veda but taken practically for granted in the non-Vedic Brahminical tradition. This was very likely originally connected with—it certainly fits well with—the way in which the evolution of the universe and the scale of time are conceived in the histories. The universe evolves, or revolves, through enormous cyclic periods of hundreds or thousands of millions of years, at the ends of which it is dissolved into its constituent elements, including the souls, and then re-evolved either by natural processes or by the action of God. There were very great differences of doctrine here between various schools of thought within the Brahminical tradition, particularly on the question whether originally, before the above cyclic periods, the souls and other atomic elements had not existed but had been created out of the supreme being or out of nothing. Very important, it would seem, for all religious and philosophical ideas in India is the vastness of the time scale assumed, which in fact agrees well with that established for the universe by modern astronomy and contrasts most strongly with the traditions of Western religions (the Babylonians had certain similar ideas, on a more limited scale). The Indian ideas of time were in fact quite early related to astronomical observations, particularly of the movements of the planets. The latter appear at first to be erratic, but on further observation and study may be seen to follow repeating patterns. Combine the movements of all the planets into an overall repeating pattern and you will find, depending on the precision of your observations and calculations, an exceedingly long cycle of time marked out in the heavens. The Indians assumed that at the beginning of some cyclic period all the planets should have been in one place, or on the same starting line (longitude), and their attempts to determine the date of this grand conjunction many millions of years ago seemed to confirm the practically inconceivable age attributed to the universe by speculative thought.[3]

Lastly we might mention that the legal traditions and many of the social customs formulated in the earliest law books give the impression of not being Aryan in origin. Thus, the conventional four stages of life (āśhrams) later regarded as part of the foundations of orthodox society (studentship—married life—retirement—renunciation) are not mentioned in the Veda. The last of these stages and the growing practice of renouncing the world at any age reminds us of the evidence for there being ascetics in the ancient Indus society rather than of any thing in the Aryan tradition.

The conception of liberation from transmigration would seem to go not simply with transmigration itself but with the vastness of the time scale recognised in Indian thought. It is almost certainly not Aryan tradition having been of a future life in some sphere of existence not altogether different from the Earth (one such sphere was the Moon) and developing into the conception of a desirable heaven attainable by means of ritual action. Speculation about liberation of the soul, on the other hand, tried to conceive of some state entirely transcending the empirical universe, such as union with the supreme being. It appears in a vague form only in the very latest part of the Veda, and is still not very prominent even in the early non-Vedic Brahminical tradition. The attainment of heaven remained the dominant idea.

After the great emperor Janamejaya (probably 9th century BC), during whose reign the Paurava Empire seems to have reached its maximum prosperity and power and to have been adorned by several of the most creative thinkers who contributed to the formation of Brahminism, there was gradual decline. The decisive term seems to have been in the 8th century BC, in the reign of Nicakṣu, when the Paurava capital, Hastināpura on the upper Ganges, wās devastated by a flood. He transferred the capital to Kauśāmbī on the Yamunā. After this event the creative period of Brahminism appears to have come to an end: lines of teachers are recorded and there was clearly some revision of Vedic texts and more of the epic and histories, but original composition seems to have been confined to the subsidiary studies, ritual, law, linguistics, astronomy and geometry. These studies were important for the history of science but of no direct consequence for Brahminism as a religion or philosophy or guiding ideology. Moreover, even among them, there is hardly any work extant which might belong to the century and a half after Nicakṣu; the great period in these special studies begins later.

After the moving of the capital the empire broke up, the local rulers and states which had been under Paurava hegemony asserting their independence. By the time of the Buddha (500 BC) sixteen major states were counted in northern India, among which one of the smaller and weaker was that of the Pauravas. There were numerous minor states. The major states (and the minor) had many different types of governments; in particular some were monarchies, others republics. Thus, the India of

Buddha was very different place from the India of Vyaśa. The states were frequently at war, and several of them sought universal hegemony. However, it was not the most orthodox states or the most legitimate dynasties which were the most successful in these struggles. On the contrary the Pauravas faded away in a haze of nostalgia and romance, and the real struggle was between the Vṛji Republic, the most powerful republican state, and the kingdom of Magadha.

Magadha appears to have been the least orthodox of the monarchies. It was situated on the periphery of the region of Brahminical influence and its kings developed a highly autocratic and centralised system of government not provided for in Brahminism. Brahminism prescribes the duties of kings rather than their powers and provides a variety of checks on their actions. In fact, the Veda does not necessarily require monarchical government, even though later the Brahminical tradition increasingly favoured it. Indeed we probably ought rather to say that under the trend towards monarchy of later times it was those Vedic schools which had been associated with the famous Paurava monarchy, not others which might have flourished under republican governments, which were favoured and have survived. The earlier Vedic texts think rather in terms of assemblies and various apparently autonomous groups in society, and of the persuasive power of speech, than of autocratic and centralised rule. The later Vedic texts, the majority of which—as now extant—show that they were composed under the Paurava Empire, are aware of republican governments in the outlying regions surrounding the central Paurava (or 'Kuru-Pañcalā') kingdom.[4]

This struggle in the Buddha's time was a contest in economic power, political craft and administrative efficiency, in which the Brahminical traditions had little to offer either to the rulers or to the people. Both its rituals and its philosophy seemed irrelevant. The question was no longer one of establishing a harmonious empire, with a emperor ruling justly according to the traditional usages of Vedic society, treating his people and vassal ruler affectionately, if some time firmly, and restrained and guided by the code of duties prescribed by the Veda and interpreted by the Brahmins. In that traditional society an individual could pursue his life in reasonable peace and freedom, seeking and to a fair extent obtaining the good things of this world, and if he confirmed to *dharma* (the Brahminical concept of duty and justice) he had been respected for it and found it conducive to his well being. But in the 6th century BC economic progress, the exploitation of natural resources and the development of industry and above all trade had let loose several new forces in society: instead of wealth being measured primarily in kind (especially in cattle) a money economy had developed. Unprecedented wealth followed its own laws of circulation, and the states tried to control it by legislation. The new class of merchants tended to become wealthier than kings, and the latter reacted to this with more arbitrary rule and confiscations on flimsy pretexts: they opposed political force to economic force. The rulers of north India experimented with various new forms of government, but the general trend was towards centralisation of power in the hands of a monarch. In this society most people found their freedom seriously and increasingly restricted, their property and lives insecure, the future uncertain and probably worse than the past.

There was much discussion of real or imaginary past golden ages and of just emperors who had made the world harmonious and happy, but the model offered by the Brahminical tradition failed to make a headway. Good men found themselves without a place. Any freedom in the increasingly centralised society ruled by money and force. For a time hopes seem to have centred on the Vrji Republic, which was based on old traditions of social harmony and respect for the individual, but in the struggle for survival against Magadha it became clear to men such as the Buddha that his position was precarious that it was only a matter of time before the greater wealth of Magadha overwhelmed it. Moreover, the basis of its defence was a pure conservatism of adhering to the ways of old and resisting the corrupting power of the new society of Magadha (exercised through bribery and sowing dissension).The Republic seemed to have no power of development which might enable it to oppose to autocracy a more economically viable form of society. The Buddha admired the Republic's ancient customs, its democratic government, its respect for wise men, but he did not see in it a political solution to the problem of human happiness. He and other philosophers of time looked elsewhere for a solution, not primarily in society but in the first place away from it. In effect they contracted out of society in order to preserve their freedom; they abandoned the quest for wealth and power and sought peace of mind and spiritual experiences. Only from an independent vantage point could they hope—as they certainly did hope—to exercise any influence on the society they left, to infuse into it bettər ideals than mssoney and violence.

The philosophical text of the Veda have been mentioned, but nothing has been said about their nature and methods, apart from the original relation to cosmogony and the latter conception of an absolute Brahmin. In the later, conservative, Brahminical tradition whatever had been received into the Vedic Canon was treated as revealed dogma (and anything else was lost). Careful reading of some of the texts on the other hand reveals a substantial amount of not merely original, but critical thought in the Veda. These evident criticisms of the Vedic tradition were explained away and harmonised with the overall dogmatic system by the later Brahminical schools, but their methods seem not to have been lost on later and remained outside these schools. The Buddha himself is recorded[5] to have held that the original Brahmins were good men and the Veda (originally) the true doctrine but that both had become corrupt and needed to be completely reformed for example, one should became a Brahmin by virtue, not by heredity. The Brahmans had become mere repeaters of texts, not creative thinkers or 'meditators' since the Veda had been compiled. What might the Buddha and his contemporaries have learned from early Vedic philosophy?

In the earliest Vedic poetry the universe has its basis in the activities of the gods. Its laws are the laws of certain gods, the universe itself was created, or more precisely 'built' (like a house) by the gods.[6] It is in the development of cosmogonic speculations from this mythology that we can most easily trace to the growth of philosophy. There is a quest for some more rationalistic explanation of the evolution of the universe, ending in the Upaniṣads with an explanation which dispenses with supernatural gods or a god and explains the universe out of itself. It is itself a living being, even a divinity, but it develops according to natural processes which can be understood by scientific observations and experiments. Accompanying this quest, or rather preceding it and stimulating it, we find expressions of doubt concerning the gods and the mythology. Do the gods exist? If they do, at least the stories about them traditionally told are untrue. What existed at first? Can anyone know this ? Can even the highest Deity know this ? Certainly the gods do not know, since at first they did not exist.[7]

Of the main steps in this line of development we may note first the poem RVS × 129 (date probably between 1200 and 1000 BC). Here it is suggested that at first there was neither a being nor a non-being, but somehow the One, a living being, came into existence, embracing everything in itself, through the influence of heat (apparently its own heat). From desire arose mind. Then a measuring line (a significant idea) was stretched horizontally across, dividing what existed into male and female principles. At this point the speculation breaks off, but it is asked: Who really knows ? Not the gods! Only he who surveys the universe from the highest heaven perhaps knows, or perhaps He does not know.

At the end of the development we may look at the doctrine of Uddālaka as recorded in the Upaniṣads.[8] (Uddālaka lived during the time of Janamejaya, probably in the 9th century BC). He first rejects a traditional (Vedic) account of evolution to the effect that originally there was nothing, non-being. If that were so, he asks, how could the being have come out of it ? So at first there was the being. Uddālaka also rejected ritualistic explanations of a phenomena: that a certain thing is so because a certain ritual is performed in a certain way.[9] The original being according to him, is that which underlies everything in the universe. It is in everything, though it is too fine to be visible. By natural processes it became many beings: first it produced heat, out of this, which also was alive like the original beings, came water and out of the latter came 'food' *(anna),* which seems by extension to include all solid matter. These three living elements, called also 'divinities', then gave rise to everything in the universe, including man and ultimately mind. Thus, there is no supernatural, external, agency but only the 'being' itself, the original matter of the universe, out of which everything comes and into which everything goes back at death.

So far the explanation is rational enough, but much more important is the way Uddālaka justifies his explanations. He appeals at each step to actual observations of phenomena and sometimes to experiments which demonstrate that things are as he suggests. In looking for the sequence of evolution he proceeds by tracing things back to their causes by actual investigation. He proves the dependence of mind on food by the experiment of fasting. By way of methodology he distinguishes the real substances from mere modifications different only in name. Despite nominal differences we can generalise about a whole range of phenomena which in fact have a common substance.

There are implied in this development the ideas and methods of science. We do not know what science except the natural science of Uddālaka himself. First the spirit of doubt and enquiry, of not accepting traditional, mythopoeic or ritualistic, explanations. Then classification and scientific generalisation. Above all observations and experiments, by which causes can be found out and inductions arrived at. The law of the gods gives way to natural law, a concept which becomes all powerful later, when Buddhism and other extra-Vedic philosophies develop.

The Buddha belonged to a new movement in philosophy which grew up under the social conditions. The Brahmins were, or had become, a hereditary priesthood, and the earlier philosophers and poets whose work is known to us, being preserved in the Brahminical literature, were either Brahmins or men who became Brahminised, at least posthumously, by being accepted into the ranks of the orthodox. The new movement on the other hand was led by men who were not Brahmins, but came from all ranks of society, and who instead on joining the Brahminical schools set up independent schools. Some Brahmins also joined these schools, but they thereby left the Brahminical tradition and were assimilated into the new movement, which was essentially a classless one.

The philosophers of the new schools were called Śramanas.

They were men who had contracted out ordinary society and become wanderers, living either by gleaning what they could in the woods and fields or begging. Their aim was to discover the truth and attain happiness, or at least peace of mind. Having abandoned social commitments they were free to spend their time thinking, trying out ascetic practices, studying nature, and of course teaching. They set up schools and trained pupils to remember and disseminate their teachings, and they also lectured in the villages and cities, even before kings if invited. The contents of this public lecturing were extremely diverse, but they tended to be ethical, to instruct people how to live, and the food or even fees they received could be regarded as a justifiable return for the teaching they dispensed.

The Śramaṇas rejected the Veda, and the authority of the Brahmins, who claimed to be in possession of revealed truths not knowable by any ordinary human means. They ridiculed the complicated rituals, and tried to show the absurdity of the Veda, as a canon of ultimate truths, by pointing out contradictions in it and drawing attention to some passages which seemed either rather futile or highly unethical, or even completely non-sensical, if supposed to be pronouncements having absolute authority (since a great part of the Veda consists of ancient poetry and legends, this was not very difficult). The Śramaṇas went further than this and declared that the entire Brahminical system was fraudulent: a conspiracy against the public by the Brahmins for the purpose of enriching themselves by charging exorbitant fees for the performance of bogus rites and the giving of futile advice.[10]

In place of this authoritarian tradition the Śramaṇas sought to find satisfactory explanations of the universe and of life by genuine investigations and by reasoning. They believed they could ascertain natural laws by their own efforts, without benefit of authority from the ancients or of supernatural guidance, and that these laws would be absolutely valid and must be accepted because anyone who cared to undertake a proper investigation could verify them.[11] In brief, their outlook was that of scientists investigating the nature of the universe, though they were guided by the practical aim of applying the knowledge they gained in sthe quest for happiness.

Like Uddālaka before them, the Śramaṇas were evidently closely in touch with, and even partly responsible for the considerable progress made in the natural sciences in their period. They were particularly interested in astronomy and mathematics and some of them were connected with medicine[12]. Their doctrines usually included some kind of description of the universe: 1of the elements out of which it is constructed, their classification, the way the universe evolves and the position of living beings in it. Again, their conception of the universe was that it was a natural phenomenon, evolving of itself according to ascertainable natural laws: it was not subject to the control of gods or a god and had not been created by such supernatural powers. If there were gods, as some of them admitted might be the case, these were natural beings on a level with men and animals, inhabiting a different region but just as subject to natural laws as men: they were not immortal, but lived and died as men did.[13]

It is noteworthy that most of the śramaṇas believed in transmigration in some form: either of a 'soul' or of a stream of consciousness from a dying body to a newly conceived one. We have noted above that by this period the Vedic or Brahminical schools also had accepted this idea and incorporated it into their tradition. Many people at this time seem to have believed that they could remember their past lives. The acceptance of transmigration perhaps effects the refusal to accept the apparently arbitrary experiences of happiness and unhappiness of men within a single life: a belief in some kind of natural law of compensation at work in the universe ensuring eventual justice. At the same time most of the philosophers of this period regarded life in the universe as on the whole unhappy, concluding that their should be, not to be reborn in it in better circumstances, which any way would be temporary, but not to be reborn at all. At this point the subject becomes difficult: what could it mean, not to be reborn in the universe ? Would one's soul or consciousness go somewhere else, go into a dormant state, or cease to exist altogether?

Out of the śramaṇa movement of the 6th century BC a large number of separate schools of philosophy developed. From the many, more or less scientific, more or less speculative, systems propounded at least five major organised schools were successful enough to become strongly established and play dominant parts in the history of philosophy in India (and sometimes outside) for at least the next two thousand years. They soon split up into sub-schools and all of them modified their doctrines in the course of time, but despite the later appearance of a few entirely new schools it was those which had originated in the period of the Buddha which thenceforth gave a general direction to Indian philosophy and provided a framework for its discussions. The Brahmins of course reacted by developing philosophical systems of their own, meeting the new ideas with adaptations of their doctrines.

In the long run, though apparently not at first, by far the most successful and important of the śramaṇa schools was that founded by the Buddha. At first the Buddha was just one of the very many wandering teachers in the Vrji Republic, Magadha and other countries of northern India during 500 BC. He collected a fair number of followers, though not as many as some of his rivals, and he promulgated a doctrine which has all the main characteristics of the śramaṇa movement, which on the surface at least is just a typical śramaṇa doctrine. He rejected all authority except experience: the student should experiment for himself and see that the teaching is true, not accept it because the Buddha says so. The universe is subject to natural laws only, by studying which one can attain freedom and happiness—the most important laws of causation, moral as well as physical. Transmigration is provided for in that consciousness continues from life to life in accordance with the laws of moral causation. The aim is to end this transmigration and attain final peace. The most essential and characteristic part of the teaching is a scheme of training and study to attain this aim.[14] The Buddha here assumes that the aim of all living beings is the attainment of happiness and his teaching is presented as a way of achieving this aim, either absolutely and finally in liberation from transmigration, final peace, or relatively in an improvement of circumstances for those not yet ready to renounce the world. Moral conduct thus follows from the desire for happiness when the laws of moral causation are correctly understood, it is not a duty, as the Brahmins maintained. As a background to his doctrine the Buddha enumerated and classified the constituent elements[15] of the universe. In the scheme of training the most important part is not moral conduct, which though essential is only a preliminary, but meditation, in which the truths about the nature of the universe and one's own being are contemplated and the consciousness becomes gradually abstracted and detached.

Notes and References

1. Romila Thapar (1966): *A History of India* (Baltimore Penguin Books), p. 40.
2. By Pargiter: *Ancient Indian Historical Tradition,* Chapter XXVI.
3. There is plenty of evidence for enormous time scales in pre-Buddhist India. On the conjunctions of planets see, e.g., Burgess' translation of the Sūryasiddhānta, 15 ff. and 328 of the Calcutta reprint, 1935, and Needham, *Science and Civilisation in China* III, 119 f., 202 (I-Hsing, a Buddhist monk), cf. also Colebrooke, Miscellaneous Essays, Vol. II, 329 ff. and 426, London, 1873, see p. 40 below for the Ājīvaka tradition.
4. e.g. Aitareya Brāhmaṇa, viii 14 (Keith's translation is not correct).
5. e.g. D. III 94, 1104 (see p.273 of the commentary on this for corruption of the texts).
6. e.g. RVS ii 15.2 f, 1159, iv 56, vi 17.7, iii 55.19 f, x 149, x 81, x 72, etc.
7. e.g. RVS ii 12.5, viii 100.3, SBr 11.1.6.9-10, RVS x 129.
8. Chandogya U.vi.
9. SBr 11.4.1 shows the traditional views upheld against him.
10. The Buddhists have preserved some typical verses to this effect in the Tripitaka (Pali J VI 206-14). The views of the Lokayata School are reported for example in the first chapter of SDS.
11. In Buddhism see, e.g., the Pali references under ehipassika, 'verifiable', in PTC Vol. 1, p. 436. For the Lokayata only knowledge verifiable by the senses was admissible.
12. See e.g. the references in REBCS, p. 51.
13. The Tripiṭaka contains satirical dialogues on the gods and particularly on Brahmā, e.g. Pali Kevaddha (D No. 11) Chinese version of Dīrgha No. 24 in TI.
14. This is a sketch of the Buddha's teaching, to be justified later.
15. The 'principles', his most original hypothesis.

3

Perspective on Pali Text in Respect of Shudras' Position

The present chapter deals with the positions of Śūdras in respect of Pali text. In this chapter, the present authoress reflects that in the myth of the tenth book of the Rigveda, while the Brahmins and nobles were the mouth and arms respectively of the original cosmogonic Male, the Vaiśyas were his thighs. There was still something lower—his feet, which gave birth to the Śūdras, the people whose work consists in the humblest manual labours. But this fourth caste is composed of a mixed mass of non-Aryans, absorbed into the Aryan organization. Only in the first three does one find the "twice-born" *(djiva)*, who at a certain point in their youth receive the initiation which makes free men of them, a real social birth added to their natural birth. That means that the Śūdras have no part in religious life. At the most they perform certain rites of their own.

A most rudimentary investigation of the facts shows us that, far from being confined to four, the castes have multiplied in swarms and are still doing so *ad infinitum,* assuming different characters according to the time and place. Thus, the men who in actual fact obey the laws of caste are not the whole body of Brahmins all over India, but a particular section of Brahmins in a particular region, practising a particular occupation. Even these sections are split up before our eyes, without their sub-dividings being subject to any strict principle. Migrations, the breaking-up of peoples at the foreign invasions, endemic scourges, wars, local economic rivalries, unequal blending with non-Aryan tribes, religious propaganda, and many other influences, the most effective of which were often the general—these are the obscure but real causes, although they are usually beyond the ken of the historian.

Not only does the caste organization not form an unalterable structure, but that abomination of abominations, mixture of castes, happens every moment. The individuals born of these mixed marriages fall into lower castes or constitute new ones. So the theoretical rule of caste is an ideal rather than a fact, but in being an ideal it is a fact, maintaining, through the infinite diversity of real conditions, a few common principles, the chief of which is the prestige of the Brahmin.

Various attempts have been made by Europeans to account for the facts of caste or the notion of caste. Sociologists and ethnologists have connected it with occupation or with race. Students of India, usually philologists, have searched the history of the country for literary evidence.

Neṣfield maintained that the decisive factor was professional specialization. In his view, occupations are classed in order of rank—hunting or fishing, stock—breeding, agriculture, manual or servile labour, trade, priesthood. The abstract character of this conception is revealed by the assertion that a succession of stages like this is inherent in the whole of mankind. Senart's replies to the arguments of Nesfield and Ibbetson are insurmountable; if the original bonds of castes lay in community of profession, those bonds would have preserved it from splitting up; but the fact is that men who exercise the same occupation in the same district, and so should be united, belong to different castes, which keep them apart. One finds Brahmans practising all trades, save those which would make them lose caste. The rules which ensure the maintenance and perpetuity of the castes have no connection with occupation.

Brahaminism, according to the tradition of Manu, holds that the three sciences which make up human knowledge are *vārttā*, *dandanīti*, the science of punishments, and *trayī*, the three Vedas or religious science. The materialistic tradition of Brihaspati recognizes only two fundamental sciences, *vārttā* and daṇḍanītī. Kautilya, in virtue of the etymology of *vārttā*, says that *artha* is the *vṛitti* of man, in other words, that it means the whole of human activity. The close connection of the two lies in the fact that *artha* raises the question of ends and *vārttā* that of means. If the object of politics is the possession of land, or dominion, a well-filled treasury and a strong army are needed, and these imply abundant material resources. The idea of this connection is expressed in mythology. The first human king, according to the Vedic legends, who is sometimes Manu and sometimes Prithu, is not only the first sacrificer, but a fire-bringing Prometheus and the inventor of agriculture.

According to orthodox principles, economic life is the affair of the Vaiśyas caste. If that caste, like the two above it, had a literature of its own, we should have valuable information, instead of being reduced to inferring the content of economic life from the form imposed on it by Brahminic theory and the policy of kings. But it is idle to sigh for the impossible; dedicated to work, the Vaiśyas caste had neither the education nor the leisure to think about anything but accounts and output.

Yet the Vaiśyas were the aristocracy of the workers. Base and arduous tasks were left for the Śūdras, the slaves (dāsya), and all the dregs of the people who were kept outside the caste system. Of these, the slaves deserve special mention. A free man *(ārya)* might be a "temporary" slave—if, for example, he pledged his person because he could not otherwise pay a fine or the costs of a law-suit, or if he was carried off in a raid. Also, if a man left his caste to enter a monastic order and then left the order or never entered it, he became a slave of the King. We should note, too, that the King must liberate every free man reduced to bondage by violence, for he is, in principle, obliged to abolish or compensate every injustice, and the proverb says that slavery is not for *āryas* (*natvevāryasya dāsabhāvah*. Kautilya, iii, 13, 65). The only case in which a free man who had become a slave could not buy himself off was where he had himself sold his person; he then became like the permanent slaves. Of these there were four kinds—born in the house, bought, captured in a raid, and inherited. In all four cases the only legal duty owed by the slave to his master was obedience, the obligation to serve him in the matter of work.

The economic life of India is chiefly agricultural. The very name of *ārya*, in which the masters of country pride themselves, means to them (root *kṛish*) the tillers of the soil, as opposed to the other occupants. Yet they came into the country as herdsmen, whose wealth lay in kine and horses rather than in crops. We must even, perhaps, suppose that the methods of irrigation on which the prosperity of the fields in the Indus basin depends were due not so much to these nomadic stock-raisers as to the settled Sumero Dravidians, doubtlessly taught by Mesópotanian experience. Whatever that may be, the Vedic Indians adapted themselves very early to the resources of the Punjab, rich in *yava* and sugarcane.

Beginning as moral and eschatological fanaticism, Buddhism was to develop on the one hand into pure metaphysics, and on the other, into a religion which grew more and more like Hinduism.

Recent works of Sylvain Lévi and his pupils, particularly Louis de la Vallée-Poussin, followed by Tuneld and Przyluski, have entirely revised our knowledge of the Buddhist councils. We are no longer content with the traditional account, according to which the discipline was laid down at Rajagriha shortly after the Master's death, and then at Vaisali a hundred years later, and the canonical books were finally established at Pataliputra in 245 BC, under Asoka. We are beginning to suspect that Buddhist traditions vary very greatly according to the place and time, and to realize that one council or another, without being a mere myth, is presented in a legendary aspect. Not only are the accounts incomplete, or late, or fanciful; they are biased, being intended as the defence of a particular tradition. Only the critical dissection of a vast mass of Indian, Chinese, Tibetan and Serindian literature will make it possible to throw some light on those early ages of Buddhism, whose air of rationalistic simplicity led the first Western historians who studied them so far astray.

J. Przyluski has noted how, as council followed council, the Buddhist centre of gravity gradually shifted westwards and this fact, as he interprets it, seems to him to be very informative. The first great manifestation of the sect, like the first attempt to set up a great monarchy, takes place in Magadha and the surrounding countries, which as we must once again recall, were little Brahminised in the sixth century. One feels that the caste system was not likely to be propitious to politics on a grand scale or to a religion embracing all mankind. Vaisali marks a first stage in the westward movement, but the account of the assembly supposed to have been held there "can only have been written at a time when Mathura was already the seat of an influential community".[1] But that city, the centre of a truly Brahmin district, was a centre of Sanskrit literature. The Mathura stage therefore marks the adaptation of Buddhism to the intellectual civilization of the Brahmins, its incorporation, not indeed in the orthodoxy, but at least in the classical thought of India. As for the Pali canon, which was to reach Ceylon, it is found in a school which is almost unrelated to that of Mathura, namely the school of Kausambi, whose influence extended to Ujjayini in the south-west. Lastly, the council summoned by Kanishka, at which Asvahosha was instructed to draw up a gloss explaining the dogma *(vibhāshā)*, was held in Kashmir, away in the north-west, in countries subject to many western influences, Iranian or transmitted through Iran.

The Buddhist legends, no less and perhaps more than the real facts, reflect the rivalries of sects. If, for example, a book tells us that Madhyantika, the apostle of Kashmir, converted Upagupta, the saint of Mathura, let us regard the statement as an anachronistic and nonsensical claim of a later church to be senior to an older church. So, too, the innocent expositors of the past did not see what lay beneath the veneration of a particular saint in a particular place. A church invoked the inspiration of Anada, Upali, or Mahakasyapa, according as it set most store by dharma or discipline or metaphysics. Ananda is the religious type of early times, full of moral inspiration and compassion; Anuruddha is the superhuman, supernatural Arhat.

The Council of Rajagriha, when viewed in the light of this new and searching criticism, becomes a legend embroidered on a wholly pagan canvas, the seasonal myth of Gavampati, the god of drought, losing his power at the beginning of the rains.[2] It is very likely that arrangements had to be made when, for the first time after the Master's death, the weather compelled the Sangha to gather together, but there is more of folklore than of history in the story of the gathering. An assembly like that which took place every year at the same season and was marked by a popular festival evidently seemed a great event, at any rate to those interested in regarding it as such, namely the clergy who wanted to distinguish themselves from the community in the wider sense, including the layman (mahāsaṃgha). When the texts have been taken to pieces in the same way for the other councils we shall perhaps be more sceptical of the genuineness of the accounts, but we shall have more correct notions of what it is most important to discover, the life of the many sects.

They seem to have evolved from an unorganised, semi-democratic state of things, in which no permanent hierarchy was possible, to an oligarchy in which the elders (Sthavira) have authority, while the saints become patriarchs. So a monastic system grows up in which the rules of discipline (Vinaya) become more and more important compared with the Law (dharma). The clergy are less interested in the edification of the faithful than in forming a nursery of Arhats, whose merit will presently be judged by gnosis or efficience rather than by punctual observance of the rules. But all generalization is rash, so different are local communities.

From the most ancient tradition, that of the Mahāsaṃghikas, in which there was least differentiation between the layman and cleric, the eastern churches sprang. In the west two stocks were to flourish particularly. The Sthaviras of Kausambi established the Pali scriptures in Ceylon, and the Sarvāstivādins of Mathura spread to Kashmir, where they founded a sect which claimed to conform to the original spirit of that tradition, and therefore called itself the Mūlasarvāstivādins. Since the Sthaviras and the Sarvāstivādins travelled to opposite ends of India, the former introducing Pali texts where they went and the latter Sanskrit, they have in Europe until recently been superficially contrasted as Southern Buddhism and Northern Buddhism.

A great deal of critical examination of the evidence is still necessary to disentangle the confused mass of sects. The question is of importance, for the canon varies according to the sects or tradition.

The present study draws up the scheme of that canonified Buddhist literature. In theory every work should, allow for variants that appear in Pali, Sanskrit, Tibetan and Chinese.

The Divisions of the Pali Canons

The whole corpus, the Triptaka or Threefold Basket, is divided into three sections—the basket of Vinaya or Discipline, of the Sutras or Stories, and of Abhidharma or the Essence of the Law, that is metaphysics.

(1) Vinaya—Suttavibhanga, explanation of the Sūtras or articles of the Prātimoksha; Khandakās, "sections" on the daily life of monks and nuns; Mahāvagga, the "great division", and Chullavagga, the "lesser division" ; Parivāra a late collection of unconnected texts and canonical tables.

(2) Sūtras—Five collections *(nikāya)*: the long collection, Dīgha (34 sūtras); the medium, Majjhima (152 homilies or dialogues); the composite, Saṃyutta (56 groups of sūtras); the numerical, Anguttara in which each section contains one piece more than the preceding; and the least Khuddaka (shorter texts). This last contains works of great importance; (i) Khuddaka pāṭha, short texts; (ii) Dhammapada, the Law in maxims; (iii) Udāna, the "spiritual" aspirations; (iv) Itivuttaka utterances of Buddha; (v) Sutta nipāta, sections of less amplitude; (vi) Vimanavatthu and (vii) Pentavatthu, tales of divine palaces and ghost; (viii) Therāgātha and (ix) Therīgāthā, verses of the monks and nuns; (x) Jātakas, stories of previous births of Buddha; (xi) Niddesa, partial commentary on the Sutta nipāta; (xii) Paṭisambhidāmagga, a work of Abhidharma; (xiii) Apadān, "Feats" of holiness; (xiv) Buddhavaṃsa, legends of thirty-four Buddhas prior to Sakyamuni; (xv) Chariyāpiṭaka, thirty-five Jātakas showing low Sakyamuni came to possess the ten perfections.

(3) Abhidharma—(i) Puggalapaññatti, the theory of individuality; (ii) Dhātukathā, an exposition of the elements or factors which condition psychical phenomena; (iii) Dhammasangani an enumeration of phenomena; (iv) Vibhanga, fragments of the same kind as the preceding section; (v) Paṭṭhāna; (vi) Yamaka questions asked in positive and negative form; (vii) Kathavatthu, a manual of controversy for the use of monks.

Such is the gist of the Pali canon. Its more ancient parts are the first two Baskets. The Abhidharma, a "supplement", an extremely subtle inquiry regarding the Law, came later as amore profound development of the doctrine implied in the Suttras (Sanskrit, Sūtras). Thus, the Kathāvātthu is supposed to be the work of Tissa Moggaliputta, a doctor of the third century BC Most of the works mentioned above must have been in existence at that time, particularly in the reign of Asoka, when the Emperor called the great, Buddhist assembly of Pataliputra. It was then that *"abidharmic"* theory took definite shape, to be a special Basket henceforward.

There is a great mass of literature, still in Pali, but outside the canon, which is a continuation of these texts and in great part a commentary on them–the *Milinda–Pañha* or Questions of King Menander, which is so characteristic of the speculative activity of the Indian sophists of the second and first centuries BC; the *kathās* (the attha and the *Nidānakathāsā*), which are explanations of the Jātakas; the glosses Buddhághosha, the great commentator of the fifth century of our era (Visuddhimagga, Samantapāsādikā, Sumangalavilāsinī, Papañchasūdani, Sāratthapakāsinī, Manorathapūranī); two Cingalese chronicles, the *Dipavaṃsa* and *Mahāvaṃsa* and many other works.

The present chapter now runs through the names of the chief non-Pali works, chiefly Sanskrit, which have often been attributed to a supposed Northern Buddhism, as if the Sanskrit and Pali literatures were fundamentally and originally opposed like the North and South of India. Most of these books belong to the Mahāyāna, the Great Vehicle, or mark the transition from it to the Small Vehicle, the Hīnayāna. None is earlier than the first century of our era.

The *Mahāvstu* and the *Lalita-vistara* are legendary biographies of Buddha. The former is the work of the Lokottaravādin Mahāsaṃghíkas of the first century and the latter belongs to the Mahāyāma Sūtras. The corpus of these Sutras contains a number of texts in which myth and metaphysics are combined—*Sudharma-puṇḍarīka*, the "Lotus of the Good Law" (beginning of the third century); *Kāraṇḍavyūha*, which is fundamental for the worship of the Bodhisattva Avalokitesvara; *Sukhāvatîvyūha*, a defence of the paradise of the Buddha Amitabha; *Gaṇḍavyūha* or *Avataṃsakasūtra*, an eulogy of the bodhisattva Mañjusri; *Karuṇapuṇdarīka*, the "Lotus of Compassion"; *Lankavatara*, an account of the supposed visit of Sakyamuni to Ravana, king of Ceylon; *Daśabhūmīśvara*, an account of the ten "lands" through one travels to attain the condition of a Buddha; *Samādhirāja*, the "King of Concentration"; *Suvarnaprabhāsa*, the "Splendour of God"; *Rāshṭrpāta-Paṛiprichā*, the question of Rashtrapala, being explanations about the state of Bodhisattva.

Most of these works were translated into Chinese from the fourth century to the beginning of the seventh. At the beginning of the Great Vehicle stands the literature of prajñā pāramitā (first and second centuries), the "Highest Degree of Knowledge", which opens the way to the great philosophies, that of the Mādhyamikas (Nagarjuna, followed by Aryadeva, between 150 and 250) and that of the Yogāchāras (fourth to seventh century), before which comes the great figure of Asvaghosha (second century).

The ancient variety of Prakrit named Pali, adopted by the Buddhists for writing the greater part of their canon, became the instrument of a whole literature.

In that literature teaching pure and simple alternates with works of imagination which, though naively didaetic, are some times charming. The Pali canon contains everything—sermons, anecdotes, hymns. If we would understand the rise of lyric poetry we can not neglect the *Thera-gāthās* and *Thri-gāthās*,[3] the hymns of monks and nuns to the glory of Buddha. Tradition already ascribed some of these to Ananda, the favourite disciple of Buddha, and Moggallana (Sanskrit Maudgalyayana), one of the first doctors of the Buddhist church. In that case they would date from some centuries before Christ. But the tradition only proves that the names of the real authors were not known and that it was desired to give this devout poetry an origin worthy of the public esteem.

It is, however, possible that in all the 107 *Thera-gāthās* there are a good many remnants of an ancient cycle. Many of the hymns consist of unconnected bits which look like fragments which have been given a tinge of severe, monotonous piety and exaggerated renunciation. Only the feeling for nature, which in the Hindu survives the death of the desires, gives a brighter tone to the drab uniformity. The "Nuns' Hymns" are much more interesting. One can distinguish different authors, mostly women, so delicate is the touch and so simple are the stories. Women were only admitted into the Buddhist community with great difficulty. The gifts of their piety were accepted readily; Buddha, according to the story, rested in the house given to him by a converted harlot. It was considered natural for rich, and even poor, women to provide for the needs of the monks. But it was not allowed that they could embrace the monistic life and found convents for themselves officially. Buddha opposed it. When Ananda asked " why do you withstand this ?" He answered, "Women are foolish, Ananda . . . . Women are envious, Ananda . . . Women are spiteful, Ananda".

Buddha's adoptive mother entreated him long before he allowed her to found an order of women. At last Ananda succeeded in overcoming his resistance, but the Buddhist canon did not thank him, and he is heaped with reproaches for his feminist attitude.

The Therī-gāthās which have come down to us reveal a knowledge of the art of poetry as set forth in the works on "ornaments" *(alamkara)*. They have a developed style such as we do not find in the inscriptions before our era. It may, therefore, be a second, later stratum of Therī-gāthās that we know.

The general theme of all these hymns, monks' and nuns' alike, is the joy of renunciation. The women add moving stories of their conversion, the opposition of their kinsfolk, the temptations of love, and so on. Some hymns are in dialogue form, particularly when a tempter comes in, man or demon. Often they are real ballads. One of the most beautiful is that of the young and pious Subha pursued by a lover, like St. Lucy or St. Bridget. She plucks out her eyes that men may not be led aside from the way of salvation, but the Master gives her back her sight.

The Gāthās are human documents. In some the monks confess their weaknesses and blame woman, the source of all evil. In others they glory in having had the courage to trample on their duties as husbands and fathers to give themselves wholly to Buddha. A certain self-assertion is noticeable. The women are simpler and more melancholy. Most took to religion after losing their children; having found consolation, they tell of their serenity under misfortune. Harlots stated with pleasure that they aspire only to Nirvana. Young girls leave the world, just as in the early centuries of Christian mysticism.[4] There are heart-rending pictures. But one also finds humour and even gaiety of a simple-minded sort. A nun declares that all that she has renounced is the upper and lower millstones and a hump-backed husband, and that for whole days she used to grind the rice and listen to her husband swearing. A monk leaves the convent to marry, but a fortnight later becomes once more convinced of the nothing-ness of things and returns to his comrades. Some of the hymns are keen satires on bad monks; one can see that Buddhism is no longer in its first stages. A commentary, doubtless not the first, on these hymns was written in the fifth century.

By the side of these works, which partake of the character of popular literature, the first centuries of our era saw the rise of an artistic and profoundly philosophic literature in Pali—the Milinda-pañha, or "Questions of Menander". It deals with the problem of personality from the Buddhist point of view. It is not only a philosophic treatise, but a work of art. The heroes are a doctor of the Buddhist church named Nagasena and the Indo-Greek king Menander, Milinda in Pali. The latter reigned between 125 and 95 BC over a large district extending from the Indus and the Gujarat country to the middle course of the Ganges. He was a Greek. He was believed to be a convert to Buddhism, but this is not certain, although he is represented on coins with a *chakra*, or Wheel of the Law.[5] In his case India—North-Western India, it is true—seems to have abandoned its traditional hostility to foreigners. If we can believe Plutarch, several Indian cities contended for the ashes of Menander, shared them among themselves, and set up a commemorative monument for each portion. The story is too much like that of Buddha to be accepted without caution. Whatever that may be, Menander was the only Greek whom India adopted.

The *Milinda-pañha* is a fine philosophic novel. We have no notion whether it has any foundation in fact. Possibly the author wanted to present the doctrine of negation in artistic form, and the persistent memory in Northern India of an Indian King of Greek race suggested that he should contrast the Greek spirit and the Indian.

Of the seven books of which the work is composed, at the the most the second and third are authentic, and even they contain late interpolations. The beginning of the first book, describing the capital, is doubtless by the first author, whose name is unknown.

The King is resting after reviewing his army. But the night is fine, and instead of sleeping he would carry out an argument with some ascetic or pious Brahmin. The courtiers take him to a famous hermit who lives near the city. The discussion starts, and the sage is soon reduced to silence, not knowing what to answer to the arguments of the King. Other renowned sages are met, with the same result. Menander exclaims in disappointment, "India is empty! People here can only prate!"

Meanwhile the Buddhist doctor, Nagasena, passing through the country, has stopped near the capital. The King is advised to visit him. Menander goes, and we witness the most remarkable, and indeed the most passionate contest that the world has seen.

"How are you called, venerable one?" the King asks. "I am called Nagasena, but that is only a name, an assemblage of sounds with no reality in it," answers the sage. And in a dialogue in which the King stands for what one may call the positive spirit and the sage for the speculative, it is proved to us that the "I" does not exist, being only a transitory manifestation of a collection of phenomena.

The most awkward questions are answered in a manner as witty as unexpected. Menander asks whether a man who dies and is born again is the same or somebody else. "Both," answers Nagasena. "You, O King, are you now the same as the little child (and so on) that you once were?" "No." "Then if you are not the same, you have had no father, no mother (etc.), and you have not lived before this moment at which you are speaking." And by a series of parallels Nagasena proves to the

King the continuity of phenomena, the only thing that we are able to admit.

Menander might have said that as soon as there is no personality there is no obligation or responsibility, and would thereby have overthrown the whole of Buddhist ethics.

While Pali was reserved for works of Buddhist inspiration, chiefly propagandist and educational, profane literature developed in Prakrit languages. Sanskrit was not given up, but, having been set up as a sacred language, it was not suited for familiar use. It did not become the idiom of chancellories and government offices until fairly late. About the beginning of our era Middle Indian came into use in the administration. This is the language used by Asoka to teach his people the Law to which he himself has been converted. His many inscriptions on pillars and rocks are written in local dialects. In any case the Prakrit works followed their Sanskrit models. Tastes were the same, being imposed by the upper classes; those who wrote on poetics (*alaṃkāra*) addressed themselves to all writers without distinction. Sanskrit, the noble language, Pali, the sacred language of the Buddhists, and the Prakrits, which were regional *kowaí*, lived side by side, although they flourished variously according to the place, the time, and the importance of the ideas which were clothed in them.

Notes and References

1. CCVI, p. 10.
2. CCVII, p. v.
3. Translated into English by Mrs. Rhys Davids, *Psalms of the Early Buddhists, i. Psalms of the Sisters,* London, Pali Text Soc., 1909.
4. Cf. R. Spence Hardy, *Eastern Monachism.*
5. Cf. S. Levi, XXV (i), xxiii, p. 43 (1891).

4

Brahminism and Buddhism in Shudras' Life

The present chapter reflects the comparitive study on Brahminism and Buddhism. This study shows the situation when Brahminism and the non-Vedic systems of Jainism and Buddhism competed with one another in spreading to the Deccan. The famous Sutrakaras, Baudhayana and Apastamba are the harbingers of the Brahmanical socia-religious system in Deccan. These law-givers lived roughly between 450 and 300 BC[1] and are believed in Maharashtra and Andhra respectively.[2] Unlike *Manudharmashastra,*[3] which was compiled much later, the Sutrakaras exhibited realistic view of the situation and followed a liberal policy of give and take in acculturating the Deccanis to the Brahminical social order. For example, Baudhayana criticised the custom of cross-cousin marriages prevalent among the Deccanis but accorded official recognition to it.[4] With Apastamba, the process of conciliation and synthesis took a long step forward. He admitted the beliefs and practices prevalent among the Shudras and the womenfolk into the Atharvaveda and recognised the Puranas as authorities on matters of religion. His declaration that he prepared the laws in accordance with the prevalent practices and conventions and because people were in need of such rules to guide them[5] and the meticulous care with which he prescribes the do's and don't suggest that the socio-relations organisation based on the conciliation of the North and the South was just in its formative stage and the aim of the rules was to regularise the new relations and build up a harmonious social order. Because of the presence of occupational groups already in Deccan, as noted above, the extension of the Varna system must have become smooth. The conclusion that in the process of 'Aryanisation of the south' all the megalithic people were absorbed into the Vaisya Varna—the third Varna of the early Vedic society[6]—is not well-thought out. It is more reasonable to assume that the Deccanis were admitted into the fold according to their professions.

However, liberal and compromising the Sutrakaras might have been, their rigid Varna regulations and exclusiveness in social relations should have proved galling to the rich Gahapati and Setthi classes and to their proud political leaders in the Deccan. They preferred, therefore, the cosmopolitanism of Jainism and Buddhism. Literary evidence points to the spread of the two religions to the South during the life time of their prophets.[7] The Hathigumpha inscription[8] says that King Kharavela brought back the images of Jina which had been carried away as trophies by Mahapadmanada (c. 430 BC). The large quantities of NBP were unearthed at Vaddamanu and Dhanyakataka,[9] early centres of Jainism and Buddhism respectively are a proof of the exodus of those religionists to the Krishna valley by about the 4th century B.C. On the hill of Vaddamanu there was Samprati Vihara[10] and the elliptical buildings at the place remind similar Vihara complexes at Rajgir (Jivakarama), Barabar Hills (Gopika Cavek), Kausambi (Ghoshitarama) and Srasvasti (Pakkikuti).[11] The Buddhist works, *Suttanipata* and *Paramarthadipaṇi* describe the advent of Buddhism into Western Deccan-Assaka and Mulaka. By virtue of being *madhyama pratipat*, Buddhism could steal a march over Jainism and gained popularity with most of the tribal states. The Bull on the coins of the Sebakas[12] may be a symbolical representation of the Buddha. The *Mahabharata* says the Mahisakas who were originally Kshatriyas were reduced to the status of Vrishalas as they lost respect for Brahmins[13]—implying that they became Buddhists. The Nagas at Dhanyakateaka and probably the Yakshas at Bhattiprolu accepted Buddhism. There is a strong view that Mahadeva Bhikshu whose famous Five Points brought about the schism at the Second *sangiti* was a resident of Caitya Saila which is identified with Dhanyakateaka.[14] The statement of the R.E.XIII of Ashoka "*Bhoja Pitinikesu Andhra Palidesu Sarvatra Devanampyasa Dhamma manusasti*" supports the impression given by Kathavatthu that Deccan became a stronghold of Buddhism.

The Buddhists appear to have preferred to have their Viharas on the upper reaches of Godavari and in the Lower Krishna basin which were rich rice producing and industrially advanced areas. Traces of ancient iron-working have been found in the region comprising the Assaka and Mulaka Janapadas and Pratistana was a great centre of industry and trade, whereas a large part of Guntur district is known from early days as Karmarashtra.[15] In addition, the Buddhists had their Viharas along the trade routes that converged at Dhanyakataka, one from Paithan across Telangana and the other from Pataliputra along the east coast, and branched off, one proceeding to Konchi in Tamil Nadu and the other to Banavasi in Mysore. Ashoka appears to have followed the east coast route in his dharmayatra to reach Suvarnagiri, described in his M.R.E. Samudra Gupta in his South Indian expedition followed evidently the same route.

On these trade routes, the Buddhist Viharas probably served as the halting places for the caravans. There is every reason to believe that at times, the Viharas lent the needy merchants not only money but also means of transport such as bullocks and bullockcarts.[16] The Viharas thus played a conspicuous role in promoting trade and industry. The Shrenis and Sarthavahas in their turn kept the inmates of the Viharas above want and thus helped them to concentrate on spiritualist exercises and rise to great philosophical heights.

Buddhism had fulfilled its historical mission of pulling down the petty tribal barriers and helped the Satavahan as to unify Deccan into an empire under their rule. They organised their administration mostly on the lines adopted by their erstwhile over-lords, the Mauryas[17] who were the first to experiment in imperial system. It is interesting that the names of the members of the *nigama* at Bhattiprolu[18] are all Sanskritic though written in Prakrit. One of the Amaravati inscriptions, belonging to the third century AD, gives the name of a cobbler (*charmakara*) as Vidhika whose father was Naga *upjjhaya*, both the names being in Sanskrit.[19] Buddhism has thus paved the way for the extension of North Indian systems and Brahminical culture in the Deccan.

The situation changed with the disintegration of the Mauryan empire soon after the death of Ashoka (c.232 BC). Taking advantage of the confusion prevailing in the North, the Asoka Janapada developed into the Satavahana empire absorbing the neighbouring Mulaka and Sebaka Janapadas. This transformation of a tribal state into an imperial system brought about a change in the religious set up also. The silence of sources about the *gotra* of the Satavahanas and the proud title Kshatriyadarpa mana mardana[20] given to Gautamiputra Satakarni would only suggest that the Satavahan as were neither Brahmins nor Kshatriyas. The Kshatriyasagara and Dvatrimshatta puttalika accounts[21] of the eponymous Satavahana are unanimous about his humble origin. During those times, such a family of humble origin naturally preferred a non-Vedic religion. According to an early Jain tradition, Satavahana, the first king of the dynasty was overthrown in a revolt.[22] That Satavahana is a personal name is proved by numismatic evidence and the descriptions of the first kings in the dynasty, Srimukha and Kanha, according to the Purnic lists, can be taken to establish his historicity. At Nanaghat, a label inscription below the image of Srimukha reads[23]: *Srimukha Satavahaano Sirimato* which may be interpreted as Srimat Srimukha, son of Satavahana. His successor Kanha is called Satavahana *kula,*[24] born in the family of Satavahana. These records suggest that Srimukha and Kanha were the sons of Satavahana, of the Jain records. But Satavahana does not find a place in the Puranic lists of Satavahana (Andhra) kings as he was a follower of non-Brahminical religion and that was also the reason for him being overthrown. It is not out of place to recall that following Ashoka's death there was in the north a movement for the revival of Brahminism, spearheaded by the Sungas of Bharadvaja *gotra*.[25] Srimukha and Kahna grew wiser by the example of their father and seem to have changed over to Bhagavatism, as suggested by their names. Even Bhagavatism is non-Vedic but efforts were just in progress at a rapprochment between Brahminism and Bhagavatism as reflected in the Nanaghat record of Naganika.[26] Srimukha's son, Satakarni I came out as a champion of Vedic ritualism probably inspired by the example of his north Indian contemporary, Pusyamitra Sunga. The innumerable sacrifices he performed and the rich *dakshinas* he gave away reveal not only the enthusiasm of a new convert but also his anxiety to win the support of the Brahmins to the newly established Satavahana authority. His queen Naganika was the daughter of Maharathi Trankairo, a name that sounds non-Sanskritic or quite aboriginal. Naganika proudly describes herself as *Yajnahuta dhupana sugandhaya*. The royal couple named one of their sons as Vedisiri—Glory of the Altar. However, the Nanaghat record registers a compromise between Brahminism and Bhagavatism. The efforts of the royal couple did not go waste as their empire could be consolidated. But none of their successors showed any interest in sacrifices. Nor do we come across any of their records registering gifts to Brahmins. They do not seem to have bothered about their social status as they never cared to have a rishi *gotra*, even while mentioning the gotras of their mothers. But the clear emergence of neo-Brahminism of Puranic theism and the growth of Purana-Agama literature as an authority on it during the 150 years following the Nanaghat inscription are revealed by *Gathasaptashati*[27] and the Nasik inscription[28] *Gautami Bala Sri*.

The Shaka rulers, the Kshaharatas and later the Kardamakas who had conquered the Western Deccan from Satavahanas took full advantage of the rising New Religion. In fact, one of the aims of the authoress of the religion was to wean away the foreigners from the attractions of Buddhism. In their turn, the Shakas with a three-fold objective become Shivabhagavatas: (i) to get the people reconciled to their rule, (ii) to get their political authority legitimised, and (iii) to get admission into the ruling elite of the orthodox social order. However, the Kshaharata prince, Rishabhadatta, son-in-law of Nahapana followed wisely the policy of patronising all the powerful religious systems in his kingdom. He gifted caves to Buddhist fraternities and instituted certain permanent endowments in their favour. At the same time, he was punctilious in observing the pious act prescribed by the Puranas, the authorities on neo-Brahminism: devotion to the favourite god; honouring the Brahmin pilgrimage to holy places and performing *mahadanas*. Rishabhadatta gifted 16 villages to Gods and Brahmins (*devatabhyo brahma nobhyah sodashagrama dana*), fed every year thousands of Brahmins (*anuvarsa brahmana satasahasri bhojayitva*), got several of them married, visited *kshetras* like Dashapura, Govardhana, Shurparaka, Suvarnamukhi and Ramatirtham where he raised *chatushshalas*, *aramas tatakas* and *undapanas* and performed *mahadanas*, which included thousands of cows and gold, lands and maiden.[29] The Karddamakas who succeeded the Kshaharatas adopted the same policy. Rudradama, evidently a *shivabhagata*, endered himself to the people by his benevolent rule.[30] The Abhiras became Vishnubhagavatas.[31] This policy of foreign tribes yielded the desired results. The Shakas were treated almost as Kshatriyas and local ruling families had marriage alliances with them. Shivashir Shatakarni, son of Gautamiputra married Rudradamanika, daughter of Rudradama.[32] Another Shaka princess of Ujjain, Rudradharabhattarika become the queen of Virapurushadtta,[33] son of Sri Chamtamula, the founder of the Ikhavaku dynasty and the performer of *agnishtoma; vajapeya* and *ashvamedha*.

The Nasik incription of Gautami Balashri pictures her son Satakarni as champion of neo-Brahminism. But Gautamiputra seems to have found political wisdom in continuing the policy of his Kshatrapa predecessors—supporting all the popular religions for the consolidation of the fortunes of Satavahanas which he himself had just restored. By about this time, as it appears, Brahmins of prestigious *gotras* like Gautama, Vashistha and Kaushika became anxious to win royal support for the rising neo-Brahminism and came forward to enter into marriage alliance with the Satavahanas. In their turn, the Satavahanas were liberal to their Brahmin queens. They allowed the latter to have their paternal *gotras* as prefixes to their names and even nominated their children as successors to the throne. The first offspring of such a Brahmin-Satavahaha alliance was Gautamiputra Satakarni and that seems to be the reason for the sudden appearance of metronymics in the form of rishi *gotras* in the dynasty.[34] The Brahmins must have entertained high hopes about Satakarni, but it is doubtful how far he had fulfilled them. The few records of Satakarni so far available[35] contain not even the slightest evidence in support of the high-sounding Brahmanical titles conferred on him in the record. On the other hand, the records register gifts only to Buddhist fraternities, that too in the Nasik region which he had conquered from the

Kshaharatas probably Rishabhadatta. Even his son and successor, Vasishthiputra Puluymavi made gifts to the Buddhists of the same region.[36] This only shows the anxiety of the father and the son-one to consolidate his authority in the newly conquered region and the other to retain his hold on the same region which was slipping out of his hands. It is doubtful whether Gautamiputra made any effort to make the titles given to him by his mother meaningful. Not even a single measure of Gautamiputra to promote the interests of Brahmins (*dvijavara kutumba vivardhana*) is so far known. On the other hand, he seems to have drawn his officers from the rich and powerful Setthi class, as indicated by the name Shivagupta, one of his ministers.[37] He is said to have stopped the admixture of castes—vinivartita *caturvarna samskara*. But his son married a Shaka princess and the names of Chatrapana Satakarni,[38] Shaka Satakarni and Madhariputra Sakasena[39] show how Shaka *mlechchos* and the Satavahanas were getting mixed up. The Satavahanas were no patrons of Buddhism, still that religion was predominant in Deccan, supported by the rich peasant, artisan and merchant classes who formed the financial backbone of the Satavahana state. No Satavahana king could, therefore, take any anti-Buddhist measures and that is conveyed to us by Balashri, when she described her son as *paurajana-nivishesa samaskha duhkhasa*—one who shared equally the weal and woe of his people. The Nasik record is the only one of the Satavahanas which mentions the Brahmins (*dvijas*) and the four *varnas*. The people of the age do not appear to have been conscious of their castes and mention only their occupations while making gifts to religious institutions. An inscription from Nagarjunakonda,[40] belonging to the Ikshvaku times mentions Brahmins but brackets them with Sramanas-beggars and the record may be taken to reflect the condition of the Brahmins, a sad commentary on the claim of Gautamiputra. The prevailing cosmopolitan spirit in society is attested by the instance of a cobbler, Vidhika visiting the Kshetra at Dhanyakatka with family and friends and making gifts. The Nasik inscription has to be studied therefore afresh and interpreted against its historical setting. About twenty years after the death of her illustrious son, the old disconsolate *rajarishi vadhu,* the Brahmin mother of Satakarni remembers her son and points him in colours which she held ideal for an obedient son and a pious Brahminical king.

As the Brahmanists, were busy in developing Puranic theism to combat Buddhism and check its progress, the Buddhists started efforts to broad-base their system and thereby retain their hold on the people. The result was the emergence of Mahayana, satisfying the sentiments and religious requirements of common people. Some scholars argue that Mahayana also was the result of the (mischievous) efforts of Brahmins to dilute Buddhism with the ultimate aim of defeating it. This view derives support from the fact that most of the philosophers who contributed to the growth of Mahayana thought and practice—Nagarjuna, Aryadeva, Bhavya, Asanga, Vasubhandu, Dinnaga and Dharmakirti—were all Brahmins. This theory sounds fantastic. In fact, Mahayana arose as a protest of the *upasakas* of the rich peasant, artisan and merchant classes against monastic orthodoxy. The Vimalakiriti Nirdesha[42] makes it clear that Mahayana was the reply to the demands of the above classes for a means of nirvana independent of monastic order. It was the wealth of these classes that had gone into the raising of magnificent stupas and Viharas and it was natural that the attitude to life of these classes only reflects in the sculpture of Amaravati, the most renowned Buddhist Kshetra in Deccan. It is, therefore, more appropriate to say that Mahayana was developed by the above classes in cooperation with prominent Acharyas, who were deeply concerned with the future. Of the Noble Gospel, in order to arrest the progress of neo-Brahminism and check the increasing popularity and influence of the Brahmins.

However, Mahayana served the cause of the Brahminists by bridging the gulf between Buddhism and Bhagavatism through devotion and paved the way for the incorporation of Buddha into the Brahminical pantheon as the ninth incarnation of Vishnu. Even by about AD 250, at Shriparvata, Buddha was looked upon as God Supreme granting the pious devotees boons such as health, victory and long life and it is not long afterwards that Buddha on Shriparvata became Shriparvata Swamy,[44] the family god of the Vaishnavite dynasty of Vishnukundins (c. AD 450-585).

The fall of the Satavahana dynasty (c. AD 255) brought about developments of farreaching importance in Deccan. Out of the ruins of Andhra empire, there sprang up several small kingdoms under Abhiras, Vakataks, Ikshvakus, Shalankeyanas, Pallaves and Vishnukundins, generally known as successors of Satavahanas. Some of them—Abhiras Pallavas and Shalankayanas—are known or have been Indianised foreigners through devotionalism, either Vaisanavism or Saivism. The others—Ikshvakus, Vishnukundins, Vakatakas and Chalukyas appear to have been indigenous tribals. These upstart ruling families seem to have struck a deal with Brahmins, the leaders at Brahminism, which was in gradual ascendency. But Brahminism developed in two directions—orthodox ritualism and popular devotionalism. Especially, the native dynasties indulged in excessive ritualism. In no other part of India and at no other point of time was such ritualistic exuberence as in Deccan during the period between AD 250 and 550. Sri Chamtamula, the Ikhshvaku king, performed Agnishtoma, Vajapeya and Ashvamedha, and vindicating the inscriptional evidence,[45] an *ashvamedha vedika* was discovered in the excavations in Nagarjunakonda valley.[46] Pravarasena of the Vakataka dynasty performed *agnishtoma, aptoryama, vajapeya,* i.e., jyotishtoma, brihaspatisava, sadhyaskra and four ashvamedhas.[47]

Ritualism reached high peaks under Vishnukundin Madhavarman and Chalukya Pulakeshin I. The former is credited with one thousand sacrificies (Katusahasra yaji) including eleven ashvamedhas, several Agishtomas, Rajasuya Paudariko, Yuddhya, Sodasi, Bahusuvarna, Hiranyagarbha,"[48] etc. The rites of Hiranyagarbha and Bahusuvarma are frequently met with the records of this period. Hiranyagarbha implies rebirth[49] evidently in a higher social order and Bahusuvarna recalls *vratyastoma* of the Vedic times. The Vishnukundins records contain suggestions about the aims of the Vedic rituals. The dynasty has admitted that they acquired political power by virtue of worshipping at the Feet of the Lord of Sripavata (Shriparvataswamy padanudhyana Vapta Prajapalanadhikaranam,[50] either the Buddha Tathagata or Buddha, the ninth incarnation of Vishnu. In the next stage, the dynasty boasted that they combined the glory of Brahmin and

Kshatriya (*brahma kshatro tejobrritam*),[51] indirectly admitting their humble origin. The culmination of this process is that Madhavavarman claims to have achieved by performing thousand sacrifices, Paramestitva[52]—the first position in social hierarchy. The dynasty has thus achieved ritual purity and got their political power legitimised.

Pulakeshin (c. 550), the founder of the Chalukyan dynasty is known to have performed *hiranyagarbha, bahusvarna, agnishtoma, agnicayana, vajapeya, Paundarka* and *ashvamedha* according to the Vedic rules[53] (*shrauta vidhanatah*) in his Campukaya, Chaluka Somesvara records that Pulakeshin I performed the 16 *mahadanas* during every Sankranti and kept the Vedic Brahmins quite busy and contended.[54] The aim of Pulakeshin also must have been fulfilled when he held equal to Brihaspati in rajaniti[55] (*nitau Brihaspati samah*) and as he took the titles Shri Prithvi Vallabha (vallabha=Lord at Shri= Lakshmidevi and Prithvi= Bhudevi=Lord Vishnu), with the implied principle of *navishnuhprithivipatith,* divine right of monarchy. The Brahmin scholars who were the probable composers of these records must have evidently conceded the high social status claimed by these dynasties and put official stamp of legitimacy on their political power. The kings granted the Vedic scholars *brahmadeyas* or Agraharas, expecting to serve as fountains of loyalty and pillars of support.[56]

Devotionalism suffered several ups and downs. The Nanaghat inscription may be taken to record the understanding between the Bhagavata (devotionalist) and the Brahmin (ritualist) and it was needed by the latter to arrest the progress of Buddhism. Each of the successors of Satavahanas had their family deity, on whose feet even the Yajvis among them meditated. These deities included Mahsena, Sambhu, Chitrarathaswamy and Shriparvataswamy. The Chalukyan *prashasti* involves three deities—Narayana, Mahasena and Hariti. Between AD 250 and 300 numerous temples were built and endowed by kings and their officers.[57] By about the beginning of the 4th century, Buddhism started declining. The Brahmin had a sense of fulfilment and no more had the need of Bhagavata support. As a result rivalry seems to have developed between the two classes of priests-Brahmina and Bhagavata—in sharing gifts. The latter or the temple priests were spoken of in disperaging terms even in some of the Puranas.[58] The Brahmin could further take advantage of the anxiety of the ruling families for social and political recognition and we have seen above how rulers pampered the Brahmin. Temples are very rarely heard during this period (AD 300-550) and the Brahmin monopolised almost all gifts. It may rightly be termed as the Age of Brahmin ascendency.

The proliferation of *agraharas* was also due to the compelling economic situation in the Deccan. Since the disintegration of the Satavahana empire, internal and external trade had rapidly declined, adversely affecting the native industry. Artisans and merchants resorted to villages and took to agriculture. The *nigamas, shrenis* and *vanijas* are no longer heard. The once busy trade routes were deserted and the centres of industry and trade languished and fell into ruins. Commercial economy yielded place to agricultural economy. It became inevitable that the kings should bestow serious attention on agriculture which became the mainstay of state economy and the chief source of sustenance to their subjects. The Ikshvaku king Shri Chamtamula is credited with *aneka hiranyakoti goshtasahasra halashatasahasra pradayi.*[59] A Pallava king of about the same time took the title Kaduvetti[60] whereas one of the early Chola kings, Karikala is also said to have cleared forests[61] and built villages and towns, evidently with the aim of bringing the land around them under cultivation. It is not unreasonable to suppose that lion's share of the land thus reclaimed was gifted to Brahmins. The Successors of Satavahanas including the early Chalukyas created a number of agraharas. The country from the confines of Utkala (Uttara Kalinga) down to the river Tungabhadra, especially the river basins came to be dotted with numerable Brahmadeyas, though the occasional occurrence of *devabhogahalas* (land gifted to temples) is not ruled out.

The *brahmadeyas* formed the nuclei of remarkable socio-economic developments. Brahmadeya being essentially an agricultural village, the demands of expanding agriculture brought the aboriginals of the neighbouring forest and hill tracts into intimate contact with centres of civilized life and were gradually absorbed into the different strata of society basing on their respective positions in the tribal organisation. The names of some of the Brahmins mentioned in inscriptions sound non-Sanskritic and aboriginal. Goginaja of Kondamudi plates,[62] Ganamadija of the Mayidavolu record[63] and Vilasharma of the Pikira plates[64] are some of such names. Interestingly, the *gotra* of Goginaja is not mentioned and it may indicate that his absorption into the Brahmin caste was not yet complete. Brahmins of Kashyapa *gotra* are frequently met with in inscriptions. The law-givers, especially Baudhayana suggests Kashyapa *gotra* for the social rehabilitation of lowly born people.[65] The Brahmins of the age took either Sharma or Arya as suffix to their names, which mean 'Vedic Scholar' and respectable' respectively. But some of the Brahmins of the age have both Sharma and Arya as suffixes as in the case of Bhavaskandsamnajja and Bhattisammajja of the Dharikatura plates,[66] which only reveals the anxiety of the persons to get recognition as high born Aryan Brahmins.

Such an acculturation of the tribal priests with the orthodox social order resulted in the rapid growth of Brahmin population as revealed by the inscriptions of the following period.[67] The pressure of increasing population appears to have compelled the Brahmins to resort to professions involving even manual labour such as carpentry. The two Salankayana records[68]—one Prakrit issued by Nandivarman and the other Sanskrit given by Skandavarman—register the grant of *agraharas* to *rathakaras,* a word generally understood as the caste of carpenters. But these rathakaras are described as belonging to different *gotras* and *charanas,* as engaged in *swadhyaya* and as having mastered the four Vedas acquired the spiritual powers of *sapa* (curse) and *anugraha* (bless). Evidently they were Brahmin scholars[69] who took to carpentry as they found it lucrative due to the increasing demand for agricultural implements.

As much of the agricultural land was alienated to the Brahmin (*brahmadeya*) and occasionally to the temple (*devabhoga*), the bulk of people became landless peasants or tenant cultivators. The imprecatory verses at the end of the records containing the threat of even physical punishment to those who disregarded royal commands (*asmadajnamati lamghetva papah sariran danda marhati*)[70] may suggest that there was some resistance to such alienation or occupation of land by the donee. But it had gradually broken down. However, there seems to have been in-built safeguards against the exploitation of the tenant by the holders of the gift lands. While registering the gift of land to a Brahmin, Gunasharma, the Ellora Plates of Salankayana Vijaydevavarman (c. AD 350)[71] stipulates that the tenant could retain half of the produce and pay the other half to the donee. The donee as well as the tenant were granted house sites and even servants. As the tenant enjoyed half of the produce he was known as *addhiyamanussa* or *arthasiri* and his right was recognised by the law-givers. The same pattern of tenancy might have governed all the gift lands.[72]

The *addhiyamanussa* system gradually improved the economic status of the peasant who naturally looked for corresponding social respectively. His master, the pious Brahmin became his idol. The peasant started imitating the life style of the Brahmin—especially his food habits and religious observances[73] and was thus getting, to use a modern word, Sanskritised, though he was denied a place in the orthodox Brahminical religious system. Instinctively, he craved for active participation in religion for which he turned to Jainism and devotional cults of Vaishnavism and Shaivism which provided not only a guarantee against social stagnation but also a leverage to intellectual awakening. By this time, Deccan was at the threshold of medieval period when the process of acculturation involving vertical social mobility and Sanskritisation received greater stimulus by the inter-state warfare.

Notes and References

1. P.V. Kane, *History of Dharmashastra,* Poona, 1930-58, I, 1, p. 56.
2. *Ibid.*
3. Manudharmashastra includes the Andhras among the mixed castes (sankirna varnas) and declares that they should live outside village (bahirgrama pratisravaih). 36.
4. B.V. Krishna Rao, *Early Dynasties of Andhradesha,* Madras, 1942, p. 55.
5. P.V. Kane, *op. cit.*, p. 56.
6. Subrahamanyam and Vidyadhararao, *op. cit.*

7. Haribhadra mentions Mahavira's visit to Mosali, identified with Maisolia on the mouth of Krishna, EI, XX, p.88.
8. SII, pp.206 ff.
9. JESI, I. *op. cit.*
10. *Arhata Vachana Quarterly Journal,* Indore, II, Fig.6.
11. H. Sarkar, *Studies in Early Buddhist Architecture,* Delhi, 1966, Ch. II. Figs. 3, 4 and 5.
12. *JNSI,* VII. p.94.
13. Anushasana-parva 33, vv 10-12
14. B.S.L. Hanumantha Rao, *Religion in Andhra*, Gunter, 1973, pp. 77-79.
15. Burgoss, *Buddhist Stupas of Amaravati and Jaggayyapet,* London, 1877, p. 110.
16. Annual Report for 1924.
17. *PIHC,* XXVIII. p. 112.
18. *Op. cit.*
19. Burgress, *Notes on Amaravati Stupa Madras,* 1882, No.2, p. 26.
20. Nasik Inscription of Bala Shri, SII, pp.196 ff.
21. R.C. Majumdar (ed.), *Age of Imperial Unity*, 4th ed., Bombay, 1968. p. 197.
22. E.J. Shah, *Jainism in Northern India, Bombay*, 1932, pp. 147-86.
23. SI.I.P.184.
24. *Ibid.,* p.183.
25. Age of Imperial Unity, p. 96.
26. *Op. cit.*
27. The Saptashati contains several *gathas* with epic and Puranic themes. It begins with the invocation of Shiva and the following *gathas* refer to Krishna and other incarnations of Vishnu: I, 42, 89; II, 12, 14, 17, 51; V,6, 11, 25; VII, 55, etc.
28. The Nasik Record Compares Gautamiputra with several Puranic heroes such as Rana, Keshava, Arjuna, Bhimsena, Nahusa, Nabhaga, Janamejaya, Sagara Yayati, Ambarisha, etc, SI. 1, p. 157f.
29. *Ibid.*
30. Junagadh Inscription, SI, 1.
31. Nagarjunakonda valley about A.D. 275. EI, XXXIV, pp.197 ff.
32. Junagadh Inscription, in SI, 1.
33. EI XX, Nagarjunakonda Inscriptions, B 6.
34. Nasik cave inscription of Kanha's time, SI, 1, p. 183.
35. Only two inscriptions are available and both are at Nasik, SI, 83, and 89, pp.191 ff.

36. *Ibid.*
37. *Ibid.* no. 83.
38. *Early History of the Andhra Country,* (Madras, 1941), 71-72.
39. Lunder's List, No.1001.
40. EI, XX, 1929-30, No.1, pp. 1-37(C-3).
41. Suvira Jaiswal, *The Origin and Development of Vaishavism*. Delhi, 1967, pp.130-131.
42. The Holy Teaching of Vimalakirti (tr. By) A.F. Thurman, London, 1976.
43. EI, XX. 1929-30, No.1, pp.1-37 (C-3).
44. B.S.L.Hanumantha Rao, 'Sriparvataswamy of the Vishnukundin Records', *JIH*, LV, pp.49 ff.
45. EI. XX, 1929-30, No.1, pp.1-37 (C-2).
46. Indian Archaeology - A review, 1956-57, p.37, pls. IV and LVI A.
47. Basim Copper Plate Inscriptions of Vindhyashakti, SI, I. p.406 ff.
48. Chikkulla Plates, EI, IV, pp. 89-93.
49. According to the Maysya, the performer of Hiranyagarbha says: *Matraham janitah purvam, martydharma surottama tvadgarbha sambhavadesa, divyadeho bhavamyaham,* ch. 275.
50. Tummaiagudem Plates Set II, epigraphia Andhrica, II, pp. 4ff.
51. *Ibid.* and Sankaranrayanan. The Vishnukundins and Their Times, Delhi, 1977, pp. 24-26.
52. Chikkulla plates, *op. cit.*
53. Badami Rock Cliff Ins., EI XXVII. pp. 4-9.
54. K.V. Ramesh, *Chalukyas of Vatapi,* Delhi,1986, p. ss37.
55. Nerur Plates of Mangalosa, IA, XXVII, pp.161-63.
56. B.S.L Hanumantha Rao, 'The Boyas in Medieval Andhra History', *JAHRS,* XXXVIII, 77 ff
57. EI. XXXIII, pp.147-49; XXXIV, pp.19-20 and 197-204; XXIV, pp. 20-22, etc.
58. R.N. Nandi, 'Client Ritual and Conflict in Early Brahmanical Order', IHR, VI, pp.64 ff.
59. EI, XX, 1929-30, No.1, pp.1-37 (B-2).
60. Several records register the agraharas gifted by Erilochana Pallava alias Kaduvett, SI. IV, No.927; *Ibid.*, Nos 561 and 620; *Annual Report* 1907, No.580.
61. K.A.N. Sastri, *The Colas*, 2nd ed. Madras, 1955, p.35.
62. EL,V,p.186.
63. *Ibid.,* pp. 84-89.

63. *Ibid.,* pp. 84-89.
64. *Ibid.,* VIII, pp.159 ff.
65. Pravara Prasna, 54.
66. EL, XXXV, pp. 1 ff.
67. Timmapuram Plates, EI, pp. 317ff; Velangavada grant c.p. 12 of 1908-1909; Vettuvada grant, c.p. 8 of 1908-1909; Ponangigrant, c.p no.3 of 1908-09; Satuluru grant, JAHRS, V. pp.101 ff.
68. *JAHRS*, XX; EI XXXI, p.1.
69. Ayyangarvaripalem (Pained Taluk, Guntur dist.) inscriptions (AR No.223 of 1892 and 575 of 1909).
70. *Journal of Epigraphical Society of India*, I, (henceforth, *JESI*), pp. 60-74.
71. *Ibid.*
72. D.D. Kosambi, *The Culture and History of Ancient India in Historical Outlines,* London, 1965, p. 83.
73. Bhandarkar; *Some Aspects of Ancient India Culture,* Madras, 1940, p. 34.

5

Buddhism and Shudras' Position in Ancient Society

The present chapter reveals the role of Buddhism in emancipation of Śūdras. This chapter, shows that the four classes, the priest (Brāhmiṇa), warrior (Kshatriya), peasant (Vaiśya) and serf (Śūdra), were crystallising throughout the period of the Rig veda. They have survived to the present day. The Sanskrit word used for them, *varna,* means "colour" and itself indicates their origin in the development of the old tribal class structure in contact with people of different complexion and alien culture. The term *varna* does not mean "caste", and has never meant "caste" by which convenient word it is often loosely translated.

However, in describing the characteristic of the above four great classes, it has been observed that by the end of the Rig Vedic period the fourfold division of Indian society was regarded as fundamental, primeval, and divinely ordained. The four *varnas* of India developed out of very early Āryan class divisions, for some class stratification exited in many Indo-European communities, and ancient Iran had four pislras or classes comparable in some respects to those of India. In India, class stratification grew more rigid when, in the Vedic period, a situation arose rather like that prevailing in South Africa today, with a dominant fair minority striving to maintain its purity and its supremacy over a darker majority Tribal class-divisions hardened, and the dark-skinned aboriginal found a place only in the basement of the Āryan social structure as a serf with few rights and many disabilities. Soon the idea of *varna* had become so deeply embedded in the Indian mind that its terminology was even used for the classification of precious commodities such as pearls and useful materials like timber. Theoretically all Āryans belonged to one of the four classes, with the exception of children, ascetics and widows who were outside the system.

Varna came to the Dravidian South comparatively late, for the earliest Tamil literature shows a society divided into tribal groups with little sense of the precedence of one over the other. Succeeding centuries saw the gradual hardening of class, until South Indian Brāhmiṇs became even stricter in their ritual observance and the untouchable even more debased than in the North.

Tracing out facts involved in distinction between such stratified classes of Indian society, the three higher castes were twice-born (dvija), once at their natural birth and again at their initiation, when they were invested with the Sacred thread and received into Āryan society. But the term "twice-born" was after reserved for Brāhmiṇs but strictly it applies to Kshatriyas and Vaiśyas and also if they have been initated. Śūdra, position during initiation of 'twice born' conception.

The Śūdra had no initiation, and was never looked on as Āryan at all. The four fold division was in theory functional.

Manu[1] lays down that the duty of the Brāhmiṇ was to study and teach, to sacrifice, and to give and receive gifts, the Kshatriya must protect the people, sacrifice and study; the Vaiśya also sacrifices and studies, but his chief function was to breed cattle to till the earth, to pursue trade and to lend money, whereas the Śūdras, duty was only to serve the three higher classes—and it was better. Manu added elsewhere[2], "to do one's own duty badly than another's well".

This epigram elaborated so beautifully in the *Bhagavad Gita*, was the leading theme of most Indian social thought; for each man there was a place in society and a function to fulfil, with its own duties and rights.

Analysing the term "initiation of twice-birth", the great right of *upanayana,* the second birth, whereby a boy became a full member of his class and of society, was confined to Brāhmaṇs, Kshatriyas and Vaiśyas. The Śūdra and lower orders could not undergo it, and were never allowed to hear or learn the most sacred of scriptures. The ideal age for the ceremony varied according to class-eight for a Brāhmiṇ, eleven for a Kshatriya, and twelve for a Vaiśyas.

Social Status of Shudras According to Patanjali

Patānjali makes clear the social status of the Śūdras in his time. Firstly, there were not excluded from Āryāvarta but were living within its social system. Secondly, there was another class of Śūdras who were living outside Āryāvarta and its society. In this regard, the author has given examples (1) Kishkindha-Gabdikam (2) Sàka-yavanam and (3) Saurya-Krñcham. Of these Kishkindha may be identified with pate khukhundoin Gorokhpore, Gabdika with Gaddis at Chamba, who were deemed as living outside the limits of Āryavarta, Saurya with Soreyya or Soron in Etah district and Krauncha with the Pater Kruncha-dvara somewhere in Garhwal. The Sakas and yavanas who are termed Śūdras were not yet part of the Āryan society and were outside Aryavarta in Patānjali's time. The Āryan society was at pains to repel the invasion of the yavnas Greeks under the leadership of Demetriun and Menander) and this hostility must have emphasized the cleavage between them. The Śakas geographically were still living outside the borders of India in the second century BC but in the first century BC we find Śàka settlement springing up at Takshasila and Mathura and Ujjaini.

Thirdly, there were Śūdras who had separate settlement of their own within their colonies (Āryanivāsa), such as a *grāma* (village), a *ghosha* (cattle ranch) a *nagara* (town) or a Samvaba (caravan camp). Examples of such Śūdras are Mantapas (undertakers), chandalas who were of the lowest grades. Fourthly, there was another class of Śūdras who were entrusted with some of the work connected with Yajanas or sacrifices as carpenters *(taksha)*, metal workers *(ayaskara)* washermen *(rajaka)* and weavers *(tantuvaya)*. There were also Śūdras untouchables who had to take their food in their own utensils and not in those of the household, while there were others who were not subject to this restriction as being more closely associated with the household (*yair-bhukle palram Saskārena Sudhyati* 11,4.10;1475).

The Pali texts written in the language of Magadha mainly describe the state of affairs in eastern UP and Bihar. But they can be considered in conjunction with the grammar of Pānini, which is a most valuable source of information for the pre-Maurya times in northern India. Even according to the most conservative estimates Panini has to be placed between 500 BC and 400 BC (Vasudevsharan Agrawal; 1968, p. 35).[3] Its picture of social and material life is more reliable because it is based on illustrations of grammatical rules. It tallies with what is known from the early Pali texts. Of course, Pañini is more relevant to Indus and western Gangetic basin, but the general trend of developments in northern India known from this text cannot be ignored.

Relating to Pāli text, it might be remarked that the teaching attributed to Gautama Buddha reflected the contemporary social outlook, and numerous imageries drawn from the world of crafts, agriculture and cattle rearing indicated in the nature of material culture that developed in pre-Maurya times. The early Pāli texts of pre-Maurya times did refer to the use of iron for purpose other than war. The term *ayanangala* or iron-ploughshare was mentioned in a later Pali text.

The absorption by Magadha of Kosala, which occupied a central position on the Ganges, and its subsequent conquest of the Anga country near the delta shows a steady eastward shift of the political axis in early Buddhist times. These states had been created shortly after a great colonizing movement on the part of the Āryan invaders, who had iron the ground from the jungle no less than from the coloured inhabitants. In such regions Brāhmiṇism had only recently been introduced and was not deeply rooted, and that is doubtless why they took so readily to Buddhism. We should note, too, that a drive on a smaller scale towards the Deccan had carried Āryan culture to the southern confines of the Ganges basin-among the Vamsas or Vatsas, whose capital, Kausambi, must have been on the lower Yarnura, and in the upper Valleys of the southern tributaries of that river about the source of the Charmnavato, where the kingdom of Avanto had been founded. The capital of that state, Ujjayini (Ujjain) seems to have been the birth place of Pali, the language in which the Buddhist canon was composed before it was found necessary to translate it into the sacred language of the Brāhmiṇs, Sanskrit (Przyluski, ccvii, 330)[4].

The Buddhism which developed in the south-western corner of the Indian world had its birth on the northern border. The region lying east of Kosala between the Himalyan heights and the Ganges contained, in contrast to the huge monarchical states mentioned above, a quantity of small republics, born of independent clans. The confederation of the Vrijis (Vajjians) consisted of eight states the chief of which, that of Lichchhavis, had its capital at Vaisali. The name of these people is like Sàka, the Indian name of a Scythian people who settled between the upper Indus and the oxus and was that time part of the Persian Empire,[5] and would invade India in the first century of our era.

Śūdras were born, or rather 'reborn', to serve the three other classes, they were burdened by a very marked social and religious inferiority. Their caste, in Vedic times, seems to have included the dark-skinned aborigines conquered by the Āryans, to whom were added later some of the poorer Āryans themselves and certain other people who had forfeited their rights for one reason or another. They were therefore not only despised from the earliest times, but also considered impure. They nevertheless took part in the Dharma; but their benefits therefrom were limited to seeking redress under the law, and, under certain conditions, the opportunity to study the sacred texts of Hinduism, namely the Puranas and the scriptures known as the Tantras, to take part in private but not public rites. This was the limit of their rights.

Their duties far outweighed these rights, for they had no possibility of freeing themselves from the servitude which was their by reason of birth. This is where the theory of Karma assumed its full significance; since being born into a particular caste was considered the fruit of acts accomplished in previous births, it was quite clear that the Śūdras had to their debit a heavy load of evil deeds from their past lives. Since this debt ruled the condition of the individual throughout his present life and could only be modified at the next rebirth, the clear implication was that there was no hope of their improving this situation during their lifetime They had one single means of achieving rebirth in a superior class, and that was to perform their allocated duties conscientiously. This idea was responsible for an understandable feeling of inferiority on the part at this underprivileged caste, more especially as the whole concept was carefully maintained by the ruling classes, and showed itself in the behaviour of everyone throughout India. We lack much information about the composition of this caste, but it appears to have included servants of all sorts. Wage-earners, workmen, labourers and minor functionaries. To these were added small clerks, tradesmen and craftsmen; some of the latter however, were able to exercise relatively lucrative trades and crafts, and even practise husbandry. On the whole they were too conscious of their despicable situation to make any attempt to escape from it, but it must not be assumed that they led an unbearable existence. Many of them worked for wealthy tradesmen and landlords, were paid a regular wage, fed, lodged (sometimes on the employer's premises, sometimes outside) and received further benefits in kind; agricultural workers, for example, were paid a fifth of their wages in goods and produce if they were fed and lodged, or a third if not. They remained attached to the same family, from father to son. Their low status compelled them to eat only the remnants from master's table, to wear his cast-off clothing and to make use only of discarded objects. The employer was supposed to treat them decently, and they were in fact protected, to some extent, by the law; he was obliged to make a contract with them, a document enumerating the names of all the employee's dependents. While the Śūdra was expected to give proof of zeal and professional competence, his master was in his turn obliged to furnish him with the instruments necessary for his work and to replace those which were out or defective. The contract laid down the number of hours to be worked and the wages to be paid, and specified the goods and produce which would normally be provided over and above the wages. If the wages were not paid or if the contract was unjustifiably terminated, the employer was liable to prosecution.

The Śūdras were subjected to what seems a relatively light taxation. On the other hand, they were subjected throughout the year to perform forced labour consisting of one or two day's work a month. Those particularly affected by this law were the workers who processed rice, flour, oil or sugar, and those who worked in spinning or weaving mills, and in factories making arms and military supplies. This forced labour could sometimes be avoided by paying a sum of money.

But the servile class was not homogeneous since, even here, distinctions were made between the (pure) or 'unexcluded' and the 'excluded'. The latter were practically identical with the 'outcastes' (untouchables).

Because of its very unworthiness, this segment of the population was only sketchily described in the sacerdotal texts, which referred to its members as 'last-born,' 'low-born' or 'those who may not approach the (sacred) vessels.' These are the people whom we designate, in modern times, by the term 'pariah' or 'untouchables.' They comprised a series of sub-castes among which that of the *chandalas* is the one most frequently mentioned. The outcastes all had trades or crafts which were despised, or even condemned, by religious orthodoxy, either because their work involved the taking of human or animal life, or because their functions involved some ritual defilement. Included in these two categories were hunters, fishermen, butchers, curriers, executioners, gravediggers, undertakers, those who sold liquor, sweepers, and, during certain historical periods, basket-makers and wheelwrights.

Among all these, the situation of the *chandalas* was the worst; in later ages they were given the name of 'untouchables' because of their impurity. They lived in isolated villages or in quarters outside the town limits, and spoke a debased tongue which was almost a dialect.[6] They were supposed to dress in clothes stripped from corpses (for they often acted as public executioners or undertakers); they were permitted to eat only from cracked bowls and dishes, and iron was the metal they could use for ornaments and jewellery. A brāhmiṇ who killed one of them incurred the same penalty as for killing a dog.

Regarded by society as the vilest dregs of the human species, they had to be most careful to avoid polluting members of the other castes by any kind of contact or even coming within their sight. For this reason, they never moved outside their villages or quarters without striking a pair of clappers together to warn people of their approach. When a man of caste chanced to glance at one of them, he was bound to carry out rites of purification. When he learnt that he had beheld a Chaṇḍāla, even unconsciously, his first action was to turn away as quicky as possible; then he would bathe his eyes with perfumed water so as to avert ill fortune; he had then to abstain from food and drink for the rest at the day.[7] His fear of defilement was so great that he dreaded the idea even that the breeze which touched him might previously have passed over a chaṇḍāla's body,[8] or again, that the shadow of one of these unfortunates might have come between his own person and the sun. As far as the Chaṇḍāla was concerned, he was held responsible for having provoked such a defilement of a man of caste, even if the offending action had been quite involuntary. In fact, he was well advised to make every effort to avoid such incidents, since, the wrathful men of caste would certainly have him beaten unconscious. Even worse, he could be quite sure that, as a result, he would be reborn in the body of an animal, and so the moment when he would be freed from the transmigration of soul (however unlikely such a prospect for him, in any case) would be put back even further.[9] It went without saying that a man of caste might not share a Chaṇḍāla's food, even if he were dying of hunger.[10]

Foreigners were placed in the same category as the outcastes, but were not subjected to the same indignities even through they were 'untouchable' by the very fact of not belonging to the Dharma and not being initiated into Veda. They were called mleccha, a term which means literally 'jabberer' and was used to designate all 'barbarians.' Many of those foreigners were ordinary travellers, others were enterprising traders or adventurers in search of fortune; but the term was applied equally to ambassadors and official delegates, as well as to monks and scholars and men of letters who had come to India either to teach or to study, mostly in the Buddhist universities. The term *mleccha* was applied more specifically to invaders, and since most of these penetrated into India through the north-western passes, it was traditional in iconography to represent them dressed in the style of the 'cold' regions, that is to say, like the Parthians who were under Iranian or Hellenistic influence. In the way, they were depicted with pronounced features intended to make clear their distant origin.

Although foreigners of noble rank were treated with appropriate honour and respect, it was still impossible for certain essential rules to be broken on their behalf : when they were received in the home of a Brāhmin family, for instance, the rites of hospitality could never be carried out fully, and no man of good caste could take a meal in their company. But a special annual feast-day was reserved for the *mlecchas*, on which they assembled together, a fact which leads us to suppose that many of them must have been long-established residents. It was, also, by no means unknown for foreigners to be absorbed into Hinduism, introduced into an appropriate caste, sometimes a high one, and assimilated into Indian society.

Finally, ascetics were classed among the outcaste because their complete detachment from society made the term 'without caste' perfectly applicable to them. They were greatly respected.

But these were only exceptions. The disinherited caste of untouchables was composed overwhelmingly of poor devils upon whom abuse and indignities were heaped and who were permitted social contact only with those of 'mixed' origin.

The statute of castes *(varnadharma)* could never really be applied strictly enough to prevent mixed marriages, and the lawgivers had, from a very early date, to face up to the facts and make the system somewhat more flexible. Although it was more or less admitted that legitimate unions between those of different castes might in fact take place, the children issuing from these unions, whether legitimate or not, were considered to have forfeited their rights because they did not belong definitely to a particular caste. Polygamy certainly aggravated this situation by those multiplying such births. The opprobrium attaching itself to those of 'mixed' origin extended to two generations. But the discredit thrown upon them did not prevent them obtaining honourable posts or exercising well-esteemed professions such as that of bard, herald, equerry, physician or scribe. This brought them much closer to the 'pure' Śūdras than to the 'excluded' classes or the 'untouchables'.

Megasthenes asserted that slavery was unknown in the India of the Mauryas. In fact, it undoubtedly did exist then, just as it did in later eras; but it did not take the same form as in Greece, so that his statement is only partly incorrect.

This class included very different types of persons. In the first category are distinguished those 'born in the house,' who were practically members of the family in which they were servants. Having been bought, or received as a gift, they were then inherited along with the goods and chattles. Their purchase price was comparatively modest, and consequently slave owning was widespread The royal palace set the example in the practice of buying slaves: these were young women destined for the harem, brought (probably from Greece) by trading vessels, often by the merchants who traded between India and Africa, and made optimistic claims as to the girls' noble birth and their talent in the arts of song and music. In the same way, a female militia charged with guarding the harem, was also composed entirely of slaves; they could be seen mounting guard on the ramparts or at the doors at private apartments, armed with a pike and wearing a helmet.[11] Their Western origin seems proved by the use of the term *yavanī* ('coming from Ionia') to describe them. It is worth noting that their costume changed over the centuries, being Greco-Roman in style until the third century or thereabouts, and then Iranian during the fourth and fifth centuries; we know this because there is evidence to show that, after the fall of Rome, this social group was reluctant to abandon this mode of dress and appealed for sartorial assistance to regions which had inherited Hellenistic traditions. Other classes of slaves in the royal and princely households were the hunchbacks and dwarfs whose job was to act as jesters and clowns, and the nurses who breast-fed the noble offspring of these households.

The living and working conditions of these slaves did not differ greatly from those of the Śūdras, which is probably what misled Megasthenes. In a certain sense they were better off than the Śūdras: they received no wages and so could more easily avoid the necessity of working when they were sick, since they were not dependent upon wage earnings for their daily bread.

Existing sources of information differ considerably in their evaluation of the slaves living and working conditions. Pali texts emphasize the hard labour often imposed on them, such as the transportation, morning, noon and evening, on the man's (or woman's) back, of the water needed each day by the entire household, and this throughout the year, even in winter when it was necessary to wade waist-high in icy water. These same texts state that corporal punishment was inflicted on slaves who neglected their duties, that they were beaten, even mutilated, sometimes killed. The threat of such punishment constrained them to obey at all costs, and kept them in a state of constant fear. It was not unusual to see them pursuing their tasks with tears streaming down their faces. As for the master, he appears to have complained frequently about his slaves' lack of interest in their work and the resulting inconveniences for himself. To believe him, very few of them showed themselves conscientious and vigilant, and most of them waited impatiently for nightfall to give them temporary relief from their duties. Worse than that, when in his presence the slaves appeared zealous and submissive, assuring him repeatedly of their devotion; yet, the moment his back was turned, they no longer cared about anything, allowing provisions to spoil and even going so far as give vent to rancorous remarks directed against him.

It seems, from allusions in certain narratives, that slave rebellions occurred on several occasions. But, on the other hand, Hindu legislation and the injunctions attributed to the Buddha himself were designed to make the slaves' existence bearable. If we are to believe these latter sources, they were relatively well treated. Though the master had the right to beat them, he might strike them only on the back, never on the head, and if he treated them too cruelly they would be withdrawn from his service.

Sometimes they were authorized to earn money freely during their spare time and to keep the whole amount: it was also possible for a female slave to receive permission to marry a free man outside her master's house, on the condition that she returned each day to perform her duties as a slave. The law protected a pregnant girl, and she could be neither sold nor given away during her pregnancy. If she had been seduced by the master, and had a child by him, the master was bound to pay her an indemnity and to free her new-born child. Ordinarily, children remained in slavery, as did their parents. As for old people, they were kept on in the master's house until their death, even when they could no longer work; if they left no descendants, their funeral expenses were paid by the master who undertook to carry out the commemorative rites for the well-being of their souls. There was a special annual festival allocated to slaves, in which they took an active part.

It would appear, then, that the lot of these slaves was not altogether harsh, especially if one compares their conditions with those generally imposed in ancient civilizations. Apart from the brutal separations which were inevitable when they were sold or exchanged,[12] they sometimes led a less arduous existence than an ordinary labourer, especially when their master endeavoured to be lust and pious. There is even a case on record of a slave inheriting his master's estate.

The law specified that slaves should have a chance to recover their freedom; they had the right to escape, but once only. If they successfully avoided recapture they could rejoin their caste (if they had one) and enjoy the condition of a free man. Those who had managed to save money from wages they had earned freely while off-duty, could buy their freedom if the sum was sufficient. Their liberation involved a small ceremony during which a special formula was pronounced; at the same time, the fortunate individual was sprinkled with water from a ewer which was then broken into pieces. His forehead was ceremonially washed, symbolizing that he was authorized now to rejoin his caste. If he entered a religious order he was allowed to change his name, so that nobody might reproach him with a servile past.

Slaves were not only bought. Many individuals entered into slavery for a variety of reasons : those convicted under the common law and sentenced to purge their offence by a term at forced labour; debtors who had been unable to repay their creditors and so entered their service, the creditors being then obliged to provide them with food and lodging; individuals who had pledged themselves as surety in a contract, a lawsuit or a bet. There were also prisoners of war, or those who had been taken as booty. Their eventual liberation depended upon the category to which they belonged and the resultant conditions of servitude: convicts were freed when their sentence was completed, debtors when they had managed to pay off their debt, and the others when the contract they had guaranteed was fulfilled, or when they had contrived to pay a sufficient forfeit. Prisoners of war kept in slavery only for a limited period of time, usually one year.

These, then, are the various modalities with which the 'statute' *(dharma)* of India society conformed. As we have seen, they were extremely complex, for the precise term qualifying each caste embraced realities that were far more gently graduated if not, indeed, hesitant at times. India's eternal paradox is reflected in them and transforms a dry enumeration of functions, rights and duties into a living, suffering human mass. The established rules were flexible or strictly enforced according to the particular era and the comparative influence of Brāhmiṇism or Buddhism. Buddhism quite naturally brought moral and spiritual comfort to those who had most to endure from the effects of a disadvantageous *karma*. It preached the abolition of social classes; and, in basing its principles of rewards for deeds performed on virtue rather than on birth or fortune, it promised deliverance from the cycle of 'rebirths' to the 'excluded' as much as to the others, on condition only that they should be pure of head and honest in purpose. But no rule was strict enough to embrace this whole human mass in well-defined categories, even in Brahminic circles where ideology might be supposed to be more rigorously applied. There was never a time when the rules were not broken. The existence of mixed classes, marriages between different castes, the occupations which Brāhmiṇs and Kshatriya were able to follow with impunity, all proved that facts were more powerful than theory.

The sources available to us give us little indication of what the feelings of the individuals themselves may have been, because according to Indian tradition what matters is the definition of types, not of particular cases. It seems probable, nevertheless, that the situation created by the division into castes was taken for granted by individuals and aroused no spirit of revolt or even of reflection. Accepting the theory of *karma* (just as Roman Catholics accept the theory of original sin) they doubtless found it natural to endure the consequences. Their behaviour was governed by pre-established rules, transmitted from father to son, which decreed that the most important objective was to conform to a particular rule of life which could alone bring the remedy of a happier rebirth. So, for thousands of years, the mass of Indian society learnt to perform to the best of its abilities the duties incumbent upon it in its particular sphere.

However, the division into castes was not the only social structure operating in ancient India. Clans, guilds family groupings were at least as important, both in social and private life, and these categories fulfilled the same need for classification which the Indian mentality demanded: to exist socially, the individual had to be included in a definite category. Very often, membership of a trade-guild was more important than belonging to a particular caste, especially where Buddhist influence was uppermost, and a man's social status was determined by his caste than by his profession. So, too, it was very important to belong to a clan or to be able to boast a long line of ancestry *(gotra)*. The guilds (*śreṇis*) offered their members the backing of powerful organizations that more closely defined than those of the castes and were backed by special tribunals and well-defined regulations. Their modalities are dealt within the subsequent section of this work concerned with economics. But, before this, it is necessary to give some account of how Indian society was normally governed and administered, what collective rules were imposed upon it, and the extent to which the penal code succeeded ensuring law and order.

The reaction of philosophers of the 6th century BC rejected the values of ordinary society, with the very important exception that they agreed, with most people, that happiness was the aim. Naturally their conceptions of happiness and how actually to attain it diverged widely from ordinary ideas. They lived as far as possible outside ordinary society, seeking truth and happiness, and most of them decided that real happiness consisted in peace of mind. Some of them returned to society as teachers, trying to persuade people that the usual ways of seeking happiness through wealth and power would not work and would in fact lead to more unhappiness. The trend of society, many of them sought to point out, was to produce more and more unhappiness, to get steadily worse. Hence, there was a need to counter this process within society (as well as outside it), to produce more happiness by applying the truths which the philosophers had discovered, this happiness being again primarily, peace of mind.

The Sramana Society

As well as teaching this reform in society, in the form of moral teachings, these *śramaṇas* sought pupils who would leave society and follow them in their wanderings. Some of them established regular communities *(saṃgha)* outside ordinary society, outside the jurisdiction of governments but having their own codes of discipline. These communities of 'monks' and 'nuns'—as we may very approximately term them in English—were at first groups of wanderers in the forests. Later they developed organised settlements, sometimes on the outskirts of towns and supposed in a regular manner by sympathetic laymen and even by governments. The Buddhist communities have an elaborate constitution based in part on that of the Vṛji Republic. The groups of Buddhist monks are independent of one another and there is no supreme head. The monks meet regularly in council and decide issues by majority vote, differences between groups being settled in the same way by convening a general congress and debating and voting on the issues. Representatives and other officers of the groups are elected by their members.[13] Thus, the Buddhist communities formed a separate society of their own, as did certain other Śramaṇa communities. The relations between these communities and governments were complicated and sometimes difficult, especially as the governments of states in and after the Buddha's time were organising society in an increasingly centralised manner. A śramaṇa community of any size and influence in the country would clearly be a disruptive element in a centralised state, especially if its constitution was republican and democratic and the state was a monarchy.

The kingdom of Magadha, in fact, gradually extended its power over almost the whole of India and thus became capable of exerting considerable control over the *śramaṇa* communities. The effect of this on the history of Buddhism must be studied below. Here we may note that it is of the utmost importance for understanding the history of India and of Indian religion and philosophy that the political unification realised by Magadha did not last. Non-unification, non-centralisation, means freedom from any single controlling authority. It makes possible intellectual freedom. It enables philosophers to be independent of governments, because if they find one government uncongenial they need not remain on its territory but can emigrate. On the other hand there were certain disadvantages for Indian philosophy in the lack of political stability which non-unification entailed and especially in the fact that the various states in India were much weaker in the face of foreign invasions than a united empire would have been. Foreign invasions were at times absolutely disastrous for the intellectual life of India and particularly for Buddhism.

The ultimate origins of the *Śramaṇa* movement are obscure and we can trace its history only from the time of the organisation of permanent communities during the lifetime of the Buddha (BC 566 to 486). There are traditions about more ancient teachers, often in very remote periods, but so far it has not been possible to establish the historicity of any of them. For the most part such traditions appear to be attempts by various schools to assert the antiquity and absolute truth of their doctrines by attributing them to legendary teachers of the past who, if they discover the truth, must be presumed to have discover the same truth as more recent teachers of the school. The ascetic practices, or even merely the renunciation of society, of the *śramaṇas*, have led to speculation that their tradition goes right back to the presumed ascetics of the Indus Civilisation, or on the other hand to the Shamanism of Central Asia and presumably of the early Āryans. This would hardly affect our understanding of the schools of the Buddha's time as new, as reacting to new developments in history by producing new doctrines. If the life of wandering in the forests was old, most of the philosophies of the 6th century BC were new, taking account of the advances of science and of the social and political changes in Magadha, Vṛji and other countries. It is especially noteworthy that our sources indicate that the establishment of organised communities of *śramaṇas* as opposed to individual wanderers was an innovation at the beginning of the 5th century BC.[14] This organisation may have been a response to the centralising policies of the states of the time.

The main organised schools of *śramaṇas* in the time of the Buddha were, besides the Buddhists, the Ājīvaka, Lokāyata, Jaina and Agnostic (Ajñāna) schools.

The Ajivaka School

The name Ājīvaka originated from the Ājīva, the way of life, of the wandering *śramaṇas*. It was taken by a large school or community founded by a group of prominent teachers in Kośala (West of Vrji) in BC 489. The leader of this school was Gośāla (died BC 488), who had propounded its central doctrine, that of fatalism, and was afterwards revered as a silent sage. The Ajīvakas believed in transmigration on a grand scaple, each individual soul passing automatically into final peace after having experienced every possible kind of life in turn (lastly that of an Ājīvaka wanderer). This series of incarnations of the soul was supposed to take nearly thirty million million million multiplied by the number of grains of sand in the bed of the river Ganges, years. The school developed an elaborate system of divination and prognostication by the interpretation of dreams and other omens. Ājīvakas were sometimes employed by kings to make predictions, but the original function of this knowledge of the future and its inescapable experiences was presumably to induce a spirit of resignation and peace of mind. The possibility of making a correct prediction was the best evidence for all events being determined in advance by Fate (Niyati).

In harmony with this determination was the doctrine of 'inaction (akriyā) originally propounded by another Ājīvaka teacher, Pūraṇa (died c. BC 503). All the supposed actions of men, 'good' or 'bad' are no actions at all, produce no effect or influence on the future (hence the school rejects moral causation). From another teacher, Kakuda (in Pali Pakudha), the Ājīvakas, took their doctrine of the constituent elements of the universe, which were uncreated, uncuttable, sterile, immoveable and rigid. These undergo no alteration or transformation and do not interact. Any supposed action passes ineffectively between their atoms. There are seven of these elements (or 'substances' kāya): earth, water, heat, air, happiness, unhappiness and soul (or life *jiva*).[15]

The Lokāyata School

The Lokāyata, the name of which probably meant originally 'natural science' or 'naturalism' (investigation of nature), was a materialist school. As opposed to the Ājīvakas they asserted complete freedom, absolute free as well as the natural way of life and were also known as the Do-as-you-like school (yadṛcchāvāda). Everything happens through the spontaneous actions of nature (svabhāva, i.e., the own-nature, of each phenomenon) The school agreed with the Ājīvakas in rejecting moral causation, but for opposite reasons: all acts and experiences are spontaneous, not determined by anything; moreover there is no soul and no transmigration which could make the working out of moral causation possible. The aim of living beings is happiness, but for this school the highest happiness attainable is that of the pleasures of the senses (kāma). The pleasure of human relationships is also particularly mentioned. Unlike the Buddhists and probably most philosophers of the time, the Lokāyata school held that there is more happiness than unhappiness in life, what is needed being discrimination and the recognition (and acceptance) that happiness is by nature transient, permanence being boring and disgusting and contrast essential for enjoyment, whilst overcoming difficulties leads to increased pleasure.

According to this school the universe is constituted out of four elements: earth, water, heat and air. All phenomena consist of combinations of these four, and consciousness is such a compound, or rather a property of the elements combined in a particular way as a living body.

The most prominent Lokayata teacher of the Buddha's time was Ajita, but he was not regarded in later times as the founder of the school. It is a legendary Bṛhaspati who was later regarded as the founder of the school and the composer of its basic text or sūtra.[16]

Involution and Evolution of the Worlds According to Sutras

The Brahmajāla Sūtra which describes the (involution) and 'evolution' of the universe and the appearance during the latter phase at the sphere at the brahma-mansion, of the gods elsewhere called Brahma-bodied. Another sūtra is the Dirgha.[17] It refers to the same involution and evolution, with the majority of beings in the world of radiance (which, it appears, is not affected by the cycles of the more material universe), but continues to describe how beings come to 'this world' from the world of radiance and how human society evolves. It does not concern itself with the gods, and its avowed object is to account for the appearance in society of class distinctions, and especially of the hereditary priesthood of the Brāhmaṇs, whose claims it was one of the primary objects of the Buddha to debunk.

'When the universe is evolving, the majority of beings pass away from their world-of-radiance bodies and come to this world. They remain for very long time made of mind, feeding on joy, self-luminous, living in the sky and staying beautiful. At the time, Vāsiṣṭhas (the Buddha is speaking to two novices, brāhmiṇs by birth), there is just one mass of water, obscurity, the darkness of obscurity (i.e., this world). The Sun and Moon are not discerned, nor the constellations of stars, nor day and night, nor the month and the fortnight, nor the year and the seasons, nor male and female. Beings are classified simply as 'beings'.

'Then at some time or other, after a long time, an 'enjoyment solid (literally 'earth', in the sense of the element)' became spread out over the water for those beings. Just like the skin ('film') on hot milk as it cools, so it appeared. It had colour, scent and taste. Its colour was like that of *ghee* or butter. Its taste was like that of pure, sweet, wild honey.

'Then a certain being, being wanton (lola, or 'restless'), thought "Sir ! what can this be ?" and tasted the enjoyment earth with a finger. As it lasted the enjoyment earth with its finger it was pleased, and desire (tṛṣṇā) arose within it. Other beings following the idea (dṛṣṭi, 'opinion') of that being tasted the enjoyment earth with their fingers. As they tasted it they were pleased and desire arose within them. Then those beings fell upon it, breaking it in pieces with their hands in order to eat it. Because of this their self-luminosity disappeared.

'When self-luminosity disappeared the Sun and Moon appeared, the constellations of stars appeared and day and night were discerned. As the months and fortnights were discerned, so were the year and the seasons. To this extent, Vāsisṭhas, this universe is evolved again.'

These beings continued for a long time feeding on the 'enjoyment earth', and as they did so 'roughness' appeared in their bodies. Colour and 'discolouration' were also discerned, so that some were beautiful and some ugly. The beautiful ones despised the ugly, and in consequence of this pride and arrogance the enjoyment earth disappeared. Afterwards a fungus appeared on the ground, like a mushroom, which had a similar delightful taste to the enjoyment earth, and beings fed for a long time on that. As they did so their bodies became still rougher and more diverse in colour (beauty), and the beautiful ones became more proud and arrogant until the fungus disappeared. Then a creeper appeared, with the same delicious taste. The same process continued and it too disappeared.

'Then, Vāsiṣṭhas, when the creeper disappeared, a rice plant appeared for those beings, which ripened without cultivation, was without any husk or coating on its grains, was sweet scented and produced rice. If this was collected in the evening for the evening meal, it had grown again and was ripe in the morning. If it was collected in the morning for the morning meal, it had grown again and was ripe in the evening. No reaping was discerned. Then those beings fed on the rice which ripened without cultivation . . . their bodies became still rougher and more coloured and discoloured, and the characteristic of the female appeared in woman, and of the male in man. And a woman bought about a man excessively, and a man about a woman. Thinking about each other excessively, passion occurred in them and lust arose within their bodies. Through the condition of lust they indulged in the principle *(dharma)* of sex. When other beings saw them indulging in the principle of sex, some threw mud, some threw ash, some threw cow-dung, crying: "Perish! Dirty!" "How could a being do that sort of thing to a being?" Now at present, too, in some countries, when a bride is led out some people throw mud, some ash, some cow-dung. So they follow ancient tradition, a primeval expression, but they do not grasp its meaning.

'What was agreed to be bad (*adharma,* bad principle, unlawful) at that time, Vāsiṣṭhas, is at present agreed to be good (*dharma,* principle, lawful; in these expressions *dharma* may have its legal sense, which we have not met before in this survey, except implicitly when referring to the 'laws' of the Brāhmiṇical tradition). At that time those who indulged in the principle of sex were not allowed to enter a village or town for a month or two months.

'Since those beings indulged excessively in (that) bad principle, they went into houses to do it secretly. Then a certain being, being lazy, thought; "Sir! why should I be troubled with collecting rice in the evening for the evening meal and in the morning for the morning meal? Supposing I were to collect rice once only for the evening and morning meals?" Then that being collected rice once only for the evening and morning meals?" Then another being approached him and said: "Come, Sir, let us go to collect rice." Enough, Sir, I have collected rice once only for the evening and morning meals." Then Vāsiṣṭhas, the other being, following that beings idea, collected rice once only for two days, thinking that would be good.'

This idea spread, and they collected enough rice for up to a week at a time, but: 'Because those beings made a store of rice and relied on it for eating, a coating and a husk enveloped the rice grain, when it was plucked it did not grow again, reaping was discovered and the rice stood in clusters (i.e., presumably was grown in fields).' The beings then assembled and lamented their gradual decadence from bodies of mind feeding on joy to their present state: 'Bad principles have appeared among the beings.' But they decided to divide the rice plants and establish boundaries (in other words they invented private property).

'Then a certain being being wanton, guarding his own

share, took another share, which was not given to him, and ate it. So they seized him and said: "Sir, you do badly, in as much as you take another share not given to you, guarding your own, and eat it. Do not do that sort of thing again." He agreed but did it again a second and a third time. He was seized and rebuked again, then some hit him with their hands, some pelted him with clods, some beat him with sticks. Since then taking what was not given, blame, false speech and resorting to force (or to punishment) have been known ('discerned').

The Origin of the Classes

The beings assembled again, discussed these bad principles that had been discerned among them, and proposed : 'Supposing we were to elect one being, who would become indignant with us when it was right to be indignant, would blame would banish when it was right to blame, would banish it was right to banish? We will grant him a share of rice.

'Then those beings, Vāsiṣṭhas, approached that being among them who was most handsome, most beautiful, most lovely, most superior, and said to him: "Come, Sir. Be indignant when it is right to be indignant, blame when it is right to blame, banish when it is right to banish. We will grant you a share of rice." He agreed, and started to perform these duties and to receive the share of rice. 'Because he was elected by the people, Vāsṣṭhas, he was called the Great Elect. Thus, the first expression applied to him was derived. Because he was the Lord of the fields (or lands) he was called Warrior (the words 'warrior' and 'field' sound similar in the original language : this is not historical but only fanciful).... Because he delighted others with principle *(dharma)* he was called King ('king' could be derived from the verb 'to delight').....'

In this way the 'circle' or class of warriors, the aristocracy, is said to have originated, but the Buddha adds that it is good principle or justice *(dharma)* which is the best thing among the people, both in the visible world and with reference to a future state.

Next the Buddha accounts for the origin of the priesthood the Brāhmins. 'Among those beings some thought that bad principles had appeared among the beings, in that taking what was not given, blame, false speech, resorting to force and banishment will be discerned. Suppose, they were to keep off bad, evil principles?' They did so and consequently the name brāhmaṇ (brāhmaṇa) was first derived for them in the vernacular languages of the Buddha's day the name might look as if it could be derived from the verb 'keep off'; this again is pure fancy). These brāhmiṇs went to the forest and lived in leaf huts, meditating. They did not prepare or cook their own food but went morning and evening to a village or town to seek it. On account of their meditating they received as a second names that of 'meditators'. Some, however, were unable to meditate, so they spent their time making books. As they did not meditate they were called 'non-meditators' (= 'teachers', this is a pun in the original language). At that time they were agreed to be inferior, but now they are considered the best. (The books they made are of course the books of the Vedic Canon).

A third class of the beings took to various kinds of business and formed the mercantile and productive class (the Vaiśyas, supposed to be connected with viśva, 'all', i.e., all kinds of business, all trades, and in this case the derivation is etymologically respectable).

Those beings who remained became hunters, the lowest occupation of all, and were called Śūdras (which in the vernacular rhymes with 'hunter' and with 'minor', i.e., law, but the historical origin of this class seems to have been that they were conquered peoples reduced to the position of helots which they really for the most part occupied in the Buddha's day; all inferior groups, together with forest and mountain tribes living by hunting, were lumped in by Brāhmaṇical theory as the fourth and lowest class).

Thus, all four classes came from the same common origin and the distinction was at first purely occupational (and the Brāhmiṇs lived a praiseworthy life of meditation and simplicity, retired from the world, very like the life of the wandering Śramaṇas of the Buddha's day). Lastly those of any of the four classes who were dissatisfied with the life of their class became *śramaṇas*, going forth from home to homelessness.

Finally, bad conduct, bodily, verbal or mental, leads to a bad destiny, good conduct to a good destiny, regardless of whether the agent belongs to one class or another. Mixed conduct leads to a mixed destiny, a mixture of happiness and unhappiness. By restraint and by developing the seven principles 'siding with' enlightenment (presumably the seven 'factors of enlightenment') anyone, regardless of class origin, can attain nirvāṇa.

This text is one at many in the Tripiṭaka directed against the claims of the brāhmiṇs to be of different origin from the rest of humanity, born from the mouth of Brahmā, having a hereditary prerogative to teach, guide and spiritually govern the rest of society. It should be noted that the Buddha's opposition is not total: rather he seeks to conciliate and win over the brāhmiṇs of his day to his new way of thinking. He flatters them that their class was formed originally from good motives and had good traditions. It is only more recently that it has become degenerate and its way of life harmful, in that the sacrifices of their ritual are harmful as well as futile, and are a travesty of the original sacrifice. Their Vedic Canon is now corrupt and perverted, though originally it may have contained sound moral injunctions, and the advice and guidance they give to others, claiming supernatural authority, is often misleading and harmful. It is an essential part of the Buddha's aim to substitute purely moral standards for all hereditary privilege, to assert the equality of all beings before the laws of nature, their equal freedom to shape their destinies within the conditions and causality of the universe as discovered by him. The brāhmiṇs are now ignorant of the truths of the universe, but they can learn them (as many did, becoming followers of the Buddha) and then join in spreading them and in exemplifying and teaching good conduct. Originally a man was not a brāhmiṇ by birth, but by a high standard of conduct, and this state of affairs should be restored in society.

Before considering any more texts concerned with the brāhmiṇs and class, however, we have others to look at which discuss social evolution further. So far we have seen what amounts to a Buddhist version of the traditions of the Purāṇas, with the evolution of the universe out of darkness, the origin of mankind, the first king (later Buddhist commentators identify the Great Elect with Manu, the founder of the Solar Dynasty).

It was probably intended to look like a corrected version, acceptable as such to those accustomed to the Purāṇas (which may have been less theistic than they are today), or even believed to be a successful restoration of the true facts from garbled Brāhmiṇical tradition in the light of 'modern scientific' investigations (i.e., the doctrines). There is no primeaval One Being, i.e., Brahmā or Brāhmaṇ, which somehow wishes to become many and becomes the universe : in the natural process of evolution Brahmā is one among many 'beings', or sequences of conditions and his idea that his wishing for company resulted in creation is an absurd error. Mankind means other but similar beings not inferior or different in kind except to the extent that their conduct may vary. All men are born equal, and born equal to the gods, to 'God' Himself. What they become depends on their own conduct. The Brāhmiṇical myths about the origins of different races and classes of men are nonsense. The first king was not of divine origin, in any sense in which all men are not divine; he did not rule as of right but was elected. The Purānas themselves preserve legends of an original anarchy in society ended by the election of the first king; here at least the Buddha could find some suggestion among the conflicting tangles of ancient tradition that what he believed to have been the true facts had once been recorded and only later were submerged in mythology.

Buddhist sources take little interest in the dynasties of kings supposed to have followed after the Great Elect. The Tripiṭika shows interest in the theory of government, in basic principles which might be illustrated from history, but not in detailed records of the past. The Mahāparinirvāṇa Sūtra, which tells us the last events in the life of the Buddha, shows the Buddha discussing the principles of republican government, so important for the Buddhist community, bearing moreover on current affairs. Other Sūtras discuss the deeds of great kings or emperors (chakravartins) of the past.

The Dirgha sūtra[18] gives an account of the reigns of three successive emperors who attempted to rule justly, presumably in the tradition of the Great Elect, but eventually failed, whereupon society plunged headlong down the path of degeneration, or more precisely of violence, which has brought it to its present perilous state. The reign of the first,[19] which lasted for thousands of years (for human life was much longer than when social degeneration had not gone very far), was illustrated by the presence in the sky of a 'wheel gem', perhaps a comet, or a nova, which circled like the Sun and Moon. The emperor knew, it seems, that this celestial phenomenon marked his reign of principle, and after some thousands of years he posted a man to keep it under observation and report if it retired or fell from its place (the Sthaviravāda commentary explains that he did this by setting up a kind of astronomical instrument at the gateway of the citadel). When told that this had happened he knew his reign hād come to end and he must abdicate, become a homeless wanderer and seek celestial pleasures instead of human ones.

He installed his eldest son as ruler and went forth as a homeless wanderer, Seer (*ṛṣi*). A week later the 'wheel gem' disappeared. The new ruler was disturbed at this and went to consult his father. The royal seer told him that the celestial 'wheel gem' was not part of his paternal inheritance. If he conducts himself according to the Āryan (or 'excellent') imperial conduct (or 'government') it is possible that the wheel gem may appear. Asked what this conduct is, he says that, depending on principle dharma, respecting and honouring principle, under the banner of principle, etc., his son should organise safety, shelter and protection among the people, for warriors who had submitted, for brāhmiṇs, householders, towns people, country folk, *śramaṇas*, beasts and birds. No unjust action should start in his realm. If anyone in the realm should be poor, money should be granted to them. He should regularly approach those śramaṇas and brāhmiṇs in the realm who had abstained from excess negligence, who were established in tolerance and gentleness who tamed, calmed and extinguished themselves, and ask advice from them: what is good, what bad, what is to be reproached, what irreproachable, what is to be indulged in (or 'pursued'), what not? By my doing what, would there long be hardship and unhappiness, or on the other hand by my doing what, would there long be benefit and happiness? Listening to them he should avoid the bad and conduct himself conforming to the good.

He acted accordingly, and the wheel gem appeared; he knew he was a (true) emperor. The wheel gem moves round to the four quarters and the emperor follows it with his army. Everywhere the hostile kings submit and ask for instruction. He tells them living beings should not be killed, what was not given should not be taken, misconduct in pleasures should not be carried on, falsehood should not be spoken, intoxicants should not be drunk, you should rule (collect taxes) in moderation (literally 'according as it has been ruled/collected').

After some thousands of years the wheel gem retires, falls from its place, and he in turn knows his reign is ending. He installs his eldest son and goes forth to homelessness. The wheel gem disappears, but this time the son does not go to the royal sage to ask him about the Āryan imperial conduct. Instead he governs according to his own opinions *(mata)* and the countries do not afterwards flourish as they did before. The privy councillors, councillors, ministers of the treasury, soldiers, gatekeepers and learned men assemble and complain. They inform the king that they, and others like them in the realm, remember the Āryan imperial conduct and can explain it to him. He agrees and holds consultation in assembly with them, and organises safety, shelter and protection.

The king fails, however, to grant money to the poor. As a result poverty becomes widespread. Then a man takes what was not given and commits what is called 'theft'. He is seized and taken before the king. The king asks him whether it is true that he has committed theft and he admits it. When asked why, he says he could not make a living. The king grants him money and tells him to make a living with it, look after his parents and family, undertake business and set up uplifting donations to *śramaṇas* and brāhmiṇs, which would lead to heaven and result in happiness. The man agrees.

Others hear that the king rewards thieves and proceeds to imitate this man. Eventually the king reflects that if he grants money to whoever takes what was not given, to thieves, in that way this stealing will increase. He decides to take preventive measures, and orders the next thief to be executed, with due ceremony.

This does not have the effect intended. In future thieves carry sharp sword and murder their victims. They band together and raid villages and towns, even cities, and commit robbery on the roads. Thus, because the king did not grant money to poor, poverty became widespread, followed by stealing, violence, murder and false speech (explained later). As a result of the prevalence of falsehood human life became shorter.

At this point the origin of false speech is explained. A man who committed theft was taken before the king to be tried and sentenced. He denies stealing, speaks a conscious falsehood. Later, malice originates in people denouncing others for theft.

As the process of degeneration continues, human beings lose their beauty as well as having their lives shortened. They are not all equally ugly, however, and the result of that is that some of them misconduct themselves with others' wives. Thus, (misconduct in pleasures) become widespread.

From this point on various other principles become widespread and life gets shorter and shorter as a result. Details of the origin of the principles are not given, but the principles are, in order of occurrence: harsh speech, nonsensical chatter, coveting, malevolence, wrong theories, unlawful passion (incestuous), inordinate desire (greed), unnatural (homosexual) conduct, un-filial conduct towards mother or father, disrespect towards śramaṇas, brāhmiṇs and elders. By the time all these have become widespread, human life is reduced to two hundred and fifty years and will decrease further to one hundred years. We have now presumably reached the Buddha's own day, when the maximum was supposed to be a hundred years.

The Sūtra continues with a prediction about the future, which is optimistic, although the Buddha believed that things would have to get very bad indeed before men came to their senses (two and a half millennia later history has surely endorsed this conclusion). Life will be reduced to ten years (sexual maturity at five). Only the most insipid food will be available. Good conduct will disappear completely, even the word 'good' (or perhaps more accurately 'the idea of the good' – neuter) will not exist among men, let alone anyone who does a good action.

Those who are unfilial and disrespectful (as above) will be honoured and praised, lust as at present those who are filial and respectful are honoured and praised. No family relationships will be recognised and men will live like goats, dogs, etc.

Human beings at that time will bear sharp hostility, malevolence, angry and murderous thoughts towards one another, such as a hunter bears towards beasts. They will hold 'sword interval' weeks when they look upon one another as beasts and go around with sharp swords taking each others' lives.

Then some of them will think: 'Let us not take.... Let no one take my life. . . . Suppose we withdraw to a thicket, or rugged mountain, and live, eating fruit and roots.' They will do so for the 'sword interval' weeks, coming out and embracing one another afterwards, assembling, singing and encouraging each other: 'It's wonderful, sir, you are alive! In this way a good principle is rediscovered among men: abstention from taking life. As a result they find their lives increase and their appearance improves, so they look for more good principles. Gradually they will rediscover all the good principles opposed to the bad principles which had become widespread before. The whole process of degeneration will be reversed until 'this Rose Apple Continent, (i.e., India, the Southern Continent of the land-mass of Eurasia) will be powerful and prosperous, with a vast population ('like purgatory'', the Buddha remarks ambiguously, thinking probably of his preference to seclusion). Vārāṇasi will be the capital, but it will then be called Ketumati. An emperor named Śaṃkha ('Conch') will rule there and the wheel gem will appear again. Samkha will conquer the whole Earth without force, without the sword, by principle *(dharma).*

To complete the well-being of mankind the next Buddha, Maitreya, will then occur in the world. He will teach the doctrine and show the 'best life' (and will have many more followers than the present Buddha). At its conclusion the Sūtra summarises the doctrine, including self-possession, meditation and the exercise of pervading the whole universe with thought charged with benevolence, compassion, sympathetic joy and equanimity.

The Buddha's idea of the perfect ancient society before degeneration took place, which is also of interest as the happy society of the future, restored after the abolition of war and violence. The conception of evolution is characteristically Buddhist in that the loss of the original innocence took place through the operation of the causal laws concerning attachment, desire, and so on. Someone became 'wanton' (*lola*) and tasted the Earth, as a result feeling (sensual) desire (*tṛṣṇa*). Here what interests us is the nature of the society of happy beings, beautiful, radiant, feeding on joy. Even when beings had become more like human beings, living on the Earth and enjoying delicious plants growing on it, there was for a long time no essential social change.

The most important feature of this society was that it was classless. The object of the first discourse is to show that the claims of the brāhmaṇs are baseless and to maintain that all beings are equal before the moral law (good conduct will lead to a good destiny, etc.). There was no priesthood, also there was no aristocracy and no king. As a kind of government there was simply the assembly of all the people, which eventually established private property and thereby ensured the doom of the ancient society. There was no work, but only food gathering at need, for each meal. The food plants were abundant and prolific, so that all needs were easily satisfied and the question of private property could not arise. Equally there was no basis for any violence or use of force, lust as in the absence of property there could be no theft. It would seem also that there was no religion, since there were no priests. Moreover, in the absence of immorality there would seem to have been no ideas of good conduct until at the end of this period sex and property originated. If there were no *śramaṇas* there was presumably no philosophy. Only in the happy society of the future, which will be happy not because it is innocent but because of moral progress, there will certainly be a code of ethics and finally a new Buddha will restart the doctrine of Buddhism (it appears to be implied that in the lowest phase of degeneration when any idea of 'good' disappears Buddhism must disappear too along with any other philosophies or religions which teach about the good; the regeneration will apparently take place without benefit of any systematic teaching, through the discovery in practice of the essential social principle of non-violence).

Principles for a Happy Society

If a happy society is to be restored, then, with or without Buddhism, the following are the moral principles which must prevail : (i) The primary principle, the first which must be established and from which the others would seem to follow or derive is 'abstention from taking life.' In a time when 'sword intervals' (=wars?) are frequent, social regeneration will be begun by people who withdraw from society, boycott the fighting. This will Increase the expectation of life, and it seems to be assumed that its advantages will be so set-evident at that time that the majority will come to follow the principle. Before that time, in the phase of degeneration, its advantages will apparently not be self-evident to very many people. A little warfare is not enough: only a massive general slaughter can produce the requisite impression. With this principle, it is natural to group its more general statements found in these texts: non-violence and non-malevolence. In addition, those who withdrew from war lived on fruit and roots, i.e., were vegetarians. (ii) Property is represented as an evil, as a basic evil from which many others flowed, but it seems that under the present conditions (lack of abundance of food) it is a necessary evil. Consequently, it must be respected and the second principle is 'abstention from taking what was not given.' Another expression for this in our texts is non-coveting. (iii) The family and marriage, though also unknown in the happy society of the past, have also to be respected. 'Abstention from misconduct in pleasures' which is equivalent to abstention from adultery in contexts like these, is the main principle. Filial respect, which is stressed in the second text, could be regarded as associated with this principle, or as a separate principle. 'Respect for the eldest' probably means conceding precedence to an elder or eldest brother. (iv) The last of the main principles is truth: 'abstention from false speech.' With this are associated avoiding all kinds of harmful speech: malicious, harsh, etc. A few other principles that are mentioned occasionally, are presumably good but not basic: the bad principles prevalent in the phase of degeneration included wrong theories and disrespect towards śramaṇas and brāhmiṇs (these might be included with false speech). Finally the emperor when instructing his vassals included not drinking intoxicants among his precepts (the reason for this, we find in other texts, is that in a state of intoxication people are liable to perpetrate bad actions). Moderation in taxation belongs rather to the principles of government.

We have found several discussions on class and arguments against any special position and privileges for the brāhmiṇs. Some of the essential points of the Buddha's teaching on this were summarised. Classes were originally occupational, not hereditary, and ought to be so again (they would then cease to be classes in the Brahmanical sense). Any person could become a śramaṇas regardless of his class origin : on this there is another *sūtra*[20] which insists on the point that persons of any of the four classes could attain enlightenment and *nirvāṇa,* if they are intelligent. Equally people of any class are reborn according to their actions, without discrimination on grounds of class.[21] Another text[22] observes that hereditary privilege is at present so far unreal that in practice who is master and who is servant depends on wealth (this observation, however, is not ascribed to the Buddha himself, but to one of the monks after his final extinction).

The Buddha's views on service are given in another Sūtra.[23] A brāhmaṇ once explained to him that the brāhmaṇs declare that there are four kinds of service: of a brāhmiṇ, of a warrior, of one at the agricultural-mercantile class (Vaiśya) or of a helot (Śūdra). The distinction is that a person of any of the four classes may serve a brāhmiṇ, a warrior may be served by another warrior or by either of the lower classes, a Vaiśya may be served by a Vaiśya or by a helot, a helot may be served only by another helot. (Thus, there is a hierarchy from the brāhmiṇ down to the helot.) When the Buddha asks whether all people concede this pre-eminence to the brāhmiṇs, the brāhmiṇ admits they do not. The Buddha then objects that the brāhmiṇs are acting as people who thrust disagreeable food on others and then make them pay for it. At the same time he does not hold that everyone should be served (by anyone) or that no one should be served. If the service will cause the person served to be better (morally), he may be served, if it will make him worse he should not be served. This applies to all regardless of class. Whether a person is a better person or a worse person does not depend on high birth, nor on superior colour (varṇa, which also means 'beauty' and 'class', so here the last may well be intended), nor on superior property. If one of high birth, etc., takes life, steals or commits other bad actions his high birth will not make him 'better'. If he abstains from such actions his high birth will not make him 'worse'.

The brāhmiṇ continues that there are four kinds of wealth, according to the brāhmaṇs, four kinds of wealth proper to the four classes: alms for brāhmiṇs, bow and quiver for warriors, agriculture and cattle breeding for Vaiśyas, the sickle and the carrying-pole for helots. It is improper for any of them to despite them proper wealth, as it is (especially) improper for a watchman to steal. Again the Buddha asks whether all people concede this, and makes the same objection when told not. The difference of class by birth tells us merely a person's origin, it means no more than the difference between several fires as 'wood fire', 'grass fire' etc. A person from a brāhmaṇ, warrior, Vaiśya or helot family may leave home for the homeless life and be successful in following the doctrine and discipline of the thus-gone. Cannot persons of all four origins develop thoughts of benevolence, without hatred, without malevolence? The brāhmaṇ admits that this is so.

In a discussion with some brāhmiṇs[24] the Buddha is told that they declare there are five characteristics which distinguish the brāhmiṇ class. A brāhmiṇ should be (i) well-born (he should be able to trace back his brāhmiṇ ancestors for seven generations on both his father's and his mother's sides), (ii) a teacher (of the three Vedas, the ancillary lexicons, books on ritual, grammar, etc., and the historical traditions), (iii) handsome, of the brahma-colour, etc., (iv) virtuous and (v) wise (in the performance of the ritual). The Buddha asks one of them whether the list can be reduced, and it is agreed (by this one, at least) that colour is unimportant and could be left out, that the Veda and birth could be left out, but virtue and wisdom are essential (from the Brahminical point of view, perhaps, a brāhmiṇ need not teach but must be able to perform the rituals). The Buddha then goes on to redefine these essentials, virtue and wisdom, on Buddhist principles. Virtue should be following the moral principles of Buddhism. For wisdom in the ritual he substitutes Buddhist 'understanding', and explains it as the four meditations and he 'three sciences' of the enlightenment (the three sciences are of course to be substituted for the three 'knowledges', Vedas, of brāhmaṇism).

We have seen already that the theology of the brāhmaṇs was incorrect, and should be replaced by the science of causation. As to the ritual, the sacrifice, the Buddha recommended to kings the substitution of economic investment, as in the story of Great Realm. However, the story continues that when Great Realm had carried out this policy, it ended the revolt and brought about great prosperity and accumulated his own treasure he still wished to perform a great sacrifice of the traditional kind. Under his chaplain's guidance this became a great festival for the whole the whole population. It was paid for entirely by the king, without levying the tithe or accepting contributions from his subjects. No animals were sacrificed, even plants were not cut down for sacrificial purposes; only butter, sesame oil, curds, honey and the like were used as offerings. No violence was used on slaves, labourers, etc., in the preparations: all the work was on a voluntary basis and what was not done voluntarily was not done at all. This, the Buddha adds, was an interior kind of sacrifice, which might satisfy those anxious to perform a Brahminical sacrifice, though it was reformed to exclude violence. A far superior sacrifice is to establish perpetual donations to those who have 'gone forth', and are virtuous, a still better one is to build a dwelling for the community (of monks), still better are becoming a lay Buddhist, following the Buddhist moral principles (as a layman), becoming a monk and attaining *nirvāṇa*.

In the Buddha's time, to judge from his remarks there is another Dirgha sūtra,[25] according to which the brāhmiṇs, or some of them, lived a luxurious life, were well dressed, well fed, had many servants, lived in mansions, and so on. This he thought was in striking contrast with the ancient brāhmiṇ seers who had composed the Veda (cf. also the original brāhmiṇs in the account of social evolution above). Now, brāhmiṇs lived like aristocrats, in fact some of them were endowed with lands out of the royal domains by kings as fiefs (there is one such in the present sūtra, another in that last referred to, another in that an Great Realm, and yet others). The ancient brāhmiṇs may have been genuine seers, but the modern ones cannot become seers merely by learning the verses and prayers of the Veda (the mantras) the ancients had composed.

The main point on the brāhmaṇs is, however, that they were no different in nature from other people. Their claim to 'purity' (śuddhi) is nonsense,[26] as is their claim to be the 'white' (*sukla*) colour whilst the other classes are 'black' (*kṛṣṇa*). According to the Buddha all four classes are equally 'pure', and what matters is their conduct. Although the Buddha thus rejected their special claims and sought to reform their entire ideology. he wished to do so by conciliating the brāhmiṇs, by restoring them, according to his version of history, to their original condition. In effect his idea was to assimilate the brāhmiṇs to the śramaṇas : to establish that anyone could become a brāhmiṇ by adopting a simple life of meditation and virtuous, tolerant and gentle conduct. The name 'brāhmiṇ' would be retained and other terms such as 'sacrifice' might continue to be used, but they should have reformed meanings consonant with Buddhist principles. In future 'brāhmiṇ' and *'śramāṇa'* should be synonymous and all those who joined this class of people, devoted to high moral aims and the quest for enlightenment and *nirvāṇa*, should follow the 'best life' (brahma life) as described by the Buddha.

It is almost superfluous to add that the Buddha did not have in mind here any administrative measures or other methods except that people would be persuaded by their own experience and observations, that his discoveries were true and his recommendations good. If emperors were to expand their realms only by principle and without the use of force, then the great debate as to what doctrines were true would proceed under conditions of the most perfect intellectual freedom. There is plenty of evidence for the Buddha's tolerant attitude in practice in these dialogues with brāhmiṇs, more in similar discussions with śramaṇas or lay followers of other schools, such as the Jainas.[27]

At the conclusion of the admonitions to a layman which we have just read, we are told the householder asked to be a lay disciple *(upāsaka)* of the Buddha. He says that he goes to the Master (Bhagavant, i.e., the Buddha) as a refuge (*śarāṇa*), likewise to the Doctrine and to the Community of Monks as refuges. Going to these three 'refuges' constitutes formally becoming a lay disciple in Buddhism. The foregoing admonitions are of course wholly applicable to the pay disciple but they are equally applicable to any layman, and to society at large. For the actual Buddhist lay disciple there is a further systematic course of instruction *(ānupūrvi kathā)*,[28] which, however, could be regarded as abstracted from these admonitions. In the Sthaviravāda version the summary of this runs: discourses on donation *(dāna)*, virtue *(śīla)* and heaven *(suarga)*; the disadvantage, meanness and defilement of pleasures; the benefit in renunciation. The Mahāsaṃghika version substitutes 'merit' and 'the result of merit' for the last two items. The essentials, however, are donation, which means primarily giving alms to monks (equivalent to providing for the physical needs of *śramaṇas*), virtue which means primarily observing the four main social principles (not taking life, etc.) and heaven. As to heaven, we saw that the way to it is virtue or good conduct. It is implied, therefore, that besides the natural laws of the sequence of pleasures of conditioned origination, whereby, as we saw, desire (for the pleasures of the senses) leads to continued involvement in transmigration and (in the Saṃyukta, at least) the forces, that is actions, lead to rebirth, there are further laws according to which various kinds of actions lead to particular kinds of rebirth. Although the monk who aims direct for *nirvána* is not concerned, perhaps, with any kind of rebirth, and such details find no place in the theory of his training, the layman who is not ready for this supreme aim is very much concerned with rebirth and is assumed to wish to go to one or other of the heavens of the gods. There are two sūtras in the Madhyama[29] which tell us a little about this doctrine of precise retribution. It is a doctrine on which the authentic Tripiṭaka has very little to say, and which perhaps had not been elaborated in more than a very general way by the Buddha himself, but which the schools of Buddhism later worked out in much detail, seeking no doubt to make their teaching to laymen more forceful by the inclusion of circumstantial particulars of the destinies attending every kind of action.

In the first of these sūtras the Buddha is asked why men are seen to live in such a variety of circumstances, inferior and superior, short lived and long lived, suffering much or little illness, having little or great wealth, having good understanding or poor understanding, and so on. His answer is that all this depends on action *(Karman)*, it is action which divides beings in this way. Asked to elaborate this he says that if for instance, a man or woman takes life, say as a hunter, he or she will be reborn in misery, an evil destiny, ruin, purgatory. Or, failing that, if he or she is again born as a human being it will be as a short lived one. In the opposite case of one who abstains from taking life, is compassionate for the benefit of all living beings, the rebirth will be in heaven or, failing that, as a human being with long life.

One who harasses other beings with violence, short of actually taking life, will be reborn, if not in purgatory then as a human being suffering from much illness, and the reverse in the opposite case. Similarly anger and malevolence result in ugliness, the opposite in loveliness. Envy *(īrṣyā)* leads to an inferior birth, lack of it to a superior one. Lack of generosity leads to poverty, generosity to wealth. Pride and arrogance leads to a socially low (despised) birth, the opposite to a high one. One who frequents *śramaṇas* and brāhmiṇs asking them about the good, the bad, etc., will be reborn with understanding and one who does not will have a poor understanding.

The next sūtra first clarifies the point whether actions of body, speech and mind are all equally significant, or whether only the latter are significant (the Buddha always stresses the mental part of action, the intention, in contrast particularly to the Jainas, and consequently was misrepresented as denying any significance to bodily or vocal actions). All are significant and may have happy, unhappy or neutral results, but only if they are voluntary (*sāṃcetanika*), i.e., is even accompanied by volition.

It continues with an explanation that the working out of the results *(vipāka)* of actions may be very complicated, so that one who takes only a short view may be misled. It is even possible that one who has taken life may be reborn in heaven—because of some good action done before or after the bad one—or that one who has done a good action may go to purgatory. Some *śramaṇas* and brāhmiṇs, the Buddha says, have been misled by such cases into concluding that there is no such thing as good action, or a result of good conduct.

The precise mechanism of rebirth as a result of past actions is hardly made clear in the Tripiṭaka. We may suppose that the Buddha believed that a bad action, such as harming another person, has an effect also on the person who does it. It may dispose him to have bad principles in the series of his thoughts, a continuing viciousness of nature. This viciousness may at death lead him to appropriate surroundings: it is also a form of strong attachment to the world, perhaps therefore disposing him towards the grossest spheres of existence as opposed to the lighter realms of the gods. A good action would have the opposite kind of effect on the person who does it, as it were an uplifting effect, conducive to detachment as well as less gross existence.

We can further illustrate the talk on heaven when teaching a layman from the following interesting sūtra in the Madhyama.[30] Śāriputra receives news that a brāhmiṇ layman of Rajagrha has become 'negligent (*pramatta*, or 'careless'): he is using ('leaning on') the king to rob the brāhmiṇ householders, and using the latter to rob the king. (An interesting sidelight on the kingdom of Magadha; it seems this brāhmiṇ was a tax collector.) The sūtra notes that his former wife had been 'confident' (presumably a Buddhist having confidence in the Buddha, Doctrine, etc.) but she had died and his present wife was not.

Śāriputra goes to meet the brāhmiṇ, as if by chance, passes the time of day with him and then enquires whether he is 'careful' 'diligent', apramatta). The brāhmiṇ asks how he can be when he has to support his parents, wife and children, slaves and labourers, do his duty to friends, relations, guests, departed spirits (his ancestors) the gods, and the king, besides looking after his own body. Śāriputra asks whether he thinks a man who had been unjust and dishonest (*viṣama*) but alleged his parents as the cause would be spared by the guardians of purgatory, likewise if he alleged any of the brāhmiṇ's other excuses as the cause. The brāhmiṇ agrees that such a man would be consigned to purgatory just the same, regardless of his excuses. Śāriputra concludes that it is better to be just and impartial *(sama)* : there are other ways to support one's parents, etc., which are meritorious and do not require bad actions. The brāhmiṇ expresses his appreciation of Śāriputra's discourse and goes off.

On a later occasion the brāhmiṇ is very ill and thinks he is about to die. He sends a message for Śāriputra to come and see him, out of compassion. Śāriputra finds him in a bad way, and discusses future possibilities: which destiny would he prefer, purgatory, to be an animal, a human being, or any of the various classes of Gods? The brāhmiṇ is intent on the heaven of Brahmā (as are all brāhmiṇs, Śāriputra thinks). Śāriputra tells him the way to union with Brahmā is to practice the exercise of pervading the whole universe with thought immeasurable, without hatred, etc., and charged with benevolence, compassion, sympathetic joy and equanimity, considering all beings as like oneself (the exercise used by monks to get rid of the 'obstacles'). The brāhmiṇ asks Śāriputra to convey his respects to the Buddha, and the monk leaves. Soon afterwards the brāhmaṇ dies, and the sūtra tells us he was in fact reborn in the world of Brahmā.

This seems rather easy for a dishonest tax collector; however, he would presumably meet the results of his injustice eventually, for heaven is far from being a final state. Or perhaps his change of heart had been so real and effective that he had balanced out his wickedness already, and his non-violent and benevolent meditation was powerful enough to overcome all trace of it.

As further elucidation of the systematic instruction of lay disciples we may proceed to another Madhyama sūtra,[31] which is curious in that it is a story told by the Buddha about a former Buddha named Kāśyapa. This Buddha had an outstanding lay disciple who was a potter named Ghaṭīkāra. Ghaṭīkāra abstained from taking life, taking what was not given, misconduct in pleasures, false speech, and moreover from intoxicating drink as a circumstance for negligence. We may note here that these five principles of conduct, rather than the presumably more original and essential group of four, were generally taken by the latter schools as indicating the essential minimum of virtue (śīla) required in order to be a lay Buddhist and known as the 'five precepts' (pañca śikṣāpadāni) or 'five virtues' (pañca śīlāni). Ghaṭīkarā has the further virtue (required of monks, but not of laymen, for whom like all the other rules for monks it is optional, though of course good) that he does not use gold and silver, moreover as a potter he avoids harming animal life when collecting his clay from the earth. The different recensions of this text add further virtues, but agree only in these six. They also agree in praising his extraordinary generosity, particularly to the Buddha.

As a further note on 'donation' (*dāna*) we may from the conclusion of another Madhyama sūtra[32] that this might consist of feeding, clothing monks, and having dwellings (vihāra) built for them. Much more elaborate rules about this are contained in the Vinaya, with reference to what kinds of gift the communities of monks accept.

Since the 'disadvantage of pleasures' was mentioned in at least the Sthaviravada version of the systematic instruction its explanation may be added from a Madhyama sūtra on unhappiness.[33] For the sake of pleasures people work hard at various trades (to earn the requisite wealth), putting up with many kinds of discomfort such as cold, heat, flies, hunger, thirst, etc. If they nevertheless fail they grieve, lament, complain, etc. If they succeed in gaining wealth they are still unhappy and melancholy when they think of the possibility of losing it, through kings, thieves, fire, flood or heirs they dislike. Then for the same pleasures people dispute with one another, fight, go to war, get killed and wounded. Or they commit burglary, robbery, adultery, etc., and if caught are violently punished. Finally as a result of bad conduct for the sake of pleasures they are reborn in purgatory.

A fuller discourse to Buddhist lay disciples is given in the Sthaviravāda Madhyama by Ānanda to the Śākyas,[34] in the presence of the Buddha and with his approval. The Aryan pupil (ślāvaka), says Ānanda, is virtuous, guards his senses, knows the (proper) measure in his food, is watchful, and is endowed with seven good principles and practices as well as the four meditations. Explaining these points he is brief on virtue, inculcates detachment through guarding the senses, suggests food should be taken so that the body may endure and not for ostentation, etc., and under watchfulness indicates purifying the thoughts on all occasions and a habit similar to self-possession, though without using this term. Coming to the seven good principles, he states these as being confident, having self-respect, fearing blame, being learned, energetic, self-possessed and having understanding.

The first of these is having confidence in the enlightenment of the thus-gone: the Master is perfectly enlightened (this is actually part of a formula which occurs more fully elsewhere:[35] the Buddha has himself discovered and made known the nature of the universe, teaches the doctrine; the doctrine is visible, timeless, verifiable, fruitful, to be experienced individually by discerning persons; the community of pupils [sic: *śrāvakas*, so apparently not restricted to the monks but the entire community of Buddhist] has practised well, practised straight, practised the method, practised the proper course... is worthy of gifts...).

Self-respect and the fear of blame check one from bad conduct. Being learned means remembering what one has heard of good doctrines relating to the best life and comprehending them. Being energetic corresponds to the principles of exertion, for abandoning bad principles and entering into good principles, also being firm in courage, etc.

Self-possession here is described in a cryptic sentence which has puzzled the commentators of the schools,[36] and might be read as: having constant self-possession and a good memory (following the Chinese interpretation; the *Sthaviravāda* substitute 'self-possession and wisdom', in Pali *satinepakka*, for 'constant self-possession').

Understanding means the understanding which penetrates origination and cessation and leads to the perfect exhaustion of unhappiness (i.e., understanding of the Four Truths and the Way).

These seven good principles have some resemblance to the 'faculties', moreover they are immediately followed here by the meditations, in other words the use of (the faculty of) concentration. Here then we have a course of training for the lay disciple, broadly corresponding to that for the monk. In fact the Āryan pupil who is all these things just set out, says Ānanda, is capable of being enlightened, of attaining the unsurpassed (i.e., *nirvāṇa*), which is safe from the yoke (of the influence of pleasure, etc.).

Ānanda concludes his discourse by elucidating this last point. The Āryan pupil capable of being enlightened, as a result of his purity of equanimity (attained through meditation) and self-possession recollects his former lives, understands the transmigration of beings according to their actions, enters into uninfluenced freedom of thought, freedom through understanding, even in the visible world, through the exhaustion of the influences, himself ascertaining and experiencing it, and remains in it. In this way he has both good conduct and science *(vidyā)*, good conduct being his virtue and science his attainment of enlightenment.

A lay disciple is thus stated here to be capable of acquiring the 'three sciences' which constitute enlightenment and of attaining *nirvāṇa*. That a lay disciple *(upasaka)* can attain *nirvāṇa*, or freedom, is also stated by the Buddha in *Saṃyukta*[37] and in the *Madhyama*,[38] but there was some discussion about this question. The Buddha appears often to have hesitated to teach laymen more than virtue, along with generosity and heaven. For example, there is a sūtra in the Madhyama[39] in which a novice monk is asked by a prince in Rājagṛha what the doctrine is. After some hesitation he expounds the training of a monk, but the prince remarks that it is impossible that a monk could have the concentration of thought described. The novice tells the Buddha of this, but the Buddha asks how one could expect anything else: it is impossible that such a prince immersed in pleasures could learn about renunciation.

Evidently, then teaching should not be indiscriminate but should be restricted to what the person spoken to could be expected to understand. Hence the stress on virtue and heaven when addressing laymen, even Buddhist laymen, despite the fact that all this is still a matter of involvement in the world, in transmigration, is only relatively good, as contrasted with evil and purgatory, his far from the supreme good of non-attachment and *nirvāṇa*. At best, the practise of this relative good was a preparation which brought the understanding of this supreme good nearer, so that a virtuous laymen might eventually be ready to benefit from hearing the whole of the doctrine.

There is a remarkable sutra in this connection in the Madhyama[40]. Of all the Buddha's lay disciples the wealthy householder Anāthapiṇḍada is one of the most famous. Early in the teaching carrier of the Buddha he bought a park near Śrāvastī, the capital a Kośala, from Prince Jeta and donated it to the community of monks.[41] He had a residence built in it for the use of the Buddha and gradually added many other buildings. The Buddha in fact seems to have spent more time here and in Śrāvastī than anywhere else: he is recorded to have spent most of his rainy seasons there, and far more sūtras give this as their place of origin than any other place. Anāthapiṇḍaḍa thus provided the Buddha with his favourite residence and the main base of his organisation. The Buddha gave him the usual systematic instruction on generosity, virtue, heaven, etc., adding the Four Truths when he saw that the householder's thoughts were ready for this. But the Madhyama sūtra just mentioned tells us of the death of Anāthapiṇḍada many years later as follows.

In his last illness Anāthapiṇḍada sends a messenger to convey his respect to the Buddha, then resident at Jeta's Park, and to Śāriputra, asking the latter to have compassion and come and see him. Śāriputra goes, with Ānanda, and speaks to Anāthapiṇḍada of non-attachment to the senses (in order to gain relief from pain), of non-attachment to all contacts (stimuli), emotions, to the elements (*dhātus*), non-attachment to five groups even to the spheres of infinity of space, infinity of consciousness, nothingness or neither perception nor non-perception. He should not be attached to this world or have consciousness depending on it. Nor should he be attached to another world or have consciousness depending on it. He should, in short, train himself not to be attached to anything that could be seen, heard, sensed, cognised, sought or reflected on by the mind, to have no consciousness depending on any of these.

After hearing this Anāthapiṇḍada wept. He had attended on the Buddha so long, and on monks with well developed minds (i.e., advanced in the doctrine), but had never before heard a doctrinal discourse like this. Śāriputra explains that such discourses are not clear to those living in the world ('house-dwellers'), but only to those who have gone forth. Anāthapiṇḍada objects that such a discourse can be clear to those in the world, there are some who have 'little dust in their eyes, who are lost through not hearing the doctrine but will be able to grasp the doctrine.

Soon afterwards Anāthapiṇḍada died and was reborn as a Tusita god (which seems pretty poor, considering that a rapacious tax collector could reach the superior world of Brahmā; however, we have learned that the working out of actions is very complicated, and may presume also that Anāthapiṇḍada still retained his attachment to sensual existence despite Śāriputra's admonitions). That night he appeared before the Buddha in the park as a radiant divinity and uttered verses praising the park which produced his joy, the doctrine and Śāriputra. The Buddha approved and so the god departed, satisfied.

This text does not make it clear whether the Buddha agreed to the request that lay disciples should here all the doctrines. Presumably he adhered to his position of judging what his hearers could grasp. There is a sūtra in the Saṃyukta[42] in which a layman, the mayor of a village (of Nālandā, it appears) takes up the same point with the Buddha, asking whether he has compassion for the benefit of all living beings. If so, why does he teach the doctrine to some thoroughly but to others not so thoroughly? The Buddha replies with a smile of a peasant having fields of differing qualities, who would sow the best one first. In the same way the Buddha regards the monks and nuns as his best field and the lay disciples as the next best, and proceeds accordingly.

The present work finds then, that at different places in the Tripiṭaka lay disciples are differently taught: sometimes virtue and heaven, sometimes the Four Truths, sometimes the law of conditionality 'whatever has the principle of origination, all that has the principle of cessation'[43], and sometimes non-attachment. Their attainments are equally various. One lay disciple, the householder Citra, was so learned that he taught the doctrine to monks.[44] In doing so he referred to the Brahmajāla Sūtra and explained a variety of advanced doctrines.

In mentioning the varieties of the Buddha's teaching and reviewing the discourse on heaven, etc., Generally regarding this more 'popular' teaching people are encouraged to believe that they themselves will somehow continue and transmigrate, as if they were permanent beings. In elementary moral teaching the Buddha does not mention the essential impermanence, the discontinuity, of the 'being' or 'person'; that there is a sequence, or a stream of consciousness stationed in sentient bodies, but no entity that endures, no real ego or soul. The unsophisticated were not expected to understand this new way of looking at experience, this critical philosophical analysis of the data. It was better, apparently, that they should believe in the crude picture of the universe generally current in the world, and not be confused by hearing the doctrine of impermanence and no soul which might lead to assume the opposite extreme of annihilationism, that there is no sequence even, no continuity at all in existence and no working out of the moral results of actions.

One or two points of major significance remain in the teaching to lay Buddhist. Śāriputra taught a brāhmiṇ, above, to attain the world of Brahmā by means of the exercises with 'immeasurable' thought (in the later schools known for short simply as the 'immeasurables': i.e., the immeasurable thought charged successively with benevolence, compassion, sympathetic joy and equanimity as four immeasurables). Lest this should be thought to debase the exercise we may glance at a discussion[45] between an architect of Śrāvastī and four monks whom he invites to a meal with him. When they have eaten, the architect asks one of the monks, Aniruddha, about some admonitions given to him before by monks. He has been recommended to develop the 'immeasurable (apramāṇa) freedom of thought, by some monks and the 'sublime (*mahadgata*, literally 'gone large', 'magnified') freedom of thought' by others. Are these the same or different? He himself thinks they are the same, only the words are different. Aniruddha then explains that they are in fact different. The immeasurable freedom of thought is the exercise just mentioned (which we remember was used by monks to get rid of the obstacles to freedom from attachment, and find here recommended to a lay disciple for the same purpose of freedom). The sublime (magnified) freedom of thought is a different type of exercise consisting of concentration on a particular material object, such as the root of a tree, a field, and eventually the whole Earth, thinking 'it is sublime (or magnified) and remaining pervading it, intent on it, with that thought. This latter type of freedom of thought varies in sublimity (magnitude) according to the size of the object contemplated. It is meant to develop the thought, to enlarge it. (The former freedom is on the other hand immeasurable, though the word infinite is not actually applied to it.)

The present work already reflected of visits to dying laymen by monks, with appropriate discourses to prepare them for death, or rather for a good destiny. It is of interest to find that lay disciples too were expected to perform this important task, and that the Buddha instructed them on how to admonish (*ava-vad*) another lay disciple who is ill, afflicted, seriously ('excessively'—*bādha*) ill. He gives the following instructions to the Śākya lay disciple Mahānāman ('Nandin' in the Chinese), who asks how a lay disciple 'with understanding' should admonish another, also 'with understanding', under these circumstances.[46] (The Sthaviravāda commentary interprets 'with understanding' as meaning simply that he really is a Buddhist).

First he should be reassured in four ways by speaking of confidence in the Buddha, the Doctrine, the Community (and virtue).[47] The formulae noted above is to be used. (For virtue there is a similar one which says it is liberating, etc., and leads to concentration). Then he should be asked whether he is thinking of his parents or of his wife and children. If he is, he should be told that he is subject to dying ('has the principle of dying') whether he thinks of them or not, and that it will be good to give up thinking of them. If he does this he can be asked whether he is thinking of (this can also be translated 'expecting', intending'—*apekṣā*) the five kinds of human pleasures of the senses (the implication is that he is seeking rebirth such as will provide enjoyment of them). If he is, he should be told that divine pleasures are superior, and that he should set hours thoughts on the (various classes of) gods, successively, each being superior to the last. Having eventually set his thoughts on the world of Brahmā, he should be told finally that is impermanent, unstable, included in (or involved in, paryapanna) an existing body (satkāya), so that it would be good to bring his thought out of the world of Brahmā and imagine (or visualize, upa-sam-hr) it as in the cessation of an existing body (i.e., nirvāṇa). If he does this, the Buddha adds, there is no difference in freedom between him and a monk who frees his thought from the influences.

Little or nothing is said in the Tripiṭaka of any regular ceremonies to be observed by lay disciples. Thus, there seems to be no record of any regular meeting and confession of offences against the discipline or virtue, such as the communities of monks and nuns held. On the other hand, occasional confessions were certainly in order, for example, that of Ajātaśatru. The Vinaya,[48] incidentally, lists eight offences against the community of monks for which a lay disciple may be punished by the monks' refusing to accept alms from him (defaming a monk without foundation, etc.). If a layman so punished afterwards confesses his offence he may be rehabilitated by a vote of the community of monks concerned. As to regular ceremonies, however, it should not be overlooked that observing the *poṣādha*, or 'sabbath' night, is sometimes praised in laymen in the Tripiṭika as one of the virtues,[49] and it seems almost to be taken for granted as a traditional ceremony. In later times it has certainly been observed by Buddhist laymen, who moreover may undertake to fulfil additional precepts, or fasts, for the occasion. The Sthaviravāda tradition records[50] that seven lay disciples (including Anāthapiṇḍada and Citra) had regular (retinues) of lay disciples (five hundred each), implying an organisation of lay communities, but there is hardly any hint of such organisation in the Tripiṭaka.

To conclude, it is worth noting a discussion between the Buddha and a brāhmiṇ[51] concerning the relative merits of the household life and going forth as a wandered (or monk). The brāhmiṇs favour (as they have always done) the household life as being most fruitful, this the brāhmiṇ says, and consider going forth less fruitful, what does the Buddha say? The reply is that one cannot be categorical (*ekāṃśa*, definite) about this but must make distinctions (*vibhajya*, dividing, differentiating). One may be successful or fail in either way of life, for example, in agriculture or commerce just as in going forth. However, after some discussion on the good principles recognised by brāhmiṇs (to which the Buddha adds compassion), it is agreed that they are found more frequently among those who have gone forth than among householders.

Notes and References

1. Manu, I, 88ff.
2. *Ibid,* x, 97.
3. Vasudevsharan Agrawal, *Paninikalin Bharatvarsh* (in Hindi), Varanasi, 1969, p. 468.
4. Przyluski (j) Le concile de Rajagṛha, Paris.
5. Far the Sacae (Sàkai) of Herodotus, 1926-8 the inhabitants of Sacastene (Seistan).
6. Citta-Sambhūta – j, no. 498, IV, pp. 244-45.
7. Mātanga – j, no., 497, IV, p. 236; Citta-Sabhuta – j, loc, cit.
8. Setaketu - j., no. 977, III, p.154.
9. Citta-Sambhuta - j, op. cit.
10. Satadhamma - j, no.179 II, p. 57.
11. *Rāmayana*, II, vi, 9.
12. D.R. Chana, L'Esclavage dans l'Inde ancienne, Pondicherry, 1957.
13. The constitution of the Buddhist Communities was codified in their Vinaya books, one of the three sections of the Tripitaka, and will be considered in more detail below (Ch. 3ff).
14. See REBCS 47ff.
15. For the Ājivakas see HAD.
16. Unfortunately there is as yet no serious full scale study of the Lokāyata published, D. Chattopadhyaya's being perverse in rejecting most of the evidence though containing much of interest. See REBCS 52-57 and *Outline of Indian Philosophy*, pp.33-40, 124-28.
17. D No. 27 (III 84 ff.), T I No. 5. Also Ak III 98 and Bhāṣya, = Mahāvastu I 338 ff, Rockhill 1ff.- MSV (SOR) 17ff.
18. D. No. 26. T 1 No. 6.
19. Dṛḍhanemi; ir. Mithilā, MSV, SOR I p. 20.
20. M. No.90 (II 128), T 26 No. 212.
21. For another sūtra emphasising this see M No. 93, T 26 No. 151.
22. M No. 84, T 99 (Saṃyukta) section 20 No.12.
23. M No. 96, T 26 No.150.

24. D. No. 4, T 1 No. 22.
25. D No. 3, T I No.20. Sanskrit fragments Turfan 495, 885,978.
26. M No. 93,126 No. 151.
27. M No. 56, T 26 No. 133 (a laina layman persuaded to follow the Buddha should not discontinue his donations to the Jaina monks); M. No 101, T 26 No.19; M No.35, T 99 section 5 No. 8.
28. D I 110, M I 379 (in sutra already referred to above: D 3, M 56), Mahāvastu III 257 with variant ending.
29. M Nos. 135 and 136, T 26 Nos. 170 and 171. A Sanskrit version of the first in Hoernle. Manuscript Remains of Buddhist Literature found in Eastern Turkestan.
30. M No.97, T 26 No. 27.
31. M No.81, T 26 No.63, Mahātvosru I 326 ff.
32. M No 52, T 26 No. 217.
33. M No.13 (M I 85ff), T 26 No. 99.
34. M No. 53.
35. See above p. 102; for the fullest form see references under ujupatipanno PTC I 373. Similar (but not identical, especially as concerns the 'community', which may be a later elaboration of the Sthaviravada school) formulae in Mahāvastu III 200 and Dharmasangiti Sutra as quoted in the Śikṣāsamuccaya, 322 ff. Cf. D I 87.
36. Sthavirovāda MA III 30 (kasmā....), for the Chinese reading see Edgerton BHSD under nipaka.
37. S.V. 410, t T 99 section 41 No. 2.
38. MI 490 ff, T 99 (Sāṃyukta) section 34 No.26.
39. M No. 125, T 26 No. 198.
40. M No. 143, T 26 No. 28.
41. Vin II 154 ff. Avadānaśataka I 313, MSV III 134 ff.
42. S IV 314 ff., T 99 section 32 No.11. Elsewhere in the Saṃyukta (S V 407, T 99 section 37 No. 11) a lay Buddhist objects when the Buddha recommends regular study of profound sūtras that this is difficult for laymen, so he is recommended, besides the five percepts, to have confidence in the 'refuges' and virtue instead.
43. D I. 110, end of T1 No. 20.
44. S IV 281ff. T 99 section 21, MSV III 21.
45. M.No.127, T 26 No.79.
46. SV. 408 ff., T 99 section 41 No. 2.
47. 'Virtue' is added only in the Sthaviravāda version.

6

Concept of Untouchability Before the Advent of Buddhism

It is known to all that Siddhartha left home at the age of 29 years in 534 BC and became Buddhist at the age of 36 years in 528 BC having gained the enlightenment and then having preached his religion and philosophy for 45 years, achieved *Nirvana* at the age of 80 years in 483 BC. There are many arguments on the question regarding the concept as well as the state of untouchability during 600 BC in the Indian social system before the advent of Buddhist religion. According to Dr. B.R. Ambedkar, the definite age of the origin of untouchability is near about 400 BC. If this thought is considered correct, there should be no mark of untouchability during 600 BC and before that, and no more doubt is left about as to what was the concept as well as the state of untouchability. But Dr. Ramsharan Sharma accepts that during the period of about 1000 BC, the Aryans hated the *Chandal* and *Polcus* and the untouchability originated between 600 BC–300 BC[5] Dr. Vivekanand, divided the untouchability in four main phase. According to him in the first phase till 600 BC, which is Vedic background, the society based on *taboos* is first seen. In the second phase, the period of 600 B.C.-200 B.C., the untouchability started and many groups adopted[6] a certain identity in this form. But if we investigate the Buddhist scriptures, this ambiguity spread in connection of the beginning of untouchability can be eliminated.

There is a complete story named *Supipya Theron and Sopak Theron* in *Chaturthon Vaggon* narrating that Supipya and Sopak, two untouchable boys, were admitted in Buddhist religion as well as the monastery by Gautama Buddha himself. Their father was a watchman in a graveyard. Dr. B.R. Ambedkar himself accepts too that *bhangee* (sweeper) *Suneet, Sopak* and *Supipya* belonged to the Scheduled Tribe and that they were admitte[7] in Buddhist monastery by Gautama Buddha himself. The story of *bhangee* Suneet's conversion into a monk, is described extensively in a Buddhist scripture and it is said that he became a great monk[8] in the long run. The greater thing is that when a *Chandal* girl, named Prakrati was asked for water by Anand, the monk and the foremost after Gautama Buddha, she refused to give water and informed him of her belonging to Scheduled Tribe. Hereupon, he told her of having no concern with her tribe and then she offered him water and finally, having been satisfied by the reasoning of Gautama Buddha, got initiation in Buddhist religion and she was included in monastery.[9] Dr. Ambedkar also describes her inclusion in the monastery extensively.[10] What is therefore concluded from these stories and data entered n Buddhist scriptures? It becomes clear that all these facts belong to the age of Gautama Buddha. He himself admitted, as quoted above, Suneet, Supipya, Sopak and Prakrati in Buddhist religion and imparted them the education of religion and good conduct. Does this not prove the untouchability was prevalent in the society in 600 BC. It is also possible from this data that untouchability, prevalent in the Indian society in 600 BC, would not have become a part of the social system in around 10–20 years, but it would have taken decades in its origin and development like other social institutions. But surprisingly, despite all these proofs, the qualified scholars have denied the existence of the institution of untouchability in 600 B.C. and before that.

Now, it can be seen as to what was the concept and the state of untouchability in India before the establishment of Buddhist religion. For information, we will have to depend mainly on Vedic scriptures as well as Upanishads. The scriptures of that age inform not only about the social, political, economical and cultural conditions of the Aryans but also provide the statements spoken by them about their opposers. We should concentrate more on anti-Aryans as it is possible that thereby some light be thrown on the concept and the origin of untouchability.

Giving the indication of the Aryan-enemies, the historian R.C. Majumdar has written:

"The Asuras, the demons, the Rakshasas and the *Naga* people opposed the cultural expansion of the Aryans strongly. Their civilisation and the culture were in different phases of the development. Some Scheduled Tribes were totally illiterate, wild and uncivilized while the civilisation of some tribes had developed a little. In old legends, from the explanation of these opposing tribes, the Asuras, the demons and the Rakshasas, the three phases of their development are obtained. In reality, these are the names of the human beings but generally, because of the Aryan-enemies, they were given such names. Its objective was to express the feeling that these people were hateable foes of different types or wild. Later, these names began to be used expressing insult and in the form of vulgar words and in other to make these people licentious also, these names were used. Finally, these words meant devils and they began to be used as synonym of the demons, affirming the collision between the Aryans and their adversaries, it is said that when the earth which is called Bharat, was attacked by the Aryans, they had to face the dreadful wild people who were called the Asuras or the Rakshasas by the former and they were driven away from that place or it seems necessary that the information of the social, economical and cultural conditions of those so-called terrible wild, illiterate and uncivilized tribes and so-called a little civilized tribes be obtained and this be also tested as to why the Aryans had enmity against, as well as the abhorrence for, these tribes. No written proofs left by these so-called wild or underdeveloped species are available for the complete information but this target can be definitely achieved by the words, *Veda Richas* (aphorisms) and the collisions adopted by the *Aryans* for their foes."

The historian Dr. Ramsharan Sharma, says that although the main question between the Aryans and their enemies was for the possession of the animals, chariots and the wealth of another type, yet their relations remained bitter due to the different caste, religion and the conservation style.[13] It is found out by the Vedic scriptures that the awful collisions and the war were going on between the Aryans and the Asuras and the latter were killed. Sixth *Mandal* of the Rigveda, contains the explanation of the movement of Indra against the main foes of the Aryans.[14] In Atharava Veda[15] also, Indra is said to be the killer of the Asuras in Shatpath Brahmana, Grahasthsutra and many Upanishads also, Indra is shown as the murderer of the Asuras.[16] Thus, he is requested repeatedly in the

Richas of the Rigveda to ruin the Das tribe (vish).[17] The fourth *Mandal* of the Rigveda explains that Indra made the *Dasyus* devoid of all good qualities and took the *Das* tribe in his control.[18] It is also described that having killed the Dasyus, he protected the Aryan tribe.[19] He is requested in the Rigveda as well as the Atharava Veda to fight with the Dasyus and expand the power of the Aryans.[20] These facts inform about the hostile relations between the Aryans, and the Asuras, the Dasyus, and the Das etc. and the hint of the wars going on between them is also met. In fact, the Aryans and their adversaries hated each other for many things as it seems from the Vedic scriptures. The Aryans belonged to the vagabond beast-rearing race and had no knowledge of either agriculture or handicraft nor did they possess any other property[21]except livestock. On the other side, the Dasyus, the Asuras, and the Das, etc., were although in different phases of the developed, nevertheless, there were the village civilisation and the fortified colonies of the people who had reached the developed phases. The Aryan-adversaries were not only illiterate and wild but also possessed the wealth like diamonds and the jewels as well as the knowledge of agriculture and the handicraft.

It is told in many Mandals of the Rigveda that the Das and the Dasyus had many fortified colonies in their control.[22] Sayan also says that there is a city named Amravati where the deities accommodated and a town named Iravati[23] of the Asuras in the Valley of the Meru mountain. The archaeologists have, in reality, discovered the remains of an ancient city by digging on the edges of the Iravati river and for accepting on the basis of the proofs available in the Rigveda, it is a major basis to accept it as the town of the Asuras. This city is called Hadappa.[24] In Rigveda, the name of this city is told Hariyupiya.[25] AM Wheeler, the modern scholar, accepts it as Hadappa of the Sindhu valley.[26] D.D. Kosambi, the famous historian, has penned that the written material and the information obtained from the archaeological discovery resemble each other to a great extent.[27] In the Rigveda, Indra is praised for defeating *mayavees* (illusory) by his *maya* (illusion) and ruining the Pipru cities.[28] In this scripture, Indra, the Vedic deity, is described as Purander, that is, the fort destroyer. Dr. Ramchander Majumdar, in his book, *Prachin Bharat,* (p. 15 Delhi, 1988), writes that the civilisation of the Sindhu valley was that of Dravid or Mediterranean tribe. Undoubtedly this civilisation resembles that one of the hint of which is obtained from the study of the *Parvarti Dravid* language and the language-speakers. The civilisation of the Sindhu valley had developed long before the arrival of the Aryans in India. Sir John Marshal and some other people, too, have reached the same conclusion by a comparative study of the civilisation explained in the Rigveda and this civilisation.

It is described in many Mandals of the Rigveda that the Aryans had their eye on the collected wealth of the fortified colonies of their foes and for its possession, the fight was constantly carried on between the two.[29] The Aryans wanted to weaken the power of the slaves of Indra and distribute their collected wealth mutually.[30] The Aryans had become greedy after seeking their collected gold and jewels.[31] On the other hand, the Aryan-enemies gave importance to their chariots, horses and animals. Same is affirmed by the Rigveda also that the *Asuras* had taken control on the city of Rajshri Dabheeti but on the way of their return, Indra having surrounded, defeated them and, having seized the cattle, the horses and the chariots, returned to Rajshri.[32] Possibly, the cities resided by the Rajshri Dabheeti, might have been belonging to the Asuras which would have been occupied by the Aryans after defeating the former. These facts clear that the vagabond Aryans required the place and the colonies for the permanent stay which could not be achieved without the struggle as well as the war. Since the Aryans lacked the knowledge of colonising the colonies and developing the rural civilisation, they either possessed the cities and the fortified colonies of the Asuras, the Dasyus and the Das or ruined them. The contemporary archaeologists as well as the historians opine that the Vedic Aryans destroyed the towns having the civilisation of the Sindhu valley, robbed their inhabitants, killed them and drove them away.[33]

Although the reason of the terrible collisions and the wars between the Aryans and their enemies, and the feelings of the bitterness and the hatred, was mainly the economical greed and the interest of the Aryans, but the racial as well as the cultural differences also were not less important for them. The descriptions of the Vedic scriptures throw ample light on the fact that the Aryan-enemies belonged mainly to different class culture.

Whichever be the creation, population of each spot was

related to the same scientific group having the same perception. It cannot be related to such different races which were having different characteristics. Secondly, in Punjab and the Sindh, the features of this population were flat nose, tall height and long head while the people of the Gujarat were having a round head. This, too, indicates the relation of the description of the Rigveda and the archaeological process. In two Mandals of the Rigveda, the Dasyus are addressed by the adjective of the Mrudhravak.[41] But the *Aryans* have used it for their foes in different forms at six places indicating that the tone of the conversation of both was different.[42] Dr. Ambedkar has written in this connection:

"It is clear that initially the Asuras spoke some language different from that of the Aryans. Prof. Mayur has quoted many paragraphs from the Rigveda in which the word *'Mrudhravak'* has been used for the language of the Asuras. According to me, it means *'hanni-prapt boli'*. According to Sayan, this is the language of those having lost their tongues. Undoubtedly, the original meaning of it has been that the *Aryans* do not follow more or less the language of the Aryans. This explanation fits correctly. The second stanza of the Rigveda also where it is said that we may win the people speaking the abusive language by pleasing *Indra*."[43]

Thus, it is described in the *Shatpath Brahmana* that the Asuras, being voiceless, remained useless. They used to cry out *Helavah, Helavah.* Their voice was puzzled and the one speaking thus, is *malechh* (untouchable). Therefore, no Brahmin should speak such abusive language as it is spoken by the *Asuras.*[44] The aforesaid facts clear that the Aryan-enemies belonged mainly to a different race, having dark complexion, swollen lips and flat noses and speaking the language different from that of the Aryans. The second reason of the bitterness as well as the dislike was different geneology.

Now, it seems necessary to see as to those foes considered hateful as well as wild by the Aryans, had what sort of culture. The criticism of the conduct and the culture of their foes by the Aryans in Vedic texts informs about the culture of the *Asuras,* the Dasyus and the Das. For a complete *Sutt* of the seventh *Mandal* of the Rigveda the Dasyus, viz., Akrutan, Ashradvan, Ayagyan and Ayajvanha, etc., the adjective is used which may prove that the *Dasyus* disliked the oblations.[45] In the first Mandal of the Rigveda,

Indra is requested to differentiate between the Aryans, devoted, as well as the Asuras, indifferent, to the oblations.[46] The Das disbelieved in oblation too. It is said about him that he, differentiating between the Aryans and the Das, approaches the oblation-canopy.[47] The priests always wished that the oblation-oppugnants be killed and postumously, their wealth be distributed among the people.[48] The Dasyus, despite their being wealthy, are called Akratu, performing no oblations.[49] It is said in the third Mandal of the Rigveda that the *keekats* don't deserve to keep cows as they donot use the cow-milk products in oblations.[50] Many such examples can be searched from the Vedic scriptures. These facts clear that the *Aryan*-enemies had no faith in oblation, performed no *hawan* (fire sacrifice) and were opposed to these ritual ceremonies. Therefore, the Aryans have repeatedly summoned to punish their enemies and requested *Indra* to occupy their wealth, kill them and weaken their power.

Then, at last, the question arises if the Dasyus, the *Das* and the Asuras, opposed the oblation, they believed in what? Did they have any religious ceremony or orientation or not? It is said in the fourth Mandal of the Rigveda that the Dasyus conducted the miraculous witchery.[51] Similar thought is entered also in the *Atharva Veda* where calling the Dasyus, the ghosts and the demons, they are attempted to be driven away from the oblation-canopy.[52] It is referred too in the *Atharava Veda* that the Dasyus are the critics of the god. Therefore, they must be offered as the victims to the deity.[53] P.P. Kani has said that the Aryans believed that the Dasyus are unfaithful, do not perform the religious duties like the former and are devoid of humanity.[54] It is explained in the first Mandal of the Rigveda, "O Indra, thou have defeated those *mayavees* who swallow the *shraad* (the offering of water, food and clothes, etc. to the Brahmanas in honour of manes) themselves, by your *maya.* Thou are the saviour of the people. Thou have destroyed the Pipru cities and protected the Bijisan from the robbers."[55] In the Vedic mythology, according to A.A. Macdonald, the verbal meaning of *mayavin* is those people having the power of illusion or *mantras.* Sayan, (*Gyanrigveda,* 1, 52.5) says that this word is used here for the Asuras.[56] In the first Mandal of the Rigveda, (11.1, 1.51.5) and the fifth Mandal (63.7), the *maya* is said to be the power of the

Asuras and such statements are present in the Vedas that the Asuras put even *shraad* in their mouths.[57] In the first Mandal of the Rigveda, (51.8.9, 101.2, 175.3), the sixth Mandal (14.3) and the ninth Mandal (41.2), the Dasyus are called Avrat and in the eighth Mandal (0.11) and the tenth Mandal (22.8) are addressed by the adjective of Anyavrat. In the Rigveda, the adjective Apravt also for the Dasyus is used.[58]

The Aryans had the enmity and the abhorrence for those Aryans opposed to their culture and wanted to conquer as well as kill them. In the tenth Mandal of the Rigveda, (83.1), the Aryans have requested Manyu, Moortiman Krodh, to assist them in defeating their both kinds of enemies, the Aryans and the Das. Here only Indra is prayed to fight with the Das and the Asuras, the enemies of his followers because they disbelieved in god.[59] Prof. Mayur has quoted such fifty eight parts from the *Rigveda* where the religious enmity or the indifference of the members of the Aryan community is abused. Many of these stanzas are available in the original part of the Rigveda (Mandals, two to eight) and many of these parts are against those unkind folk who are called aradhsam or apragatah. In many Mandals of the Rigveda, the expressions of the enmity of the Aryans against Panis appear. According to the authors of the Vedic Index (1.472), the word Pani is the synonym of one owing riches, but who neither offers the *havya* (articles used as oblation) to the god nor donates to the priests as a consequence of which they might be worthy of loathing of the *sanhita*-creators.[61] According to the writer of the Vedic Index (1.472), the word pani is so extensive that it also signifies the Adivasi or the malicious Aryan tribes.[62] The wealth of such Aryan-enemies used to be grabbed and they used to be made pauper like those subsequent to Aryans.[63] In the tenth Mandal of the Rigveda (69:6), it is said that the Agni grasped the property situated on the flat land and in the hills, for the welfare of his subjects and defeated their enemies, the Das and the Aryans.[64]

All the aforesaid facts clear that the Aryan-enemies, the Das, the Dasyus, and the Asuras and some Aryans were against the Vedic culture, performed necromancy, the atheists disbelieving in god, illusory and those grabbing or swallowing the *shraad* themselves. According to the Rigveda (1.51.8-9, 101.2, 175.3;

6.14.3, 9.41.2, 8.70.11, 10.22.8, 5.42.9; 40.6), they were *Avrat, Anyavrat* and *Apvrat* as either they had no belief in Aryan tribal law or custom, or some different racial custom or had separated from *vratya* life after development.

D.P. Chattopadhyay has authored that the area of the Sindhu civilisation was very expansive and that is why neither its inhabitants would have been killed completely nor it is possible that their thoughts, beliefs and religious rituals would have disappeared from this country.[65] Then, at last, what happened with these surviving Aryan-enemies? Dr. Ramsharan Sharma, searching the solution of this problem, has written that on the one hand, many of the surviving people would have been bound to accept the slavery and on the other hand, in the Aryan community, the natural tendency of the *vish* would have been to merge in low class. The tendency of the Aryan-priests and the warriors would have been to mix with the high class of the ancient community.[66] He has quoted many citations from the Vedic scriptures making it appear that many Das from the ancient community were attempting to merge in the Aryan community. It is possible also that most of the Das, the Dasyus, the Asuras and some Aryans against the Aryan-culture, having accepted the slavery of the Aryans, would have made the efforts to adopt their language and the culture as they owned neither fortified colonies nor political power, the cattle and the land and the wealth like gold and diamonds. Many people becoming the Aryan-slaves, were categorised as the Sudra tribe, in the social system based on their classes, the chief castes among Hindus, viz., Brahmana, Kshatriya, Vaisya and Sudra. Dr. Ramsharan Sharma, throwing light on the origin of the Shudras, has written that the condition of the Aryans or pre-Aryans was such due to the internal as well as the external collisions. Since the chief reason of the collision was regarding the ownership of the cattle and later the land, those from whom the land and the cattle were seized and those becoming powerless, used to call the fourth class in new community. Then those families owning the cattle and the land more than their capacity to maintain the same, felt the need of labourers and in the end of the Vedic period, they began to be called the *Sudra*.[67] It is very much possible that the Das and the Sudras have been named step by step on the base of the tribes of these names which might have been in close contact with the

Indian Aryans and the people of the pre-Aryan population from the chronological order and the afflicted Aryans also would have been merged in these classes.[68]

But one question remains unanswered as to those Aryan-enemies who were driven away or who were made in different phases of the development spread in expansive areas, or who did not accept the Aryan-slavery, quit their beliefs, traditions and oblations, met with what end? In this connection, Dr. D.P. Chattopadhyay's indication is significant. He says that nevertheless, if we accept that the people of the Sindhu civilisation are called the Asuras in the initial parts of the Rigveda, yet it is natural to guess that their successors too, after them, would have been called the Asuras. Even same description would have been present also in subsequent Vedic Brahmaneey literature and so it is not illogical to raise the question here whether the activities of the Asuras explained in the Upanishads and the scriptures like the *Geeta,* written subsequently, might have been the remains only of the period of Sindhu civilisation.[69] Substantially, in subsequent years, the feeling of the hatred and the enmity of the Aryans for these enemies also appears in the Brahmaneey texts. In the background of the Vedic period, it will not be illogical to search the concept of the untouchability by keeping in attention the feeling of pervaded hatred of the Aryans for their opposers and their culture because the hate and the malice of the Aryans of which kind appears for their enemies in the Vedic period, similar appears in *Parvarti* period against the untouchables and Scheduled Tribes.

Dr. Ramsharan Sharma has written that in the background of the inferior culture of the primary tribes, increasing feeling of the hatred for the labour and the very old thoughts related to prohibition and impurity, the peculiar feeling like untouchability ascended.[70] He denies the origin of untouchability as explained in sacred texts because here the people born of the parents of different tribes are called untouchables.[71] But the learned author has not cleared the inferior culture of the primary tribes nor does he take pains to inform about the danger the Aryans had from that culture. Is not so that the primary tribes had the same culture as was had by the Das, the Dasyus and the Asuras. The labour work was being performed not only by the primary tribes but also by all people of the Sudra class. But the Shudras were not announced untouchables. Therefore, it seems necessary that the culture of the Asuras, the Das and the Dasyus be investigated a little because Dr. Ambedkar, pointing out the abhorrence of the Brahmins for the Buddhists as one main reason of the origin of untouchability, quotes a couplet quoted by Manu in *Prayashchit Mayukh* of Neelkanth. It is said in this couplet, "If any person will touch any Buddhist, the *pashupat* (a devotee of Shiva, one of the *Upanishads* of Atharava Veda), the *lokayat,* an atheist and the *Mohapatki* (one who is guilty of crime of the highest degree), he will be pure after the bath." It clears that the Aryans had the eye of hatred for the *lokayats* as well as the atheists and the former became impure just by touch of the latter. According to Dr. D.P. Chattopadhyay, the *lokayat* is the notion of the Asuras and says that this was physical or *ihlaukik* (pertaining to the present world) originally and their oblations also were *ihlaukik.* Madhvacharya, presenting the thoughts of the *lokayats* in a fit and logical manner, says that the *lokayats* did not consider any other source of knowledge legitimate except the direct sensual knowledge and therefore, they regarded true those material things only which can be known only by the medium of the senses. According to them, there is no true proof of the god as well as the soul nor is there any existence after death. As a possible result of this, *lokayats* neglected all religious as well as moral values and believed in sensual comforts only.[74] It is clear from Madhvacharya's comment about the *lokayats* that they were also atheist as well as materialistic.

There is a famous couplet for the *lokayats,* "As long as there is life, enjoy the pleasures. Use pure ghee, does not matter if thou are buried in debt". But on knowing the science of ethics of the *lokayats,* it seems that it is publicised to defame them. D.P. Chattopadhyay has written that in order to prove that the effect of the *lokayat* doctrine was very deep as well as widespread, many proofs can be given. One is the word *lokayat* itself, that is, prevalent in the world. The constant efforts of its oppugnants, to present the horrible shape of the *lokayat* and to defame as well as deny it, is another proof. Had the *lokayat* been one having the shallow principle, in which it is believed that 'of course, borrow but enjoy', then we cannot clear that despite it, how their effect was so deep and extensive or then why all sects of the Indian philosophy did not take the *lokayat* very seriously.[75]

The *lokayats* had their own racial morality which they kept very strongly. In the tribal community they lived in, the murder of one's relatives was considered an immoral crime. Due to this very reason, at the time of the war of Mahabharata, the lokayat Charvak *Shanti Path* criticised Yudhishthir sharply. The incident explained in of the *Mahabharata* is as follows:

"After the great war of Kurukshetra when the Pandavas were returning victorious, thousands of *Brahmins* had gathered in the city to bless Yudhishthir, Charvak being one of them. He approached ahead and without the permission of other *Brahmins,* addressing the emperor, said, "This group of *Brahmins* is cursing thou as thou have killed your relatives. What have thou achieved by killing kinsmen and yours elderly people? Thou should die". The gathered *Brahmins* remained wondered at the sudden roar by that furious Charvak. Yudhishthir received by the horrible shock and he wanted to die. But by then the other *Brahmins* were balanced and they informed the king that Charvak was not their real representative but some demon in deceptive appearance as well as the friend of Duryodhan, Yudhishthir's enemy. The Brahmins convinced the king that they were praisers of their great deeds, and thereafter they captured Charvak and reduced him to ashes by burning.[76]

D.P. Chattopadhyay has written in this part of the *Mahabharata,* Charvak has not said anything suggesting even a little that the life-philosophy of the *lokayats* was concerned only with, "eat, drink and enjoy, who has seen tomorrow?". On the other hand, if we want to see only the moral values placed in these words, these values were definitely of racial life where the people lived in groups of relatives or a *Kabeela.* Yudhishthir's misdeed Charvak expressed his fury on, was about the destruction of his relatives as well as the murder of his elders. His allegation was not regarding the destruction of human life only, had it been so, his viewpoint would have been regarded non-violent. Definitely, the allegation was in the context of the assassination of the relatives and therefore, we consider it as the expression of the moral values of distinguished tribal life.[77]

G. Thomson, in *Askillas and Athens* (pp. 34–35), has written about the tribal morality:

"In the entire history of the tribal community, the relations of the *kabeela* are regarded as the most sacred ones. Greenvekh, writing in connection of the primary tribal life of Norway, says the murder of any of the *kabeela* member would create the atmosphere of great fury and hatred. With the immediate entry in the *kabeela,* the life achieves the supreme place of holiness which can never be defied. Assassinating anyone in *kabeela* is considered against religion, blindness and suicide. In this condition, the natural reaction takes place with as much definite sharpness as it happens after the needle is pierced in any nerve of the body".[78]

These facts clear that in those *lokayats* or atheists despised by the people of Aryan culture and due to whose touch, the later became impure, the tribal morality and the collective life was strong. Such *lokayats* and atheists used to oppose the people of Aryan culture furiously because the fourth class people were constantly violating the racial values.

In many Mandals of the Rigveda, the Dasyus and the Asuras are addressed by the adjective of Avrat, Anyavrat and Aprvat, etc., being ordinary. By these adectives, many development phases of Aryan enemies are informed about. Some of the Dasyus and the Asuras had reached very progressive phases. Those not keeping the tribal collective values, would have been called *Avrat* or *Apvrat* by the Aryans and those obeying the same, are addressed by the adjective of *Anyavrat* possibly as it may signify some other *vratya* or racial group. According to P.P. Kane, Katyayan said that all the words like *shranee, poog, gann, vrat* and *sangh,* had the same meaning and that originally was 'any group' or 'class'.[79] Sayan, too, has not ascribed any difference between the *gann* or the *vrat.*[80] Therefore, in the third *Mandal* of the *Rigveda* (26.6), alongwith the appreciation of the *gannas,* the *vratas* too are praised greatly that in prayer we wish the power of the wind and the prosperity of the fire in every *vrat* and every *gann.* Thus, abreast the *gan,* the *vrat's* excellence is sung in tenth *Mandal* (34.8) and (34.12) of the Rigveda. It is also explained in the Atharva Veda as to how the *vratya* went to the east, the south, the west and finally the north and achieved abundant fame. The citations of this majesty-song of the *vratyas* by the Vedic saints are as follows:

"He (*vratya*) got up. He stepped towards the east. The *Vrahad* (a Vedic couplet) and the *Rathantar* (another Vedic couplet) as well as Aditya (the son of Aditi) and all deities followed him. Whoever insults such well-read *vratya,* insults the *Vrahad* and the *Rathantar* as well as the Aditya and all deities. One, aware of the same, is inhabited by the *Vrahad* and the *Rathantar* as well as the *Aditya* and all deities. In east, the faith is his concubine, the friend his minstrel, the conscience his apparel, the day his turban, the night his hairs, the yellow colour his chest, the lotus his jewel, the present and the future his two servants, the heart his uncontrolled vehicle, Matrishvan and Vavman, the pullers of that vehicle, the wind his chariot, the sun his *ankush* (the iron hook by which the elephants are controlled by his driver) and the honour and fame his carriers, one, aware of same, achieves fame. (translated by Hivtony 774).[82]

Thus, in the Atharva Veda, the *vrat* or the *vratya* is praised and the Vedic sages have criticised the Dasyus and the Asuras disobeying the *vrat* and the enemies obeying some other *vrat.* But in the subsequent period, this situation seems to be reserved while in the ordinance of the *Mahabharata* as well as the literature of religious ceremonies, this indication is found that the people called the *vratya* were unholy and fallen as well as degraded.[83] According to the *Aapstamb* holy maxim, the *vratya* is that person whose ancestors had not met with *upnayan-sanskar* (investiture with the sacred threat).[84] It is told also in *Manusmriti* that the *vratya* were those people who were immoral and therefore they were out of the horizon of the Aryan community. In Yagvalkya Smriti also, supporting the same statement, it is informed that only the degraded people having no morality, were the *vratya* who were neither taught the Vedas nor permitted to perform any religious ceremony during the oblations and the mutual reconciliation with them according to the social custom was prohibited.[86] In Bodhayan religious text also, supporting that old principle, it is said that the *vratya* were none but the people born of men-women of different classes.[87]

The facts mentioned earlier conclude what? The sages of the Aryan culture of the Vedic period have defamed those disobeying the *vratya* or dismissed from *vratya,* but in the subsequent period, those obeying the *vratya* were to be called degraded as well as the fallen ones, devoid of Vedas and *upnayan-sanskar* born of men-women of different tribes, that is, were considered the so-called untouchables or Scheduled Tribes. This absolutely surprising aspect seems to have stood in front. But if it is promoted onwards by the process of minute investigation, a prudential as well as true conclusion of those opposite circumstances can be achieved. The Aryans of the Vedic period were living in tribal community at that time and they were obeying the collective custom of the tribal community and therefore, they were singing the euology of the *vrat* or the *vratya*. At that time their many enemies, especially the Dasyus and the Asuras were rising above the tribal standard or had risen above those who did not obey, or were violating, tribal *vrat* tradition, were reprimanded as *Avrat* by the Vedic Aryans. In conjunction with, maximum people of their enemies, the Dasyus or the Asuras, those who being in the underdeveloped phase, were keeping the *vrat* of the tribal community different from the Aryans, were criticised later as *Anyavrat.* But subsequently, when the people of the Aryan community had reached the new stratum of the development and they got rid of the moral values as well as the customs of the tribal community, unsurprisingly, they separated themselves from those *vratya,* criticised as well as hated them. Since the Aryan-enemies, being in the underdeveloped phase or those having been driven away, could not relieve themselves from the *vrat* custom of the tribal community nor were they left to have any opportunity for development, they were forced to spend the *vratya* life. Therefore, the hatred by the people of the Aryan culture for the people spending such *vratya* life, making the later untouchable as well as the Scheduled Tribes[88] or using the words *varn-sankar,* signifying the insult, were natural only. When the people of the Vedic culture could have hated those people who were bound to spend vratya life, of their own geneology untouchable or degraded ?

D.P. Chattopadhyay has written that the primary Vedic people had unequal progress in their social life. Some of them had progressed while some lagged behind and had to spend *vratya* life. Those who progressed, had developed hate possibly for those lagging behind because it is announced in this *Brahmana* that those spending the *vratya* life, were degraded as they undertook neither agriculture nor trade. Substantially, by the description of the *Brahmana* scriptures, the learned author has proved that same Aryans also were spending the *Vratya* life. In *Tandaya Mahabrahamana* as well as Katyayan short sutra (xxII. 4.27-8) a process named "*Vratya Stom*" is inscribed in which the method of the elevation of the *vratya* is described and which is related clearly to the *Arya-vratya.* A story is narrated in *Tandaya Mahabrahmana* "when the deities proceeded towards the heaven, some of their dependents on the earth and they had to spend the *vratya* life".[90]

Thus, it is clear from the aforesaid statements that although the authors of the holy writs of the *parvarti* period were calling themselves the successors of the Vedic people, they grudged the *vratya* organisation of those very *Vedic* people and all those classes spending the *vratya* life were considered by them as fallen, hateable as well as hybrid or untouchable whether they belonged to the classes opposed to Vedic culture or some other Aryan tribe. Will cherishing the tribal morality as well as the *vratya* life be called inferior culture? Yes, at least the authors of the holy writs used to think this way only.

If we return again to that statement of Manu and find out as to why the *lokayats* and the atheists observing the morality of the tribal community, were considered untouchable and unholy, then the concept about untouchability also can be cleared and other aspects of their reasoning can be brightened. In *Shukraneeti Saar* (45.55), in the list of the scholars and the arts, it is quoted that the reasoning of the atheists was very strong. In their writs, the existence of the god and the authority of the Vedas is rejected. They had their creative side also: *Sarva Svabhavik Matan,* that is, the principle according to which everything is managed by natural law.[91] Kautilya, in his *Arthashastra* (1.1), along with naturalism as well as the *yog*, has also described the *lokayat* and called it the science of the logic, that is, meditation.[92] In *Manusmriti* (2.11), the *Hetu* scripture as well as the *Hetukas* are described who were the atheists according to the Vedic viewpoint.[93] In *Bhagvata Puran* (11.18.38) also, alongwith the Buddhists and the *Jainas,* the *Hetukas (lokayats),* too, are described and the word hypocrite is used for them.[94] In *Manusmriti* (1.30 and 2.11), it is said that the strict legal law be enforced against these logic teachers and none should talk to these atheists (hypocrites), violating the caste religion, hypocrites and *Hetukas.*[95] Many such references, used for the *lokayats*, the atheists and the *Hetukas* in holy writs, can be searched. Whatever was being stated by the writers of these holy writs, resembles the atheist, the witchery performed by the Dasyus, the Asuras and some Aryans described in the Vedic scriptures because in the Vedic period also these people were seen with abhorrence. The reason is clear that the Dasyus, the Asuras, etc., believed neither in the Vedas nor the Vedic deities, nor did they perform oblations or had faith in god and in the progressive period also, the *lokayats,* the atheists or the people called the *Hetukas* were oppugnant of the Vedic culture and the god. The *lokayats* were against not only the god or the oblation but also opposed to the principle of the *atma* (soul) of the Vedic culture. In this context, the story of Indra and Virochan explained in *Chhandogya Upnishad* is worthy of quotation:

Prajapati said, "The soul which is sinless, immortal, devoid of grief, appetite-desire, whose objective and the ideal is supreme truth, that only should be searched. There should be desire to achieve the knowledge of the soul only. One who achieves the same, gains all the regions and the wishes".

Both the deities and the Asuras heard him and said, "Come, we discover that soul by whose knowledge the man achieves all the worlds and the desires".

Then the Indra, out of the deities and Virochan, out of the Asuras approached Prajapati, Without any conversation with each other, visited him with *aradyay* (holy water).

Then both, as pupils having possessed the desire of the achievement of the sacred knowledge, cherished the celibacy for 32 years.

Then the Prajapati asked them, "What desire made thou live"?

They answered, "The soul which is sinless, devoid of suffering, appetite and greed, whose objective and ideal is the supreme truth, should be discovered. There should be the desire to achieve the knowledge of that soul only. The achiever obtains all the worlds and the wishes. O God, the people say that these words are yours. We have been living with the desire of the attainment of that soul".

He said, "That, which is apparent in eyes, is soul in whose connection I have said. That is immortal and fearless. That is Brahma".

"But O God, who is that seen by us in water and mirror"?

"See thouselves in the vessel of water. Whatever thou don't

understand about the soul, let me know".

Then they looked into the water-vessel. The Prajapati asked them, "What are thou looking"?

They replied, "O *Prabhu,* we can see everything in it. One soul is exactly like us. Even the hairs as well as the nails are like those of us".

He told them, "Both of thou decorate thouselves with ornaments and beautiful apparels and then look into the water-vessel".

Then they, having decorated themselves with beautiful ornaments and clothes, looked into the water-vessel. He asked them, "What are thou seeing"? They answered, "Exactly as we are, decorated wth ornaments and outfits".

"Same is soul," the Prajapati said, "immortal and fearless, same is Brahma." Then they departed with a tranquil heart.

He beheld them going and said, "They are returning without understanding anything and knowing the soul. Whoever will be having this Upanishad, whether he be deity or the Asura, will be destroyed. Then Virochan came to the Asuras with the quiet heart. He told them about the Upanishad, "One makes the soul happy on this earth only. This had to be attended only, one who makes the soul felicitious on this earth, serves it, achieves both the world".

Therefore, today also on this earth the relatives of that person, who do not donate, has no reverence, and performs no oblation, call him irreligious and this is the Upanishad of the Asuras. They decorate the corpse with clothes and jewellery gained in alms and believe that hereby they will attain the second region also.[96] Thus, Shankaracharya, in his commentary on Brahma Sootra, has described the *lokayat* doctrines thrice and everytime said that according to them, there is no soul separate from the body. He has told clearly that the philosophy of the ignorants and the *lokayats* is that only the learned physical body is the soul. In Vrahad Aranyak Upanishad also, the same idea is inscribed which are the thoughts of the oppugnants in the form of the former side. Here Yagyavalakya told Matraiyee, "The man, having progressed from these elements (past), again disappears in the same. There is no consciousness after death. *Na pretya sangya asti.*"[97] In soul relating talks, explained in Brahmjaal Soott, Ris Davids, the scholar of the Buddhist scripture, has discussed such thoughts only where *tam jeevan tam shareeram* is referred to.[98]

Thus, the aforesaid data clears that the *Asura* doctrine was that of the *lokayats* who considered the body and the soul as the one and without the body, did not accept the existence of the mind. This is affirmed by the explanation of F. Maxmuller also:

Some material people (*lokayats*) who regard the body only as the soul, do not believe in existence of any soul separate from the body. They think that the consciousness (although in the earth and other external facts) cannot be seen in any of the single element or their groups. It can come in them when they come in the body form. Thus, the consciousness is produced out of them. They say that the knowledge is just like drunkenness (which is produced by mixing some ingredients in a definite proportion) and the man is only a body whose characteristic is consciousness. Thus, apart from the body, there is no existence of any soul which can visit any region or achieve salvation and which makes the body conscious. Only the body is intellect as well as the soul. According to them, this concept is based on this maxim, "Due to existence only there is the body". Because where due to the existence of one thing, another thing exists, and if due to the non-existence of former, the later is absent too, we say that the former is the property only of the later. For example, the lustre and the heat we call the properties of the sun and just as the life, speed, consciousness, memory, etc. (which are considered as the properties of the soul by those having faith in the existence of the separate soul), exist only in the body, not out of it and the body is the synonym of these properties and if they cannot be proved to be separate from the body, then the conclusion is that these are the mere properties of the body and that is why the soul is not separate from the body.[99]

Clearly, the *lokayats* would have adopted these thoughts as successors from those notions of the Asuras and the Dasyus continuing from the very old period, which was the non-Vedic thinking and of another culture opposed to the Aryan-culture. The people of Vedic culture could have hated such people. In *Geeta* (16.7), whatever the Lord Krishna, addressing the Arjuna, has told about the Asuras as well as their thoughts, maximum statements out of them are spoken with the feeling of hate only. He said that the Asuras were unable to differentiate between the desire and the self-control. They had no knowledge of the holiness, morality and the truth.[100]

The Asuras, the Dasyus and their *parvarti* followers, the *lokayats*, etc., were also opposed to the godly principle of the world-creation. They did not believe in the universe-system created by the Prajapati of the Aryans. On the contrary, they believed the science of the world-origin. In many of the above-quoted citations, it has been cleared that the *lokayats* and the atheists believed in *dehvaad* (pertaining to body). Analogous to the creation of this *dehvaad,* they used to see the creation of the universe. It is affirmed clearly by the *Geeta* at least. In *Geeta* (21.8), the extract of the science of the world-origin of the Asuras is given thus: *"Aparaspar sambhootam kin anyat kamm hetyuam"*. That is, the world is created by the alliance of the man-woman, and the reason of this creation can be none except the lust or desire. According to the *Geeta* (16.17), the second thing is that the Asuras had no faith in god and the other world, nevertheless, they had their own distinguished oblation-activities and those oblations are for the name only.[101]

D.P. Chattopadhyay has authored that this means that these oblations, according to the thinking of the Asura-haters, were not as much bad as they cannot be called oblations.[102]

The science of the universe-creation of this kind described in the *Geeta* seems to resemble that one of the *tantravad* (theory of the *tantra*). The *tantravad* also is being continued from the ancient period in India.

S.B. Dasgupta guesses that this can be older even than the Vedas.[103] P. Bandopadhyay, clearing the world-creation science of the *tantravad,* writes that in human community, the new life is originated by the man-woman alliance. This very process is also for the origin of the universe and there the man-woman alliance in limitless cosmopolitan empty sky, originally that which was the great quivering, embodied the form of the lust of love in the human body. Just as due to the love and the lust in human community, new names and new forms are created, similarly, in the primary man as well as the nature also, due to the lust and the love, the great quivering created the new names and the forms in the whole universe. In some systems, substantially the *Shiva* (man) and the power (nature) as well as the male and the female, the comprehensive description of the equality of the alliance is provided. The alliance between the *Shiva* and the power as well as the male and the female became the causes of the world-creation as well as the birth respectively.[104] (Rachnavali 'Bangla' 2.294)

The aforesaid facts conclude that also in subsequent period of the Vedic age, all people did not believe the Vedic culture and the *Brahmneeya* thoughts, but non-Vedic reasoning was principle in the society and the common people were *ihlaukik* or voluntarily physical. They were believing the notions like *lokayat* or the *tantravad* where the theory of the body as well as the *dehvadmoolak* science of the universe-creation was prominent. Actually, the *lokayats* were the necromancers as seems from scriptures. S.N. Dasgupta has written:

Gunratan, in his commentary on *Shad Darshan Samuchchaya* has called Charvak the atheist doctrine whose followers knew only about the eating-drinking and did not believe the truth of the vice-virtue. They regarded that the knowledge attained directly through the medium of the senses, true and nothing else. They drank, were non-vegetarian and conducted sexual intercourse cleanly. Every year on a fixed day, all congregated performed intercourse with the woman freely. Their behaviour was like those of common people and hence called *lokayats*.[105]

In this account, the shapes of the theory of the universe are lucid and D.P. Chattopadhyay, has written in this connection that the sexual freedom of the *lokayats* described by Gunratan indicates one interesting aspect. This freedom cannot be the symbol of the moral distortion because the people possessing such distorted thinking, donot need to fix a day of a year for their activities. And if that sexual freedom was some celebration, then eating meat and drinking wine, too, must have been some celebration. Thus, in Gunratan's writings, we get three 'm' of the necromancers. As we all know that the five activities of the necromancy are called *panchmakar* or five 'ms' because the names of these activities start from m and these are: wine, flesh, copulation, gesticulation and fish.[106]

In logic mystery, *Deepika* (300) also, the statements of the same kind about *lokayats, kapaliks* (the followers of the Shaiva sect who carry with them human skull, eat flesh and drink wine) atheists or necromancers, are given and hereafter the *lokayat* sect. First of all, the atheists, *kapaliks* who apply cinders on their body and are ascetics and many of whom are degraded Brahmanas, don't believe the vice and virtue of the man. They say that the universe is made of four or five elements. Some of them, Charvak, etc., consider the sky the fifth element. They say that the universe is created by five elements. According to them, in these elements the consciousness is produced in the same manner in which the power of intoxication is created in any thing. The man, is nothing else, but the body having consciousness. They drink wine, eat flesh and conduct free sexual intercourse, even family adultery. Every year they congregate on a certain day and any male can conduct the sexual intercourse with any female of his choice. They have no religion. They believe the lust only. They are called *Charvak,* the *lokayats,* etc. Drinking and eating only are the objectives of their lives. They are called *Charvak* because they chew. *Charu,* that is, they keep on eating without thinking. They regard the virtue-vice as the merit-demerit of the large items. They are also called *lokayats* or *lokayatik.* They are also called *vaharspatya* because their doctrine was ascertained by the *Brahaspati* originally.

All the aforesaid statements related to the theory of the universe of the *lokayat* provide not only a lucid information about their thoughts but also tell that these were the notions of the common man as well as the culture. The facts actually clear that they were the thoughts of those opposed to the Vedic and the *Brahmneeya* culture and therefore, the common people believing this thinking must be those out of the community based on four classes, mainly Vedic or *Brahmneeya.* They would be opposing not only Vedic or *Brahmneeya* ideas but also criticising the *Brahmneeya* social system based on four classes or high-low openly. A. Avlaan in *Principle of System* (17) has penned:

We see that in *tantravad,* this principle was considered superior that in this doctrine as well as its religious performance and customs, all the people can participate equally, whether they be males and females, their caste or tribe does not matter. These ideas were more perfect than those narrow Vedic prohibitions. The English authors have spoken of Vedic prohibitions as oppugnants of *tantravad* mostly.

The shape of *lokayat* doctrine or *tantravad* represents definitely the collectivity, brotherhood or equality of the Scheduled Tribe community where the male-female can participate equally and don't believe any caste-difference. D.P. Chattopadhyay has authored in this connection:

In *tantras*, Chandali, Dombi, Rajki and Savri, etc., are given paramount importance. These are female names. They are the goddesses of those lower classes who are engaged in self-evident occupations. It is said that the rise of the *tantras* of *kukhjik* doctrine took place in 'the potter, a lower class of the Hindus' and therefore, the people of this tribe are called *kulali kamnaya.* It is instructed in *kukhjik tantra* that the religious rituals should be performed in the house of any potter. The name of one founder of *Nath* sect, which is the form of *tantravad* in its original shape, was *Gorakh*, that is, the shepherd. In another story, Bengal's initial prose, related to this sect, in *Mainmati Gaan,* Rani's coronation was performed by *Hadi*, a member of that class which was considered the most abominable. In many matters of the necromancy activities, it is seen that the duty of the priest is conducted by a member of the lowest category. It is expected that due to this kind of relations with the bribes considered the most contemptible there was no caste-difference in lower classes.

Although in the aforesaid account, those lower and hateable tribes, the names of the goddesses of which are considered very important for the *tantravad,* are based on the very latest scriptures but it also indicates the perpetuality of the Indian culture continuing from the ancient period. We have seen that the *lokayat* or *tantravad* is the feeling of the non-Vedic and non-*Brahmneeya* culture which is flowing as a river in the society of the modern period incessantly. Therefore, giving the importance to the Scheduled and abominable tribes here is the continuity of that ancient flow which began from the Dasyus and the Asuras and collecting the peculiarities of the Scheduled Tribes, via from the Chandal, Pulcus, Rajki, Sari and Dombi, has reached till today. The second important thing is that the hatred and malice of the Vedic and *Brahmneeya* culture have been continuing from the culture of the Asuras and the Dasyus to the development of the *lokayat* and *tantravad*. If we keep in view the unequal progress prevalent in the Indian history, it may be easier to follow these things. The author of *Imperial Gazeteer of*

India, 1881 has written correctly: "Thus, India is a large museum of different tribes where we can study the human history and culture from the lowest stratum to the highest one. These examples are not the skeletons of the dry bones but a living society according to the very different circumstances of which we have to adjust our administration as well as law".[110]

It has been seen that the Das, the Dasyus and the Asuras knew the witchery and therefore, the Vedic people hated them a lot and drove them away from the oblation-canopy, considering them the spirits. R. Brifo, in the connection of witchery, has written: In the entire world, this proof is seen that in comparative initiative phases, the agriculture was understood to have depended on witchery. Thus, the witchery was provided the importance of a peculiar kind in prime agricultural phase. All uncivilised people believe that the agriculture as compared to any other work, depends more on miraculous power and nature rather than the labour and the expertise of the man. In *The Mothers* (3.92.3),[111] G. Thomson, comparing the occupation of beast-rearing with the agriculture, has thrown light on the origin of witchery: "As long as they possess cattle, fodder and fodder-ground, they compare the agriculture, that is, the sowing and ploughing, as well as reaping of crop with that of the beast-rearing and regard it as a slow, painful and uncertain work. Agriculture requires the patience, farsightedness and belief. Therefore, in agriculture community, the witchery developed extensively.[112]

Since the Vedic Aryan people were mainly the herdsmen, they knew very little about the agriculture and therefore, they must also be unaware of the witchery and that is why, they hated the Dasyus and the Asuras as the latter knew the witchery. In *parvarti* period, although in Upanishads, the *Brahmneeya* scriptures and the Atharva Veda, it has been suggested to enchant the *mantras* and perform the religious ceremonies during agriculture, the relation of the witchery with the primary agriculture and tribal community or the classes considered to be lower, continued. Abreast the *lokayats* and the necromancers, the witchery, too, was believed to be inferior culture. Whatever be, only the desire of enhancing the *ihlaukik* comforts and prosperity echoed, and not spirituality and attaining the salvation. Therefore, the monks were instructed clearly in Buddhist scriptures not to learn these modes.

In Vinay Pitak's *Chulvagga,* such instructions are lucid: "O *bhikshus,* thou will neither study nor teach the modes of the lower category, making predictions, judging omen and ill-omen, using mantras, palmistry, offering victim to the deity, performing witchery, acting as a fraud leech, etc".[113] It clears that actually the witchery like other non-vedic notions, relating to the agriculture as well as the physical labour, was being continued in the society form Vedic to the *parvarti* period for decades incessantly. D.P. Chattopadhyay has written: "In the initial phase (agriculture) labour activities were full of the belief for witchery and its related activities. But in spite of being full of ignorance and uncivilised hypothesis, the witchery related to agriculture, due to which *tantravad* originated (because its relation was with the physical labour) remained physical. The symptoms of this easy materialism appeared in *dehvaad* of *tantravad* which came immediately after the contemplated side of witchery related to agriculture. Afterwards, this very *tantravad* living in altered social atmosphere, changed exactly into its own oppugnant side. That which the natural materialism earlier, engaged in adopting the devotion, worship, salvation and other spiritual thoughts. Nevertheless, the remains of the original materialism never vanished completely as in the subsequent period also, the relations of the *tantravad* with the abominable tribes and labourers remained maintained.[114]

Thus, it is clear from the above-mentioned description that the Aryans of the Vedic culture, having defeated the pre-Vedic people, occupied the fortified colonies and the property of their enemies as well as their political power. Consequently, the Aryans of the Vedic-Aryans and subsequent enemies to the Aryans, that is, the Das, the Dasyus and the Asuras had to accept their salvery. But the Dasyus, the Asuras and the Das who were in the stratum of the development spread in the extensive area, continued to spend the scheduled tribal life as earlier although the ways of their natural progress had closed. Due to the occupation of the power and property by the Vedic-Aryans, the development phases of the other Asuras had blocked and they were obliged to live an undeveloped and scheduled tribal life in unequal progressive stratum. This is the only reason that their tribal culture remained witchery, *ihlaukik, lokayat, tantravad* or atheist. Since the Vedic Aryans had unlimited loathing and enmity for the culture and beliefs of the non-Vedic as well pre-Aryans, in *parvarti* vedic period also, the people believing the Vedic culture continued their despise for the *lokayat, tantravad,* theist and those against the Vedic culture. Even the people of Vedic culture, having reached the high stratum of economical and social progress, began to hate the Aryans and those subsequent to Aryans who cherished the tribal morality as well as the *vratya,* and called them degraded while they themselves were able to reach here only after entering the same tribal community and the *vratya* custom. Therefore, only from this background of the strifes going on between the Vedic and the non-Vedic culture, that is *lokayat, tantravad* and other tribal community, and the feeling of hatred, the concept of the untouchability is clear. It is clear from the quotations of many sources that those Chandal, Rajki, Shabri or other despicable tribes or the people undertaking the physical labour, are called untouchable in holy writs and other scriptures, have been having clear relation with tribal community, morality and aforesaid non-Vedic culture.

Now, it is necessary to see due to the feeling of hatred of the parvarti of the Vedic culture for non-Vedic culture, the untouchability did not originate in Vedic period, while the Aryans' despise was continued for non-Vedic culture and the people at that time also. Therefore, it seems necessary that these statements be investigated in *parvarti* period. The literature and the *Brahmneeya* scriptures of subsequent Vedic period, which are generally the creations of generally between 1000 BC to 600 BC,[115] provide many significant description. In many scriptures of this age, the feeling of loathing of people for the *Chandal* and *Polcus* folk appears and their inferior social and cultural life-stratum is known about. In Vajsaneyee Sanhita (30.21), Tantreeya Brahmana (3.4.7) Chhandogya Upanishad (5.10.7; 5.24.4) and Vrahdaranyak Upanishad (4.3.22), the abhorrence of the people of Vedic culture for the Chandal appears clearly.[116] It is said in Chhandogya Upanishad (6.10.7) that the people having good behaviour, will be regenerated as the *Brahmin,* the *Kshatriya* or the Vaisya, but those having mean conduct, will be produced in the contemptible womb of the dog, pig or the Chandal.[117] In Vajsaneyee Sanhita (30.21) and Tantreeya Brahmana (3.4.7-17), expressing the contempt for the Chandal, it is said that they can be victimised in *purushmedh* (sacrifice of a human being) oblation.[118] Hereby the quotation of the *Atharava*

Veda (12.1-37) is affirmed in which it is said that the Dasyus, condemning the god, should be victimised to the deity. It seems that the Chandals must have been the successors of the Dasyus and believing their ancient godless materialistic culture. In Vajsaneyee Sanhita (30.17), Tantreeya Brahmana (3.4.1-14) and Vrahdaranyak Upanishad (4.3.22), the hate is expressed for the *Polcus* which informs about their inferior socio-cultural condition.[119] In Aitraya Brahmana (7.18), Andhra, Pundu, Shabar, Pulind, Mutib, Dasyu and Antas are called the inferior tribes and is said that those sons defying the Aryan discipline or opposing the fathers were considered the Dasyu and the Antas.[120]

In this scripture only, it is described that Shunaha Shep, the son of Ajogartta of Angirat *gotra,* was sold by his father as a commodity against three hundred cows for the *Varuna* oblation. But the deity released him who was adopted by Vishwamitra and given the first place in his hundred sons as well as we also provided the right of the eldest son. But his fifty sons refused to accept him as their eldest brother.[121] Vishwamitra got furious and cursed them that their successors would be of the inferior caste as those of Andhra, Pundu, Shabar, Pulind, Mutib, Dasyu and further, that they would be out of the dwellings of the people of the Vedic culture or nearby as in Aitraya Brahmana (33.6) and Vrahdaranyak Upanishad (1.3.30), it is explained nearly that the pre-Aryan Scheduled Tribes were settled on the borders of the dwellings of the Aryan people. Chandal as well as the Polcus, too, were, in the beginning, the people of the pre-Aryan Scheduled Tribes.[122]

The enmity and the contempt of the people of the Aryan culture for these Scheduled Tribes appears clearly. Although the Vedic sages sang the ecology of the *gannas,* but in subsequent Vedic period, they began to be seen with the feeling of hate and insult. Those people living in *gannas*, or spending the Scheduled Tribal life, were regarded as unholy, uncivilised and disbelieved the moral values of marriage. The clear picture of the viewpoint of the people of the Vedic culture for the *Vaaheek* and *Madrak* public can be seen in the following description of the *Mahabharata,* narrated by Karna:

"In Dhrutarashtra's palace, the *Brahmanas* used to describe countries and many kings of the ancient period. Out of the *Brahmanas,* an old and outstanding man, describing the primary history, told these words in connection of Vaheek and Madrak people: "Everyone should always remain far from the Vaheek people. They are impure and have no relation with the rectitude, and stay far from the Himvant, the Ganga, the Saraswati, the Yamuna, the Kurushetra, the Sindhu and its five subsidiary rivers. I remember those days of my youth when there was constructed a slaughter-house for the cow-meat and a place for the collection of the intoxicant liquids on the outer gaters of the houses of the Vaheek kings (sardars). Once I had to stay among the Vaheek people due to any confidential work. By living there I gained an excellent knowledge of their conduct. There is a city named Sakal, a river named Apag and a tribe named Vaheek which is known as Jarantik. Their behaviour is contemptible. They drink the wine named Gaudh and eat the fried barley with it. They also eat the cow-meat with the garlic. They eat the flour with the meat mixed bread as well as the rice after boiling, begged from the people. They have nothing like morality. Their women, getting intoxicated, laugh and dance in a nude position outside their houses. They do not apply any paint of a fluid, wear necklace and always getting intoxicated, sing the vulgar songs of different kinds and their voice is as sweet as that of any donkey or camel. In sexual intercourse, they are completely shameless and impatient, and in other things also, they work as they want. They lose their consciousness due to the effect of the alcohol and use the loving adjectives for one another. The degraded wives of the *V*aheek people, having become ecstatic, address their respective husbands and the latter, even in pure days, exercise no patience and the women remain busy in dance. O king, all inhabitants of Sakal country, young and the old, thus drink alcohol, sing songs and shout. Where can the morality be seen in such people ? You should know this. But I should also inform about another *Brahmana* who told us in royal assembly of Kuru:

Where there are the forests of the Peelu trees and five rivers—the Shatardh, the Vipasha, the Irawati, the Chanderbhaga and the Vitasta and the sixth river is Sindhu and in those areas, there is territory named Aratta, far away from Sim Himwant. In those areas, there is no morality and religion. The deities, manes and the *Brahmins* do not accept any gifts from the degraded people or the people born to the girls of the other tribes by the Sudras or the Vaheeks. They never perform the oblations and are very irreligious."

That enormous *Brahmin* said this also in the Kuru assembly:

"These Vaheek people do not hate eating in large and deep wooden utensils, plates of mud and the pots licked by the dogs, or in which the ground barley and other grain is stuck. These people drink the milk of sheep, female camel and donkey, and use the curd produced by same milk. These degraded people have many illegitimate children. There is no food or milk not used by them. They are stupid and ignorant and therefore, one should always remain aloof from them".

"But, I should also speak in connection of another *Brahmina* who told me something in the royal assembly of Kuru:

"....In Vimata river, there are the ghosts named Vaahi and Heek. The Vaheek people are born of both of them. They are not generated by the creator. How can those born by this low stratum, have the knowledge of the duties described in holy scriptures and books ? We should always remain far from Mahishkas, Kalingas, Keralas, Karkotakas, Virakas and other irreligious people".[123]

Thus, in this period, the contempt of the *Brahminas* and the Vedic-culture people for those living in tribal Community organnas is sen clearly. D.P. Chattopadhyay, about the view point of this hatred for the Scheduled Tribes, writes: "But originating the feeling of hate from the moral vision in the hearts of the Brahmins who described in connection of the people of these Scheduled Tribes, was a gesticulation. As if it be seen according to their viewpoint, the attitude of the Brahmins for these Scheduled Tribes was not of high moral stratum. It is clear from Kautilya's *Arthasastra* that the secret duties of these *Brahmins* were to spy these Scheduled Tribes as disguised saints or hermits and to corrupt them by illegal wine and nymph (married, unmarried and prostitutes), and thus to ruin them morally.[124]

Although the *Brahmins* and the followers of their culture hated the Vaheek folk deeply as the latter lacked immorality related to sexual intercourse, these civilised supervisors had their tribal past with the same customs. D.P. Chattopadhyay has written correctly: "The people of civilised tribes see their contemporary Scheduled Tribes from this viewpoint (they are shameless in the activities of sexual intercourse) only and this viewpoint about the sexual relations of our contemporary aboriginals is not very different from that of some modern scholars but the reality is that the discourse which was believed to be contemptible, was a form of the matrimonial relations before the establishment of the custom of marrying a woman.[125] By these statements described actually in the Mahabharata, the past of the observer Brahmins is known: We have heard that there was a great sage named Uddalak. He got a son named Shwetketu who himself was a high class hermit. One day, a Brahmin came. He, holding of the hand of Uddalak's wife, was taking her with high-handedness. This excited Shwetketu's fury. On seeing him angry, *Uddalak* said: "O son, do not be angry. This custom has been continuing since the primary age. In this world, the women of all ranks are free. O son, in this kind of matter, as far as the classes of the men are concerned, they behave like animals." But Shwetketu rejected this custom and founded the present custom in connection of men-women in this world.[126]

Thus, in *Mahabharata,* Pandu told Kunti, supporting the custom prevalent among the Vaheek people: "Now I would tell you about those ancient usages described by our sages who possessed the knowledge of every rule of our morality. In ancient period, the women were not living closed in their respective houses nor did they depend on their husbands and relatives. They could come and go anywhere freely, and enjoy their lives as they desired. At that time they did not remain united to their husband as the chaste ones, nevertheless, O *priyadarshini* (lovely-looking), they were not regarded as sinful women as they conducted according to the traditions of the ancient period. The same tradition has been continuing among the birds and the animals without any malice today also. This custom accepted by the tradition has been called supreme by the great sages. O *sujaghna*, this tradition is professed with respect by the residents of the northern Kuru today also. This tradition of the women side has been continuing from the times immemorial. The current custom is established subsequently only.[127]

It is clear from the aforesaid description that in post-Vedic period, the Brahmins and the people of Vedic culture began to hate the tribal community and their culture. The feeling of despise for the Vaheek people appearing in people of Vedic and *Brahmneeya* culture, applies actually with the communities of all those maximum Scheduled Tribes and the *gannas* equally. While the people of Vedic culture, having entered themselves all those stratums, had reached the standard of civilisation. But why did it happen? The answer can be searched in this description of *Dialectics of Nature* (Moscow, 1954, pp. 238-39) authored by Fredrick Angeson:

"The nations and the kingdoms got developed by the tribes, then the law and politics were produced, and in conjunction with, the strange thoughts in connection of human goods germinated in human. This notion was 'religion'. All these were the hypothesis of the human head which seemed to have spread over the human community and before them, the goods created by the labourer class, became secondary. Particularly then, while in very old period of community development, the labour observance adjusted by the human cerebrum, he wanted to get it done by others and escape himself. All credit of the rapid progress of civilisation was given to sensorium, that is, the development of brain affairs. People became habitual, not to know their duties or the consequences of their needs, but those of their thoughts. Thus, there came a time when an idealistic viewpoint about the world emerged which after the decline of the ancient values, has spread over the human brain distinctively."

Substantially, in post-Vedic period, the Aryan tribal community adopted the form of solid nation-kingdom based on four classes, where the idle Brahmin-Kshatriya class, came into existence and the physical labour was thrown on the shoulders of the numerous *Sudras.* This idle class, having retired from the physical labour, emphasized on the brain affairs and having created the imaginary consciousness like *Brahm* and soul, believed themselves to be superior human beings. In conjunction with this, they developed the hate for those performing the physical labour and from this view of the hatred, began to see the people of undeveloped tribal society, contrary to Vedas, as degraded, wretched, unholy and untouchable. The retirement of *Brahmin* and *Kshatriya* class from the physical labour, was the separation from the ancient values and when it had happened, due to the enemity with the tribal community and their culture, contrary to Vedas, being continued from the ancient age, hating them was obvious. D.P. Chattopadhyay has written: "The primary *gannas* were destructed and on their remains, the kingdoms emerged. But due to imbalanced development, nearby the primary Indian kingdoms and mostly in their area, there were many places where Scheduled Tribes resided although the representatives of the government power hated them. On religious or semi-religious stratum, this loathing for the *gannas,* was expressed in hate for *ganpatis* or *vinayaks.* On the other side, on moral or semi-moral stratum, the abhorrence for the common customs and beliefs of the aboriginals, and mainly, the matrimony related moral conduct, was the consequence of that religious worship".[128]

Subsequenty, due to the arrival of the people of the Vedic culture at the new stratum of development, by the feeling of despise produced for the physical labour, not only the people of *Sudra* class in their four-class based society became victims of their hate and disability, but this feeling also announced its culture-opposers, that is, the descendants of non-Vedic Das, Dasyus, Asuras Rakshasas, etc., as absolutely inferior and contemptible and finally, they began to be declared as untouchables. Since the people of this non-Vedic culture had been against the Vedic or *Brahmneeya* culture traditionally and were living in *vratya* and tribal community of low stratum of physical labour which professed easy materialistic thoughts, *lokayat* or beliefs of *tantravad,* it was obvious for those people of Vedic or *Brahmneeya* culture who, by now, had become rural class, to hate the ruled or exploited people and it was in favour of the ruler class to declare their culture inferior or contemptible.

Now the Scheduled Tribes of the non-Vedic culture were hailed by the names of Anva, Vahya, Antyavasin, etc. In holy scriptures, having announced them as Scheduled Tribes collectively, they are addressed by the adjectives of Anva, Bahya, Antyavsayin, etc. In holy writs, the oldest scripture is *Vidhi* by Gautama which is believed to be 600 BC[129] possibly. Here the *Antya* (lowest) tribe is regarded the great sinner.[130] Here only, Gautama had said that these tribes should be given unholy costumes.[131] In Aapstamb holy writ, the people of Chandal Scheduled Tribe are called *Antah* and it is told that they lived on the last point of the village.[132] In Vashishtha holy writ, *Antah* people could be present in their law suits only as the witnesses.[133] Here only (18.3), the Antyavsayin tribe is called to be born of Sudra male and Vaisya female. In Gautama holy writ (20.1; 23.32) it is said that the Brahmin father living with Antyavsayins or conducting the intercourse with the woman of that class, should be expelled. In Aapstamb holy writ (1;3.9.18) they are called Bahya.[134]

It is said on the basis of these proofs that the untouchables were called Antya or Bahya collectively, that is, they were living outside the village or the town.[135] It is also said that they did not become untouchable as a consequence of living on the edges of the villages and towns or the policy of expelling them out intentionally from their colonies. It looks that the whole population of the villages of the primary tribes were declared untouchable by the Brahmins.[136] But Dr. B.R. Ambedkar does not consider the Antah, Vahya, Antay or Antyavsayin people as untouchables and calls them 'unholy' tribes.[137] He tried to conduct expansive investigation about these words used in aforesaid scriptures. He has said that "the substance of this is that neither holy scriptures help us to decide as to who the untouchables were nor do the Smritis. Thus, the holy writs and the Smritis do not assist us to decide even that those classes called Antyavsayin, Antyaj and Bahya, were untouchable or not".[138]

But the inferior tribes described in holy scriptures or ancient Buddha codes collectively lived outside the village or the town and among them Chandal, Shavpak and Pukkast were declared untouchables decidely. The remaining explained tribes, too, began to be called *Varn-Sankar* (born of parents of different races) and untouchable in Smritis in Parvarti period. In ancient Buddha scripture, *Majjimnikaya,* belonging to former period of Maurya dynasty,[139] Chandal, Nasad, Veinn, Rathkar and Pukkas tribes are mentioned repeatedly and called inferior tribes.[140] It is also said that these people belong to low lineage and inferior tribe. It is said in *Sanyuktnikaya* that Chandal and Pukkas who are kept in the index of *varn-sankar* tribes in holy books, were not included in the *Sudra* category,[141] and Panini has called them the Sudra, residing outside the cities and the villages. By their touch, the brass vessel of the *Brahmins* became impure forever.[142] In a famous Jaina scripture, *Suyagaddham* (2, 2.27) which was compiled possibly in 400 BC along with Shabar, Dravid, Kaling, Gaudh and Gandhar, the Chandals are described too. In Buddha scripture, Vinay Patak, belonging to the former period of the Maurya dynasty (4.5), woodman, potter, weaver, cobbler and barber are categorised as inferior. Although in *Deeghnikaya* (1.51), the work of weaver, woodman, potter and barber is put in the list of common arts, it seems that the work of cobbler would have been considered certainly of the inferior rank. Therefore, the aforesaid facts clear that the Antya, Bahya and Antyavsayin, the people of all different Scheduled Tribes, were residing separately from and outside, the Aryan colonies. In primary age, only some people were considered untouchables but in Parvarti period, all other Scheduled Tribes became untouchable step by step. It clears that the aforesaid ideas of Dr. Ambedkar are untrue. In holy writs, the origin of the untouchability is defined and it is said that the people of untouchable tribes are *varn-sankar* born of parents of different classes. In Gautama holy book, it is said that if any *Sudra* creates a son by a woman different from his class, he will be degraded.[143] In *Bodhayan* holy writ, it is explained that the child born to a Kshtriya woman by a *Sudra,* is called *Maagadh.*[144] Here also it is said that the progeny born to a *Brahmin* woman by a *Sudra*, will be called Chandal. Similar description is entered in Vashishtha holy writ also.[145] It is stated in Gautama holy writ that the issue born to the *Sudra* woman by Brahmin, Khsatriya, Vaishya and Sudra is called step by step Parshav, Pawan, Karan and Sudra.[146] Similar description is also found in *Bodhayan* holy scripture (2.2.32). Here it is said also that a son born to any Sudra wife by a Brahmin is called *nishad.* Same statements are found also in Gautama holy writ (4.26) and Vashishtha holy writ (18.8). The descriptions like Nishad son born to any Sudra woman is called *Pulkat* and the issue born to *nishad* wife by a Kshatriya is called *Urga* and the son born to a Shudra wife by Vaisya is called *Rathkar.*[148] Thus, it is said that the child born of Vaisya father and Kshatriya mother is called Vedehak, and the child born of Brahmin father and Vaisya mother is called Ambashth. In Bodhayan holy writ it is said that the child born to Ambashth wife by Vedehak is called *Venn.*[149] Thus, in holy writs, the origin of those tribes born of different parents, is described in descending and ascending order but ascending order, that is, the marriage of low class man and high class woman is seen insignificantly and the begotten child is called inferior.[150] Many of these tribes are categorised as untouchable.

Viewing the description of the origin of *varn-sankar* and untouchable tribes in holy writs, Richard Fik has written that many of these *sankar* (hybrid) tribes belonged to the backward Scheduled Tribes which were included in four-class system by blending with the *varnas* (classes)[151] in a way with difficulty by an agreeable way. Dr. Ramsharan Sharmas, opposing the particulars entered in these holy writs, has written that the definition of untouchables found in holy writs, cannot be accepted as here those are called untouchables who are born of different classes.[152] Dr. B.R. Ambedkar, too, conducting the comparative study of the commentary of holy writs as well as the Smritis, has denied the *varn-sankar* principle of origin of untouchability[153] and told that the untouchability came into existence as a result of the collision with the *Brahmin* religion due to the eating of cow-meat and adoption of Buddhist religion by scattered people (the defeated folk in strifes among *kabeelas*).[154] But we have seen initially that before the advent of Buddhism, the untouchability had come into existence and as far as the relation of untouchability with the eating of cow-meat is concerned, this cannot be accepted as the reason of its origin. In this connection, Dr. Ramsharan Sharma's statement sounds logical that may be due to their constant eating of cow-meat, their number must have been increased in future but this cannot be accepted as the definition of their origin because except the Gautama holy writ (22.13), nothing which can prove that eating cow-meat in Brahmin community in this age was prohibited, appears anywhere.[155] Dr. Vivekanand Jha, too, is of a similar view and has written that in Vedvyas Smriti, the first time, the maximum people, eating cow-meat, were announced untouchable.[156] This is considered the creation of around 200 B.C. Dr. Vivekanand Jha, too, rejects the definition of the origin of untouchability found in holy writs and tells that in any context of untouchable tribe the principle of *varn-sankars* is not related obviously whether they be ascending or descending series, but this notion informs of their inferiority certainly due to which the list of the untouchable tribes is propagated.[158] Although by the holy writs, it is found out that the untouchability had spread from the north-India to the west because Aapstamb and Bodhayan are considered the writers of western India but as compared to northern-India, by this time, the untouchability was not spread much in west.[158] But N.K. Dutt has written that the feeling of hatred, producing untouchability, was not in the Indian Aryans originally, but it entered through the medium of Dravids among whom *chhuaachhoot* (the act of touching the untouchable) is prevalent today also.[159] But Dr. Vivekanand Jha has regarded the aforesaid hypothesis wrong and false.[160] Dr. Ramsharan Sharma has also asserted: "But there is no such proof that in the Brahmin dominated society, before the assimilation of the Dravids as well their adoption of Brahminhood, the untouchability was prevalent in west". On the contrary, the viewpoint of Bodhayan and Aapstamb, the western authors of sacred precepts, in the matter of food and touch, is not as much conservative as that of two northern authors of holy writs, Vashishtha and Gautama.[161] G.S. Dhurya has penned: "The high class people, who claimed to be Aryans, believed some artisans and professions worthless and finally, the origin of the feeling of untouchability is based on the principle of considering some occupations unholy".[162] But he has not given the reason for the same.

We have seen earlier that the people of Vedic-culture hated the Das, Dasyus, Nag and the Asuras, etc., non-Vedic people unlimitedly and this contempt continued till the Parvarti period. Second thing was that having defeated their adversaries as well as seized their wealth and power, the Vedic-culture people established themselves as the ruler class completely and by blending the conquered Aryans, those subsequent to Aryans and labourer Aryans, formed a *Sudra* category, and loaded them with the burden of all physical labour. Consequently, the Brahmin-Kshatriya, the ruler class emerged organisedly. They started hating Shudras who performed the physical labour and separated themselves from them. those Scheduled Tribes who were spending their lives on a very low stratum and cherishing the *Vratya* life, and who were residing outside colonies of Vedic-culture people and had been constantly professing a different culture, *lokayat, tantravad,* atheism, were insulted by the Vedic-culture people who had reached the developed stratum, in the background of traditional despise with drastic contempt. By the Aryan-attack, the natural growth of the primary scheduled tribes had stopped and they remained in the phases of imbalanced economical development and therefore, they remained behind as compared to the Vedic-culture people. Backward arts and the professions linked with physical labour filled the people of Vedic-culture with the feeling of unholiness and loathing, and they, addressing them successively Bahya, Antyavsayin, Antyaj, etc., hated them and believed them to be untouchables. But this answer remains unanswered as to why they were called *varn-sankar* in holy writs. Although the aforesaid scholars have accepted the definition of origin of untouchability entered in holy writs, this is surprising that these very scholars have accepted other statements of holy writs and believed them to be original and important sources.

But it is not possible that such description entered in holy writs is absolutely wrong while their other statements are used as an important source. The aforesaid details of holy writs may not be completely true but they have really got some partial truth. We have seen that the *Vedic-Aryan* people themselves had reached from the state of Scheduled Tribe to the stratum of a class. So, can't it be possible that after reaching there, they must have the remains of the Scheduled Tribe? If in Aryan-class system, the proofs of the remains of the Scheduled Tribe are found, it will be difficult to deny that they must also have the tribal quality like remains of sexual freedom, which would be appearing hateable in new value like class-system. The famous historian D.D. Kosambi's Statement to clear this context is worthy of quotation : "It is found out from the entire Indian history that the tribal elements were blended in ordinary community. This is the base of the main quality, that is *varn-sankar,* of Indian community and is the essential essence of ancient Indian history".[163]

D.P. Chattopadhyay has written that the Scheduled Tribes are having single *gotra* (clan) but its sub-tribes, called *kabeelas,* are having many *gotras.* All members of the *kabeela* believe strongly that they are the progeny of the same ancestor. Their original forefather is believed to be some plant or animal generally and the *kabeela* is named after that forefather only and finally the main quality of ancient India is its assembly. All the works of *kabeela* are managed by this assembly. Thus, the *kabeelas,* even on tribal stratum, have their respective assemblies, superior to all the members of the Scheduled Tribe. The greatest punishment in these tribes is expelling from the tribe.[164]

If investigation be conducted minutely, it looks clearly that the aforesaid quality of the Scheduled Tribes, that is four-class based Aryan social system, has also its own fundamental characteristics. The people of the Brahmin class were also divided in small *gotras* which were completely having many *gotras* and were generally known by name of some animal.[165] Thus, the system was prevalent among other classes, kshatriya and Brahmin also, and even among people regarded as *Sudra* also.[166] It is also generally known that all classes were having their respective assemblies and the custom of greatest punishment, 'expelling from the caste', was also prevalent. It is said in Gautama holy writ that the Brahmin father living with *Anyavsayins* or conducting the intercourse with the woman of that class, should be expelled from the caste.[167] D.P. Chattopadhyay has written that the greatest quality of the tribal community is its assembly and the their hardest punishment is expulsion from the *kabeela.* In Santhal and other Scheduled Tribes, this form of punishment is practised today also.[168] In *Encyclopaedia of Religion of Ethics,*[169] J. Hastings has written about the expulsion prevalent in caste-system: "In caste, the discipline is maintained by the medium of recognised leaders and chief. Sometimes they take charge of their designation and have some fixed tasks and duties but generally, especially in some working tribes, a sort of committee or Panchayat is formed which looks after all aspects and the affairs of the tribal discipline. The decision of the Panchayat is final and its right cannot be challenged. For the minor violation of the rules of the tribe and its preventions, a sort of purification function is arranged and the tribe members are given a treat. But for the serious crimes or impudence, one is excommunicated from the caste, that is, the members of that tribe have no relation with the punished member. Neither anyone eats food with him, nor does he smoke nor talk to him. The people remain aloof from him just as they do from a leper and his life becomes so miserable that he becomes ready to accept any condition. If his crime is so heinous that even atonement cannot get him redemption, he is included in some low caste or has to be converted into a Mohammedan, or has to hide in the cities where the restrictions of the caste as compared to those of the villages are week and not so hard. (E.R.E. 3.252)[170]

Thus, the tribal remains included in class as well as the caste-system appear to be clear reason of the obstruction of economical development. Similarly, seeing in holy codes, marriage and sex related all provisions, compositions, discipline and punishment, it can be guessed easily that the four-class based social system was having the remains of sexual-freedom. All the people of these classes were violating the matrimonial life based on the class and discipline of the sexual-intercourse. Thereby they were professing the remains of their respective tribal-sexual cleanliness. It does not matter if in this period the newly-established values of their social system were considering their aforesaid behaviour as immoral, inferior or contemptible.

The Upanishads are also called Vedant. The following part from the *Vamdevya Shaman* of Chhandogya Upanishad is worthy of quotation:

He invokes: This is the call out.

He requests: This is proposal.

He lies down with the woman: This is beginning.

He rests on the woman: This is removing curtain.

He reaches the end: This is destination

He finishes: This is conclusion.

In connection with this quotation, I.E. Whom has written in *Thirteen Principle Upanishad* (3.13) that this is *Vamdevya Shaman* based on sexual enjoyment. One, understanding the *Vamdevya Shaman* thus centred on sexual enjoyment, produces the man like him by every sexual enjoyment. He lives a complete life, becomes long-lived, achieves the accomplishment of progeny and livestock and gets fame. One should not remain aloof from the copulation with any woman. Actually this is in his law. In Atraya Brahmana also, similar sexual enjoyment is provided importance. Anushtrap (couplet) asks one to step towards one's fiery ordeal. He separates first two feet and therefore, the woman opens her thigns. He creates last two feet and therefore, the man unites his two thighs. This is intercourse. One aware of the same, achieves issue and livestock.[171] Similar description is found in Koshitki Brahmana,[172] Satpatha Brahmana,[173] etc. These statements clear that the sexual celebration as well as sexual freedom were as much important in Aryan tribes as in other castes of the world. D.P. Chattopadhyay has stated correctly, "In reality, the Vedic literature is full of similar statements. The contemporary supporters of Indian culture generally try to bury the proofs to protect their Aryan-ancestors from so-called stigma of this kind of beliefs and activities. But it would be better to accept as well as face the proofs rather than to remain confused by the imaginary story of ancient inheritance".[174]

Thus, it is clear from the aforesaid data that in four-class based social system, the remains of the sexual freedom were certainly present which were believed to be as hateable and inferior in the view of the values of new class-system as after reaching this stratum, the *vratya* life and tribal collectiveness was being looked at. We have seen that in *Karan Parv,* in *Mahabharata,* how sexual freedom prevalent among Vaheek folk is shown contemptible and low, and declared to be anti-Vedic culture. Similarly, in the four-class system, ascending and descending marriages, and sexual enjoyment were considered not only a violation of Aryan-discipline but against the violators, the punishments like atonement and expulsion from caste were also prescribed. Such expelled people, having withdrawn from the four-class system, must have been obviously merged in those tribal communities which were considered contemptible and inferior like them because they were also practising the 'sexual freedom and sexual celebration based *tantravad*'. We have seen earlier how fifty adopted sons of Vishwamitra, for disobeying their father, were cursed that their generations would be Andhra, Pundu, Shabar, Pulind, Mutib, Dasyu and Antas like the inferior tribe.[175] It becomes clear hereby that many people, transgressing the discipline of Brahmins or class-system, would have been boycotted, whether that discipline be the violation of class-religion, father's order or matrimony or sexual enjoyment. The Brahmins and other people would have been hating them unlimitedly. The feeling of similar abhorrence must have been one reason of making those tribes untouchable because among those tribes residing outside the Aryan-colonies and their towns, the culture, contrary to Vedas, backward economic system and sexual freedom were present strongly, and at the same time, the background of traditional enemity also existed. Therefore, not only the excommunicated people were called *varn-sarkar* by the Brahmins and the authors of the holy writs, but also their generations were called by the same adjective and simultaneously, those tribes in whom the boycotted people had taken shelter, were also announced *varn-sankar* and *jaati-sankar.* Here *varn-sankar* signifies not only the sons born of people of different castes but also the attainable condition of lowness, inferiorism and contempt.

Now it is necessary to see that the situation and the social, economical and political condition of untouchable tribes in 600 BC. It is clear from the descriptions entered in holy books that the untouchable people addressed by the adjectives of Antas, Antya,

Antyavsayin, Antyaj, etc., resided outside the Aryan-colonies or the towns or on the last points. Originally, these people were spending the tribal lives. It is found out by the holy writs of this age that Chandal had undoubtedly included in untouchable tribe.[177] It is said in Apstamb holy writ (2.1.2.8) that it is a sin to see and touch Chandal and in Gautama holy writ (15.24) it is also said that it is an ill omen seeing him throwing the dead body.[178] In Apstamb holy writ (1.3.915), Gautama holy writ (16.19) and Vashishtha holy writ (13.11)[178], meeting with Chandal is denied and on his residence or where he is staying, the study of the Vedas is not permitted.[179] It is described in Apstamb holy writ (2.1.2.8) that with the immediate eye on the Chandal, the study of the Vedas should be stopped.[180] In Gautama holy writ (14.30), it is stated that if by touch of any Chandal, the body become unchaste, that can be purified by taking bath with the touched clothes.[181] It is affirmed by the Bodhyan holy writ (1.5.9.5) that the *Chandals* were considered unholy. It is told here only (2, 2.4.14; 2.4.12.3) that taking food sitting with Chandal and establishing matrimonial relations with him is a heinous crime. Similar statements are entered in Vasishta holy writ (20.17;23, 40-1).

In Jatak Buddha tract, it is described that the dialect of *Chandal* is of different type which indicates that they belonged originally to pre-Aryan tribe.[182] In Jatak (4.397) it is quoted that Chandals are from the extremely wicked class.[183] In Jatak (3.233) it is explained that the wind passing by touching the body of Chandal was believed to be polluted.[184] In Jatak (4.376) falling down of vision on Chandal, is regarded an ill omen and therefore, the daughter of a moneyed-man in Benaras, washes her eyes on seeing the Chandal because the sight of an ignoble man polluted her eyes.[185] In Jatak (4.390) it is described that if Chandal happens to see a particular food or drink, consumption of that item was restricted and ignorant consumption caused the punishment of social ex-communication.[186] In Jatak (2, 82–84), the description of a Brahmin is entered who, due to suffering of hunger, ate something defiled by Chandal and to protect himself from the scorn of his tribe members, committed suicide.[187] Although Jataks are the subsequent creations to 600 BC but Chandal related description resembles the conditions explained in holy writs.

It is said that initially the Chandals were hunters and fowlers, but in Brahmin dominated society, the former was assigned the duty of throwing the human as well as animal corpses.[188] They performed the duty of removing and burning the corpses and sometimes they were asked to sweep on the roads.[189] In Jatak, his work is told to swish the criminal and to amputate. It is also said that some Chandals earned their living by the profession of jugglery and tumbling.[191] It is described in Buddha code *Anguttar Nikaya* (4.376) that when the children of a Chandal, wearing the rags and holding the begging bowls in their hands, enter the village or the town, they proceed with bending heads.[192] It appears hereby that the children were bound to beg as their parents must be unable to fill their bellies with food by their means of livelihood. It is said in *Anguttar Nikaya* (3.206) that the man deprived of any quality, religion and morality, was called Chandal.

The other inferior species, put along with the Chandal, in the index of Buddha scripture, are—Pukkas, Naisad, Veinn and Rathkar.[193] It is said that the Pulkas and Pukkas appear to be from such primary tribe making their living by hunting or manufacturing cane-items but subsequently they were engaged in the task of removing the flowers from the temple as well as the royal palace.[194] In Buddha scripture, *Ther Gatha,* the famous monk named Suneet is said to belong to low tribe like Pukkas[195] who is linked with untouchable tribe, calling him from the bhangi (sweeper) tribe.[196] Although other scholars have written that the Pukkas cannot be regarded as untouchable despite their being of low social standard[197] because they were appointed for removing the flowers from the temple courtyard.[198] But it is clear from the Buddha scriptures that the Pukkas and the Pulkas were of the untouchable caste who possibly cleaned the filth by sweeping and in the same manner only removed the stale flowers from the temple or royal palace. These people, too, lived outside the Aryan colonies or cities because the way Suneet is shown getting initiated, provides the proof therefore.[199]

Sopak or Shavpak were believed definitely to belong to untouchable tribe although no information about this tribe is available in Vedic scriptures.[200] From the description of Chatutthovaggo of Buddha scripture *Thergatha,* it is clear that two untouchable boys named Sopak and Supipya, were from the Sopak tribe and their father kept watch on the graveyard. The Veinn is also said to belong to inferior tribe in Buddha scripture. It was possibly a Scheduled Tribe and its members spent their life by hunting and cane-work. It is also called *varn-sankar* in holy writs. In *Majjim Nikaya* (3, pp. 169-70) and *Anguttar Nikaya* (2, p.85), it is said: "If that stupid takes birth in the human womb after such a long period, he goes to the house of low tribe such as Chandal, Nishad, Veinn, Rathkar and Pukkas. They are regenerated to spend a deficient life as a vagabond and destitute person. They get complete food and clothes by chance only". It clears that Nisad, Veinn and Rathkar like Chandal and Pukkas, were spending their lives in inferior state and decrepit economical condition. Although the proof of these tribes being untouchable is not clearly available in this age, nevertheless due to their entry in list with the Chandal and Pukkas, they can also be considered undoubtedly untouchable. In *Mahabharata* (12, 59, 102-3), Nisad is said to be pre-Aryan tribe, having the features like short height, coal like dark complexion, red eyes, raised cheeks, flat noses and brass colour hairs.[201] By Jatak (2, p.200; 6, p. 71) it is found out that the Nisads too spent their lives as hunters and resided in their respective villages. Vrashal, too, is called ignoble in Buddha and Jaina scriptures. It is said in *Deegh Nikaya* (1, 92–3) and Jaina scripture *Ayarang Sutt* (2, 4.1.8) that *Vrishals* are born in inherent slave and inferior lineage and deserve to be insulted as dog, thief, dacoit, swindler, hypocrite, etc.[202] In Vasal Sutt of Buddha scripture *Suggnipat,* the *Vrishal* are pointed out as angry, hostile, sinful, blaming meritorious persons and illusive, etc. They seem to be categorised as Chandal. It becomes clear hereby that the Vrishal tribe people were spending low standard life and professing the culture continued from prime age and having witchery, illusion, etc., which was the symbol of lowness and inferiority according to Vedic-culture people. In conjunction with this, the Vrishals had the enemity against Brahmins and opposed their culture. Even they must not be believing Buddhist or Jaina religion philosophy and are called hypocrites and cheats therefore.

The other low tribes or Scheduled Tribes mentioned in holy writs and other scriptures, were not considered untouchable in this age although they were definitely in inferior condition. In Parvarti period, they became untouchable step by step.

Thus, it is clear from the aforesaid facts that in 600 BC

untouchable people resided outside the Aryan colonies or towns. Their social life was tribal based. They professed the culture, contrary to Vedas and traditionally, had been assuming witchery and *ihlaukik* charm. They had enemity against four-class social system and their culture from traditional inheritance. They complied with the *lokayat, tantravad,* atheist and other materialistic culture and tradition. Like other Scheduled Tribes, the untouchable Chandal, Pukkas, Sopak, Nisad, Veinn, etc., Scheduled Tribes were also busy in collective activities and men-women equally participated in all social and other activities.

Economically, the untouchable species were undeveloped to a great extent. They were in different backward phases of economic development. Chandal, Pukkas, Veinn and Nisad people earned their calling mainly by hunting and cane handicraft but Vrishal people were engaged in undeveloped phase of agriculture because they also knew witchery and illusion which is professed to be agriculture related originally. They were very far from religion and god, and opposite to the thinking of soul and Brahm. Their thinking according to their economical condition, hunting, agriculture, undeveloped handicraft, etc., also was mainly *ihlaukik.* Due to the Vedic-Aryan attack and the possession on the power and wealth, the natural phase of the economical development of untouchable Scheduled Tribes together with the prime Scheduled Tribes, stopped, and therefore, they remained stuck to their personal tribal profession but due to economic infirmity and unnatural demolition of the tribal community in conspiratory manner by the ruler classes of Vedic culture, the people called untouchables, having withdrawn from tribal community and profession, became compelled to adopt the task of cleanliness of Aryan-colonies, custody of graveyeard, begging and other inferior handicrafts. Even the Chandal species were engaged in the inferior physical duties like protection of graveyard, burying the corpses and removing the dead animals, etc. Similarly, the Pukkas people were employed in the work of cleaning the roads and temples. But the economic misery of these untouchable tribes continued.

Politically, the untouchable tribes became slaves. Due to economic decay and conspiracy of the Brahmin-Kshatriya ruler classes, their tribal community became feeble and scattered and collective power came to an end. They became subordinates mainly of Aryan colonies and political power of four-class people, while the respective power of other tribes was still maintained which had to be demolished in future. Its horrible form appears to us in Kautilya's *Arthasastra* while the tribal sets were being broken by hook or by crook. In this connection, D.D. Kosambi's comment is absolutely suitable: "Generally, such gangs are very powerful and could not be destroyed by military power. Same is completely proved by Sikandar's expedition in Punjab. When *Arthasastra* said that by a direct attack, these assemblies cannot be defeated, this was not an exaggeration.[203] In Karan Parva of *Mahabharata,* by the feeling of hatred expressed by *Brahmins* and members of royal family for Vaheek folk, it is affirmed that the *Brahmins* and the *Vedic*-culture people had unlimited contempt for non-*Vedic* and opposers of its culture and those tribal *gannas* and people living the *vratya* life.

Notes and References

1. *Baudh Darshan,* p. 15 (Allahabad, 1989); Rahul Sankratyayan.
2. *Acchhoot, Kaun aur Kaise?* p. 198 (Lucknow, 1989).
3. *Ibid,* p. 199.
4. *Shudron ka Pracheen Itihas,* p. 57 (Delhi, 1979).
5. *Ibid,* p. 116.
6. I.H.R.-2 *Stages in the History of Untouchables,* p. 31.
7. *Bhagvan Buddha aur Unka Dharam,* pp. 146-47, Bombay, 1986; translation B.A. Kosalyayan.
8. *Suneet Thero, Dadhash Nipato, Thergatha.*
9. *Shardool-Karan Apdan.*
10. *Op. cit.,* pp. 153-56.
11. *Vedic Age,* p. 313 (Nandan, 195).
12. E.R.E.-2 p. 157 (Edinbara, 1908-18); (S.) J. Hastings.
13. *Ibid.* p. 11.
14. *Rigveda,* 6.22.4.
15. *Sacred Books of the East,* 8.79, 83, 137, 215, 222 (Oxford, 1879); editor-F. Max muller.
16. *Ibid,* 26.399, 16.193, 29.342, 15.
17. *Rigveda,* 2.11.4, 6.25.2, 10.148.2.
18. *Ibid,* 4.28.4.
19. *Ibid,* 3.34.9.
20. *Ibid,* 1.103.3; *Atharva Veda,* 20.20.4
21. Ram Sharan Sharma: *op. cit.,* p. 15.
22. *Rigveda,* 1.103.3; 2.19.6; 4.30.20; 6.20.10; 6.31.4.
23. Max Muller: *op. cit.,* 7.110.
24. *Lokayat,* p. 47, Macmillan Publication (Calcutta, 1973); Devi Prasad Chattopadhyay.
25. *Rigveda,* 6.27.4.

26. *The Indus Civilization,* p. 18 (*Cambridge History of India ka Purak Khand, Cambridge, 1953).*
27. *An Introduction to the Study of Indian History,* p. 68 (Bombay, 1956).
28. *Rigveda,* 1.51.5.
29. *Ibid,* 4.30.3; 5.40.6; 10.69.6.
30. *Ibid,* 8.40.6.
31. *Ibid,* 1.33.7-8.
32. Sharma: *op. cit.,* p. 9.
33. Chattopadhyay: *op. cit.,* p. 47.
34. *Rigveda,* 9.41.1-2.
35. *Ibid,* 9.73.5.
59. *Ibid,* 10.38.3.
60. *Sharma*: *op. cit.,* p. 13.
61. *Ibid,* p. 14.
62. *Ibid.*
63. *Ibid,* p. 13.
64. *Ibid.*
65. *Op. cit.,* pp. 47–48.
66. *Ibid,* pp. 15–16.
67. Sharma: *op. cit.,* p. 30.
68. *Ibid,* p. 31.
69. *Op. cit.,* p. 48.
70. *Ibid,* p. 117.
71. *Ibid,* p. 116.
72. *Ibid,* p. 100.
73. *Ibid,* p. 48.
74. *Ibid,* p. 9.
75. *Ibid,* p. 26.
76. *Ibid,* p. 28.
77. *Ibid.*
78. *Ibid.*
79. *History of Dharamshastra,* Part 2, p. 66 (Poona, 1941).
80. Chattopadhyay: *op. cit.,* p. 132.
81. *Ibid,* p. 134.
82. *Ibid,* p. 133.
83. *Ibid,* p. 131.
84. *Ibid.*
85. *Manusmriti,* 2.39.
86. *Yagyavalakya Smriti,* 1.38.
87. *Bodhayan Dharamsutra,* 1.9.15.
88. In all holy writs, *Manusmriti,* etc. the *varn-sankar* is called untouchable.
89. *Op. cit.,* p. 132.
90. *Ibid,* p. 131.
91. *Ibid,* p. 21.
92. *Ibid.*
93. *Ibid.*
94. *Ibid.*
95. *Ibid,* p. 22.
96. *Chhandogya Upanishad* 8, translated by Wheum; Chattopadhyay: *Op. cit.,* 35–36.

97. Chattopadhyay: *Op. cit.,* p. 38.
98. *Dialogues of the Buddha,* Part 1, p. 167 (London, 1899).
99. Max Muller: *Op. cit.,* 38, 269.
100. Chattopadhyay: *Op. cit.,* p. 40.
101. *Ibid,* p. 41.
102. *Ibid.*
103. *Ibid,* p. 40.
104. *Ibid,* p. 41.
105. *A History of Indian Philosophy,* 3, 4, 533 (Cambridge, 1922-55).
106. *Op. cit.,* 42.
107. *Ibid.*
108. *Ibid,* 260.
109. *Ibid.*
110. *The Imperial Gazetteer of India,* 4, 174 (London, 188) Modified 1907–8 W.W. Hunter.
111. Chattopadhyay: *Op. cit.,* p. 211.
112. *Ascillus of Athenes,* pp. 21-22 (London, 1941, second edition).
113. F. Max Muller: *Op. cit.,* 20, 151–52.
114. *Op. cit.,* p. 277.
115. Sharma: *Op. cit.,* p. 42.
116. Vivekanand Jha,: *Op. cit.,* p. 14.
117. Sharma: *Op. cit.,* p. 57.
118. *Ibid.*
119. Vivekanand Jha: *Op. cit.*, p. 14.
120. Sharma: *Op. cit.*, p. 58.
121. *Ibid.*
122. Vivekanand Jha: *Op. cit.*, p. 14.
123. Chattopadhyay: *Op. cit.*, pp. 127–29.
124. *Ibid,* p. 129.
125. *Ibid.*
126. *Ibid,* p. 130.
127. *Ibid.*
128. *Ibid,* p. 134.
129. Sharma: *op. cit.,* p. 82.
130. *Gautama Dharamsutra,* 4.28.
131. Sharma: *op. cit.,* p. 139.
132. *Ibid,* p. 116.
133. *Ibid,* p. 115.
134. Jha, *op. cit.* p. 16.
135. Sharma: *op. cit.*, p. 115.
136. *Ibid,* p. 116.
137. Ambedkar: *op. cit.*, p. 182.
138. *Ibid,* p. 173.
139. *A History of Pali Literature,* Binding-1, pp. 30–33 (London, 1933); B.C. La.
140. *Majjim Nikaya,* 2, 152, 183-84; 3, 169-78; (S.). V. Tracnor and R. Chamars, Pali Text Society (London, 1888–1896)
141. *Sanyukt Nikaya,* 1, 102, 166.
142. *Panini Vyakaran* (*Patanjali Bhashya* 1 to 2), 4–10.
143. *Gautama Dharamsutra,* p. 27.

144. *Bodhayan Dharamsutra,* 1, 9.17.7.
145. *Vashishta Dharamsutra,* 18.1.
146. *Gautama Dharamsutra,* 4.21.
147. *Bodhayan Dharamsutra,* 1, 9.17.13-14.
148. *Ibid,* 1.9.17.5-6.
149. *Ibid,* 1.9.17.12.
150. *The Social Organisation of North-Eastern in Buddha's Time,* p. 51 (Calcutta, 1920); Richard Fik.
151. *Ibid,* p. 9.
152. *Ibid,* p. 116.
153. *Ibid,* p. 176.
154. *Ibid,* p. 199.
155. *Ibid,* p. 116.
156. Jha, *op. cit.,* p. 31.
157. *Ibid,* 16–17.
158. *Ibid.,* 17.
159. *Origin of Growth of Caste in India,* 1, pp. 106–107 (London, 193); N.K. Dass.
160. *Op. cit.,* p. 17.
161. *Ibid,* p. 116.
162. *Caste of Class in India,* p. 159 (Bombay, 195).
163. *Op. cit.* p. 25.
164. *Ibid,* p. 161.
165. *Ibid,* p. 163.
166. *Tribes and Castes of the Central Provinces of India,* pp. 24-39, (London, 1916); R.V. Rasel and Heera Lal.
167. *Gautama Dharamsutra,* 20.1; 23.32.
168. *Op. cit.,* p. 169.
169. *Ibid,* pp. 169–70.
170. Chattopadhyay, *op. cit.,* p. 53.
171. *Rigveda Brahmanas,* H.O.S. 25, p. 159 (Cambridge, 1920); A.B. Keeth.
172. *Ibid,* pp. 423–24.
173. Max Muller, *op. cit.,* 12, p. 194, 257.
174. *Op. cit.,* p. 53.
175. Sharma: *op. cit.,* p. 58.
176. Jha, *op. cit.,* p. 15.
177. *Ibid.*
178. *Ibid.*
179. *Ibid.*
180. *Ibid.*
181. Sharma, *op. cit.,* pp. 112-13.
182. *Ibid.*
183. *Ibid,* p. 113.
184. *Ibid.*
185. *Ibid.*
186. *Ibid.*
187. *Ibid.*
188. *Ibid.*
189. *Ibid.*

190. *Ibid.*
191. *Ibid.*
192. *Ibid,* 114.
193. *Majjim Nikaya,* 2, 152; 183-84; 3, 169-78.
194. *Jatak*-3, 195; Sharma, *op. cit.,* p. 114.
195. Ris Davids, *op. cit.* 1, p. 102.
196. Ambedkar, *Bhagvan Buddha aur Uska Dharam,* pp. 146-47.
197. Jha, *op. cit.,* p. 16.
198. Sharma, *op. cit.,* p. 114.
199. Suneet Thero, *op. cit.*
200. Jha, *op. cit.,* p. 16.
201. Dutt, *op. cit,* 1, p. 107.
202. Sharma, *op. cit.,* p. 112.
203. Chattopadhyay, *op. cit.,* p. 136

7

State of Untouchables in 200 B.C.

From 600 B.C. to 200 B.C., struggle against high-low and caste-difference was managed continuously in leadership of Buddhism. Except rulers of the Shung dynasty, generally all rulers offered protection to Buddhism, provided economical and moral assistance and helped completely to bring mobility in this social and cultural movement. This is the very reason that Buddhism, having crossed the Indian boundary, could be spread in many countries. Against inhuman social institutions like caste-difference and untouchability, in cultural arduous task, Buddhism provided topmost speed to, all from high classes and tribes of India to Sudras and untouchables, participated and this could take the shape of a great social-cultural movement. It is necessary to see as to what changes this socio-cultural movement having been continuing for about eight hundred years, could bring in Indian society as well as in the state of untouchability. Whether Buddhism could bring any changes or not, can be cleared only by finding out that in 200 B.C., whether untouchable tribes existed or not, and if they did, how was their social, economical, political and cultural condition? In this period, maximum information about the state of untouchables is achieved through *Manusmriti* as this is considered the creation of 200 B.C. to 200 C.[1] Besides, also on the basis of information obtained from Patanjali's commentary on the aphorisms or Panini's Sanskrit grammar, Bhas's dramas and Buddhistic scriptures Milind Palho, Divyadan, Mahavastu and Sadharampundrik, it can be found out about the state of untouchables because these texts are regarded of 200 B.C. to 200 C., too.[2] Apart from this, information can be collected also from *Vishnu Smriti, Jagyavalakya Smriti* and *Narad Smriti* because B.P. Kane has pointed out the creation period of these scriptures 100 C. to 300 C.[3]

In *Manusmriti*, old *varn-sanskar* (a hybrid) tribes, viz., Nishad, Parshav, Ugra, Ayogav, Shrit, Chandal, Pukkas, Kukkutak, Shavpak and Venn are described. In *Manusmriti* (10.49-51) it is said that the tribes, *viz.,* Nishad, Ayogav, Med, Andhra, Chunchuon, Madguon, Shrat, Pukkas, Dhigvan and Venn, etc., should settle in big trees, graveyards, cremation grounds, mountains and gardens outside the villages. It is stated in *Manusmriti* (10.51), "Chandal and Shavpak will stay outside the village. They will have to be made good for nothing. Their property will be dogs and donkeys." It is also told in this Smriti that "they will have to wear the clothes taken off from the dead bodies, have food in broken pots, their jewellery will be of black iron and they will always have to roam about in several places."[4] It is described that "any man, occupied with religious jobs, will not have any sort of relation with those, that is, untouchables. They (untouchables) will have their conduct mutually and perform their marriages only with those equal to them."[5] It is said in *Manusmriti* that *varn-sanskar* people will be served their food by any servant in broken pot and they will not enter village or city during night nor will they be able to wander there.[6] But during daytime they can go to villages or cities for working but they will have to keep with them the token given by king. They will have to take corpse of such people outside by carrying, who have no relatives of own.[7] It is also said that by king's permission, only they will always have, according to the ethics of government (as propounded by the sage Chanakya) to murder criminals and that they will be able to take clothes, bed and jewellery of those criminals.[8] In footnote of *Sacred Books of the East* (24.415), G. Buhler has written that generally Chandals and Shavpaks were asked to wear some special sort of dress to differentiate between them and others.[9] In *Manusmriti* (4.79), it is said that graduates, who were mainly Brahmins, should not associate with Chandals, Pukkas, Antyas and Antyavsayins. Thus, Manu has repeated old decisions of holy texts. Probably he would be desiring no relation between Brahmin and untouchables. Manu decided that while performing *shradhkaram* (offering water, food, etc. to the Brahmins in honour of manes), Brahmins should not be visible to Chandal, village-pig, cock and dog.[10] Here Manu has repeated those old talks of sacred texts, according to which Brahmins performing religious acts or reading Vedas should not be visible to untouchables. It is said in *Manusmriti* (2.276) that if any

Brahmin performs sexual intercourse with any Chandal or Antya woman and accepts victuals, etc., he will be degraded from Brahminhood and if he does so intentionally, he will have to achieve that state of Chandal or Antya, too. But it cannot be penetrated hereby that such relations with Brahmin tribes and Chandal and Antya women were not considered condemnable as is said at one place.[11]

Like sacred texts, in *Manusmriti,* Antya and Antyavsayins are called *varn-sanskars* and informed that they are originated by internal mixture of tribes. In *Manusmriti* (10.15), it is stated that the issue called Dhigvan by daughter of Ambasht tribe and woman of Ayogav tribe. It is said that the Dasyu male and Ayogav female produce a progeny called Sarandhra, Vadehak male and Ayovav woman called Maitreyak and Nishad male and Ayogav woman produce Bhargav or Das.[12] It is explained in *Manusmriti* (10.37) that Chandal and Nishad born of Vedehak woman produce children like Sopak and Ahindak step by step. It is described that a child born of Nishad man and Vadehak woman is called Karavar and similarly, child born of Vadehak woman is called Andhr and Med step by step.[13] In *Manusmriti* only (10.39), it is told that the son born of Chandal male and Nishad female is called Antyavsayin whom they see hatefully too as he is outsider, that is, out of four class system. In this very scripture it is explained that Soot, Vedehak, Chandal, Maagadh, Shitu and Ayogav tribes produce descendents from the tribe only, who are considered more contemptible and more despicable than their father are kept outside class-system.[14] In *Manusmriti* (10.31) it is said that Brahmins and inferiors produce fifteen kinds of low tribes by women of high tribes but their names are not caused to be counted. It appears hereby that in this period also sexual freedom was prevalent to some extent and marriages (in which the bride belongs to a high family and the bridegroom is of low descent) or children born due to sexual intercourse were considered untouchables or outsiders.

In *Manusmriti* (3.16) it is said that the son born to a Vaisya by Sudra woman, must be expelled from caste. In Manusmriti (9.178) it is described that for a Brahmin his alive son, Sudra is equivalent to a carcass and therefore he is called Parshav. Similarly, it is said that one who kisses the lower lip of a Vrishal woman, 'corrupt' is formed by his breathing and thereby a son is born and no atonement is available therefore.[15] But Patanjali states that the Das and Vrishal women were used for pleasures of high class people.[16] It clears that this prohibition with Vrishal woman was only for Brahmins.[17] It is said that if any Brahmin performs copulation with any reserved woman of these classes, smaller than him, he will be charged fine of 500 *pan* but on committing this sort of sin against Antyaj, that is, untouchable woman, fine will be increased to 1000 *pan.*[18] In *Manusmriti* (11.79), it is prescribed that if any Brahmin spends a night with a Vrishal woman, he will get rid of such a sin in three years by living on alms and reading holy texts daily. It is clarified hereby that people of Vrishal tribe, like other untouchable tribes, were considered ignoble and inferior and wanted to put Brahmin separate from this mean tribe.

In *Manusmriti* (8.279) it is prescribed that the part by which people of Antyaj, that is, low tribe, cause harm to high tribes, will be cut. It is also said that if any man (inferior) born in low lineage, tries to sit on that place where any man (superior) of high tribe is sitting, after scorching his buttock, he will be exiled or king will get his buttock wounded.[19] Although Kulluk has considered Sudra[20] inferior but this must have been applied also to untouchable tribes implicitly. It is described in *Manusmriti* (8.270) that if any Sudra insults any Brahmin by abusing him, his tongue will be cut. It is also prescribed that if any Sudra discusses names and tribes of Brahmin scornfully, the ten fingers long hot red ironed nail will be stuffed in his mouth.[21] If Sudra teaches Brahmins their duty arrogantly, the king will get hot oil poured in his mouth as well as ears.[22]

Aforesaid criminal law provided for Shudra tribes must have been applied also to those untouchable tribes. It does not took possible that these criminal laws be applied to Shudras, and untouchable and external people be free from these while we find that contemptible and hostile explanation is present in sacred texts and Smritis against untouchables. K.P. Jasyasvaal, the historian, opines that these rules are enacted for those Shudra scholars propagating religious principles, that is, Buddhist Shudras or Jaina Shudras and other Shudras of this sort, who claim equality with high classes.[23] K.V. Rangswami Ayyangar in *"Aspects of the Political and Social System of Manu"* (32) has written that these rules are mentioned against those political rivals of Manu, who insult established system.[24] It appears herefrom that oppugnants of Manu and Brahmneeya culture and royal dignity, must have been followers clearly of Buddhist and Jaina religions as well as tribal people of non-Vedic culture staying outside villages or cities, for whom such hard rule was enacted.

In *Manusmriti* (10.55) it is informed that people of Chandal tribe performed the task of throwing the corpse of such men having no relative. They performed the duty of hanging or killing criminals by the permission of the king[25] and also the job of hunter and butcher.[26] It is told when in Brahmin-dominated society, Chandals got place probably due to their being hunter and fowler, they were given the task of throwing dead bodies of animals and humans.[27] From description of *Ramayana* (1.58.10) and Chav-Chaddak-Chandal, it appears that they are always seen connected to the duties of removing and burning corpses.[28] By Andgad da Sajo (65) it is found out that Pann called Chandals performed same duty too.[29] In *Manusmriti* (10.56-39) it is described that the Chandal, Shavpak and Antyavsayins performed the job of hanging criminals and later they were given clothes, bed and ornaments of those criminals. People of Nishad spent their lives by catching fish and the livelihood of Bheds, Andhrs, Mridguas was hunting of wild animals.[30] In *Manusmriti* (10.49) it is said that people of Shitu, Ugra and Pukkas tribe made their living by catching and killing animals living in caves.

But all untouchable and so-called *varn-sankar* tribes were not only hunters or fowlers but many people were engaged in many important arts. According to *Manusmriti* (10.48), people of the Ayogav tribe were engaged in wood art. It is said that Dhigvan and Karavar tribes performed the work of leather art.[31] Pandu Sopak tribe made their livelihood by work of stick art.[32] In *Manusmriti* (10.34) it is stated that Margav or Dah the spent their lives by work of boatman, who were addressed by the name of Kaivart by the people of Northern Indian. In this very scripture it is described that people of the Venn tribe performed the duty of making public demonstration[33] and Maitreyak people rang bell when dawn drew and sang the euology of great dignitaries in harmonious voice.[34] It is described that people of Sairandhra tribe were considered expert in makeup and serving the master but the main source of their livelihood was snaring of shaning the animals.[35] It is found out from *Manusmriti* (4.218) that the cobbler tribe performed the work related to leather art. It clears that this was significant and that three untouchable and inferior tribes were engaged herein. It is described that people of Soot tribe made their livelihood by work of chariot construction.[36] Magadh people made their subsistence by work of local business and the Vadehak tribe performed the duties of serving women of royal palace and supervision.[37] In *Sacred Book of the East,* H. Karn has told that Chandals, the followers of Buddha, hated Kokkutiks that is hen-breeder, *Sankariya, Shodiks* that is wine sellers and their duties were regarded as inferior.[38] In Sadharampundhik, the Buddhist scripture, it is described that butchers, pugilists, dancers, wrestlers, *nirgranthas* and *lokayats* were seen hatefully by followers of Buddhism.[39] It is affirmed also by the account of Ateendra Nath Bose.[40]

In *Manusmriti* (4.215–16) it is stated that the grain of ironsmiths, *Nishad,* actors, goldsmiths, basket-makers, hunters, those taming dogs, wine-sellers, washermen and dyers of clothes is prohibited for graduates. Here only (4.218) it is described that by consuming food of cobbler, fame is decreased. In *Manusmriti* (4.219) it is described that by eating food of artisans, washermen and prostitutes, the graduate becomes childless, his strength reduces and he is degraded from the other world respectively. Here (4.222) it is also said that if graduate eats food of any of these unintentionally, he has to fast for three days but if intentionally, he has to perform a difficult atonement 'scanty urination accompanied by pain'. Thus it looks that along with untouchable artisans, the food of other artisans, probably Shudra tribe, was prohibited for graduates. It is said that the Brahmin lives in company of three classes and repudiates all low people; he is honoured but on practising against this, he having been corrupted, reaches state of Shudra.[41] It is found out from this that abreast untouchable tribes, to accompany Sudras also, symbolised inferiority and degrading for Brahmins. In *Manusmriti* (8.363) it is said that Buddhist and Jaina female recluses must not be conversed with because they were regarded dismissed generally from low tribes and having considered them these Buddhist recluses, were seen with bad sight.[42] It appears herefrom that Brahmins as well as people of Brahmana culture hated *aajeevak, nirgandh, Lokayats,* followers of Buddhist and Jaina religions, accompanied by untouchables, unlimitedly. This is exhibited by the fact that even talking to Buddhist and Jaina female recluses was considered a crime, then in Prayashchit Mukh of Neelkanth, it is said in a couplet of arrogant *Manusmriti* that if any man touches any Buddhist, a devotee of Shiva, male, *Lokayat*, atheist or one who is guilty of a crime of the highest degree, he will be pure by bath only.[43] In *Milind Panho,* authored by Nagsen, a renowned Buddhist recluse, it is said that one born in low tribe and belonging to the lineage having no tradition, is not worthy of being called king.[44] In *Manusmriti* (7.54) it is described that the king should appoint seven or eight ministers of this sort, whose ancestors were faithful officers of the king, who are expert in management of weapons and who belong to prosperous family as well as are experienced. In *Manusmriti* (7.54), the old talks of holy texts that members of four classes and people of untouchable tribe can witness in court cases of their communities, are repeated.[45] In Narad Smriti among described list of untrue witnesses are included magicians, dancers, wine sellers, oilmen, drivers of the elephant, cobblers, Chandals, Sudra, farmers, Sudra sons and those expelled from caste (degraded).[46]

In *Manusmriti* it is described that society consists of four classes.[47] On its basis, it is conclued that *varn-sankar* tribes or untouchables were included in Shudra class.[48] But in *Manusmriti*, Antyaj is used as Chandal who is shown in context of washerman, ironsmith, dancers, Burudh, Kevartt, Bhill and Med in subsequent scriptures.[49] In this scripture (10.29–31), it is said that Soot, Vedehak, Chandal, Maagadh, Shrit and Ayogav tribes are outsiders who are considered out of four classes by annotators as Meghatithi, Govindraj and Kulluk.[50] In *Manusmriti* (8.385), deciding the punishment for crime of Parastrigaman, Shudra and Antyaj are differentiated. In matters of witnessing also, the Shudra and Antyavsayin are differentiated. Patanjali has called exiled Shudra, Chandal and Mritap and considered the use of his eating bowl prohibited for high classes.[51] In Manusmriti (10.51), for these Shudras, the word *appatra,* that is, those people whose pots cannot be reused, is used. On the basis of these aforesaid proofs only, it is said that *varn-sankar* tribes and untouchables were categorised as inferior Shudras and on bais of their separate accommodation, backward culture and ancient religious communities, former were differentiated from common Shudras.[52]

Calling the doctrine propounded by Manu about four classes and other *varn-sankar* tribes or untouchables, 'agreeable trick', R. Fik has written, "Directly, it is clear that this doctrine does not provide the correct picture of real state. It is also not difficult to find out as to how this sort of system developed. It is clearly found out by names of some certain *sankar* tribes as to what the material was by which this system was formed. This material in all phases, is based either on geographical or tribal relations, places or names of people and by these only the names of tribes and sub-tribes occu red, for example, Maagadh, Nishad, Vadehak, Ambasthh, Mall, Livi and Chandal. Abreast, to some extent, also on the basis of professional classes, the names of tribes developed, such as Soot meaning charioteer, Venu meaning flute maker, Nat meaning dancer and Kaivartt meaning fisherman. This or such groups were intoxicated in their lives separate from Aryan society although hate was exhibited for their progeny or profession. Their own identity was clear and living but avoiding them silently or chaining them under any of four classes was impossible. Then this doctrine was enlarged and mixed tribes were linked with four original tribes and having made agreeable resolutions about origin of their families or professional groups, they were made recognised tribes."[53]

It is possible by aforesaid particulars that in sacred texts and *Smiritis* untouchables and *varn-sankar* tribes were made recognised tribes by agreeable contrivance but more than half picture of social, economical and political conditions of these so-called *varn-sankar* tribes is dependent on these very sources. We have already seen that many tribal remains were present in four classes, sexual freedom being one of them. Despite strict provisions of sacred texts and Smritis, sexual freedom would have been present in low level people of all classes, especially women, due to which the word *varn-sankar* would have been used for produced children. But in tribal people and those having backward economical state, settled near and outside, abreast all tribal qualities and remains, sexual freedom would have been clearly appeared too, by seeing which Brahmins and other so-called superior people would have hated as having seen sexual deformation in their four-class society. Therefore, they would have started calling those tribes *varn-sankar.* In period of *Manusmriti* also, the state of many new tribal people appears because *varn-sankar* list of Manu includes many new tribes. We can agree with statement of Fik that writers of Smritis, having addressed these tribes by name of *varn-sankar,* broken as well as kept them under Sudra class, made them recognised tribes. By aforesaid commentary of Dr Ramsharan Sharma also, the renowned historian, similar kind of conclusion emerges when he calls untouchables and *varn-sankars* "inferior Sudras". This is indeed the truth that the manner in which Manu has described the origin of these so-called *varn-sankar* tribes, is exaggerated and confusing. But the reason of this exaggeration and confusion is class-system and sexual freedom present in tribal society settled outside, which has been continuing for ancient period. D.P. Chattopadhyay has asserted correctly, "Those who claim to be supporters of Vedic tradition, for them to express anger on sexual principles and activities of *tantravad* would be illogical particularly, because initial vedicle people themselves believed in these very talks, too and also practised accordingly."[54] Therefore, among the authors of Smritis, fury developed against unrestricted activities of sexual intercourse which was natural and people embraced in that, called inferior, *varn-sankar* and untouchable. This was natural too because these writers were now claiming to be called civilised and learned having developed from the level of initial Vedic people.

It is clear from aforesaid interpretation that Vedic and Brahmneeya culture as well as thoughts are being opposed in this period also. In this period also, Lokayats, atheists and people of Buddhist and Jaina sects were protesting Brahmneeya and Vedic system based on four classes and making a bitter attack on high-low and caste-different prevalent herein. Therefore, writers of Smritis and supporters of Brahmneeya system hated them unlimitedly. This ruler class of society and culture had banned even talking to them as well as meeting and keeping relations with them was prohibited. Just as the ruler class of Brahmneeya culture hated *varn-sankars,* similarly, they hated those having opposing culture as well as thoughts. It is clear also from aforesaid account of R. Fik that the so-called *varn-sankar* tribes were non-Brahmaneeya and non-Vedic culture too. Having seen these very proofs, Dr. Ambedkar became confused and he even said that the hate of Brahmins for Buddhists was a fundamental reason of origin of untouchability.[55] Although in proofs presented by the famous scholar in favour of this thought, the hate for Lokayat, *pashupat,* Buddhists and atheists has been exhibited,[56] but he concluded this by taking in account only the feeling of hatred for Buddhists. We can agree with it that due to feeling of loathing for these sects, untouchability would have been clearly increased because in *Parvarti* period, untouchability adopted not only a solid shape but the number of untouchable tribes also increased.

It is clear from the aforesaid description entered in Manusmriti that the untouchable or so-called *varn-sankar* tribes lived outside Aryan colonies or cities. They stayed by making their huts in big trees, cremation grounds, buildings, side of mountains or gardens. Generally the life and social system of untouchable tribes was separate from four class social system and of a different sort seen by people of Brahmneeya culture hatefully. Untouchable tribes such as Nishad, Parshav, Ugra, Ayogav, Shrit, Chandal, Pukkas and Venn were living mainly tribal life and therefore, tribal qualities, whatever collective life, maintenance of spell and prohibition as well as religious performance based on sexual freedom, that is, keeping of Lokayat and tantravad would have been mainly present in them. Therefore, people of Vedic and Brahmneeya culture hated them. It is said that due to their separate accommodation, backward culture and ancient religious sect, that is, non-Vedic culture, they were considered separate from Sudra class as well as deserving more hate.[57] Therefore, there is no possibility of any suspicion that they were still connected with tradition and culture of ancestors, viz., Dasyu, Asuras, Rakshasas, Nag, etc, irrespective of their being inferior, backward and having low standard of life-style as compared to their oppugnants. In this connection, following example of Fredric Angels is worthy of quotation:

"Tribal *kabeelas* and their social customs were sacred and unfit to be violated for them; there was a supreme power established by nature itself and for which everyone was loyal by mind, action and speech. People of this age may appear grand but they are not different from one another any way. As Marx said, They are still connected with navel-string of ancient society. Power of these ancient societies was to be dissolved and it was done. But this was performed by medium of such influences which appear to us declining process from outside, decline of straight, simple moral grandeur of ancient uncivilised society. Interest of low category, such as excessive greed, cruelty, sexuality, uncommon hostility, robbery of joint property, has crossed over new civilised, divided society."[58]

The substance of comments made by Fik on provisions of *Manusmriti* can be cleared by aforesaid explanation of Angels. How Manu made so-called *varn-sankar* tribes who were overjoyed in their lives separate from Aryan society, recognised tribes by trick by agreeable way, because to avoid them silently or to tie them under any of four classes was impossible. But why only Manu is to blame for this? Manu made such provisions under those very policies which had been continuing since before decades, violent form of which appears to us in Kautilya's *Arthasastra*.[59] D.P. Chattopadhyaya has written about hatred expressed for tribes and objective of conspiratory attack of breaking their society in Kautilya's *Arthasastra*. "In India like today, earlier also the tribes were settled in many areas. This sort of tribal areas must have been very extensive as well as achieving prominence. Generally state powers were limited to some areas locally and wherever ruled area of any state was very big, as that of famous empires, tribes were inside the state administration there also. Therefore, tribal people always created the problems for state rulers. It is known by Kautilya's *Arthasastra* that these problems were very complicated in reality. Now the question arose as to what should be done with tribal people? Kautilya spoke of two things. First, after dissolving the unity of these tribes, they should not be let to stay together. If it happens, then despite defeat in war, they will again attract towards tribal unity which is natural and then they will pick up weapons for re-achieving their lost freedom. Therefore, the first duty, was to scatter the tribal people. Herefrom we reach second thing which is the most important one of Kautilya's policy in connection of tribal people. What are the methods Kautilya spoke of by which these tribal people had to be resettled? He said that these people should be settled in small villages, each consisting of five or ten families and engaged in agriculture (*panchkulim daskulim va krishyayam nivesyet*); these villages should remain separate and therefore, they should be self-dependent."[60]

In connection of tribes, Kautilya's two policies, although in words of Marx, symbolised excessive greed, deformed enmity, cruelty, robbery of joint property but tribal power and society had to be dissolved and they were dissolved and it is clear from *Manusmriti* that by a preplanned method, they were provided places under big trees and in buildings, cremation grounds, gardens, etc., outside the Aryan colonies or cities for their resettlement. They began to be used for agriculture and agricultural artisans. This was not their natural disintegration discisively which were the result of progress in production processes but this was the situation to break tribal people by attacking on their society from outside as well as to oblige them for staying in very small and separate villages.[61]

But it cannot be concluded hereby that all tribal society were decomposed by trick. It is also possible on the basis of exposition of sacred texts that the entire village of tribe was declared untouchable or *varn-sankar,*[62] because they are addressed by names of "Antyavsayin", "Antya", etc., and Manu has called them "Bahya" (external), " Antyavtayin", "Antyaj", etc., too.

It is clear from the account of *Manusmriti* and Buddhist texts that their economical life was very hazardous. They were in different phases of economic development. Due to Aryan attack and obtaining power, their natural economic development had been obstructed and they were bound to spend a backward economic life. It is lucid from *Manusmriti* that dogs and donkeys were the only property of Chandals and Shavpaks. Earlier they were in profession of hunter and fowler but by breaking their tribal lives, they were engaged in duties like carrying and burning corpses, sweeping roads and executing death-sentence of criminals by king's permission in Brahmneeya system. They were not employed in any production work. They wore those clothes taken off from the bodies of carcasses or those criminals awarded death-sentence adorned iron ornaments, had their food in broken pots and used their bed. Their economic life was very pitiable. Nishad, Med, Andhr, Mridgu, Chanchu, etc., were spending their lives as hunters. Nishad performed the work of fish catching and people of other tribes made their subsistence by hunting wild animals. But many untouchable tribes were artisans and businessmen. Dhigvan, Karavar and cobblers made their livelihood by work of leather-art. Soot constructed chariots. Soot and Ayogav tribes were engaged in wood art. Probably they must be manufacturing agricultural instruments and wooden instruments for domestic use. Pandu Sopak used to make goods of stick art. They must be making their livelihood by manufacturing winnowing basket, small basket, etc., used for domestic purposes. Bhargav and Kaivartt were boatsmen. They must be undertaking works like catching fish, taking ready goods from one place to another via water passage, getting people to cross rivers and drains, etc. People of Venn tribe undertook the duty of making public announcements. Possibly they must be beating drums on the occasions of religious functions and marriages, etc., as the people of Dom or Chamar tribe still do. Maagadh people were occupied in local business.

But in spite of breaking aforesaid artisan tribes by Brahmneeya system by agreeable or conspiratory method, why did their art and profession remained unchanged? The answer can be searched by description of G. Thomson:

"In initial phase of tribal society labour-division was only between female and male. But professions decisive by development of beast-rearing, agriculture and handicraft became hereditary. This inclination emerged particularly in *kabeelas.* As Greenvel has told that advent of shrenees took place through kabeelas. Structural difference between them is that membership of *shrenee* occurred not by taking birth only. It is possible that son, having adopted the occupation of his father, becomes member of that *shrenee.* In very old *kabeelas,* generally people of other *shrenees* were included too. Since *kabeelas* performing handicraft were present extensively in developed phase of tribal system and therefore it is not difficult to accept that these sort of *kabeelas* were also present in ancient Greece. And if it was not so, there were definitely some ancient *kabeelas* by which artisan *kabeela* developed latter."[63]

By keeping in view the aforesaid explanation and list of artisan tribes presented by Thomson; D.P. Chattopadhyay has penned, "Thomson, by this viewpoint only, has told about artisan tribes and *kabeelas* of ancient Greece such as Homredai (bard), Askale Piadai (physician), Iyamidai, Branchidai and Krontidai (astrologer), Unaidai (veena player), Karikes and Thiyokerikes (messenger or one making public announcement by beat of drum) and there is no doubt that soot (charioteer), Venu (flute manufacturer), Nat (dancer), Kaivartt (fisherman) tribes were either real professional *kabeelas* or remains of those *kabeelas* engaged in handicraft in form of professional tribes whose examples appear to us in India today also. In matter of this kind of clans, there were many matrimony related strict *bahigotreeya* (many clans) rules. In such tribes sub-tribes profession related strict rules also were remains of tribal social system."[64] Therefore, it is clear from the aforesaid proofs that unchangeability of arts, handicraft or professions of untouchable tribes were remains of their tribal or *kabeela* life and these remains stayed as it is because their natural economic development could not take place. Their tribal life was broken by external attack of Vedic or Brahmaneeya people or deception as a result of which they could not cross backward phase of unbalanced economic development.

It appears from the aforesaid data of Buddhist scriptures *Milind Panho* and *Manusmriti* that inferior tribes and people of low lineage could not appointed on any important post in contemporary state system. It is stated clearly in these codes that king or his ministers cannot be belong to any inferior lineage or tribe. Untouchable species began to be ruled by four class people politically. Local Brahmneeya rulers started ruling them directly. Their tribal powers vanished and now they transformed in ruled ones. They became dependent not only economically but also got gripped in chains of slavery. In Kautilya's *Arthasastra,* due to exhibited policies of breaking tribal ssociety and power and then resettling them, it is useless to expect that political power of untouchable people be maintained. It is not so that this talk remained only with policies fixed by Kautilya or Manu. Before Kautilya from many decades to subsequent decades, these policies would have been remaining a part of state system. In this connection, the statement of D.P. Chattopadhyay is worthy of quotation: "By description of attack by Ajaatshatru (on Vajjeeyjano), it appears that the policy ascertained by Kautilya extensively, had been used by Ajaatshatru long before. It is found out hereby that through this policy Kautilya provided a shape of doctrine, which had been brought in practice long before. Probably its clarification can be this that Kautilya himself has quoted a long list of his preceeding religious instructors by whose policy or doctrine called propounded by Kautilya could be in truth older than that. Besides, this is also the basis of thinking that real use of Kautilya's policies took place for many decades even after him. We also come to know of his policies becoming modest in Sanskrit poetry such as Kiratajurneeyam, Shishupadvadham, etc.[65]

Thus, it is clear from investigation of all aforesaid proofs that in 200 C. untouchable tribes which were addressed by various names such as Antyaj, Antyavsayin, Bahya (external), etc., stayed outside villages or cities of Brahmneeya system, who were seen very hatefully by four class people. They had no religious or cultural rights in the four class society. They had been professing mainly non-Vedic and non-Brahmaneeya thoughts and culture traditionally. Their economic condition was very decrepit and hazardous. They worked on many levels such as whatever inferior service, throwing out dead animals or humans, burning carcass, giving death-sentence to criminals, sweeping roads, etc., prevalent in the hunter, artisan, tradesman, and Brahmaneeya society of economic development. Politically they had attained slavery of Brahmneeya state power. Their living standard was of a very low level. They helped in agriculture and agriculture subsidiary works through different arts.

But their culture and religious beliefs remained oppugnant of Brahmin religion and Vedic culture as earlier. Although, they were accepting many thoughts and beliefs as superstitions, Lokayat doctrine, atheist doctrine, Buddhist doctrine, etc., because these very doctrines were according to their development phases as well as professed morality and fraternity of tribal life but they were protesting Brahmneeya supremacy and personal interest, libido and Vedic culture believing in religious ceremonies, very strongly. In *Manusmriti,* against Sudra and non-Brahmaneeya culture and Lokayatik, athiest, *pashupat* and Buddhists, what sort of hate appears, it is found out therefrom that from 200 BC to 200 C an awful war was going on between these two cultures due to which the Vedic and Brahmin cultures were receiving spirituous attack. Having become insane, all writers of Smritis, in their scriptures, not only repeated talks of reinforcing all those restrictions and prohibitions of sacred texts strictly but also approved the right of punishing or having weapons for Shudra and Brahmins who had become a part of Brahmneeya system by now if any irreligious does not believe in social system. In this period, legal and political condition of Sudras was improved to some extent as is found out by account of Manu and other writers of Smritis.[66] Probably in this period, binding of class system sank by foreign attacks and foundation of privileges of high class weakened by tribal chaos.[67]

In fact, the period from 200 BC to 200 C can be called a motion period in Indian history. Due to motion and instability, pungent hate and prohibition appear in Brahmneeya scriptures against those irreligious and oppugnants and in conjunction with, some political and legal rights appear to be given to them for taking support of Sudras. This is the reason that in scriptures of Parvarti period, not only the number of untouchable species seems increasing but solid form of hatred for them also comes to light in Gupta period.

Notes and References

1. Ram Sharan: *op. cit.,* p. 174.
2. *Ibid,* p. 174.
3. *Ibid,* p. 258.
4. *Manusmriti* (10.52) editor, V.N. Mandlik, Bombay, 1886; translator, G. Buhler, *Sacred Books of the East,* 25, Oxford, 1886.
5. *Ibid,* 10.53.
6. *Ibid,* 10.54.
7. *Ibid,* 10.55.
8. *Ibid,* 10.56.
9. Sharma: *op. cit.* p. 196.
10. *Manusmriti,* 3, 239: *op. cit.*
11. Sharma: *op. cit.* p. 197.
12. *Manusmriti,* 10, 33-34: *op. cit.*
13. *Ibid,* 10.36.
14. *Ibid,* 10.26–29.
15. *Ibid,* 3, 19.
16. Sharma, *op. cit.*
17. *Manusmriti,* 3, 17–19.
18. *Ibid,* 8, 385.
19. *Ibid,* 8, 281.
20. Kulluk on Manu, 8.28.
21. *Manusmriti,* 8.271.
22. *Ibid,* 8, 272.
23. Sharma, *op. cit.,* p. 185.
24. *Ibid.*
25. *Manusmriti,* 10.56.
26. *Ibid,* 5, 131.
27. Sharma, *op. cit.,* p. 113.
28. *Ibid.*
29. *Ibid.*
30. *Manusmriti,* 10.48.
31. *Ibid,* 10.36.49.
32. *Ibid,* 10.37.
33. *Ibid,* 10.49.
34. *Ibid,* 10.33.
35. *Ibid,* 10.32.
36. *Ibid,* 10.47.
37. *Ibid*
38. H. Karn: *Sacred Books of the East,* 21, 438, Oxford, 1884.
39. *Sadharam Pundrik,* pp. 181 : 311-12 translation H. Karn, 1884.
40. *Social and Rural Economy of Northern India,* 2, pp. 463-64, Calcutta, 1945.

41. *Manusmriti,* 4, 245.
42. *Manu and Yagyavalkya,* pp. 167–68, Calcutta, 1930: K.P. Jayasvaal.
43. *Ambedkar: Acchoot Kaun aur kaise?* p. 100, Lucknow, 1989.
44. *Milind Panho,* 3. 358: translation, T.W. Ris Davids, *Sacred Books of the East,* Oxford, 1890–94.
45. *Manusmriti,* 8, 58.
46. *Narad Smriti,* 1, 178: 180–85.
47. *Manusmriti,* 10.4.
48. Sharma: *op. cit.* p. 197.
49. *Ibid:* p. 216.
50. *Ibid.* p. 197.
51. *Ibid.*
52. *Ibid.*
53. *The Social Organisation in North East India in Buddha's Time,* pp. 8–9, Calcutta, 1920.
54. Lokayat, 59.
55. *Op. cit.,* pp. 103–04.
56. *Ibid,* p. 100.
57. Sharma: *op. cit.,* p. 197.
58. *The Origin of the Family, Private Property and the State,* p. 258, Moscow, 1952.
59. *Arthashtra Adhikaran,* 11: translation, Shyam Shastri.
60. *Op. cit.,* p. 140.
61. *Ibid,* p. 141.
62. Sharma; *op. cit.,* p. 116.
63. Ascillus and Athenes, pp. 44–45 (Lokayat se Uddhat).
64. *Op. cit.,* p. 140.
65. *Ibid,* p. 140.
66. Sharma: *op. cit.,* p. 205.
67. *Ibid*

8

Untouchability for Śūdra Contexting with Pali Text

The present chapter deals with the untouchable Śūdra we are shown that they were the early representatives of the people who were later called untouchables, out-castes, depressed classes, or Scheduled Castes. Buddhist literature and the early Dharma Sutras show that several centuries before Christ there already existed groups of people who, though serving the Āryans in very menial and dirty tasks, were looked on as quite outside the pale. Sometimes they were called the 'fifth class' (pañcama), but most authorities rejected this term, as if to insist that they were excluded from the Āryan social order altogether.

Numerous groups of these people are mentioned, by names which are non-Āryan in origin, and were probably those of aboriginal tribes which came under the sway of the advancing Āryans. Chief of these groups was the caṇḍāla, a term which come to be used loosely for many types of untouchables. The caṇḍālas was not allowed to live in an Āryan town or village, but had to dwell in special quarters outside the boundaries. Though some caṇḍālas had other means of livelihood in theory their main task was the carrying and cremation of corpses, and they also served as executioners of criminals.

According to the law-books, the caṇḍālas should be dressed in the garments of the corpses he cremated, should eat his food from broken vessels, and should wear only iron ornaments. No man of higher class might have any but the most distant relations with a caṇḍāla, on pain of losing his religious purity and falling to the caṇḍāla's level. By Gupta times caṇḍālas had become so strictly untouchable that, like lepers in medieval Europe, they were forced to strike a wooden clapper on entering a town, to warn the Āryans of their polluting approach.

Certain classes of outcastes or untouchables seem to have gained their unenviable position through the growth of the sentiment of non-violence—for instance the *nisāda,* who was a hunter, the fishing caste colled Kaivarta, and the leather worker (kārāvara). The Pukkusa, who appears as a sweeper in Buddhist literature, may have fallen in status because members of his class made and sold alcoholic liquor. More difficult to account for are such base classes as basket-maker *(veṇa)* and the chariot-maker *(rathakāra).* In early Vedic times the latter were the most respected craftsmen, but soon fell to the status of the impure Śūdra or out-caste.

By the beginning of the Christian era the out-castes themselves had developed a caste hierarchy, and had their own out-castes. Manu[1] mentions the *antyāasāyin,* a cross between a caṇḍāla and a nisāda, who were despised even by the caṇḍāla themselves. In later India every untouchable group imagined that some other group was lower than itself, and this stratification evidently began quite early.

Even the lot of the untouchable was not altogether without hope. Though he was denied access to the temples and the comforts of orthodox religion, Buddhist monks preached to him, and the more enlightened wandering ascetics would give him instruction. The untouchable dying in defence of brāhman. s, cows, women, and children secured a place in heaven. Orthodox texts contain frequent warnings on the evils which arise when Śūdra and outcastes grow too powerful, and this would seem to show that a do not might occasionally become influential.

Another class of untouchables was the *mleccha,* the word commonly used for outer barbarians of whatever race or colour. As an invader he was loathed, but once he had come into contact with the Indian ways and was less strange and forbidding, his status could improve. In fact, it was not blood which made a group untouchable, but conduct. Generally there was no chance of an individual rising in the social scale, but for a group this was possible, over a number of generations, by adopting more orthodox practices and following the rules of the Smrtis. Thus the Indian class system was always somewhat fluid.

An early legend tells of Viśwāmitra, a Ksatrya who, by penance and piety, became a brāhmiṇ and a seer (*ṛṣi*) to boot; but as time went on such raising of one's status became more and more difficult, and finally virtually impossible, though convenient fictions sometimes permitted kings and chiefs of low status to find legendary Kṣhatriya ancestors and advance in the class hierarchy. While it became very difficult for the individual to rise, it grew progressively more easy for him to fall. Every breach of the manifold regulations of one's class entailed impurity outcasting, either permanent or temporary. The lawbooks give a long lists of penances for the restoration of the unfortunate offender, ranging from trivial ones, such as bathing, or touching the Ganges water, to others so rigorous that they must usually have resulted in the death of the penitent. Secular literature, however, tells many stories of high class people infringing the rules of purity without doing penance, and no doubt, the more sophisticated townsmen often took his class responsibilities lightly.

The continual injunctions to the king to ensure that "confusion of class" *(varṇa-saṃkara)* did not take place indicate that such confusion was an ever-present danger in the mind of the orthodox brāhmaṇ. The class system was indeed a very fragile thing. In the golden age the classes were stable, but the legendary king vena, among his many other crimes, had encouraged miscegenation, and from this beginning confusion of class had increased, and was a special feature of the Kali-yuga, the last degenerate age of this aeon, which was fast nearing its close. The good king, therefore, should spare no effort to maintain the purity of the classes, and many dynasties took special pride in their efforts in this direction.

Before the tightening of the social system in the Middle Ages confusion of class was comparatively frequent, and some forms of inter-class marriage were expressly permitted. The type of marriage known to anthropologists as hypergamous, when the husband is of a higher class than the wife, was by no means disapproved of on the other hand hypogamous marriage, when the wife's status was higher than that of the husband, was always frowned on. The former was "in accordance with the direction of the hair" *(anuloma),* smooth and natural, while the latter was "against the hair", or "brushing the wrong way" *(pratiloma).* This distinction is to be found in other societies; for instance in Victorian England the peer who married an actress rarely incurred the same scorn and ostracism as the lady who married her groom.

The earlier legal literature permitted *anuloma* or hypergamous marriage, provided that a man's first wife was of his own class. Generally brāhmiṇs were forbidden to take Śūdra wives, but one lawbook allowed even this, and Bāṇa, the 7th century poet, who was a brāhmaṇ, had a stepbrother by a Śūdra mother. Various mixed classes, many of them the forerunners of later castes, were said to be the products of marriages of this type, and their members were not looked on as in any way unclean, but enjoyed a position intermediate between that of the two parents. Of the groups thought to have descended from hypergamous marriage only the Niṣāda, in theory a cross between a brāhmaṇ and a Śūdra woman, was thought to be impure.

Hypogamous or *pratiloma* marriage, on the other hand, produced offspring whose status was lower than that of either parent. Thus, the caṇḍālas were believed to have described from marriages between Śūdras and Brāhmin. women. The only exceptions were the class of charioteers, or *sūtas,* thought to have sprung from the hypogamy of *Kṣatriyas* and Brāhmins, and the bards or Māgadhas, descended from Vaisyas fathers and kṣḥatriya mothers, both of whom were well respected. The complex system of sub-classes low in the social scale, out of which the Indian caste system developed, was believed to be wholly the result of "confusion of class". This tradition was accepted by early indologists, but as we shall see, is completely unfounded.

Relations between classes and social groups in later Hinduism were governed by rules of endogamy (marriage was only legitimate within the group), commensality (food was only to be received from and eaten in the presence of members of the same or a higher group), and craft-exclusiveness (each man was to live by the trade or profession of his own group, and not take up that of another). Megasthenes noted seven endogamous and craft-exclusive classes in India—philosophers, peasants, herdsmen, craftsmen and traders, soldiers, government officials and councillors. His sevenfold division is certainly false, but he gives evidence to show that in Mauryan times the class divisions were already hardening. Even in the Gupta period, however, the regulations were by no means rigid. Hypergamous intermarriage was recognised, the rule of craft-exclusiveness was often ignored or circumvented by the convenient escape clauses of *āpaddharma,* and in the earlier lawbooks the Brāhmaṇ was permitted to accept food from any Āryan. It was only in late medieval times that it was finally recognised that exogamy and sharing meals with members of other classes quite impossible for respectable people. These customs and many others such as widow-remarriage, were classed as *kalivarjya* - customs once permissible, but to be avoided in this dark Kali age, when men are no longer naturally righteous.

This chapter uses the word which in most minds is most strongly connected with the Hindu social order. When the Portuguese came to India in the 16th century they found the Hindu community divided into many separate groups, which they called castes, meaning tribes, clans or families, The name stuck, and became the usual word for the Hindu social group. While attempting to account for the remarkable proliferation of castes in 18th and 19th century India, authorities credulously accepted the traditional view that by a process of intermarriage and sub-division the 3,000 or more castes of modern India had evolved from the four primitive classes, and the term "caste" was applied indiscriminately to both *Varna* or class, and *jāti* or caste proper. This is a false terminology; castes rise and fall in the social scale, and old castes die out and new ones are formed, but the four great classes are stable. They are never more or less than four, and for over 2000 years their order of precedence has not altered. All ancient Indian sources make a sharp distinction between the two terms; Varna is much referred to, but *jāti* very little, and when it does appear in literature it does not always imply the comparatively rigid and exclusive social groups of later times. If caste is defined as a system of groups within the class, which are normally endogamous, commercial and craft-exclusive, we have no real evidence of its existence until comparatively late times.

Caste is the development of thousands of years, from the association of many different racial and other groups in a single cultural system. It is impossible to show its origin conclusively, and we can do little more than faintly trace its development, since literature paid scant attention to it; but it is practically certain that caste did not originate from the four classes. Admittedly it developed later than they, but this proves nothing. There were sub-divisions in the four classes at a very early date, but the Brāhmiṇ *gotras*, which go back to Vedic times, are not castes, since the *gotras* are exogamous, and members of the same *gotra* are to be found in many castes.

Perhaps the first faint trace of caste is to be found in the careful cataloguing of trades and professions in later Vedic literature, as if their members were looked on almost as distinct species. In the Pāli scriptures many trades and professions are described as living apart; thus, we read of villages of Brāhmiṇs, potters, hunters and robbers, and of separate quarters in the towns for different trades and professions. Many trades were organised in guilds, in which some authorities have seen the origin of the trade castes; but these trade groups cannot be counted as fully developed castes. A 5th century inscription from Mandasor[3] shows us a guild of silk-weavers emigrating in a body from Lata (the region of the lower Narmada) to Mandasor, and taking up many other crafts and professions, from soldiering to astrology, but still maintaining its guild-consciousness. We have no evidence that this group was endogamous or commensal, and it was certainly not craft-exclusive; but its strong corporate sense is that of a caste in the making, Huen Tsang, in the 7th century, was well aware of the four classes, and also mentioned many mixed classes, no doubt accepting the orthodox view of the time that these sprang from the intermarriage of the four, but he shows no clear knowledge of the existence of caste in its modern form.

To the present day the life of the lower orders is much more affected by caste than by *Varna*—it is not being a vaisya or a Śūdra, but being an *ahīr*, a *kāyasth*, or a *sonār* which matters, and corporate feeling is centred around this caste group, whether based on region, race, profession or religion. The same strong corporate sense existed among the Mandasor silk weavers, and evidence of its existence at an even earlier date can be gathered from many sources. Indian society developed a very complex social structure, arising partly from tribal affiliations and partly from professional associations, which was continuously being elaborated by the introduction of new racial groups into the community, and by the development of new crafts. In the Middle Ages the system became more or less rigid, and the social group was now a caste in the modern sense. Professor J.H. Hutton has interpreted the caste system as an adaptation of one of the most primitive of social relationships, whereby a small clan, living in a comparatively isolated village, would hold itself aloof from its neighbours by a complex system of taboos, and he has found embryonic caste features in the social structure of some of the wild tribes of present-day India. The caste system may well be the natural response of the many small and primitive peoples who were forced to come to terms with a more complex economic and social system. It did not develop out of the four Āryan *varṇas,* and the two systems have never been thoroughly harmonized.

By the end of our period many of the present-day caste groups were already in existence. Even the Brāhmiṇ class was much subdivided into endogamous groups, often based on locality and race, with many different practices. The Rajputs were divided into clans which, if not regularly endogamous, were castes of a sort, and the Vaisyas, Śūdras, and untouchables had evolved hundreds of castes. They were governed by local communities of elders, usually hereditary, which had the power to expel members and regulate caste rules, and whose decisions, from the time of the *Arthashāstra* onwards, had the force of law.

After the large joint family, the caste provided social security, helping destitute members and providing for widows and orphans. A man expelled from his caste was also automatically expelled from his family, unless the whole family accompanied him in his social ostracism. He was lost to society, and could only consort with the lowest of the low. Though he might sometimes retain some of his former wealth he was isolated, a tree torn up by the roots. Permanent loss of caste was the greatest catastrophe, short of death and the major chronic diseases, which could happen to a man.

Early Tamil literature gives no evidence of caste, but the growth of Āryan influence and the development of a more complex political and economic structure produced a system in some ways more rigid than that of the North. By the Ch period an important feature of South Indian caste structure had appeared, which has survived to the present day. In the Dravidian country families claiming to be *kshatriyas* were few, other than the ruling families, and Vaisyas, were equally rare. Nearly the whole of the population were Brāhmiṇs, Śūdra or untouchables, and the Śūdra castes, which formed the mass of the people, were divided into two great caste groups, known as the right and left hands. The great animosity and rivalry which still exists between these groups is atleast a thousand years old. On the right are the trading castes, some weaving castes, musicians, potters, washermen, barbers, and most of the cultivating and labouring castes; on the left are various castes of craftsmen, such as weavers and leather workers, cowherds, and some cultivating castes. We have no evidence of how this strange bisection of society arose.

Hypergamy never wholly disappeared. In Malābār, where matrilinear succession has continued almost to modern times, men of the great Brāhmiṇ caste of Nambūdiris have regulary married the women of the dominant secular caste, the Nayyars. In Bengal the Rāḍhī caste of Brāhmiṇs and the important and respectable castes of scribes (Kāyastha) and doctors (Vaidya) are divided into subcastes, which are hypergamous. The system is known as *kulīnism,* from the name of the highest subcaste of the Brāhmiṇs *(kulīna);* it was by tradition imposed by the Bengal king Vallāla Sena (12th century), but is no doubt a survival from much earlier times.

The organisation of castes independent of the Government, and with social ostracism as its most severe sanction, was a powerful factor in the survival of Hinduism. The Hindu, living under an alien political order imposed from above, retained his cultural individuality largely through his caste, which received most of the loyalty elsewhere felt towards king, nation and city. The caste was so strong that all attempts at breaking it down, until recent years have ended in failure. Equalitarian religious reformers of the late Middle Ages, such as Basava, Rāmānand, and Kabīr, tried to abolish caste among their followers; but their sects soon took on the characteristics of new castes, and in some cases divided into castes within themselves. The Sikhs, despite the outspoken centiments of their *gurus* and the adoption of rites deliberately intended to break down caste prejudice, such as the ritual meal eaten in common, did not overcome caste feeling. Even the Muslims, for their equalitarian faith, formed caste groups. The Syrian Christians of Malābār early divided into sections which took on a caste character brought their caste prejudices with them, and highcaste converts held themselves aloof from those of the lower orders. When in the 16th century Roman Catholic missionaries began to make converts in South India.

Only in the last fifty years has the caste system shown real signs of breaking down, thanks to the many inventions of the West not designed for use in a society divided into watertight compartments, the spread of Western education, growing national sentiment, and the intensive propaganda of enlightened leaders. The process is not yet complete, and it will be many years before all traces of caste feelings are eradicated; but when Mahatmā Gāndhī, in many ways socially conservative, persuaded his followers to sweep their own floors and clean their own latrines, he sounded the death knell of the old Hindu social order, which for all its faults, has preserved the identity of Indian society over centuries of foreign domination.

Megasthenes declared that there were no slaves in India. He was certainly wrong, but Indian slavery was milder than the form to which he had been used, and slaves were much less numerous than in the civilizations of the West; hence he may not have recognized the *dāsa* as a slave. There was no caste of slaves; though the *Arthashastra* declares that servitude is not in the nature of the Āryan (in which term the humble Śūdra is explicitly included), an individual of any class might in certain circumstances become a slave, although most slaves were no doubt of low caste.

The word *dāsa* originally meant a member of the peoples conquered by the Āryans in their first invasions of India. Its later connotation no doubt developed from the reduction to bondage of the many dāsas captured in battle, and here we find the probable origin of Indian slavery. The *Mahābhārata* declares that it is a law of war that the vanquished be the victor's slave,[4] and the captive would normally serve his captor until ransomed. But there were several other classes of slaves in their times. Children born of slaves normally became the slaves of their parents' masters. Slaves might be bought, given away, or mortgaged. A free man might sell himself and his family into slavery in times of dire distress. He might also be reduced to slavery for crime or debt, but in these cases his servitude might be only temporary. All these types of slavery are recognized in the Smriti literature and elsewhere.

As in other slave-owning civilizations, the slave might become an important man, and there are even references in stories to slaves serving as royal counsellors. Slaves might sometimes perform work of economic importance, such as agriculture or mining, but they were usually domestic servants or personal attendants. The slave was, in fact, a subordinate member of his master's household. His maintenance was his master's responsibility, and if he died sonless it was incumbent on the master to perform funeral and commemorative rites for the welfare of his soul. According to most lawbooks, a slave's property ultimately belonged to his master, and he might be bought, sold, loaned or given away; but master's had no rights over the lives of their slaves, and were not allowed to abandon them in old age, as was done in many ancient civilizations. "A man may go short himself or stint his wife and children, but never his slave, who does his dirty work for him."[5] Some lawbooks even limit the right of a master to give corporal punishment to his slave. "A wife, a son, a slave, a servant or a younger brother may, when they do wrong, be beaten with a rope or a cane, but only on the back and not on the head. If a man beats them otherwise he should be punished as a thief."[6] The main mission of a slave is commended by the textbooks as a pious act, and in any case a person enslaved for debt became free when he had paid the debt with his labour.

The *Arthashastra,* in many ways more liberal than the religious lawbooks, lays down regulations appreciably milder than those we have outlined. The sale of children into slavery is explicitly forbidden except in dire emergency. Slaves are entitled to own and inherit property, and to earn money freely in their spare time. Slaves of the upper classes cannot be forced to perform defiling duties. The chastity of slave-girls is protected – the master who rapes a slave-girl must set her free and pay her compensation, and if she has a child by her master, even with her own consent, both mother and child became free. A promise made by a man in dire necessity to sell himself and his family into slavery is not binding.

The humane regulations of the *Arthashastra* probably unique in the records of any ancient civilization, are perhaps survivals of Mauryan laws, and it is therefore not surprising that Megasthenes declared that there was no slavery in India. India, unlike most ancient civilizations was never economically dependent on slavery; the labour, farm worker, and craftsman alike were normally free men, and the Latifundia of the Roman magnate had no counterpart in India. Slave markets are not mentioned in early sources, and though provision was made for the sale of slaves they do not seem at first to have been a regular article of commerce. In the early centuries of the Christian era, however, there was trade in slave-girls between India and the Roman empire in both directions, and slave markets existed in the 16th century Vijayanagara empire.

There are numerous references in literature to slaves being badly treated by their master's, and the slave's lot must have been often a very unhappy one; but he was probably better off in India than in most parts of the ancient world. Indeed in many contexts it would seem that the word *dāsa* implies rather a bondman or serf than a chattel slave.

The Hindu social order was complicated by other features which had no original relationship to class or caste, but were roughly harmonized with them. These are the institutions of *gotra* and Pravara, which were in existence in late Vedic times, and probably earlier, and are very important to the orthodox Brāhmiṇ to this day.

The original meaning of *gotra* is "a cowshed, or are a herd of cowshed," in the *Atharva Veda,* the word first appears with the meaning of "a clan," which has retained a special connotation. Some ancient Indo-European peoples, such as the Romans, had exogamous clans, as well as generally endogamous tribes. It may well be that the *gotra* system is a survival of Indo-European origin which had developed specially Indian features.

Gotra as it existed in historical times was primarily a Brāhmiṇic institution, adopted rather half-heartedly by other twice-born classes, and hardly affecting the lower orders. All Brāhmiṇs were believed to have descended from one or other ṛṣi, or legendary seer, after whom the *gotras* were named. The religious literature generally speaks of seven or eight primeval *gotras,* those of *Kasyapa, Vasistha, Bhrgu, Gautama, Bharadvaja, Atri* and *Viswamitra,* the eighth *gotra,* that of Agastya, is named after the sage who is said to have taken the Vedic religion beyond the Vindhyas, and who is a sort of patron saint of the Dravidians. His name may have been added to those of the original seven as the South became progressively Āryanized. These primeval *gotras* were multiplied in later times by the inclusion of the names of many other ancient sages.

Though the *gotras* perhaps evolved from local units within the Āryan tribe, they had quite lost their tribal character by historical times, and Brāhmiṇ from the furthest parts of India and of different caste groups might have the same *gotra.* The chief importance of *gotra* was in connection with marriage, which was forbidden to persons of the same *gotra.*

The position was further complicated by Pravara. In the Brāhmins daily worship he mentioned not only the name of the founder of his *gotra,* but also the names of certain other sages who were believed to be the remote ancestors of his family. The formula generally contained three or five names, and set up a further bar to marriage, for the same names would occur in the Pravaras of families of other *gotras.* According to the custom of some *gotras,* marriage was impossible with a member of another *gotra* having one Pravara name in common, while others barred intermarriage only when there were two common names in the Pravaras. Thus, matrimonial choice was much restricted, especially when in the Middle Ages the endogamous caste system was fully established.

The social prestige of the Brāhmiṇs led to the respectable classes adopting a *gotra* system of some sort. Kṣatriyas and Vaisyas, took the same *gotra* names as the Brāhmiṇs; their *gotras,* however, were not based on the claim to descent from an ancient sage, but merely on the *gotra* of the family of Brāhmiṇs which traditionally performed their domestic rituals. As imposed on non-Brāhmaṇic families the system was quite artificial. Non-Brāhmaṇ families were also expected to take the Pravaras of their domestic priests, but this rule counted for little. The real *gotras* of the Kshatriyas and Vaisyas, were secular *(laukika)* ones, founded by legendary eponymous ancestors. Legal literature takes little note of these secular *gotras,* but numerous references in inscriptions show that the term was used in the sense of "sect" or "clan," and that many non-Brāhmiṇ *gotras* existed which do not occur in the lists of any of the lawbooks.

Early lawgivers take a comparatively liberal view of breaches of *gotra* regulations. A man marrying a woman of the same *gotra* must perform a *cāndrāyana* penance, and observe fast of a month's duration, and henceforth maintain his wife as he would a sister;[8] no stigma attaches to the child of such a marriage. With ruthless logic, however, later jurists declare that this applies only to inadvertent marriage within the *gotra;* when the relationship is known, the sin is equivalent to that of incest.

Notes and References

1. Oldenberg, H., *Zur Geschichte des indischen kastenwesens,* XXIX Vol. li, 267.
2. Senart, E., *Les Castes dons l'Inde,* new ed., Paris, 1927.
3. Shama Shastri, *Evolution of Castes,* Madras, 1916.
4. Bodas, *Historical Survey of Indian Logic,* XVIII, Vol. xix.
5. Dasgupta, *Yoga Philosophy,* Calcutta, 1930.
6. Deussen, P., *Das System des Vedanta,* 3rd ed., 1920, Leipzig.
7. Pargiter, F.E., *Ancient Indian Historical Tradition,* Oxford, 1922.
8. Papson, E.J., *Ancient India,* Cambridge, 1914, and others. *The Cambridge History of India.* Vol. I. *Ancient India,* Cambridge, 1922.

9

Buddhist Religion and Abolition of Untouchability

The founder of Buddhist religion Gautama Buddha was born in 600 BC during which in conjunction with important economical and social changes, the speculation and preachings of saints and erudites came in sight. Every philosopher is affected by the trends of his time. In 600 BC generally all thinkers and philosophers were sunk in speculation of Soul, World and God. The number of doctrines as well as thinkers was equal. On the contrary, there were many philosophers and thinkers who were opposing the notions of Soul, World and God having been continued for years and for common public-life, were proving their uselessness. These philosophers made the common public-life their main target and were paying more attention towards their troubles. Out of them, Gautama Buddha became the most successful and renowned philosopher who emphasised on the problem of misery and its prevention. He has said himself, "I emphasise more only on prevention of misery."

Gautama Buddha was not in favour of blank literacy and regarded the movement of logicians on many philosophical problems to be thoroughly investigated, useless. The questions whether this world is immortal or mortal' finite or infinite, soul and body are one or different and Buddha exists posthumously or not, were established by Buddha avyawcat (secret). In Chulmalvkya Prett Scutt, Clearing the doubt of son Malukya, Breedha said, "O *Malukya putt,* the view and belief that universe is immortal or mortal, cannot help in religious practice. If it is believed that world is immortal, then also no freedom from old age, death, mourning or crying is available. Thus, despite our belief that world is not immortal, body and soul are one or they are different and that Buddha is regenerated after death or not, birth, old age, death and crying are always present. So, *Malukyaputt,* I did not go in their discussion because that discussion cannot bring any sort of stability in celebacy. That discussion would not create asceticism, prevent sin and help in achieving peace, intellect, enlightenment and salvation."[2] When Proshthhavad asked, "Why has God kept it secret?" Buddha replied, "Proshthavad, this is neither meaningful nor religious, nor useful for celebacy nor it is for indifference, alienation, prevention, patience, enlightenment and salvation. That is why I have not defined that."[3] In reality, if the man afflicted from misery, getting entangled in questions of philosophy, is not stupid, then what is he? In his very childhood, Buddha suffered from mother-loss. On getting mature, he found that every man is victim of birth, old age, death, crying, conceit, etc. Due to malice and thirst, dreadful sight of deception and war is produced. Tribal collectiveness, equality and brotherhood are replaced by personal selfishness, greed, hatred and war. The strifes are going on between kingdoms and the men. The kingdoms are breaking the tribes and destroying their remains completely. In the name of caste and lineage, the high-low, touchable-untouchable and social condition of Brahmana and *Vrishal* are becoming strong and tribal equality and brotherhood are breaking up. All people are suffering from grief and searching the way for redemption therefrom. Innumerable untouchables and backward people have been separated from the community on the base of caste and culture and they have achieved neither a respected life nor do they have any opportunity to improve their life and develop. Having dispossessed them of property, respect and knowledge, they have been made slaves, servants and ironsmiths. On seeing this condition, Gautama Buddha says, "Oh, how dreadful the fire is? All are burning. The eyes are burning. The beauty is burning. The science produced by eyes and beauty is burning. Which fire is burning all of them? They are burning by the fire of desire, malice and delusion. They are burning from the consequences like birth, old age, grief, crying, suffering, conceit, etc."[4] Therefore, he inspired the man to know the answers of misery related questions and not to illustrate the philosophical problems. According to him, the objective of philosophy is 'cessation of sufferings'. Illustrating this fact by an example beautifully, he has said in *Chulmalukya Putt Sutt.* "O Malukya Putt, if any man tosses due to piercing of poisonous arrow in his body and trustworthy friends call a surgeon but if the patient says, "I won't let him touch my body as long as I don't get the answers to these questions, "Who shot me an arrow? Was the Brahmina or Kshatriya, Vaishya or Sudra, dark or fair? What kind of bow he had? What material was the cord of bow made of?", etc., then O *Malukya Putt,* in that condition he would die without getting answers to these question."[5] Therefore, Gautama Buddha threw a bird's eye-view on the complicated problems (philosophical and socio-economical) of his age and undertook Buddhistic movement.

It is said that Buddha dedicated himself for the goal of *bahujan hitay, bahujan sukhay* (welfare and happiness of people), and human welfare and achievement of comforts. In Sarnath, imparting the first preaching of his religion, spent one year and in the end of the year, leaving that place, addressing thus his sixty disciples (in 4 months), he said, "*Bhikshus,* wander about for the benefit and comforts of many people, commiserating on universe, and happiness of divine men. Don't go two together. I am going to Uruvela, a military village, for religious preaching, too."[6] He made *shankha* sound against four-class system, caste-variation and untouchability prevalent in contemporary society. He shivered while seeing unequal life system loaded on Chandal, Pukkas, Vrishal, etc., untouchable species and celebrating jubilation of humanity, he said, "O disciples, just as big rivers, irrespective of their number, Ganga, Yamuna, Achiravati, Saryu, Mahi, etc., reach the ocean, they abandon their old names and achieve a single name, 'ocean', similarly, O disciples, these four tribes, Kshatriya, Brahmina, Vaisya and Sudra leave their houses by described rules of Buddha and enter the house-deprived position, they sacrifice their old names and lineage and their one name remains, *bhikshus,* who are the followers of Buddha of *Sakya* lineage."[7] The famous scholar, Ris Davids said, "First thing is that as long as their religion and group and confederation are concerned, and on which they had a complete control, they neglected all special benefits and facilities produced by birth, occupation and social reputation completely and finished all interruptions and inabilities created as a result of religious or social pollution related desired rules."[8]

Attempts made in Buddhist Religion for abolishing untouchability

It becomes clear from all these contexts that Gautama Buddha also concentrated on social diseases in the establishment age of his religion and philosophy, and against those diseases, conducted the strife. Now we should see that against untouchability and caste-variation how the struggle of the Buddhist religion was and what attempts Buddha and his religion made for the abolition of these social maladies.

1. The Elements of Abolition of Untouchability in Buddhist Philosophy

Although we have seen above that Gautama Buddha had indifference for spiritual and philosophical talks, yet he developed a great speculation mode which provided relief to the man afflicted from vanishing tribal equality and freedom and replaced real suffering and pain by universal misery and spiritual principle. Then first of all, we should discover the elements of abolition of untouchability and caste-variation in Buddhist philosophy. It can't be possible that the logic given and movement begun against caste-variation and high-low, have no theoretical or philosophical base.

In the long period from 600 B.C. to 200 C., many branches of Buddha philosophy had developed. Although in posterior Buddhist philosophy, philosophical notions are very important, yet they seem to be different and opposing in many talks from initial Buddhist philosophy. In spite of this, *Chaar Arya Satya, Prateetyasamutpad, Anityata, Anarmavad,* etc., are many philosophical proofs which are professed by all branches, does not matter if their illustrations are different. Therefore, keeping an eye on subsequent the Buddhist philosophy, we should investigate primary Buddhist philosophy to see as to how long the elements of prevention of untouchability are present there.

Karn states, "When Buddha achieved previous enlightenment, he prepared two precepts and distributed among all. These are *Chaar Arya Satya* and *Prateetyasamutpad,* having twelve links. They were the fundamental truths of his preachings."[9] First one is related to the problem of suffering and second was an illustration of a series of reason and consequence the objective of which was to illuminate as to what was the root of suffering or vice. The saint, Rahul Sankrityayan, has written, *"Anitya, dukha, anatma* (transient, suffering, soulless), it includes the entire philosophy of

Buddha".[10] Whether there be *Prateetyasamutpad* or *anitya, dukha, anatm,* all these philosophies are lying close together to four Arya truths of Buddha. The suffering, suffering-community, suffering-prevention and suffering and way of prevention, only are the four Arya truths which are called by him 'Arya-truth'—supreme truths. These are the extract of the Buddhist religon and in their absence even the imagination of Buddhist religion is impossible. Clearing their importance, Buddha himself said, "By these only, disinterest, destruction of desires, end of sufferings, mental piece, knowledge, intellect and salvation can be possible."[11]

The Four Arya Truths

Then, first of all, we have to investigate these four Arya-truths only to see whether the caste-variation and opposing elements of untouchablity are present in them or not?

(a) First Arya-truth. In his famous sermon of *Ammachakka Pavattanama Sutt,* Gautama Buddha, elucidating *dukh arya-satya,* said, "O *bhikshus,* in connection of suffering, it is absolute truth, birth is suffering; old age is suffering; sickness is suffering, death is suffering; meeting on unloving is suffering; departure from beloved is suffering; not achieving one's desire is suffering; in brief all five passion are suffering."[12] Portraying the miseries, he said, "Since a long time you tolerated the death of parents, son and daughter...tolerated the wretchedness of enjoyment and disease, departure from beloved, meeting unloving, weeping and wailing, the tears you caused to fall, are more than the water of the seas."[13] Buddha says that those feelings we believe to be pleasant, are painful. The pain is there for achieving a happy feeling. If somehow that thing appearing to represent the comfort, is achieved, then also the fear of losing that thing and worry is always present. Therefore, he said, "The comfort creates fear.[14] Loss of matters of sensual comforts also creates sorrow.[15] Entire world is schorcing by the fire, then where is the opportunity to celebrate the gaiety?[16] It is clear from the aforesaid explanation of suffering by Gautama Buddha that on one side, the suffering is generalised or universalised, on the other hand, the real problem of grief was changed into an ideal problem. Untouchable tribes must have been breathing a sigh of relief that poverty, insult, suffering created by expulsion from society and education, and dispossession of wealth are sufferings as they saw in those sorrows created by departure from beloved. Whether be king or beggar, touchable Brahmina, Kshatriya, Vaisya or Sudra tribes or untouchable *Chandal, Pukkas, Vrishal* etc., all are equally victims of sorrow created by birth, old age, death, war, meeting unloving and departing from beloved. When all are afflicted from pain, what is the need of being more sad by untouchability? Untouchability is just like other social, economical and physical sufferings. Hereby untouchable species must have been satisfied definitely. That is, seeing the happiness, prosperity, education and social respect of touchable high tribes, *Brahmina, Kshatriya* and *Vaisya*, may not understand themselves contemptible and inadmissible. This comfort is poisonous sweets of matters. Buddha said, "The beauty, word, smell, taste and touch of these five senses, eyes, ears, nose, tongue and skin respectively, achieved by the man, is called by me the poisonous sweets of matters. For these matters only, a king with another, Kshtriya with Kshatriya, Vaisya with Vaisya, mother with son and vice-versa, father with son, sister with brother and friend with friend fights. What does not happen for these matters?—Brawling and scuffle take place, weapons are used and people are also killed, otherwise, the pain has to be born till death. For this poisonous sensual enjoyment only, man commits dreadful crimes by heart, voice and body in this universe and after death is attainable to misery."[17]

What was the achievement of desire for untouchable tribes? The people of untouchable tribe wanted back their lost property and respect. They wanted to get the right of learning and teaching too. They wanted to be rulers like Aryans and progress economically. But in contemporary system, the fulfillment of these desires was impossible and therefore, this was the suffering for them. Had they achieved these desired goals, they would have been sad again by the fear of losing them. Then what was the use of their achievement? Buddha's this statement must have definitely affected the ruined and untouchables. "A youngman earns his living by business, agriculture or service. In his profession, he has to bear massive problems, then also he attempts day and night to achieve the material of sensual enjoyment. Despite of performing such labour, if he does not attain his desired item, he, becoming mournful, gets occupied with senseless thoughts. If he achieves fame in his efforts and desired article, he is worried day and night lest that article should be looted by some wicked king or thief, be destroyed by fire or flood, or caused harm by his friends having enmity. His mind always remains suspicious and afflicted from these thoughts and if his doubt comes true, his sorrow knows no limits."[18]

Due to violation of discipline of Aryan four-class system and reason of undeveloped living and culture, untouchables were seenin contemptible form, boycotted and separated from all social sections. There was Aryan superiority and feeling of self-conceit. Gautama Buddha, having generalised or universalised misery, attacked on this supremacy and pride of Aryans. He proved by extensive explanation of suffering that there is no difference between the sufferings of untouchable tribes and Aryan Brahmins, Kshatriya and Vaisya-Sudra and that untouchables and touchables, both are equally victims of suffering. By this universalisation of misery, Aryan prominence received an assault and their views against untouchable tribes got changed, behaviour became humble and hate was reduced. In a *sutt,* Buddha has said about the suffering of Aryans and untouchables, "I see in this world that wealthy people have collected many items and property but they do not give anything to others out of that and this is their mistake. With a great curiosity, they keep on adding plenty of resources and augmenting their luxuries day by day. The king, although has won all kingdoms of this earth, and established his rule everywhere, his hunger would not be satisfied and he would try to achieve whatever is beyond the sea. The king and many other people become the morsel of death with their unfulfilled desires and relatives, friends, companions, none can save this dying man and his successors possess his property. But one who dies, does not take away with him any money and property, nor do his wife, son, wealth or kingdom go with him. He achieves only the fruits of his deeds."[19] It is not possible that this explanation of suffering did not affect the Aryan rulers and their cultural superiority.

Thus, having defined first *Arya Satya* (truth), that is, suffering, extensively, Buddha proved that the happiness is temporary and changes into unhappiness finally. All things are transient and variable, and therefore, everything should be counted as suffering. He changed real contemporary problems in an ideal one and linked external happenings with the internal changes of man. Consequently, the sorry plight of the common man of that age was changed into plight to fit to be investigated thoroughly. Now people of untouchable tribe could not give blame to the Aryan-system for their miserable plight, but by leaving their undeveloped living and culture, religious performance, witchery and body related physical speculation, could be bound to think over ideal suffering and problem fit to be investigated thoroughly. They got such ideal speculation and problem which was totally different from the religious ceremonies and culture of their enemy class and Aryans. Before this ideal problem and suffering, social-economical problems and hurdles were nothing and so became subsidiary. In conjunction with, this ideal suffering, untouchables and touchables were able to stand on the same footing. None was greater or smaller nor was anyone high or low.

(b) Second Arya truth—dukh-samudaya. Gautama Buddha, talked about his second *Arya* truth, *dukh-samudaya,* that is, in connection of reasons of suffering extensively. He has analysed the reason of suffering through a doctrine which is called *Patichayasamutpad* in Pali and *Prateetyasamutpad* (The Doctrine of Dependent Origination) in Sanskrit. *Prateetyasamutpad* is made of two words—*Prateetya* and *Samutpad. Prateetya* means due to presence of one item, origin of another one, that is, on arrival of one, second one is originated. Thus, the doctrine of *Prateetyasamutpad* is based on dependent origination. Rahul Sanskrityayan has said, "Although Buddha does not believe the dependent origination of continuous descendent but yet he believes that due to this, that happens and after the destruction of one, another is originated. The same principle is called by Buddha *Prateetyasamutpad*".[20]

In Buddhist philosophy, the doctrine of *Prateetyasamutpad* is very important. This is the base of Buddhist philosophy and later cannot be imagined in the absence of former. Buddha himself has said in this connection. "One who sees *Prateetyasamutpad,* sees religion; one who sees religion, sees *Prateetyamutpad.* This is five passions (beauty, agony, knowledge, influence of previous birth, learning) *Prateetyasamutpann* (produced as a continuous flow)."[21] In *Mahavagga,* the extract of this doctrine is given thus: "Then in the first quarter of night, Buddha paid attention directly and reversely on series of 'reason'. Ignorance creates influence of previous birth, later consciousness, personality, personality six areas (six senses of perception), these six areas touch, touch knowledge,

knowledge desire, desire affection, affection existence or fear, existence birth, birth old age and death, agony, pain, misery, depression and disappointment. This is the origin of this entire *dukh-samudaya.* Then, by destruction of ignorance, that is, by complete desertion of libido, influence of previous birth is destroyed, hereby consciousness is perished, by destruction of consciousness personality comes to an end, by end of personality six percepts of senses are destroyed, by this destruction touch is perished, then knowledge becomes dead, by death of knowledge greed is devastated, by devastation of greed affection is no more, by absence of affection existence disappears, by disappearance of existence personality is destroyed, by destruction of personality birth does not take place and finally the birth, old age, death, agony, misery, discouragement and frustration are destroyed. Thus, this entire *dukh-samudaya* is destroyed.

It is clear from the aforesaid facts that old age and death, that is, the reason of suffering is *jaati.* Taking birth is called *jaati.* Had the man not taken birth, he would not have faced worldly sufferings. The reason of *jaati* is *bhav* or existence. The man has to take birth because the inclination to take birth is present in him. This inclination is called *bhav*. The reason of *bhav* is attachment. To be fond of worldly items is called 'attachment'. The reason of attachment is 'greed' which is longing for word, touch, etc., matters. Herefore only, the man rushes blindly behind worldly matters. The reason of 'greed' is agony which is called previous sense of perception. By the senses, the man achieves happy feeling which keeps his desires alive. The reason of 'agony' is 'touch' which is created by the contact of items with the senses. The reason of 'touch' is six areas. The addition of five senses of perception and mind is called 'six areas'. Five senses are external organs and mind is internal organ. These six senses contact with matters and 'touch' is created. The reason of six senses is 'personality' which is the group of 'mind' and body. The senses reside in body and mind. Had personality not existed, the advent of these six senses would not have taken place. The reason of personality is learning and the reason of learning is *sanskar.* Sanskar means to manage. Sanskar is accepted as the influence of previous birth. Due to the actions of previous life, *sanskar* is formed. The reason of *sanskar* is lack of knowledge or confused perception. To understand unreal thing to be real, unhappy to be happy and soulless to be soul, is ignorance. Due to reason of not knowing the real identity of things, ignorance, having reflected, constructs *sanskar*. Ignorance is the fundamental reason of all sufferings and series of dependent origination of *Prateetyasamutpad* concludes here. Here are twelve links and first is *'jara-maran'* (old age and death) or *dukh* (suffering) and last is *avidhya* (ignorance). Twelve series of *Prateetyasamutpad* are pervaded in past, present and future lives. *Avidha* or *sanskar* are related to previous life, *jara-maran* (suffering) and *jaati* (birth) to future and rest learning, personality, six senses, touch and agony, greed, affection or existence to present. The advent of series of dependent origination takes place between the past, present and future. Past is the reason of present and present that of future. This doctrine is also called the cycle of birth and death because this decides the cycle of birth and death of man. It is also called the cycle of religion because it takes place of religion. *Prateetyasamutpad* is also called the twelve sources because it analyses the twelve links to find out the reason of suffering each of which is called *nidan* (diagnosis). This doctrine is also called the cycle of world and the cycle of existence. It is clear from the aforesaid explanation of *dukh-samudaya* or *Prateetyasamutpad* that the human life is action based. This doctrine of dependent origination of twelve links of *Prateetyasamutpad* is widespread in the form of dependent origination in past, present and future. The present is the fruit of previous actions and future the fruit of present actions. Therefore, this doctrine establishes the *karamvad* (Mimasa school of philosophy which attaches importance to action). According to this doctrine, everything happens according to reason. On destruction of reason, the thing is destroyed too and changed into other form. Therefore, *Prateetyasamutpad* establishes *anityavad* (the theory of perishableness) which is later changed into *shanikvad* (the theory of moment). When everything in this world is momentary, the imagination of soul in form of persistent power is impossible. Therefore, by this doctrine permanent or lasting soul is denied and *anatmvad* (the theory of no-self) is established. According to Buddha, this world is managed by the rule of *Prateetyasmutpad* and the entire world is ruled by origin and destruction. Then to determine God who is permanent and constant, the creator of this destructible and variable universe, is unreasonable. Therefore, by the doctrine of *dukh-samudaya anishwarvad* (Atheism) is established.

Thus, we see that *Prateetyasamutpad* is base of Buddhist religion and philosophy which professes the universe and human life based on *karamvad, shanikvad, anatmvad* and *anishwarvad.* Now we should see whether these elements affect high-low, caste-variation and untouchability or not.

***(c) Karamvad* and untouchability.** In Buddha'time, the principle reason of origin of suffering is supposed to be action. In Buddhist philosophy also, action was clearly accepted as the immediate reason of universe. In frequent repetition of a line of *Nikaya,* it is said, "Action only is owned by creatures. It is their inheritance, lineage, kinsmen and support. Action only divides creatures, makes them inferior and supreme".[23]

But the *karam* of Buddhist philosophy was totally different from that of Vedas, Upanishads, and doctrine of non-scriptures. In Vedic doctrine, action is regarded the merchandise of a doer having the form of creature and invisible power created by him, but in ancient Buddhist contexts, action is not supposed to be religion of any *anuvartman* doer.[24] The philosophy of Vedic-Aryan culture professed four-class system and said that the Brahmins are born of the mouth of God and Sudras of His feet. *Brahmanoustra* Mukhmasidbahu *Rajanya Krit Uru Tadasya Yadhaishyah Padbhyam Shudro Ajayat.*[25] Therefore, Brahmins are superior and Sudras inferior. Supporters of Vedic religion also said that due to virtue and vice of previous birth, one is born in Brahmin lineage and Sudra or untouchable tribe respectively. On the contrary, it is stated in *Sanyukta Nikaya* that action is not performed by soul. This body is neither yours nor of others. It is just an old action. By regarding creature and body neither one nor different, chastity does not reside. This is not done by soul or others. It is originated due to ignorance and in absence of ignorance, body will be destroyed".[26] In Buddhist philosophy, the base of action is greed and greed, on the one hand, is based on ignorance and on the other, on the experience of happiness. Buddha regarded the extract of action the mental determination or mental decision of doing action which was called consciousness. He has said, "O *bhikshus,* I have called consciousness the action, action is done consciously, by body, by speech, by mind".[27]

In *Sanyukta Nikaya,* Buddha says, "I do not tell about the cessation of suffering without reporting the fruit of the collective actions and done consciously. For everyone cessation of suffering is possible only on the actions getting weak which are performed knowingly".[28]

It is clear from the aforesaid explanation of *karamvad* that *karamvad* of Buddhist philosophy is absolutely different from Vedic, non-scripture, Brahmana and *Upanishadic karamvad. Karamvad* of Vedic, non-scripture, etc., is based on 'soul' and vice-virtue, regeneration four-class system or genealogical action and god or oblation, etc., but in Buddhist philosophy, *karamvad* is *'anatmvad* or *anishvar* (not done by others)' and its fundamental reason is greed. It is born due to ignorance and will be destroyed by obstruction of ignorance.

Thus, by Buddhist *karamvad,* regeneration of soul, previous actions, action in god-formed system and four-class action, and genealogical action were denied by which caste-variation, high-low feeling and view of untouchability received a violent attack. Attacking on actions of previous birth, Gautama Buddha said, "If it be believed that whatever is the agony of happiness-unhappiness or indignity, is due to consequence of previous birth, then O *bhikshus,* those who are murderers, thieves, immoral, liers, backbiters, harsh-spoken, chatterers, greedy, culprits and possessing heretic vision, might be so as a result of previous birth. Therefore, O *bhikshus,* those who believe that everything happens as a consequence of actions of previous birth, then according to their doctrine, they should not have personal desire or personal effort. They would not have to perform any task nor would they be indifferent to any work".[29] Denying action or variation based four-class system, lineage or tribe, and birth, Buddha has said, "Neither by matted hair, nor by lineage or birth anybody becomes Brahmin. One having truth and religion, is pious and Brahmin. I do not call anyone Brahmin just because he is born of Brahmin mother. I call one having as well as desiring nothing, Brahmin".[30] Opposing high-low and untouchability based on caste and birth, Buddha has said in *Vasal Sutt,* "By birth only one is neither Vrishal or Chandal nor Brahmana. Action makes one Chandal and action Brahmin".[31] Untouchable tribes did not believe in Vedic oblations or religious performances and they were *lokayats* professing necromancy and *mantras*. They were against

Vedas and oblations. It is said in couplet of Charvak doctrine of *Sarvdarshan,*

"Pashushchennihatah Swarga Jyotishtome Gamishyati. Swa Pita Yajmanen Tatra Kasmanna Hinsyate. ... Trayo Vedasya Kartaro Bhagddhurt Nishacharah.

That is, if the animal killed in *agnishtom yagya* (a ceremony in which oblations are given to fire), attains heaven, why does he who performs sacrifice, not kill his father? ....There are three doers of Vedas, flatterer, wicked and demon." Gautama Buddha said too that by animal-killing in oblation, one performing sacrifice, practises inauspicious *kama-vacha-mansa* (body, speech, mind) actions and hence unlucky. He has said in a *sutt,* "One who kindles fire for oblation and stands the post to which the victim which is to be immolated, is tied up, uplifts three inauspicious suffering-producing weapons. What are they? They are bodily, verbal and mentals arms. One who starts oblation, thinks that so many bulls, calves, heifers, he-goats and sheep be killed. Thus, first of all, he uplifts suffering-producing unlucky mind-arms. Thereafter, to kill these animals by his speech, he himself starts killing them and finally uplifts inauspicious suffering-producing body arms.

"O Brahmin, these three fires are fit to be abandoned. They are: sex, malice and infatuation. One subdued by sex, performs *kaya-vacha-mansa* sin and gets posthumous catastrophe"...[32] In *Abhidharamkosh,* generally three kinds of actions are described, auspicious, inauspicious and secret. Here Buddha has defined auspicious and inauspicious actions repeatedly.[33] Explaining inauspicious actions, Gautama Buddha has said, "O houeholders, what are three kinds of irreligious practices performed by body? 1. Someone murders, is involved in creating horrible atmosphere, torturing poors and beating, or 2. Steals, commodity which does not belong to him, whether present in vilage or forest, takes away without asking its owner, or 3. Commits infidelity, performs adultery with woman defended by parents, sister, husband or trusted ones. Thus, performs various irreligious practices by body."

"And O householders, what are the four kinds of irreligious practices performed by speech? 1. Any man lies. He is witnessed in committee, assembly, confidential board or royal palace that whatever you know, tell. What he does not know, he tells about that he knows. And what he does not see, he says that he has seen. Thus, for himself, for someone else or for little achievement, he lies intentionally, or 2. He backbites. Having heard these people, to create difference in them, he tells them all. Thus, he divides people living unitedly and excites disputants. He enjoys in promoting dispute and holds talks to promote dispute, or 3. He brawls. He speaks words, full of wickedness, harsh, pungent, heart-piercing, furious and disturbing happines, or 4. He chatters unnecessarily. He speaks on inappropriate time and talks not materialized after mending them. His speech is irreligious, against propriety, unworthy of attention, inelegant, uselessly extensive and harmful. Thus, by speech four kinds of irreligious practices are performed."

"And, O householders, what are three kinds of irreligious mental practices? 1. One speculates about money of someone else. He wants to achieve the sources of wealth of another person. Or 2. He has malicious mind. He thinks these animals be killed, destroyed. Or, 3. He possesses sceptic vision. He is occupied with atheist notions of absence of donation, religion, fruits of vice-virtue, this world, the other world, etc. Thus, various types of irrefigious practices are performed by mind."[34] Thus, murder, theft and infidelity, are three inauspicious body actions. Untruth, back-biting, brawling and unnecessary chattering are four irreligious speech practices. Greed of money of others, desire of their destruction and miscreant view, are three irreligious mental practices. These are ten inauspicious actions and being free from them are auspicious actions. Therefore, there are ten auspicious actions opposite to aforesaid ten inauspicious actions.[35]

Karamvad is established on the base of inauspicious, auspicious and secret actions in *Buddhist* philosophy. Secret actions, related to universe, soul and palingenesis are ten in numbers too. Having known these secret actions as useless and unfriendly, Buddha kept silent on questions related to aforesaid three subjects. In conjunction with, Buddha, explaining in auspicious and auspicious actions completely, defined *karam* as the base of being high and low, superior and inferior, touchable and untouchable and Brahmin and Chandal. The base of touchability and untouchability, and superiority and inferiority is inauspiciousn and auspicious actions and not Aryan-non-Aryan caste-variation, coming into existence of tribe and four-class system. That is why Buddha, having seen the situation of high-low and untouchability prevalent in contemporary society, says, "Do not ask tribe, ask one's practice only. Just as fire is created by wood, similarly, the man of inferior lineage becomes steady, wise and virtuous saint."[36] One performing auspicious actions, is called Brahmin by Gautama Buddha. He has said, "I call Brahmin one who has renounced the world and who has become free from all sorts of bonds. One who has become fear-free and indifferent to worldly attachment and love, I call Brahmin."[37] He says further, "One who has deserted malice and contempt, whose nature is cool and who is devoid of distress, such world-victor brave man, I call Brahmana."[38] The man free from mental-verbal-bodily inauspicious actions, is called Brahmana. Buddha has said, "One who sins neither by mind nor by speech nor by body; and has controlled mind, speech and body, I call Brahmana".[39] Thus, the man clung in inauspicious actions is called untouchable, Chandal and Vrishal. Buddha has said, "One who is hot-tempered, hostile, accuses meritorious persons, possesses sceptic view and illusive, is actually Vrishal, that is, Chandal."[40] Those murdering creatures, committing infidelity, robbing villages and cities, telling lies and due to self-conceit, praise themselves and condemn others, are Chandal, untouchable or *Vrishal.*"[41]

Thus, it is clear that Buddhist *Karamvad* made a violent attack on original beliefs of untouchability, high-low and caste-variation. Untouchable tribes were considered low and inferior while *Brahmins, Kshatriyas, Vaisya* and *Sudra* tribes considered themselves superior and high. Buddhist *Karamvad* called this system and concept prevalent in society based on birth and tribe, wrong, denied and divided the people of all tribes and sects in superior and and non-superior and high-low on the base of auspicious and inauspicious actions. Second important thing is that four-class people considered the labour performed by untouchable tribes contemptible and their own duties supreme. But *Buddhist* Karamvad did not regard living duties by performing labour and toil hateable whether they be performed by four-class people or Chandal, Pulkas, etc., Vrishal or untouchable people. According to *Buddhist Karamvad,* those committing ten kinds of inauspicious and auspicious actions, are mean, inferior and contemptible, and Brahmins and superior people respectively, irrespective of their belonging to untouchable tribe, *Brahmin, Kshatriya, Vaisya* or tribe called *Sudra*. Third and last significant thing is that the base of culture of untouchable tribes was hard work and based on that material rituals accompanied by atheism, theory of no-self and necromancy on which the notion of world-origin was based. Due to struggling for these cultural thoughts considered backward and inferior by people of Aryan culture and opposing Aryan-culture, they had to become untouchable. In Buddhist *Karamvad,* some divine power and propagation of soul is denied whereby thoughts of untouchables would have got strength. In conjunction with, oblation activities and theory of deity, symbol or supremacy of Aryan-culture, were also denied and categorised as inferior thoughts and actions. Hereby the thoughts of Aryan for untouchables got improved and high-low, and caste-variation reduced to a great extent. Necromancy and witchery (illusion) were also criticised under the category of inauspicious actions by which untouchables got an opportunity to abandon their thoughts and achieved superiority by committing auspicious actions. That is, by calling both *Vedic* religious ceremonies and religious celebrations of untouchable tribes, inferior actions, both cultures and their people were brought on same level and *Vedic* prominence received a shock. In conjunction with, denial of godly power and theory of soul, untouchable culture (*lokayat* culture) got strength.

2. Anityavad (the Theory of Moment) and Untouchability

According to *Prateetyasamutpad,* every thing or incident is based on dependent origination. When reason is destroyed, the existence of thing or incident is destroyed too. Therefore, all things of universe are destructible, perishable, temporary and mortal. Thus, in Buddhist philosophy, the doctrine of *anityavad* (theory of perishableness) has resulted from *Prateetyasamutpad.* Defining this, Buddha has said, "One who can be old, will be old, one who is to die, will die certainly. Something which is destructible, will destroy definitely."[42]

Gautama Buddha, dividing all universal things in senses, volume and metal, has called them perishable.[43] There are five senses: beauty, *vedna, sangya, sanskar* and *vigyan.* Beauty includes four elements: earth, water, air and fire. *Vedna* is the experience of happiness-unhappiness. *Sangya* is knowledge and *sanskar* means longing. *Vigyan* means consciousness of mind. There are twelve volumes including six senses, eyes, ears, nose, tongue, skin and mind. Beauty, word, smell, taste, touch and mind are *vedna, sangya* and *sanskar.* When six senses contact with their matters, six kinds of consciousness are originated and these are: eye-consciousness, ear-consciousness, nose-consciousness, tongue-consciousness, sex-consciousness and mind-consciousness. Thus, there are eighteen metals and these senses, volumes and metals include all universal things. Thus, beauty, that is, *vedna, sangya* and *sanskar* by contacting with earth, water, air and fire, produce *vigyan* which Gautama Buddha has called *anitya sanskrit* or *Prateetyasamutpann* or religion which prevents.[44]

According to *Anityavad,* every thing of world is perishable, destructible, whether it be immoveable or life. Buddha says, "Beauty,...*vedna* ...*sangya* ... *sanskar* ... *vigyan* (these five senses) are not permanent, immortal, unchangeable and this is scholarly (talk). I say same, too. Despite of saying and understanding so, one who does not see or understand, what can I do for such stupid...blind, ignorant man?"[45] This *anityavad* of Buddha was developed into *shanikvad* by his followers and finally into *shunyavad* (nihilism) by Nagarjuna. Everything of universe is not only destructible or perishable but also momentary. Clearing this, Buddha said, "O *Bhikshuon,* this is better that ignorant (men) may assume the body of these four elements as soul (permanent element) but intellectually this is wrong. Why so? This body of four elements is seen present for even one...two... three...four...five...six...seven years but which is called intellect, mind or *vigyan,* also in day and night (by first) second is born, second is destroyed."[46] It is clear from this that this *shanikvad* or *anityavad* is not mere external change (continuous flow) of a single original element but complete destruction of one original element and complete new production (separate flow) of second. Every moment new is born and new is destroyed.

It is clear from the aforesaid explanation of *Anityaval* that (a) all things of universe are perishable or destructible and momentary. (b) Human life and culture of community are destructible and changeable, too. Everyday, every moment is changing. (c) Human consciousness and thoughts also do not always remain same and are destructible and changeable.

Now the question arises as to what was the effect of this *anityavad* on high-low, caste-variation and untouchability prevalent in contemporary social system. Like other universal materials, human life, social system and thoughts were also called perishable and momentary by Buddha. Throwing light on momentariness of body, Buddha said, "This momentary body is the house of disease. This body is to be defeated by rotting. It is unsurprising as the body is *jeevan marnaant* (lives and dies)."[47] That is, human body is destroyed by passing from childhood, youth and old age whether one be untouchable Chandal, Pukkas or touchable Brahmin, Kshatriya or Vaisya. In front of perishableness and momentariness of body, all human beings equal. Transitoriness does not provide any important place or relaxation to Brahmin or Kshatriya called superior tribes. Then why to be proud of such body and to hate untouchable tribes? Gautama Buddha said, "One who prides on such momentary and contemptible body, and disregards others, what can be the reason except his stupidity?"[48] Whether one is born in superior or high lineage or in any distinguished place, whether one is called belonging to low sect or born in unholy place, all are victims of *shanikvad* or *anityavad.* None is bigger or smaller. Buddha says, "Perishableness is neither a religion observed in a city nor *kuldharam* (hereditary rites of Hindus observed in a family). The nature of all human beings and deities is to die one day or the other.[49] The walls of Aryan-non-Aryan, touchable-untouchable and high-low are erected by people for their tribe, family and relatives, and property and respect have been seized from untouchable tribes but their own relatives cannot save them nor can they be defended by those for whom lie was told and sin was committed. Buddha has said, "Neither son nor father nor relative can safeguard. When death comes, neither the people of tribe nor family can be protectors."[50] In this condition, why high-low and what sort of hate for untouchables?

According to *anityavad* or *shanikvad,* all items and human beings of universe are destructible and variable. Then, can the society formed of those very men and materials be permanent? Never, society and culture, concept and thought, whether they are of untouchable tribes or those of four-class people calling themselves supreme, all are changing moment by moment and day by day. One society or organisation is destroying, second is developing. Today what is superior, will be inferior tomorrow and tomorrow another one will be superior and what is inferior today, is not permanent, and tomorrow that will be superior by destroying inferiority. It is said, "What appears to be eternal and permanent, is destructible too. Who appears great, is to be ruined too."[51]

It is clear from the aforesaid data that on one side, by attacking on tribal and cultural haughtiness and superiority of touchable tribes by *anityavad* or *shanikvad* and telling about their destruction, an attempt was made to bring revolutionary change in their thoughts by which the hate prevalent for society and culture of untouchable tribes was reduced and many people became *Baudh-bhikshu.* On the other hand, a new hope that their lowness, pitiableness or awkwardness were temporary and so could be changed, developed in the hearts of untouchable tribes. By this philosophy of perishableness, they understood that the arrogance of touchable tribes is perishable and temporary and that they can also be inferior tomorrow by destroying their superiority.

3. Anatmvad and Untouchability

According to *Prateetyasamutpad* or *dukh-samudaya,* all materials of world are perishable and momentary. Nothing remains same in any two moments, does not matter if we cannot experience the change entered in that material during these two moments directly. Like other substances, soul is destructible and variable too. Although Gautama Buddha, having not presented a straight explanation of this question whether soul is mortal or immortal, believed it to be 'secret', nevertheless, denying soul related beliefs of other communities, his explanation clears his thoughts about soul.

At the time of Buddha, two kinds of soul related concepts were prevalent in society. On one side, there were people who believed that inside and outside the body, there is eternal and immortal conscious power the entry of which makes appear warmth and rational bodily action. When that power leaves body according to actions and enters another body, the abandoned body becomes cool and dead devoid of bodily action. They called this immortal conscious power *atma.*[52] This type of thoughts were believed by Aryan four-class people, *Brahmins, Parivrajak* and preceptors of other doctrines. On the other hand, there were numerous people of non-Aryan culture, viz., *Lokayats,* atheists, Asuras, etc., who believed that there is no soul separate from body, warmth and bodily action are born due to alliance of different elements in body and that due to increase of magnitude of these elements, body becomes frigid or dies. Thus, soul is not any different commodity from body and this is mortal, perishable and dies with the body only.[53] But the founder of Buddhist philosophy, Gautama Buddha, on one hand, permanance of soul and on the other hand, destruction of soul with body, leaving both beliefs, chose the middle path. Buddha tells *Bhikshu* of *Katyayan* lineage, "O *katyayan,* public generally goes upto two edges of theism or atheism. But Buddha, leaving both passages, sermons through middle one."[54] He said, "The soul is not permanent, unchanging material due to main reasons originated by union of five senses—beauty, *vedna, sangya, sanskar* and *vigyan* is a power which like other things of universe, is a flow originating and perishing every moment. This flow is perishable and soulless. Having preached about four Arya-truths to *bhikshus* divided in five categories, Buddha has said, "Therefore, *bhikshus,* by reality and *samyak* (complete) knowledge, it should be known that any stationary item past, unknown, reproduced; in, of or outside body; coarse, thin, inferior, excellent, ulterior, near, all that is not mine, I am not that and that is not my soul. O *bhikshuon,* the scholar knowing thus becomes indifferent to subject of stationary substance (beauty), *vedna, sangya, sanskar* and *vigyan* and becomes free due to alienation."[55]

In Buddhist philosophy, five senses, beauty, *vedna, sangya, sanskar* and *vigyan* are perishable and painful and therefore, the power (soul) produced by union of these five senses, is neither immortal nor mortal, but soulless. On asking by Minander (Milind), Yavan ruler, Nag Sen, Buddhist eclesiast, explaining soullessness, has said, "Just as the name of association of axis, wheels and cords is chariot, similarly, there is no soul except multitude of five senses."[56] In *Chulsachchak-Sutt,* Buddha says, "Beauty is soulless, *vedna* is soulless, *sangya...sanskar...vigyan...* all religions are soulless."[57] Denying the doctrine of soul established by hard labour of Vedic religion and Upanishad, Gautama Buddha said, "What my soul experiences, is subject of experience and here and there, experiences about the subject of (its) good and bad actions, that my soul is permanent, immortal and unchanging, will remain as it is for infinite years—this is little intellect (stupid belief)."[58]

Thus, it is clear that in Buddhist philosophy, soul has no place.

In Vedic culture, Upanishads, etc., soul means an immortal unchanging spirit (soul) different from body which was denied by Buddhist philosophy by calling it false belief little intellect. By tearing prominence of Vedic and Upanishadic self-speculation to pieces and assuming the combined form of this body and mind, originated by the union of aforesaid five senses, a changing spirit or conscious power, Buddhist philosophy favoured untouchable tribes having thoughts of *lokayats* or atheism. People like Asuras, Das, etc. opposing Vedic culture and beliefs, were declared untouchable by Aryan priests and rulers, and expelled from Aryan four-class system. Having opposed the soul related thoughts of Aryan culture, Buddhist philosophy provided the philosophy of *anatmvad* (theory of no-self) which resembles the thoughts of untouchables. Hereby many *Aryans* and learned people developed generosity for untouchable tribes and many became *Bhikshus* and followers of Buddhist religion. Touchables and untouchables were equally attracted by Buddhist religion. It is a different thing that *Lokayats* and atheists did not believe in regeneration while in Buddhist philosophy, it was believed in, not due to experiencing of permanent soul, but because of greed and ignorance, like lighting lamp by lamp. Thus, it is clear that *anatmvad* of Buddhist philosophy striked on root (soul) of Aryan-Vedic religion by axe due to which taking birth in untouchable tribe was a result of previous birth which was being carried by soul. This helped a lot in prevention of untouchability.

4. Atheism and Untouchability

In Buddhist philosophy, the rule of God is prohibited and this universe is managed by law of *Prateetyasamutpad.* This universe is variable and perishable, and ruled by law of origin and destruction. S.N. Dasgupta has written, "Buddha, like Mahaveer of his contemporary Lichchhavi tribe, not only disbelieved in god, but presented many logics against this identity."[59] Valse Pussiyan, calling Gautama Buddha, an alert atheist, has said, "In form of a philosophical system, Buddhist religion is fundamentally against the thought of God or Supreme Spirit. Thus, he resembles western viewpoint."[60] But Geden, rejecting these views, has written, "This concept is possibly wrong that it is known by original preachings of Gautama Buddha that he was atheist completely and definitely and that he thought that this universe is made of material substances and god has no existence. It is possibly correct to say that he called this universe physical and he adopted this thought from ancient *Sankhya* (one of the six schools of Hindu philosophy propounded by the sage Kapila) philosophy where everything is assumed the product of soul and physical element (man and nature) and no divine power is considered necessary. But this second concept that the "founder of Buddhist religion wanted to express clearly atheist thoughts", about the attitude of Buddha, appears to be based on description available in Buddhist scripture. According to this description, whatever Buddha thought about the other world, soul or imperceivable, he did not reply to the questions of his disciples or threw any light on them although he was able to do so. Therefore, about imperceivable god, who cannot be touched, darkness and uncertainty remained as it is.[61]

Although Geden has rejected the talk of presence of atheist thoughts clearly in Buddhist philosophy but accepts the presence of ancient or original *Sankhya* materialism. If materialism was adopted from ancient *sankhya* in *Buddhist* philosophy, then definitely atheism would have also been adopted. It is a possible conclusion that atheism is the result of materialistic thought of universe. D.P. Chattopadhyay, explaining Buddha's atheism, has written, "Although Buddha repeatedly told himself that he has achieved complete enlightenment and that even he has become all-knowing, then there is no reason to say that Buddha had had any sort of doubt in his mind regarding the question of god, If despite this he assumed useless the god related speculation by his disciples, this proves that Buddha himself had no faith in existence of god. Believing in god and yet regarding his existence useless for human destiny, is impossible. This is true that Buddha always tried that his disciples should concentrate on practical problems like prevention of suffering and considered speculation and meditation self-delusion. Despite this, Gautama Buddha gave minimum theoretical base to his practical programme. As we will see that in this programme god had no place."[62] In Vedic and Upanishad scriptures, god is believed as permanent and complete and at that time this very thought was prevalent in four-class society. But in Buddhist philosophy supposing god to be creator of universe is called ridiculous because believing so, change and destruction, happiness and unhappiness, auspicious and inauspicious, etc., should be reduced. Having centralised these original feelings, thinker and writer of Buddhist philosophy,

Ashvghosh has kept logics of Buddha in Buddha*charit,* "Had universe been created by god, no change or destruction would have happened here. Suffering or calamity, right or wrong, nothing should take place, because pure and impure, all materials would have been created by same god. If suffering and enjoyment, love and hate, which originate in all living creatures, are provided by god, then he himself would have been experiencing happiness and unhappiness, attachment and contempt, too and if it is so, then how can he be called complete?

If god is creator of the world, and all creatures have to bend their heads before the power of their creator, then what is the need of rectitude? Committing good or bad actions will be same because they are caused to be performed by him and no difference would be between these two before him. But if suffering and pain happen due to some other reason, then there is definitely something not made by god. Then whatever is in existence, why should not that happen without god? If he is creator of the world, he works with or without objective. If he works with objective, it cannot be called complete because the necessary placed meaning of objective is to compensate some deficiency. And if he works without objective, that will be like some lunatic or new born child. Besides, if god is creator of the universe, then why should people not dedicate respectfully before him and why should they make an appeal before him at the time of misfortunes only? Thus, on the base of logic, god is proved false and all diametrically opposed statements of this type should be brought to light."[63]

Although Buddha*charit* of Ashvghosh, was created after many decades of Buddha, that is, in first decade of Christian era and the logics presented in it, do not matter if they were pronounded by Gautama Buddha, yet definitely are the logical results of his original preachings and were certainly tenable among his *parvarti* followers. In *Tik Nipat Sutt,* putting question mark on existence of God, Buddha has said,[64] "O *Bhikshuon,* those who say and believe that whatever happiness, unhappiness or insult, is undergone by man, is all produced by god, I ask them whether they think so. And when they say 'yes', I ask them whether they have become murderers, thieves, unchaste, liars, back-biters, abusers, talkative, desirous for others' money and possessors of wicked vision just because of their creation by god. O *Bhikshuon,* if it is regarded true that this is created by god, then (for virtuous act) preservance and excitement would not be present and this would not be understood as to certain act should be done and not done.

"Challenging his (god) being permanent, *swayambhu* (self-existent), infinite and existence beyond comprehension, Ashvghosh has put the logics of Buddhist philosophy in Buddha*charit* thus, "Buddha told Anathpindak, if *swayambhu* means something different from living things, then by teleology its existence cannot be proved. How can we know that something not related to other things, exists? The world known by us is a system of entire world relations. We do not know something which is, or can be, unrelated. How can the thing which is independent, unrelated to none, construct such things which are related to, and dependent on, one another for their existence? Is this *swayambhu* one or many? If it is one, then how can it be the reason for different things as we know that there are different causes for different things? If there are different *swayambhu* for different things, then how can they be related to one another? If *swayambhu* is covered on all things and entire sky and omnipresent, how can he create them because there is nothing for creation. Besides, if that *swayambhu* is devoid of qualities, all his creations should be devoid of attributes too. But substantially all things of this universe are limited with attributes. Therefore, the first reason of these things cannot be this *swayambhu.* If this *swayambhu* is assumed different from qualities, then how does he constantly create those things having qualities and express himself by them? Then, if that *swayambhu* is unchanging, then all things should be unchanging too because the nature of consequence cannot be different from that of reason. But in this universe all materials are changing and mortal. Then how can this *swayambhu* be unchanging and immortal? Besides, if this omnipresent *swayambhu* is the reason of all materials, then why should we try to achieve salvation? As this *swayambhu* resides in ourselves, we should constantly bear every suffering and pain created by him patiently."[65]

In reality, by aforesaid description entered in Buddha*charit* created by Ashvghosh, the proofs of god opposing, that is, atheism become clear which is imitation of those original thoughts of Gautama Buddha described in *Tiknipat Sutt*-61 of *Anguttarnikaya, Tevijj Suttant* 1/13 and *Devdlh Sutt* 101 of *Majjim Nikaya*.

It is clear from the aforesaid data that in Buddhist philosophy the existence of god is prohibited and no divine power is paid any attention. Thus, the theory of atheism of Buddhist philosophy supports atheist and *lokayatik* thoughts, though it does not believe in their theories of physics and comfort. Due to god opposing atheist and *lokayatik* thoughts of untouchable people, four-class people, Brahmins, Kshatriyas, Vaisya and Sudras declared them untouchable and contemptible. But Buddhist philosophy made a rigid attack on the reason of untouchability by starting the war of thoughts against god's existence. Hereby not only the morale of untouchable people got encouraged but pride of touchable culture received a massive shock. Denying Vedic culture and *Upanishadik* Brahm (god) notion, Gautama Buddha presented many god-opposing arguments. He declared god related thought of *Vedic* culture of four-class people absolutely false. On asking about Brahm or god by Vashishta, Gautama Buddha replied, "But Vashishta, is there anyone out of those Brahmins, conversant with all three Vedas, who has seen Brahm? ...Has any of their single teacher has seen *Brahm* face-to-face? ...Then has none seen Brahm? Has none met Brahm? Then how do you accept the statement of Brahmins is based on truth? Vashishta, just as in queue of blinds, none walking ahead, in middle, or behind sees. Conversation of these Brahmins is just ridiculous, devoid of essence of even word. Vashishta, does it not resemble the love of man for unseen woman?"[66] Having received such logical answer, both Brahmins, Vashishtth and Bhardwaj, got initiated in Buddhist religion. That is, tis reasoning affected touchable people comprehensively. They abandoned god related false notions and became atheists the natural consequence of which was reduction of their hate for untouchable tribes. These touchable people developed same vision for both Brahmins and Chandal, touchable and untouchable and became missionaries of theory of atheism of Buddhist philosophy.

Having denied existence of god or Brahm, Buddhist philosophy rejected the creation of *Vedic* social system based on four classes, which was called to be created to Brahm or Prajapati (Brahma).[67] Teasing Brahma as creator of the universe, Bhardwaj and Vashishta told Buddha, "Friends, the creature born firstly, thought of himself as Brahma, supreme spirit, conqueror, undefeated, one who can see everywhere, endowed with full powers, lord, producer, creator, chief, manager, self-lord and father of those present and to be born in future. All these creatures are born of me only. Then does it mean that Brahma is the father of those who are present and to be born in future? ...Thou say that this respected, conqueror and unconquered, is the father of present and future creatures. He who has created us all and who is Brahm, is permanent, everlasting, perpetual unchanging and will remain as it is till eternity. Then why are we who are created by Brahma and who have come from Brahm's house, perishable? Why is *maran-dharmo* (death) there?"[68] Thus, putting a question mark on permanance and existence of Brahma, the creator of four classes. Buddhist philosophy concluded divine miracle of Vedic class-system and hurt its supremacy deeply. By these arguments, not only untouchable tribes realised the freedom from sense of inferiority but Aryan prominence received a massive shock too.

By denying god thus, supremacy of Vedic oblations and religious celebrations performed for his sake was also denied which was unliked by untouchable tribes. The morale of people professing *Lokayat* and non-Aryan culture got excited. Now untouchable people, not considering god the reason of their poverty and inferiority, could achieve redemption by being self-dependent.

(c) Third-Arya-truth: Dukh-nirodh (prevention of suffering). Buddhist philosophy starts with pessimism, first Arya-truth, suffering but concludes with optimism. Knowing this universe as full of grief, Buddhist philosophy has no relaxation of mourning or direction but knowing the reason of suffering, the preaching to injured man to throw it out by arrow of suffering is placed there. Therefore, third Arya-truth, *dukh-nirodh* is accepted as extremely auspicious which is called *nirvana.* This is the ideal of every human life. This is the ganglion of the Buddhist religion.

Now it is necessary to know as to what *dukh-nirodh* or *nirvana* is and whether it helps in abolition of untouchability or not. *Dukh-nirodh* is explained thus, "Just as suffering is accumulated, similarly, it is also prevented, that is, prevention of ignorance prevents *sanskar.* Prevention of *sanskar* leads to prevention of *vigyan*, prevention of *vigyan* to prevention of *naam-roop,* prevention of *naam-roop* to prevention of six senses, prevention of six senses to prevention of touch, Prevention of touch to prevention of *vedna,* prevention of *vedna* to prevention of greed, prevention of greed to prevention of indifference, prevention of indifference to prevention of existence, prevention of existence to prevention of birth and prevention of birth to prevention of all sufferings, viz., old age, death, misery, self-conceit and *upayas,* etc. This is called *nirvana."*[69] Answering the *nirvana* related question of Minander, Yavan ruler, Nagsen, the famous Buddhist-monk, said, "Yes, Highness, getting prevented is nirvana. All ignorants are clung in consumption of matters, enjoy and sunk in that. They remain in that flow, take birth repeatedly, become old, die, mourn, lament very much and do not get salvation from suffering, restlessness and trouble. They are always surrounded only by misfortunes. Majesty, but erudites do not cling in enjoyment of matters. Thus, their greed is prevented. Prevention of existene stops birth. Then to get old, die...all sufferings get obstructed. Excellency, actually getting prevented thus is *nirvana."*[70]

According to Buddhist philosophy, there are two kinds of *Nirvana: Klesh* (distress) *nirvana* and *skandh nirvana.*[71] Redemption from ten afflictions (enmity, jealousy, delusion, arrogance, pride, lie, vision, *styanbhidh,* rudeness, doubt, shamelessness) is called *klesh nirvana* which is achieved not in second life but in this life only. If anyone only in his life-time conquers all these ten afflictions, he gets free. Although living in this universe, he is unconnected to worldliness. This type of free man is called *arhat* (venerable). After *nirvana*-achievement, body remains established because it is the result of greed of previous birth. As long as greed is there, body is present. *Skandh-nirvana* is achieved by the end of this life which is called *parinirvana* (final beautitude) or *skandh-nirvana.*

Explaining the state of *nirvana,* Buddha has said, "The mind attainable to this state does not deviate by difficulties of profit-loss, repute-disrepute, scorn-praise and happiness-unhappiness and being devoid of woe, sin and fear, becomes the best omen."[72] In *Dhammpadd,* he says, "By complete knowledge, who have pacified the fire of enemity and malice, mind and speeche, actions of such people freed from bondage of wordly life, become silent."[73] Substantially, one who retires from the religious path of origin and destruction, is devoid of sorrow and always remaining free. All his senses have become weak and suffering and anguish are meaningless for him."[74] In *Deeghnikaya,* Buddha says about the form of *nirvana,* "One who torments neither himself nor others, wanders with sorrowless, happy, cool, felicitious and godly soul.[75] All old actions of venerables decline and new actions don't originate; they are neither attached in next birth nor do they have any desire. Therefore, all these steady people are attainable to *nirvana* like an extinguished lamp.[76] Just as extinguished lamp goes neither to earth, nor to'sky, nor to directions and.foreign countries. Just by decline of attachment (oil), achieves peace. Similarly, the venerable attainable to *nirvana* goes neither to earth, nor to land, nor to directions and foreign lands and by decay of distress, achieves peace.[77] Therefore, *nirvana* means not the end of life but this is a state attainable only in life time. This idleness is not the state too. For achievement of *nirvana,* one has to abandon inauspicious actions and contemplate four Arya-truths. After achieving knowledge, he, instigated by feeling of common weal, appears to execute auspicious actions. After *nirvana*-achievement, Gautama Buddha, instead of getting idle, got determined for suffering-prevention of people of universe. By riding which boat, he crossed the sea of suffering, he did not break it but used completely for good of miserable people. He preached his disciples, "O *Bhikshuon,* you visit all four sides, wander, for the welfare and comfort of all. Devoid of selfishness, urged by your mercy, make complete, well-cleaned, controlled, pitiful, friendly and rational life manifest."[78] Urged by feeling of welfare of mankind, Buddha, wandering himself, put his preachings among public. He gave a message of hope to afflicted people. He founded many Buddhist-monasteries and for public sponsored many disciples here and there.

Thus, it is clear that *nirvana* prevents all sufferings of man. By termination of all reasons of suffering, enemity, malice, etc., *Nirvana* gets redemption to any man from sufferings. *Nirvana* has no place for caste-variation or high-low, rather it is for mankind only. Whether he be Brahmin or Vrishal, of touchable Aryan tribe or untouchable tribe, like Chandal, Pulkas, etc. *Nirvana* is for all who, by indifference to inauspicious actions, have annulled the reasons of suffering. In *Nirvana*-achievement, tribe, lineage, sex, etc., have no relaxation or restriction. Untouchable people can acheve *Nirvana* by committing auspicious actions too. Thus, in *Nirvana*-achievement, no binding of untouchability exists and before *Nirvana,* touchable and untouchable, high and low and Brahmin and Vrishal, all are equal. Last goal of Buddhist philosophy is achievement of *Nirvana* and that is different from salvation of four-class people or that of Upanishadik people. In Aryan-system, achievement of salvation is limited to three classes, Brahmin, Kshatriya and Vaisya only and Sudras or untouchables were disowned of it while *Nirvana* has no such difference or restraint. Thus, this theory of *Nirvana* proved the notion of salvation of Aryans, trivial and false. Notional supremacy of Aryans received a stiff stroke. In conjunction with, wise touchables were deeply affected by this thought and they, having changed their false viewpoint of high-low and touchable-untouchable, provided a reverent place to untouchables. Due to this very reason, Buddhist religion took the shape of grand movement in which people of all tribes and classes participated.

In *Nirvana* of Buddhist philosophy, god is not required nor is there any need of distinguished place, that is, heaven or hell after *Nirvana* is achieved. But in four-class Aryan religion, god, Brahm and other world are indispensable. In *Nirvana,* having rejected the imagination of god and the next world, salvation is achieved only in this life and universe. That is, Nirvana has single place of action of man. Thus, the thought of Buddhist philosophy hurts Aryan-religion a lot. In conjunction with, the communities, atheists, *lokayats,* oppugnants of Aryan-culture, who regarded salvation and heaven, imaginative, were taken to the level of untouchable and lowness, their morale got much strength. By denial of god and other world, people began to make self-efforts for emancipation from misfortunes. It is regarded a supreme duty of one who has achieved nirvana, to get clung in actions related to common weal and provide the message of redemption from sufferings to people of universe.

For men emancipated from enemity and malice, or men achieving *Nirvana,* there is no difference between touchable and untouchable, high and low, and Brahmin and *Chandal.* They wander for welfare of humanity and give messages. Equality and same feeling for all are their attributes. The man who has achieved *Nirvana,* whichever tribe or community he belongs to, spends rest of his life peacefully and happily due to prevention of all sufferings. Therefore, in Dhammpad, *Nirvana* is called the state devoid of joy, ultimate happiness, complete peace and greed, hate and delusion.[79]

Due to their opposing thoughts and hate of Aryans for culture and malice, the concept of untouchable was developing. Gautama Buddha, explaining *Nirvana,* has made a stiff stroke thereon, "*Bhikshus,* the man with mind charmed by greed, wicked by malice and foolish by delusion, remains woeful by his and others' sufferings, and experiences mental agony and pain. But if greed, jealousy and delusion are destroyed, man will not be unhappy by his sufferings or by those of others, nor will he experience mental agony and pain. Thus, *Bhikshus, Nirvana* is attainable in this life, not in next life, sounding good, attractive and an intelligent heretic can obtain this."[80]

(d) Fourth Arya-truth: Way of Suffering-Prevention. Way of suffering-prevention is backbone of Buddhist philosophy and the science of ethics. Gautama Buddha has explained a path having eight parts for the state of suffering-prevention and *Nirvana*-achievement. This path is called way of suffering-prevention or *ashtangik marg* (path having eight parts). Throwing light on its importance, it is said that supreme way is *ashtangik marg,* supreme truth for Arya-truths, supreme religion alienation and supreme man one who is chakshuman *(*Buddha*).*[81] This way of suffering-prevention is way of termination of reasons of suffering by walking on which Buddha himself achieved *Nirvana.* Therefore, Buddha says, "If you will walk on this path, you will be able to end suffering. I have preached this after getting complete knowledge of painful thorn. This is open to every man, whether he be touchable or untouchable, Brahmin or Chandal, or householder or hermit. All people can experience *Nirvana* by walking on it and spend a peaceful life by obtaining emancipation from their respective miseries.

Untouchability was by all means new and great suffering of social system of that time. It is necessary to discover as to what this suffering-afflicted man achieved by way of suffering-prevention. But first of all, it is necessary to see as what the way of suffering-prevention is. Buddha has said about this, "Bhikshus, Parivarajak must not used these two ends (overlimit). Who are these two ends? First is, clung in lust for sexual enjoyment. This end is extremely trivial, vulgar, for wretched people, not noble and disastrous. Second end is to bear suffering by punishing body. This is tragic and not noble too. By abandoning both of these, the path of *madhyama pratipada, ashtangik marg,* should be adopted. This *madhyama pratipada* provides light to eyes as knowledge. Hereby patience, identification, rousing from sleep and *Nirvana* are achieved."[83] According to Gautama Buddha, "Complete vision, complete determination, complete speech, complete *kamant,* complete *ajeev,* complete exercise, complete memory and complete meditation—these are *Arya ashthangik marg.*[84] This *ashtangik marg* is divided into three particular parts, named *pragya, sheel* and *samadhi* (meditation). *Pragya* consists of complete vision and complete determination. *Sheel* consists of complete speech, complete *kamant,* complete subsistence and complete exercise and *samadhi* consists of complete memory and complete meditation. This very contemplation of kindness, meditation and intellect is called middle path.[85]

(i) *Pragya: Pragya* means consummate knowledge.[86] To know real form of material and universe and to determine to spend life according to that, is consummate knowledge or *pragya.* According to Gautama Buddha, ignorance is the principle reason of all afflictions and as a consequence of this, false vision comes into existence. One affected by false vision, considers unreal material real, soulless soul, immortal universe permanent or mortal unhappy feelings happy and therefore, for real knowledge, end of ignorance or false vision is necessary and it is possible by complete vision only. At the time of establishment of the teachings (of Lord Buddha which he commenced at Banaras), telling *Parivrajaks* the purpose of complete vision, Buddha has said, "Actually destruction of ignorance is the objective of complete vision. This is anti-false vision. And ignorance means that man may not know the suffering, remedy of suffering-prevention and these Arya-truths."[87] Substantially, knowledge of suffering, knowledge of reason of suffering, knowledge of suffering-prevention and the way taking to suffering-prevention, this Arya-truth, complete knowledge of four truths is called *samyak drishti* or *pragya.*[88] Bodily, verbal and mental, correct knowledge of good-bad action is called correct vision (*samyak drishti*). Violence, theft and infidelity, and opposite to them, non-violence, not to steal and vision devoid of infidelity, are bad bodily actions and good bodily actions respectively. Under verbal vicious acts, are false speech backbiting, bitter speech and chattering and opposite to this, speaking truth, not back-biting. Soft speech and not chattering are *vachik* virtuous acts. Thus, greed, revenge and false concept are mental bad actions and devoid of greed and retaliation, and appropriate concept are mental good actions.[89] Determination to maintain *samyak-drishti,* first of all, in life, is modified in *samyak* sankalp (complete determination). Determination to keep entire knowledge of four Arya-truths in life is called *samyak sankalp.* Therefore, *samyak drishti* and *samyak sankalp* are put under *pragya.* Nishkaramta-related, that is indifference related determination, non-violence related determination and toleration-related determination are called *sanyak sankalp.*[90] That is, determination devoid of sexual desire, anger and violence is *samyak sankalp.* The man cannot take the profit by the knowledge of Arya-truths without *samyak sankalp. Pragya* is above all development of human mind and its way is obstructed by enmity, malice and violence. When distresses as enmity, malice and delusion are far away, complete rise of *pragya* brightness takes place and then man achieves the knowledge of real mystery and transitoriness, suffering and soullessness of universe. *Pragya* has the power to extirpate greed. *Pragya* is the concept devoid of false vision or knowledge. When *samyak drishti* comes into existence,false visions including enmity, violence and revenge come to an end and it is called *pragya.* In *Brahmjalasutt* of *Deegh-nikaya* and *Pottpad,* sixty-two kinds of false visions are described but they include three main false visions also explained in *Anguttar Nikaya, Tik Nipat* and *Mahavagg.* They are:

1. To regard the actions of previous birth the reason of happiness and unhappiness of man;
2. To consider god the reason of happiness and unhappiness of man.
3. To accept nothing as the reason of happiness and unhappiness of man.

Buddha has said, *"Bhikshus,* these three *teerthaytan,* meaning, false vision having accepted which man does not act. Which are they?

1. There are many wise Brahmins also in this world who have such argument and vision that whatever happiness or unhappiness or difference man experiences, the reason for all that is previous actions.

2. There are many wise Brahmins who possess such argument and vision that whatever happiness or unhappiness or difference man experiences, god is responsible for all that.
3. There are many wise Brahmins who possess such argument and vision that whatever happiness or unhappiness or difference man experiences, there is no reason therefore."[92]

Having ended such false concept, man can develop *samyak drishti* or *pragya.* Then only man can leave imaginative false actions, viz., epigious ceremonies, sacredness of *shastras,* soul, god and permanence and be one doing actions, genuinely. Dr. Ambedkar has said "*Samyak drishti* means that the man considers useless the activities of religious ceremonies, gets freedom from false concept of sacredness of *Shastras,* emancipate from false belief and not understand that anything happens against laws of nature. Man be free from such false concepts which are just the imaginations of human mind and which do not have any kind of relation with man's experience or reality. His mind and thoughts be free."[93]

It is clear from aforesaid investigation that in Buddhist philosophy, *pragya* means not ordinary knowledge but knowledge based on wisdom and conscience. By rise of *pragya,* man terminates false notions, viz., soul, god, reasonless thing and incident, performance of religious ceremonies, etc. and believes in thoughts based on reality. By emancipation from soul, god and religious ceremonies, dependence of man comes to an end and he becomes totally free. For reasonable speculation, achievement of redemption from suffering and construction of a healthy society, where bodily, verbal and mental vicious thinking as well as actions are lacking, high-low and, malice and contempt come to an end and man is led towards virtuous actions and speculation. The second important thing is that *pragya*-achievement has no caste or race-difference or high-low, rather it is obtainable and available for the entire humanity. Third thing is that by the notion of *pragya,* soul, god, happiness-unhappiness due to previous actions, religious ceremonies,etc., prevailing in Aryan culture were denied strongly. Hereby thoughts of atheists, *lokayats,* untouchables, etc., oppugnants of Vedic culture were encouraged. Now untouchable people were able to speculate freely and attempt for emancipation from great suffering, untouchability.

(ii) Sheel: Sheel means virtue or continence. Man short of virtue or continence is called a rake. The supreme ideal of human life is continence or honesty. In Buddhist philosophy, birth in any tribe, lineage and class indicates no greatness or smallness rather it is achieved by modulation of *sheel*-maintenance, that is, by proportion of keeping the rules of virtue.[94] Under *sheel, samyak* speech, *samyak kamant, samyak* subsistence and *samyak* exercise are kept.[95]

To keep mind, speech and body well-cleaned by pious actions completely, that is, not to shrink even a little from the path of virtue, is called *sheel.* For virtue, mendacity, back-biting, speaking bitter words and chattering, speech devoid of these four flaws of speech, that is, *samyak* words are to be spoken.[96] Sheer maintenance of *samyak* speech does not suffice but desertion of these three vicious actions, violence, theft and sensual enjoyment, *samyak kamant,* that is, non-violence, not accepting the commodity not given and abandoning sensual pleasure, are considered necessary *sheel.*[97] For *Nirvana*-achievement, alongwith *samyak* speech and *samyak kamant,* complete abandonment of inauspicious path for livelihood is considered indispensable. Desertion of false means of livelihood and spending life by good and honest livelihood, is *samyak* subsistence.[98] Under this, business of arms, man or animal, meat, wine and poison, etc., are kept as false means.[99] Under *sheel,* leaving accepted bad habits, rejecting unaccepted bad habits, adopting unaccepted good habits and maintaining accepted good habits and increasing them, are four kinds of efforts too. These four kinds of mental efforts are called *samyak* exercise.[100] Buddha has said, "Concentrate on speech, control thoughts and do not commit any bodily sin. If man keeps clean three paths of actions only, he can achieve path referred to by Buddha."[101]

Replying to the Brahmana-chiefs of Shala village of Kaushal habitation, Gautama Buddha told about rectitude, "As far as rectitude is concerned, a man (1) remains indifferent to every kind of man or animal violence, abandons punishment or sword, innocent, kind and in his heart, for every creature mercy and resides; (2) deserts theft, does not accept anything belonging to others not given to him, and spends his life honestty; and (3) remains away from sex related delusion and does not conduct sexual intercourse with unmarried girls depending on parents, brother-sisters and other relatives and those girls who have been engaged or who are wearing the necklace of betrothal.

As far as the verbal rectitude is concerned, a man (1) abandons lie and remains alienated to untruth. When asked to witness before a committee or village-assembly or family-assembly or royal-assembly or his category, he, if unknowing something, says that he does not know and if he knows, he says that he knows; if he has not seen, he says that he has not seen and if seen, he says that he has seen; he does not lie intentionally due to any greed or in his interest or that of others; (2) does not back-bite, hear here and tell there to create dispute between people, break peace and stimulate restlessness. He speaks only with the intention of establishment of peace and enjoys in getting reconciled and becomes happy; (3) His tongue is not bitter. His speech is lovely, friendly, heartily, virtuous, favourable, liked by others and without bitterness; and (4) He is not talkative nor does he talk meaninglessly. He always speaks regarding religion and ethics, something according to time, unforgottable, full of knowledge, correctly and beneficial. "As far as mental rectitude is concerned, he (1) is devoid of greed and never wants to occupy the property of others; (2) does not give any place to malice in his mind, always wants his surrounding creatures be living peacefully and happily and safe against every kind of enmity and torture; and (3) possesses a *samyak drishti* and correct determination and concepts."[102]

Throwing light on the need of virtue and its profit-loss, Gautama Buddha has told the devotees of Patligram, "O householders, a wicked man has to face these evil consequences. He bears a great financial loss due to error. He earns a disrepute which makes him lower in the eyes of the world. Whichever group he approaches, whether it be Kshatriya-assembly or Brahmin-assembly or householder-assembly or labourer-assembly, everywhere he goes hesitatingly and worriedly. He is scared. This is third loss. While dying, he is peaceless and remains woeful at the time of death. This is fourth loss.

O householders, now think of those profits obtainable to gentle virtuous man. "Gentle well-behaved man collects a lot of money as he is unerring. He becomes renoned. Wherever he goes, he is paid respect. Whichever assembly he approaches, whether it be Kshatriya-assembly, or Brahmin-assembly or householder assembly or labourer-assembly, he is without hesitation and fear. Then, he is mentally peaceful. While dying, he abandons his body with mental peace. Whoever causes him, one who is harmless and innocent, suffering, becomes victim of a great accident or gets his brain scattered or bears a great financial loss."[103]

It is clear from aforesaid explanation that in Buddhist philosophy, virtue is provided a great importance. Virtue or rectitude makes one superior, learned and great and one devoid of virtue is low and stingy. Virtueles man even if born in high lineage, or Brahmin, Kshatriya or Vaisya class, yet he is low and attains disrepute. But one born in low lineage, if virtuous, maintains complete speech, complete *kamant,* complete subsistence and complete exercise, is high and.superior. Buddha has said, "Not born in high lineage, but if a man determined on religious path, practices religion correctly, is praiseworthy and venerable."[104]

Having accepted the touchstone of superiority and height of virtue, Buddhist philosophy rejected the touchstone of prominence of Vedic race, soul, god, religious ceremonies, etc. This gave a jolt to the base of untouchability and untouchable people got a way to get freedom from untouchability. Now they could achieve redemption from the great suffering like untouchability by maintenance of virtue as well as challenge the Aryan-cultural supremacy. Virtue of Buddhist philosophy included tribal fraternity and morality also present in untouchable community. Maintenance of virtue had no caste-difference or Vedic religious ceremonies of soul, god, heaven or oblations, which were seen by untouchable people with contempt and which was the cause of their untouchability. Speaking the truth, the virtue of Buddhist philosophy was nothing but tribal equality and morality which were broken by people of Aryan culture. Therefore, the explanation of virtue in Buddhist philosophy encouraged untouchable tribal excellence.

(iii) *Samadhi: Samyak smriti* and *samyak samadhi* are called *samadhi. Samadhi* means meditation, that is, concentration of good mind, installation of mind and conscious religion equally and completely in a prop.[105] Body, agony, mind and religion wandering vigilantly and cautiously in actions of these four, is called *samyak smriti.* Buddha has said, "To be pure, achieve emancipation from mourning and suffering, destroy conceit, obtain pure path and meet *nirvana,* the path of *smriti-upasthhanon* only is a single true path."[106] These four recollection-assemblies are: (1) to inspect personal body by reasonable mode, that is, to be vigilant in bodily duties, viz., getting up, sitting, acting, sleeping and walking, etc; (2) to inspect agony by reasonable mode, that is, to be vigilant in experiences of happiness-unhappiness; (3) to inspect mind by reasonable mode, that is, regarding the mind having enmity as it is and mind without it as it is, considering the malicious mind as it is and mind without malice as it is, knowing the mind with delusion as it is and devoid of it as it is and remaining vigilant against all these mental states; and (4) to become *dharmupashayi* or to inspect humours by reasonable mode, that is, to be vigilant in functions of mind, viz., sex, anger, greed, delusion, pride, supercilliousness, remorse and doubt, etc.[107] Besides, four Arya-truths, suffering, reasons of suffering, suffering-prevention and way of suffering-prevention, by perusal by reasonable mode are kept in *smriti.*[108] Thus, *samyak smriti* means thing, alongwith universe to be always conscious in connection of realistic form of life and its experience and not to let vicious thoughts originate. Dr. Ambedkar has said, "*Samyak smriti* means to pay attention on everything. This is true vigilance of mind. To keep watch on inauspicious thoughts originating in mind, is second name of *samadhi.*"[109]

Four recollection-assemblies are the phases of *samadhi.* Concentration of good mind is *samadhi.* To meditate in auspicious religions, that is, *samnovrattiyon* is *samyak samadhi.*[110] There are first, second, third and fourth, *dhyanrupi* four stairs of this *samyak samadhi*. First contemplation consists of doubt, thought, attachment, comfort and concentration. In second contemplation, doubt and thought disappear and these three humours of mind, attachment, comfort and concentration remain. In third contemplation, attachment decays and comfort and concentration remain. In fourth contemplation, comfort vanishes too and indifference and concentration remain.[111] At the time of establishment of teachings (of Buddha which he commenced at Benaras), Gautama Buddha, explaining the importance of *samyak samadhi,* he said, "O *Parivrajaks,* one who wants to achieve, complete vision, complete determination, complete speech, complete *kamant,* complete subsistence, complete exercise and complete recollection, he has to face five hurdles in his path.

These are greed, malice, idleness, remedy and indecision. It is necessary to win or break these hurdles which are, in reality, strong restraints. To get free from these restraints, the only way is *samadhi.* But *parivrajaks,* it should be understood that there is great difference between *samadhi* and *samyak samadhi.* They differentiate a lot.

...Empty *samadhi* is a negative state because it does this much as to keep connections postponed temporarily. Herein permanent alteration of mind is not placed. *Samyak Samadhi* is an emotional thing. It provides the practice to mind to meditate with concentration of good actions and thus ends the inclination of mind to get attracted towards bad acts produced by connections.[112]

It is concluded from the aforesaid information that by meditation remembrance of destruction of body, momentariness of universe and real form of happiness-unhappiness remains maintained inside the body. Hereby alongwith the concentration of mind, the feeling of indifference is exhibited. It is not the expression of carelessness for others but alienation where loving-unloving is nothing. This is the state of emancipation from defects like enmity, malice, greed, delusion, etc. Since due to enmity, malice, greed and delusion, tribal fraternity in contemporary society was being broken; collective property was being swallowed and converted into personal property; to keep their superiority and discipline maintained, those professing non-Aryan and opposing culture were being tortured by people of Vedic culture; contempt was being propagated against them and even some tribes were being made untouchable. These principles of Buddhist philosophy regarded those all deteriorations not only painful and declared them inferior thoughts but also having abandoned that, gave the message of emancipation. This affected both, touchables and untouchables extensively.

5. Psychological attempts of abolition of untouchability

One important aspect of untouchability is psychology. Human society, when due to enmity, malice and delusion, is trapped in various types of false beliefs, he becomes so miserable, afflicted and unable that he stops to act by wisdom and conscience. Despite possessing intellect, eye and carnal power, he cannot differentiate between right-wrong and true-untrue, see advantage-disadvantage, and does not try to prevent his suffering, respectively and gets trapped in traditional customs and superstitions. A handful of clever and cunning leading people of society enact various types of provisions and rules in the name of tribe, religion, god, destiny and consequences of previous birth, enforce them on maximum people and having abducted the interest and comforts of maximum people by deception, enjoy imappropriate comforts. Exploiting class, clothes, its selfishness, hypocrisy and complexity the robe of tribe-superiority, god and religion which, in future, appears in the form of religious actions and tradition of entire society. Exploiting class proves its lordship, supremacy and rightness of exploitation by sacred texts and tradition while exploited and depressed class, having accepted that traditional superstition, becomes victims of inferiority complex and having believed their poverty and sorry plight as the fruits of god and destiny, become idle. These psychological effects are so deep that they continue for decades. What else can be the reason that when Prakrati, the Chandal girl, asked by Anand *bhikshu* for water, refuses to give, having informed him of her belonging to Scheduled Tribe? Acharya Hazari Prasad Dwivedi, learned scholar of Indian culture and Hindi literature, has analysed this psychological aspect in the following words:

"Whoever wants to know the Indian religion and literature, cannot lead without knowing this doctrine (fruits of actions). Its far consequence has affected the entire Indian society. This has certainly diverted the humour of Hindus thus that its comparison cannot be found in the entire world. For thousands of years, due to acceptance of this doctrine only, the thought of furious revolution did not rise in tribes considered low by birth. Everyone knows that he is not away from the fruits of his actions. Chandal makes an appeal of his actions for his sorry plight. Brahmin makes an appeal of his actions for his high rank, too."[113]

Buddhist Principles on Emancipation of Untouchables

Gautama Buddha, the founder of Buddhist religion, was aware of the complexity of this mental sickness of high-low, caste-difference and untouchability which was prevalent in contemporary society. He was aware of this truth that the conspiracy including determining caste-difference and high-low fair in religion as well as tradition by scriptures like Vedas, etc., calling class-difference the creation of god and providing lowness and untouchability the fruits of previous actions, was being operated by exploiting classes and Aryan rulers. He had understood that all these games were being played by Brahmins by which *bahujan* society was being exploited, tortured and insulted. He found that Brahmins were ecstatic due to pride of supremacy and on the other side, the tribes like Vrishal, Chandal, etc., having become victims of inferior mentality, had mistaken themselves for untouchable, inferior and low. Therefore, he blew bugle against high-low, caste-difference and untouchability.

To treat this mental disorder, on one side, like a psychiatrist, he attacked on self-conceit of Brahmins who were spreading untouchability and giving it a form of social organization and on the other side, tried to get emancipation to untouchable people from feeling of inferiority and dullness. Against high-low, blowing the bugle, Buddha said, "Do not ask tribe, ask one's practice only. Just as fire is created by wood, similarly, the man of inferior lineage becomes steady, wise and virtuous saint."[114]

(a) Touchstone of high-low is actions and not tribe and birth. To get emancipation from low mentality of caste-difference and untouchability, Gautama Buddha gave the base of touchstone of supremacy as well as inferiority of actions. He did not accept social difference or system like Aryan-non-Aryan, Brahmina-Sudra and touchable-untouchable by birth nor did he regard same the consequence of previous acts.[115] In Buddhism, practice or behaviour were considered the touchstone of high-low, Brahmin-Sudra and touchable-untouchable. Anyone can be Brahmin, Sudra or superior by virtue and Vrishal or Chandal, uncivilised and trivial by vice. But in contemporary society, Brahmin or Vrishal, touchable or untouchable and high or low was considered by birth and Brahmins, by low selfishness, made this thought the base of four class system and society. Gautama Buddha denied it and presented the thought of *karamvad* (virtuous act) based on virtue and public interest before the society. Not connecting the word Brahmin with tribe, he linked it with good conduct and virtuous act and denied 'Brahmin' based on birth and tribe strongly.

Addressing Vashishta and Bhardwaj, two youths, Buddha has said, "I do not call Brahmin due to his birth of mother and vagina, he is pleasure-seeking. I call Brahmin one who has renounced the world and who has become free from all sorts of bonds. One who has become fear-free and indifferent to worldly attachment and love, I call Brahmin.

One, having cut nandi (enmity), *vartra* (rope or greed), *Sandan* (twelve kinds of *paghas*) and *hanukram* (*jaba* used to tie on the mouth) and thrown yoke, has become Buddhist, is Brahmana according to me. One, who bears abuse, beating and restraint, without corrupting mind and whose forgiving in his soldier, is Brahmin according to me.

One, not furious, ascetic, kind, very learned, patient and having last body, is Brahmin according to me. One, who, like water on the leaf of lotus and mustard on the point of saw, is not clung in sensual pleasures, is Brahmin according to me.

I call him Brahmin, who has achieved supreme material, viz., sincere consummate learning, intelligence and knowledge of virtue and vice. One, not involved in family and outsiders, wandering without destination and having no desire, is Brahmin according to me. One, remaining non-combative among oppugnants, devoid of punishment among anchorites and uncollected among collected ones, is Brahmin according to me. Like mustard one the point of saw, who has thrown enmity, malice, arrogance and spite, is Brahmana according to me. One, delivering soft, ceremonious and true speech, not causing any pain, is Brahmana according to me. One, not accepting anything whether big or small, fat or thin, auspicious or inauspicious not given to him, is Brahmana according to me. One not thinking of heaven-hell and devoid of hope as well as affection is Brahmin. One, devoid of greed, having known very well speaks of Nirvana and has achieved thick nectar, is Brahmin. One like moon, is beautiful, pure, clean and unchanging and whose desire of all births is destroyed, is Brahmin. One, who has deserted the path of delusion creating troubles for this inaccessible universe and who is conversant with the world, contemplative and successful, is Brahmin according to me. One who, having deserted pleasure and becoming houseless, has transformed into a saint and whose enjoyment and birth are destroyed, is Brahmin. One, abandoning greed and becoming houseless, is renunciated and whose greed and re-birth are destroyed, is Brahmin. One, having deserted human pleasures, has abandoned even the profit of divine enjoyments, and who is disconnected to all kinds of pleasures, is Brahmin. One who has neither sexual passion nor indifference, has cool temper and is devoid of distress, who is such world-victor brave man, is Brahmana. One knowing very well the birth and death of creatures, is devoid of attachment, hapy and learned, is Brahmin. Whose fate is unknown by deities. Gandharva and human beings, who is venerable, is Brahmin. One before, after and in middle of, whom, there is nothing, who is devoid of encircling and acceptance, is Brahmin. One, superior, valiant, eminent, great saint, conqueror, not trembling, graduate and Buddha, is Brahmana. One who knows birth, forsees heaven and hell, whose birth is decayed, who is learned saint and whose sins have ended, is Brahmin."[116]

It is clear from the explanation of aforesaid 'Brahmin' that one who is virtuous, maintains rectitude, knows about four Arya-truths and who is Buddha's follower, i.e., has achieved *nirvana,* is Brahmin. The founders of four-class society and considering themselves supreme as well others low and contemptible, so called Brahmins are not Brahmins. By taking birth in any tribe, lineage or superior community, one does not become a Brahmin as was being believed by the people of contemporary society since tradition. As that time those reading the *Veda-Richas*, believing in Prajapati, Indra and Usha, etc., as god, performing oblations or religious ceremonies and creating the false and imaginative stories of soul and *Brahm,* called themselves Brahmins and considered supreme but in Buddhistic philosophy, these things were provided no importance nor were the professors of above thoughts called Brahmins. The talks not given importance by people of four class society, were fraternity and equal feeling, absence of feeling of high-low, desertion of personal interest and greed, and maintenance of rectitude, etc., and which are given important place in *Buddhist* religion and accepted as the touchstone of superiority and Brahminhood, Buddha says:

"One who is meditative, holy, stable, satisfied and devoid of bodily dirt, and who has achieved truth, is called Brahmin by me. One, who sins neither by mind nor by body and nor by speech and who has restraint on mind, speech and body, is Brahmin according to me. Neither by keeping matted hair, nor by a certain sect or birth, one becomes Brahmin. One who has met truth and religion, is sacred as well as Brahmin. Who has killed hate, and having known very well, is called having unknown status and achieved dense nectar, is Brahmin according to me."[117]

It is clear from this example of *Dhammpad* that anyone

maintaining mental, verbal and bodily rectitude and remaining separate from every sort of immoral and inhuman acts, is Brahmana. Having been born even in Brahmin lineage or caste, who believes in high-low and inferior-superior, and hates others, is not Brahmin or supreme. People, despising Scheduled Tribes, cannot be Brahmins. Those hating their oppugnants cannot be called Brahmins or superior. He who has killed his feeling of contempt, broken the captivity of high-low, inferiority and superiority, and achieved *nirvana,* is a Brahmin. It is clear that putting Chandal, Pulkas, etc., under low tribes, hating them and calling them untouchable, cannot be the talk of supremacy. This was a false thought which people of all four classes accompanied by Brahmins, began to accept. Having called this feeling crime and false, Buddhist religion started struggle against untouchability and caste-variation. Having exposed high-low and inferior feeding of the people of four class society, Gautama Buddha made complete attempt to change them mentally. He called the man superior or inferior by actions only. Buddha says:

"By birth none is Brahmin or non-Brahmana. By action only one is Brahmin or non-Brahmin. By action one is farmer, carpenter, thief, soldier, sacrificing priest and also the king. Entire universe is operated by action only. Just as chariot walks by keeping base on axis, similarly all creatures keep base on their actions."[118]

Just as none is Brahmin or supreme by birth, similarly by birth none is low or untouchable. In Aryan social system, this thought was being proclaimed by so called Brahmins that birth or tribe only make one low and untouchable. These people had declared the Vrishal and Chandal tribes untouchable and low. Vrishal and Chandal were considered inferior and untouchable by birth. Gautama Buddha objected to this false and inhuman thought of Brahmins and touchable people. He offered the doctrine that by birth neither one is prominent or Brahmin nor inferior, low, untouchable and Vrishal. Replying to *Aggik Brahmin,* Buddha says:

Who is hot-tempered, greedy, immoral and back-biter, processing false vision and fraudulent, consider him Vrishal. Who is Shudra or Brahmin, causes harm to, and devoid of mercy for, creatures, consider him Vrishal. Who destroys huts of villages and is torturer, know him as Vrishal. Whether be in village or in forest outside village, who takes commodity of someone, that is, steals, know him as Vrishal. One who, having taken loan from someone, not returns, by saying that he does not have to give anything to lender, escapes, know him as Vrishal. Whoever, due to desire of anything, murders or robs anyone walking on road, know him as Vrishal. Whoever for his or others' interest, or due to greed of money witnesses falsely, know him as Vrishal. Who tortures the wife of his friends or relatives by force or consent, know him *Vrishal.* Who, despite of possessing money, though in prime of his youth, cannot nurture his old parents, know him as Vrishal. Who on asking about good religion, teaches bad religion, and educates as mystery, know him as Vrishal."[119]

Vrishal, that is, aforesaid explanation of untouchable or inferior, has no relation with one born in Vrishal tribe or any untouchable community, rather one born in any tribe or society achieves inferiority or untouchability on committing aforesaid actions. Here untouchability or lowness does not mean any social or personal system or institution but is linked with those inferior actions which hurt human relations and feelings, create chaos in society and produce dispute and restlessness. Clearly the base on which Brahmins or four class people made untouchables, viz., Chandal, Vrishal, Pukkas, etc., Buddhist religion, having rejected, tried to shatter it to pieces. Brahmins' visit to houses of others and their acceptance of hospitality but not offering them same due to their visit, considering themselves supreme due to self-conceit and calling others low, are called trivial and low invisibly, and accepted those performing such acts, as Chandal or Vrishal. Buddha says:

"Who accepts hospitality by visiting others' houses, but if those come to his house, does not respect them, what is he if not Chandal? Who due to feeling of self-conceit, praise himself and condemns others, should be known as Chandal. Who is furious, stingy, jealous, dishonest and shameless, and who does not care a little about the fear of slander, he should be understood Chandal. Who, being unable, calls himself able, is thief in Brahmlok, and this sort of man is called Vrishal or very low Chandal. By birth neither one is Vrishal or Chandal nor Brahmin. By act only man is Chandal or Brahmin."[120]

(b) Caste-difference is not natural but artificial. High-low and caste-difference prevalent in contemporary society used to be accepted as permanent and natural. The tribes considered mean and untouchable, believed it to be a natural curse because no way of freedom from that inferiority and lowness, was appearing to them. Such mentality was prevalent also in touchable people, viz., Brahmin, *Kshatriya,* etc., and so called superior people. To treat this mental disease, Buddha told Vashishta and Bhardwaj, the Brahmin youths, "O *Vashishta,* there is caste-difference in one another in tribes of creatures, (similarly) also in grass and tree, but they do not assert. In big-small cattle, there is the mark of tribe and castes are different. *Padodar,* that is snake, having long waist, fishes living in water, *patrayan,* that is fairies wandering in sky, too, have the mark of tribe and their tribes are different, but unlike these tribes, human beings do not have the mark of different tribes. Hair, nose, lips, eyebrows, neck, shoulder, waist, stomach, bosom, head, coition, hands, feet, fingers, hips, thighs, a letter of the alphabet or voice have no sign of tribe. All corporeal creatures have symptoms separating the tribes but in man, those kinds of symptoms separating the tribes do not appear. In man difference is only in name."[121] Thus, Buddhist religion openly operated a publicity movement against false mentality prevalent in Indian society. On base of bodily construction, all men belong to one caste, 'mankind', whether they be Aryan or non-Aryan, touchable or those regarded untouchable, or Brahmin, Kshatriya, Vaisya or Chandal, Vrishal, Pulkas. Unlike other creatures, they do not have caste-difference nor do they have any sign of big-small. Therefore, among them, differences like superior-inferior, high-low, touchable-untouchable, etc., are false, hollow and inhuman. Human beings who are addressed by different names, are due to name and actions of universe only and artificial. It has no relation with superior-inferior and high-low. Name and actions can be changed and considering it natural is stupidity. By taking birth even in Brahmin lineage, due to different action, different name can be used for address. Buddha says:

"Vashishtha, in human beings, who makes his livelihood by cow-breeding, know him as farmer and not Brahmin. Who makes his livelihood by art, know him as artisan and not Brahmin. Who makes his livelihood by business, know him as *baniya* and not Brahmin. Who performs the duty of messanger, know him as messanger and not brahmin. Among human beings, who lives by others' money without giving, know him as thief and not Brahmin. Who lives by bow-arrow, know him as soldier and not Brahmin.

Vashishtha, who is priest, know him as beggar and not Brahmina. Who enjoys village and nation, know him as king and not Brahmin. By his act someone is farmer and someone artisan. Someone is businessman and someone attendent. This universe is based on action only. By his act only, a man can be Brahmin and another non-Brahmin."[122]

It is clear that Buddhism made complete efforts to drive off false supremacy and inferiority from minds of people by opposing natural conditions of caste-difference and mentality. Aforesaid talks are very important for emancipation from caste-difference and feelings of untouchability being spread by fraud and hypocritically by four class people. Aforesaid arguments of Buddha not only penetrated hope in untouchables and people tortured by feeling of caste-difference but many Brahmins, Kshatriya and Vaisya were impressed mentally too and they, having got initiated in Buddhism, participated in thoughtful war being operated against high-low and untouchability.[123]

(c) Touchable and Untouchable: all tribes are equal. It is described in Rigveda that Brahmin originates from the mouth of gigantic man, Kshatriya from his arms, Vaisya from his thighs and Sudra from his feet. This *mantra* is found, except in *Samveda,* in remaining three Vedas with a little change.[124] In four class society from subsequent Vedic period to 600 BC, high-low and class-difference appear clearly among four classes. This very class-difference took the shape of caste-difference and in 600 BC the effect of inhuman social institution like untouchability on society came to sight. To take birth in Brahmin, Kshatriya and Vaisya tribes, was considered the symbol of fruits of good actions while taking birth in Chandal tribe, was the result of vicious act which was regarded contemptible like pig and dog.[125] Similarly, Pulkas tribe is called hateable and untouchable, too.[126] It clears that touchable tribes Brahmins, Kshatriya, Vaisya and Sudra considered themselves superior and high, and untouchable tribes inferior and despisable. Among touchable people also, difference of high-low and big-small was prevalent where Brahmin was supreme and the highest and Kshatriya, Vaisya and Sudra, were regarded low, step by step. But in Buddhist religion, similar difference and caste-separation were provided no importance. Gautama Buddha rebelled openly against social curse prevalent in temporary society. He expressed not only oppugnation against this division based on birth and tribe but gave some respect to Aryan-non-Aryan, touchable-untouchable, Brahmin and Vrishal, behaved equally and on the base of actions, called superior and inferior and not superior and untouchable. Addressing Ashvalayan, the Brahmin youth, supporting the superiority of Brahmin, Buddha said: "Then what do you believe, Ashvalayan, if Kshatriya king who has achieved coronation, assembles hundred males of various tribes and tells them, "You all, who are born of *Kshatriya,* Brahmin and royal lineage, come and make fire of bark of wood of sal or *sakhu* or sandalwood or lotus, and produce lustre, and you also come, who are born of Chandal, Basor, Rathkar or Pulkas lineage, take drill of drinking bowls of dog, pig and washerman or wood of castor oil plant, lit fire and produce lustre. Then what do you accept, *Ashvalayan,* the fire produced in drill of sakhu, sal, sandalwood and lotus, by males born of Kshatriya, Brahmin, Vaishya or Sudra lineage, and lustre created, would be inflammable, censurable and radiant. And, the fire produced in drill of *swapan* bowl, *shakur-pan* bowl, castor oil plant wood, by males born of Chandal-Nishad, Basor-Rathkar-Pulkas lineage, and lustre created, would not be inflammable, censurable and radiant? Would this fire would not be able to be used as *agni*"?"[127]

Before this logical question of Buddha, Ashvalayan could not stay. Agreeing with Buddha's ideas, he regarded both, touchable and so called superior tribes like Brahmins, Kshatriya, Vaisya and Shudra as well as untouchable tribes like Chandal, Pukkas, Basor, Nishad, etc., equal. Therefore, accepting aforesaid logical discrimination of Gautama Buddha, Ashvalayan said, "No, O Gautama! the fire created by those born of Kshatriya lineage, will be inflammable, that is having flame. That fire can be used as *agni* too and that fire created by those born of Chandal lineage, will be archiman, too, that is having flame. All will be able to be used as fire."[128]

It is known by aforesaid example, as to how Gautama Buddha tried to remove the feeling of untouchability and high-low from mentality of four class touchable people of contemporary society. He knew that just by giving appropriate honour to untouchable people or their coming forward against untouchability, untouchability and contemptible feeling will not end but they would have to be brought ahead against those whose minds were being eaten by white ants of untouchability and who were spreading such inhuman feeling against men of another culture and those opposing their culture, and termite of untouchability would have to be ended from their minds. Keeping in attention these kinds of talks, the followers of Buddhism operated publicity movement against untouchability and gave untouchables the message of getting equal opportunity. In conjunctiorl with this, Gautama Buddha called the thoughts of touchable tribes, Brahmin, Kshatriya, Vaisya and Sudra wrong and imparted them the education of *samyak gyan* (complete knowledge).

(d) Caste-difference is useless, it is a binding. In contemporary society, to give caste-difference the social institutional shape, especially the people of Brahmin tribe were making efforts. They used to determine this social difference and high-low appropriate and argue and discuss in its favour. They proved Brahmin supreme on the base of class and tribe, and knowledge and logic and considered other tribes inferior and called untouchables low and mean. Therefore, Gautama Buddha has centred logic opposing caste-difference and high-low, and denounced any publicity therefore against socalled prominence. Buddha has given many apprehensions against uselessness and meaninglessness of racism. The dialogues between Sondand accompanied by Brahmanas and Buddha are worthy of mention here:

"Brahmin, a man possessing how many parts (qualities) is called Brahmin by Brahmin people and he, saying, "I am Brahmln", speaks the truth and does not lie?" Buddha asked Sondand.

Then Sondand felt that Oh! As I desired, expected, intended, requested—Oh similar, had shraman Gautama would have asked the question in my own learning of three *vedas*", so Sudra*man* Gautam is a king me in erudition of three *Vedas* only. I will definitely satisfy his mind by my answer. Then Sondand got up and having thrown a glance towards assembly, told Buddha, "O Gautama, Brahmin people call one Brahmin possessing five parts (characteristics). What are they? Brahmin be (1) born of those parents belonging to good families; (2) teacher, conversant with *mantras* and three Vedas; (3) beautiful, handsome and possessing very white complexion; (4) virtuous; and (5) literate, learned and first or second in accepting donation for performing oblation."

"Brahmin, by leaving one out of these five, can remaining four qualities be called Brahmin too?"

"Can be called, O Gautama, out of these five, complexion is left. What will it do? If Brahmin denounced any be well-bred on both sides, teacher, conversant with *mantras,* virtuous and erudite, he is called Brahmin by Brahmin people."

"By leaving one out of these four, can one having three qualities be called Brahmin?"

"Can be called, O Gautama, out of these four, *mantras* can be deserted. What will *mantras* do? If Brahmana be well-bred on both sides, virtuous and erudite, one possessing these qualities is Brahmin."

"Brahmin, by abandoning one out of these three, can one be called Brahmin?"

"Can be called, O Gautama, out of these three, tribe is deserted. What will it do? If, Brahmin be virtuous and erudite, one having these two attributes is called Brahmin."

On saying so, those Brahmin*s* told Sondand,

"Sondand, do not say so. You contradict complexion, mantras (Vedas) and tribe. By one way you accept Gautama's arguments only."

Then Buddha told those Brahmin*s,* "If Brahmin*s,* you feel that Sondand is having little knowledge, unable to speak and unwise and that he cannot discuss with shraman (sage) Gautama, he should stop and you discuss with me. If Brahmin*s,* you feel that Sondand is very learned, eloquent speaker and literate, he can discuss with shraman Gautama, then you stop and let him discuss with me".

On saying so, Sondand told Buddha,

"Gautama, you stop and keep silent. I will assert the answers of these questions on oath." Then he told those Brahmin*s,* "You people do not say so, you contradict Sondand class. I do not contradict complexion, *mantras* or tribe."

At that time, Sondand's nephew Angak manvak (a youth of sixteen years of age), was sitting in that assembly. Then Sondand told those Brahmins, "Do you all see my nephew Angak *manvak*?"

"Yes, they replied.

"Angak a youth of sixteen years of age, is beautiful, handsome, sweet, absolutely white-complexioned and beautiful. In this assembly, none, except Gautama, is equivalent to Angak as regards complexion. Angak manvak, is conversant with scriptures, at home in *mantras* and well versed in three Vedas and fifty History accompanied by Vedic lexicon-sacred performance-alphabet-difference. He is at home in medal, vocabulary, and *Shastras* related to *Lokayat* dignitaries. He is well-bred on both sides. I know his parents. Even if he performs violence, theft, visits other woman, lies or drinks wine, what will complexion and tribe do there while Brahmin is (1) virtuous, and (2) literate and erudite, and first or second in accepting donation? One possessing these qualities is called Brahmin by Brahmin people. He saying, "I am Brahmin", speaks truth and doesn't lie."[129]

Thus, Gautama Buddha, having rendered answerless those proud of caste-superiority as well as encouraging caste-difference, managed struggle against the thoughts, viz., high-low, superior-inferior, touchable-untouchable, etc. He, having defeated Brahmin literates and scholars by his arguments, encouraged them to get down against racism and untouchability. He himself challenged people for fighting against his social institution based on exploitation and selfishness from among exploiting and selfish class. He proved on thinking level that creating caste-difference between mankind is based only on false resolution but also a hurdle in human and social development. Buddha and his followers cured narrowness of people's mentality psychologically. Buddha, attacking violently on casteism, racism and lineage-superiority, said; "Ambashthh, incomparable learing-wealth is not called tribe, racism and haughtiness. 'You are not worthy of me'. Ambashthh, where coming and going, and marriage takes place, this casteism, racism, pride, you are worthy of me, you are not worthy of me', he said. Ambashthh, those bound by casteism, lineage and pride, are far from learning-wealth. Ambashthh, casteism, racism, haughtiness and coming-going of wealth are bindings. Only by leaving all these, incomparable learning-wealth can be met."[130]

(e) Brahmanas have no right to decide servitude and profession of others. Brahmins had divided majority of people of contemporary society into four classes, that is, tribes, in which Brahmin, called supreme by keeping himself at the highest place sequentially and declared Sudra inferior by keeping him at the lowest place. Not only this, they had decided the duties and rights of the people of all four classes. What will the people of four classes do, their duties for another class and which money in the form of right is attainable to them, had been decided by Brahmins in four-class society. Not only this, Brahmins had declared those untouchables who opposed their culture. Gautama Buddha, founder of Buddhist religion and his followers presented logic against this agreeable and independence of Brahmins and lit the lamp of public-awakening. In *Majjim Nikaya,* a part of publicity by Buddha is available in which a dialogue between him and a Brahmin named Esukari took place. It is as follows: "Once Buddha lived in Anathpindak's hermitage, in Jetvan of Shravasti. At that time Esukari approached him and having asked about well-being, sat aside and said, "O Gautama, *Brahmins* speak of four kinds of services (servitude): Brahmin's, Kshatriya's, Vaisya's and Sudra's. They say that Kshatriyas serve Brahmins and also Vaisya and Sudra. O Gautama! Brahmins speak of Kshatriya's service thus, Kshatriya serve Kshatriya, Vaisya and Sudra serve too. O Gautama! Brahmins speak of Sudra's service thus, Sudra serve Sudra only. ...O Gautama! what do you say in this matter ?"

"Do the Brahmins permit Brahmins of entire world that they intimate these four services?"

"No, O Gautama!"

"Brahmin, whoever spends one part of meat for one having no money, poor and despite his unwillingness, and tells him, "O man, this is the meat for your eating and you pay its cost." Thus, Brahmin, without the permission of other shraman Brahmanas of the world, Brahmins intimate these four services. Brahmin, neither I call all services serviceable nor unserviceable. Brahmin, by serving which benefit is achieved and not lost, I call that serviceable. By serving which loss is achieved and not benefit, I call that unserviceable. Brahmin, if Kshatriya be asked as to by serving whom and due to which service, he achieves benefit and not harm, will he serve or not? Then Brahmin, he will also give exactly this answer: "By attending whom and due to which service, bad happens and not good, I will not serve him and by serving whom and due to which service, bad happens and not good, I will not serve him and by serving whom and due to which service, good is achieved and not bad, I will serve him." Brahmin, if Brahmana, Vaisya and Sudra be asked too.

"Brahmin, I do not call belonging to high lineage good nor do I call it bad. Brahmin, I do not call kind tribe superior (to be of high class or good complexion) nor do I call it sinful. Brahmin, Neither I call taking birth in rich lineage good nor do I call it bad.

"Brahmin, one born in high-lineage is creature-murderer, thief, adulterer, liar, back-biter, scurrilous, talkative, greedy, malicious and possessing false resolution, too. Therefore, Brahmin, I do not give credit to high-birth. One born in high-lineage, is devoid of violence, theft, infidelity, lie, back-biting, bitter speech, chattering, malice and false resolution, too. Therefore, Brahmin, I do not call high-lineage sinful or bad." "Brahmin, some of high colour are killers, thieves, adulterers, liars, back-biters, scurrilous, talkative, greedy, malicious and possessing false resolution, too. And some having high colour are devoid of violence, theft, infidelity, lie, back-biting, bitter speech, chattering, greed, malice and false resolution, too. Brahmin, these sorts of persons are available in rich lineage also. Therefore, I do not call high complexion or one born in rich lineage sinful or bad.

"Brahmin, neither I call all serviceable (fit to be served) nor unserviceable. Brahmin, by serving whom, due to service, devotion, virtue, knowledge and sacrifice progress, I call serviceable."[131]

It becomes clear from aforesaid example that Gautama Buddha declared the duties decided by Brahmins for four classes inappropriate and called that unprivileged attempt. He clearly told that whatever services have been decided by Brahmins, should be performed as the touchstone from the viewpoint of profit and loss. If someone is benefitted by service and servant is developed, service must be conducted definitely. But the service causing harm to servant, must not be performed. By saying so, Buddha made an axe-stroke on services fixed by Brahmins for themselves to be taken from four classes and called them unjust as hereby other inferior tribes clearly had no benefit and the maximum loss was caused to Sudra tribe. In contemporary society, only Brahmana called himself of high complexion as well as born in high lineage. Buddha determined their decision wrong and said that bad people are also available in high colour and high lineage, by serving whom no class has any benefit. Clearly the services fixed by Brahmins neither provided any help in development of knowledge and virtue of servants nor caused economical and social development which might help in increase of feeling of devotion and sacrifice. Therefore, Buddha called these service conditions based on colour and tribe, and formed on high and low, improper and operated widespread publicity against them. In conjunction with this, instead of gripping lives of people in clamp, inspired them to work for profit and well-being and to serve. Similarly, fixing subsistence for four classes by Brahmins was called wrong by Buddha. Summary of dialogues between Etukari Brahmin and Buddha is worthy to be seen:

"O Gautama, Brahmins speak of these four riches or livelihood... alms is personal money of Brahmins. Arrow-quiver is wealth of Kshatriyas, agriculture and cow-breeding of Vaisyas and reapinghook and basket of Sudras. If these four classes be careless against their personal wealth, they are unsatisfied like thieves. What do you say in this connection?"

"O Brahmin! have people given to Brahmins the right of informing about these four riches or livelihood?"

"No, O Gautama!"

"Then this work of Brahmins is equivalent to asking a poor man for the cost of the meat loaded on him despite his unwillingness to eat it O Brahmin! I say that Arya supreme religion only is personal wealth of all. Men born in Kshatriya, Vaisya and Sudra lineages are called Kshatriya, Brahmana, Vaisya and Sudra step by step. Just as fire born of wood, *shakalika,* grass and dried cowdung cakes is called—woodfire, *shakalikagni,* grassfire and cowdung-fire respectively, similarly these nouns are there. But if men of these four sects be retired from sin, violence, etc., then do you feel that out of them only Brahmins and not others, will be able to make friends?"

"O Gautama! it is not so. Man of any caste can make friends."[132]

Thus, Gautama Buddha called not only prominence of Brahmin tribe or lineage wrong but also opposed provisions of special rights formed by Brahmins for themselves logically. Buddhism called resource of service and subsistence based on mutual agreement and interest proper, and not the work like heaping on offers the service and livelihood as they wished. Thus, having opposed the different attitude of the system created by Brahmins and discipline, Buddhist religion also put a question mark on fitness of that system. Inhuman social institution like untouchability based on contempt or difference and touchable-untouchable, received a deep shock too. Brahmins had no right of creation of untouchability morally nor did they seek permission of untouchable tribes and other people of society for the same. This was an independent and immoral act like entrusting a part of meat on a poor man despite his unwillingness to eat it and thereafter, demanding its cost from him. Therefore, the morale of untouchable tribes got instigation by this resistance-movement operated by Buddhism and in conjunction with this the contemptible viewpoint of touchable tribes received a deep jolt.

(f) Superiority of Brahmin is Erroneous, all Four Classes are Equal. Buddhism made various efforts of equality and same feelings. It criticised all hurdles coming in the way of equality and same feelings. To denounce all walks like high-low, superior-inferior, caste-difference, untouchability, etc., which denied human sensitivity on inappropriate bases and immoral standards as well as having decomposed society, obstructed its development, Gautama Buddha and his followers attempted constantly throughout their lives. In contemporary society people mainly were divided in four classes based on high-low. People separate from four classes, four class people considered inferior. Gautama Buddha operated throughful war against the feeling of highness and lowness as well as superiority and inferiority prevalent in society based on four classes. He denied the supremacy of Brahmanas and regarded four classes equal. In this connection, the conversation between Buddha and Ashvalayan is worth mention.[133]

"O Gautama! Brahmins say, "Only Brahmana is superior class and other classes small. Only Brahmin is white class and other classes dark. Only Brahmin is sacred and not non-Brahmin. Only Brahmins are legitimate sons of god, born of his mouth, created by him and his theory of kindness." What do you say in this matter?"

"But Ashvalayan, the wives of Brahmins have periods, become pregnant, produce children and feed them. Thus, generation of

Brahmins like that of other classes takes birth from mother's womb. Then if Brahmins say that they are born of Brahma, is it not surprising?"

"O Gautama! You say what you want but Brahmins had conviction that Brahmin only is supreme class."

"Ashvalayan, then what do you believe? You have heard that there are only two classes in Yavan, Kamboj and other countries on boundary and they are—Aryan and *Das* (slave). Aryan can be *Das* too and vice versa."

"Yes, I have heard so".

"Ashvalayan, what proof Brahmanas have for saying that only Brahmin is superior class."

"Ashvalayan, do you accept now that if *Kshtriya* be creature-murderer, thief, adulterer, liar, back-biter, scurrilous, talkative, greedy, malicious, and possessing false resolution, havng died leaving his body, will he be born in hell or not? If Brahmins, Vaisya or Sudra be creature-murderers, will they be born in inferno or not?"

"O Gautama! if *Kshatriya* is creature-killer, he will be born in hell and Brahmins, Vaisyas and Sudras too."

"Then Ashvayan, what proof Brahmins have for saying so?"

"Yet Brahmins say same."

"Ashvalayan, what do you accept then? If Brahmana is alienated to creature-violence, then, having achieved salvation, can he be born in heaven or not and Kshatriya, Vaisya or Sudra and four classes or not?"

"No O Gautama! If Kshatriya is alienated to creature-violence too, he, having achieved salvation, can be born in heaven and Brahmin, Vaisya, Sudra four classes too."

"Then Ashvalayan, what proof Brahmins have for saying so?"

In aforesaid conversation, Buddha has denied the superiority of Brahmins and called inferiority of non-Brahmins improper. He has accepted clearly that people of four classes are equal. No particular class signifies highness or any sort of lowness. Calling Brahmins' origin from Brahma's mouth is wrong and similarly, telling that origin of Kshatriya, Vaisya and Shudra from his arms, thighs and feet respectively is false and sheer deception. People of four classes are born in same manner and brought up, then why do Brahmins call themselves superior and Vaisya, Kshatriya and Sudra inferior? Similarly, Buddha also presented this logical talk that had only these four classes been present in universe, it would have been accepted that they are created by Brahma but in Yavan, Kamboj and other countries situated in boundaries, there are two classes only—Aryans and slaves. Out of those Aryans, anyone can be slave and vice-versa. In those countries, no complicated and unchanging caste-system exists. Then definitely this unchanging system based on four classes is temporary only which cannot be accepted as god-created. Similarly, if those Brahmins, Kshatriyas, Vaisyas and Sudras committing good acts, having been indifferent to creature-violence, will be born in so-called heaven, and people of four classes committing bad acts will be born in so-called hell, how is superiority of Brahmins and inferiority and lowness of other classes proved by these talks? Similar kind of other arguments were held by Buddha with Ashvalayan and finally, he, accompanied by other Brahmins had to accept the talk of equality of four classes and they became devotees of Buddhist religion.[134]

Buddha not only opposed the divine doctrine of origin of classes but also discovered the reason of origin in social development. He told that due to birth of personal interest in man, many social problems, personal wealth, greed, laziness and theft came into existence and consequently, origin of Kshatriya class took place by *mahasammat* and thereafter Brahmins, Vaisya, etc., originated.[135] Gautama Buddha, having established the theory of evolution of class-origin, not only determined Brahmins' superiority false but also presented the way of changing class-system before society. Since the four class system prevalent in contemporary society was the product of physical and social condition, this talk suggests that only if physical and social condition be changed, then by changing class-system and caste-difference, equal society can be formed. Therefore, class-system was founded by which *'Mahasammat'*, there the element of ending social-system is hidden. But Gautama Buddha was not satisfied hereby. He told clearly that no people of any particular class are superior but in man only religion is superior. In this connection, the portion of his discussion with Vashishta is as follows:

"Vashishtha, you belong to Brahmin tribe and lineage and want to be renunciated by being homeless and devoid of Brahmin lineage. Do Brahmins do not condemn or tease you?"

"Yes, Bhante, Brahmins, as suits them, condemn me with their complete amusement and tease."

"Vashishta, how do Brahmins condemn and tease?"

"Bhante, Brahmins say, "Brahmin only is superior class and other classes inferior. Brahmin only is white class and other classes dark. Brahmin only is sacred and not non-Brahmins. Brahmins only are sons born of Brahma's mouth, Brahmjaat, Brahma-created and his successors. You (Vashishta himself) have become low by falling from superior class. These men with shaved heads are born of lotus, low, dark and Brahma's feet. This is not compatible to you (Vashishta) that you, having abandoned superior class, belong to low class. Bhante, Brahmins scorn in this manner and tease."

"Vashishta, those Brahmins due to forgetting old talks, say so, "Brahmins only is superior class.

"Vashishta, Brahmin-wives have periods, become pregnant, produce children and are seen feeding them. Those Brahmins, even having born of vagina, say, "Only Brahmin is superior class." They tell lie about Brahma. They sin by mendacity.

"Vashishtha, Kshatriya, Brahmin, Vaisya and Shudra, are four classes. In Kshatriyas also, many commit creature-violence, theft, infidelity, lie and possess false resolution, Vashishtha, thus they are seen committing those tasks which are bad, defective, unserviceable, ignoble, dark, producing bad fruits and scorned by scholars. Vashishta, many Brahmins, Vaisyas, Shudras commit creature-violence, lie, theft and infidelity and possess false resolution, too. Thus, they are seen performing those jobs which are wicked and scorned by scholars.

Shakya sons are shraman, you say so. Vashishtha, in whom Buddha's devotion is accumulated, fixed, established and firm, he can't be deviated by any sage, Brahmin, deity, beating, god or anyone else in universe and only his statement is right, "I am born of god's mouth, created by religion, formed by religion and successive son of religion." What for? Vashishta, religion, sex, *Brahmkay, dharmbhut* (religious)—are the names of Buddha only."[136]

It is clear from the above conversation that Buddha accepted the touchstone of congeniality and not complexion, tribe and caste. He regarded all classes and tribes equal on the base of caste and colour and none is bigger or smaller. Telling superiority of Brahmins based on false resolution, he opposed the feelings like class-difference, high-low and black-white. Attacking on feeling of self-conceit of contemporary Brahmins, he told that these Brahmins are dismissed from ancient Brahmin-religion and that they are destroyed due to their greed and selfishness. Replying to rich Brahmin, Gautama Buddha said :

"Ancient saints were temperate and ascetics. Leaving five-sex characteristics (beauty, word, smell, taste, touch), they performed their duties. At that time Brahmins possessed neither cattle nor gold and silver, nor grain. Their only wealth was their continuous and regular study of the Vedas. They protected Brahm-wealth. Food prepared for them devotedly, was offered to them by people while demanding. Prosperous people and nations adored them by clothes of various colours, bed and abode. Brahmins were protected by unfit to slaughtered, unconquerable and religion. They were never stopped on gates of the houses. They maintained celebacy for forty-eight years. Neither they approached another woman nor did they buy any. They performed sexual intercourse only with mutual love. Except menstrual period, during prohibited period of meantime, they never conducted copulation. They appreciated celebacy, virtue, simplicity, humbleness, religious austerity, softness, mercy and forgiveness.

One, out of them, who was supreme, firm and valiant Brahmin, did not perform copulation even in dream. According to his practice, walking Brahmins, praised celebacy, virtue and forgiveness. Having demanded rice, bed clothes, ghee and oil, they performed oblations religiously. They killed no cows on 'oblation present sacrifice'. 'Just as parents, brothers and other relations are there, similarly, cows are our close friends too. Medicines are created by cows. These very cows give grain, strength, colour and comforts.' Having known so, they did not kill cows. Sukumar, Mahakaye, Varnvan, renowned Brahmins, as long as they were present in universe, remained engaged in their duties and people lived happily. Having seen gradually king's wealth, ornamented women, chariots having beautiful and incomparable stitching and best yoked horses, and houses divided in departments and lofty buildings, Brahmins' minds changed. They developed thirst for ample human enjoyments accompanied by beautiful women and surrounded by a flock of cows. Then, having composed *mantras,* they visited to Ikshvaku and said, "You possess abundant wealth, perform oblation," On being informed by Brahmins, the king possessing numerous chariots, performed *Ashvmegh, Purushmegh, Sambhapas, Vajpay* and *Sarvmegh* (different kinds of oblations) and offered them money.

Cows, bed, clothes, ornamented women, beautiful constructed chariots united by best horses and palaces divided in parts and high buildings, various riches were donated to Brahmins. They liked to collect money. The desire of those greedy Brahmins increased thereby. Having composed *mantras,* they reapproached Ikshvaku and said, "Just as water, earth, gold riches are there, similarly, cows are for man and is the commodity for their consumption. You owe a great wealth. So perform oblation." Then having been inspired by them, king, possessing several chariots, killed thousands of cows in oblation. Cows which hurt neither by foot, nor by horns, nor by any other part, which are dear like sheep and provide milk full pitcher, king killed them by weapon, holding them by their horns.

Then deities, manes, Indra, Asuras, Rakshas, shouted, "Unrighteousness happened that weapon fell down on cow." Earlier three disease were present, desire, hunger and old age. By violence of animals, they transformed to ninety-eight. This irreligion was devoid of old punishments approved by religion. Priest kill innocents and destroy religion. Thus, this is trivial act scorned by old scholars. People, wherever find such priests, scorn them. Thus, due to destruction of religion, Sudra and Vaishya got separated. Kshatriya scattered too. Wives began to insult husbands. Kshatriya, Brahmins and others who were guarded by clan, having neglected community, were controlled by sexual-enjoyments."[137] By these talks, Gautama Buddha has tried to prove that Brahmins, having become warp and waft by attachment of personal property and pleasures, have become indifferent to religion. Due to origin of personal selfishness and libido, abreast with the Brahmins, other classes have become indifferent to religion as well as victims of sexual-pleasures, too. In this condition, with false vision, false pride and wicked actions have entered in them due to which social interests have been put aside. For fulfilment of their interest only, oblations and religious ceremonies are created, *mantras* formed and appeal of heaven and hell made and thereby limitless loss of society is happening and its development is obstructed. Determining Brahmins responsible for destruction of religion and society, Buddha has made heavy slander and told that even dogs have five religions of Brahmins too but these are not found in later despite of discovery."[138]

"*Bhikshus,* five ancient Brahmin religions are seen this time in dogs. Which five? *Bhikshus,* earlier Brahmins approached Brahmin-wife and none except herself. But, now they approach both. But, *Bhikshus,* dogs approach bitches only and not those (who are not bitches). *Bhikshus,* this is first ancient Brahmin-religion appearing in dogs now.

Bhikshus, earlier Brahmins approached menstruating woman and not one having no periods. But now they approach both. But *Bhikshus,* dogs approach only the later and not the former one. *Bhikshus,* this is second ancient Brahmin-religion appearing now in dogs.

Bhikshus, earlier Brahmins neither bought nor sold Brahmin-woman and performed sexual intercourse with mutual love. Now-a-days they buy as well sell Brahmin-woman and perform sexual intercourse also with mutual love as well as want of love but dogs do not buy or sell bitches and perform sexual intercourse with love only. *Bhikshus,* this is third ancient Brahmin-religion appearing now in dogs.

Bhikshus, earlier Brahmins collected no money nor did they collect silver-gold. But nowadays they collect money as well as gold-silver but *Bhikshus,* nowadays dogs donot collect money or silver-gold. This is fourth ancient Brahmin-religion appearing now in dogs.

"*Bhikshus,* Brahmins used to search for morning and evening food during morning and evening only but now, they, having eaten full stomach, take remaining home but *Bhikshus,* dogs, search for food for evening and morning during evening and morning only. This is fifth Brahmin religion appearing this time in dogs and not in Brahmins.

"*Bhikshus,* these five ancient Brahmin-religions appear in dogs nowadays."[139]

By this kind of satire, Gautama Buddha attacked on superiority and pride of contemporary Brahmins. By various types of conjectures, he denied caste-system based on high-low and superior-inferior prevalent in society and called all four classes equal. After his death, his followers continued their publicity movement against four class-system based on caste-difference and high-low. According to them, four classes are artificial and equal. Challenging the self-conceit and superiority of Brahmins, they kept their publicity movement progressing. Conversation between Buddhistic recluse Katyayan and Avantiputra, king of Mathura, is a good example of this. A part of that conversation is as follows:

"O Katyayan, Brahmins say, "Only Brahmin is superior and classless, he is white and other classes dark, he is sacred and not non-Brahmin. Brahmins are legitimate sons of Brahma."

"Then what do you accept, Highness, if *Kshatriya* be prosperous by riches and kingdom, can he, by getting up and sleeping before and after master, obeying him and working according to his mind, and also dear, appoint another Kshatriya or Brahmin or Vaisya or Sudra as a servant, for attending or not?"

"O Katyayan, if Kshatriya wants, then Kshatriya will be his dear (servant) too, and Brahmin, Vaisya and Shudra too."

"O Katyayan, if Brahmin wants, then Brahmin will be his servant too, and Vaisya, Shudra and Kshatriya too."

"O Katyayan, if Vaisya wants, then Vaisya will be his servant too, and Sudra, *kshatriya* and Brahmin, too."

"Highness, if Shudra wants servant by his money?"

"O Katyayan, if Shudra wants, then Shudra will be his servant too, and Kshatriya, Brahmin and Vaisya too."

"Then what do you accept, Highness, due to happening this, are all four classes equal or not, what do you feel here?"

"Definitely, Katyayan, due to happening this, four classes are equal. Here no difference is seen."

"By this way also, Highness, you must understand that this is only ado—'Brahmin is superior class'.[140] Thus, Katyayan, the Buddhistic recluse, proved before Avtiputra, the king of Mathura, by other four apprehensions that the talk of superiority of Brahmins prevalent in society is false. It is just a noise and has no relation with truth. Katyayan has cleared in those conjectures that people of all four classes can achieve superiority by performance of virtuous actions and be attainable to inferiority by wicked actions. People of all four classes, on committing crimes, viz., theft, will be deserving punishment equally and any particular class would not be freed from punishment. Similarly, in aforesaid portion of conversation, he has told clearly that any class, on becoming prosperous economically, will be able to appoint other classes for service. Having been satisfied by his arguments, Avantiputra took initiation in Buddhism too.

In contemporary Buddhistic followers of Ashoka, the king, feeling opposing caste-difference and high-low, remained as it was present in period of Gautama Buddha. From conversation between Yash, the minister and Ashoka, the emperor, described in *Divyavdan,* it becomes clear that contemporary Buddhist shraman and devotees did not believe in caste-difference. The substance of these dialogues is as follows:

"Ashoka, the emperor, because Buddhist recently and he touched feet of all Buddhistic recluses. On seeing this, Yash, the minister, said, "King, there are people of all tribes in Shakya shramans. Your bending coronated head before them is not proper." Ashoka gave no reply. In a short while, having procured the heads of he-goats, sheep, etc., he got them sold. Then having procured the human head by minister, asked him to sell that. A little cost of animals, viz., he-goats, sheep, etc., was obtained but human head was not bought by anyone. Then Ashoka said that that head be given to anyone free of cost. But none, taking that free of cost, was found by minister. He conveyed same to Ashoka. Then he said, "Why do not people take human head despite of being given free of cost?"

"Because, they hate this head."

"Do people hate this head only or will they hate all human heads?"

"Highness, if any man's head be cut and taken to them, they will hate similarly."

"Will they hate even my head?"

The minister hesitated in answering this question. When Ashoka assured him of protection, he replied, "Highness, people will hate your head same way."

"Then if I respect Buddhistic recluses by keeping such head in their feet, why do you feel bad?"[141] It is clear from all aforesaid examples of dialogues that Buddhism took support of many arguments to remove inhuman thoughts of high-low and caste-difference of society based on four classes. From Gautama Buddha to Ashoka, who loved all, Buddhistic followers operated an open publicity movement against class-superiority and class-pride of Brahmins. Having denied Brahmanik doctrine of class-origin, they called it the reflection of social problems, viz., personal interest, personal property, greed, theft, etc. Due to this, Brahmin-created theory 'origin of four classes by Brahma' was denied and a hard attack was made on their prominence. Not only this, Gautama Buddha called them responsible for destruction of ancient religions of society, viz., tribal morality, equality and fraternity, etc. Hereby common public became vigilant against false notions and institutions created by Brahmins. This is the only reason that many Brahmins as Ashvalayan, Vashishta, etc., having deserted society based on traditional false thoughts and high-low, got initiated in Buddhist religion and participated in thoughtful battle being operated against caste-variation and untouchability. Clearly, having attacked on prominence of Brahmins, Buddhism moved untouchable people also and in conjunction with, tried to remove the feeling of untouchability, hate and caste-difference, and false resolution from the minds of touchables, viz., Brahmins, Kshatriya, Vaisya, etc. Since the base of untouchability was high-low, superior-inferior, touchable-untouchable, etc., having called them useless and proved all four classes equal, Buddhism tried to end the false base of untouchability.

(f) Man is Not Superior by Food and Religious Ceremonies. Some devotees and Brahmins, Buddha's contemporaries, believed in sacredness of food and regarded meat as prohibited. They believed that abreast austerity, purity of food is necessary and that meatless food brings virtue. Having believed in touchstone of purity of food, they called themselves superior, holy and great, and categorised flesh-eaters as inferior, unholy and low. Similarly, Brahmins and people of other tribe considered religious ceremonies, viz., oblations, worship and bath, etc., sacred and having completed them, called themselves superior. Those non-*Vedic* people, not performing these religious ceremonies, were regarded inferior, mean and untouchable by Brahmins. Society was cursed by this sort of superstition, being divided in touchable and untouchable, and superior and inferior, and entire universe was moving towards hell by mutual contempt and malice. In this condition, Buddhism commenced thoughtful movement against these misbeliefs. He did not give importance to purity of food and religious ceremonies but supported good practice. This is affirmed by conversation between devotee Tishya and Gautama Buddha which is as follows:[142]

Tishya, an ascetic, became disappointed on knowing that Gautama Buddha does not prohibit food containing meat and fish. To know the truth in this matter, he reached Jetvan Vihar, Shravasti, where Gautama Buddha stayed and said:

"Whoever, beans and fruits, leaves and roots, worth of eating, vegetable growing on any branch of tree-having achieved these things religiously, eats, does not lie for comfort. O Kashyap, you eat sumptuous and delicious food offered and prepared by others. One who eats this kind of rice-*pulao,* eats *aam-gandh.* O *Brahmbandhu*! You eat rice cooked by mixture of bird-meat and say that *aam-gandh* is not appropriate for you (myself). O Kashyap, ask you as to what sort of this *aam-gandh* is of yours?"

Replying to him, Buddha said, "Committing creature-violence, beating, cutting, tying, stealing, telling lie, cheating, deceiving, practising burning-killing and infidelity are *aam-gandh* and not non-vegetarian food. "Losing continence in sensual matters, becoming greedy for soft things, relating to unholy duties, having false vision, not being simple and imitating—this is *aam-gandh* and not non-vegetarian food."

"To be bitter, strict, backbiter, unfaithful, cruel, proud, unkind and one not giving anything to anyone, this is *aam-gandh* and not non-vegetarian food."

"Anger, pride, rashness, anti-feeling, cheating, malice, boasting, excessive self-deceit, wicked company—this is *aam-gandh* and not non-vegetarian food."

"Wickedness, not repaying debt, defaming others, dishonesty, making excuses, commiting this sort of sins by close people in this universe, this is *aam-gandh* and not non-vegetarian food."

"Those who have no mercy for creatures, who, having robbed others, torment them and who are wicked, horrible, brawl and insult others, their act is *aam-gandh* and not non-vegetarian food."

"To attack creatures greedily and maliciously and always be ready to commit wicked acts—after death takes from darkness to hell—this is *aam-gandh* and not non-vegetarian food."

"By alienation to flesh and fish, remaining naked, having bald head or matted hair, applying *bhabhut* (the ashes of cowdung smeared on the forehead and other parts of body by ascetics), wearing deerskin, worshipping fire, keeping austerity of all types for achievement of nectar, enchanting *mantras,* offering as a victim to a deity and performing oblations according to season, he, whose doubts are not removed, cannot be purified."

"Who has controlled senses and fixed in religion, who enjoys maintenance of rectitude and who has deserted attachment and killed suffering, that patient man does not attach to wicked and renowned materials."

Having heard that speech without smell and destroying all sufferings, that ascetic Brahmin saluted Buddha politely and there only he accepted renunciation.

It is known by this example that in contemporary society thoughts related to purity of food had appeared on the basis of which feeling of superiority and inferiority was being publicised. It could not be chief feature of society at that time but same had to happen in coming decades. Along with austerity, importance was attainable to *Vedic* religious ceremonies and oblations, and their performance had become a symbol of superiority. Due to understanding these talks and duties useless as well as opposing, people of many communities were being called untouchable and inferior. But Buddha and his followers proved this thought false. They clearly proved the purity and superiority of food, Vedic religious ceremonies and austerity false and said that is rectitude that purifies people, makes them superior and frees them from all sorts of sufferings, and not pure food and oblations or religious ceremonies. Conversing with Brahmins, Buddha has said:

"Do not ask tribe but practice. Wood creates fire and man of low lineage becomes steady, learned, virtuous and saint, too. He, who, by truth, is chaste and has subdued the senses, has reached end of knowledge and achieved celebacy, he has achieved oblation and has been conducting sacrifice in donation-bowl since ages. "Definitely this oblation of mine is very adored and *su-hut* that I saw an erudite like you. Due to not seeing like you, other people would have eaten remains of oblation. O Gautama! you have food, you are Brahmin." ... Brahmin said.

"...Brahmin do not get purified by burning wood. This is external material. Literates do not point out that purity which is internal one from outside. Brahmin, having left wine-jealousy. I lit internal flame. Daily having fire and solitary mind, I keep celebacy. Brahmin, this pride of yours is heap of chalk, anger smoke, mendacity cinders, tongue a wooden sacrifical ladle and heart place of light.

By self-suppression, man achieves light. Brahmin, having virtue as a place of pilgrimage, is lake of religion, appreciated by gentlemen where, devotees, having bathed, without becoming wet, reach over. Brahm is dependent on (supreme)-achievement, truth, religion, forbearance and celebacy. Therefore, you end these oblations, that is, salute Buddha's followers. I call them charioteer fit to be killed."[143]

In above conversation described in *Sanyukt Nikaya,* Gautama Buddha declared oblation and religious ceremonies useless and criticised on that base caste-superiority and tribe-pride. He provided important place to rectitude and virtue and said clearly that man born in low lineage can achieve superiority by keeping rectitude and virtue, too. Truth, forbearance, sacrifice, celebacy and learning are called by him oblation and not that performed by wood and fire sacrifice. Buddhism operated thoughtful movement against all external presumptions like bath, etc. Emphasising on internal purity by maintenance of rectitude, virtue, etc., external purity was called useless. Criticising external purity, Buddha asked Brahmana Sangarad:

"Brahmana, as people say, is it true that you believed in purity by water and purify by water only? Maximum time of your day-night is spent in bath only."

"Sharman Gautama, this is true."

"Brahmin, what benefit do you see in bathing day and night?"

"Shraman Gautama, this is thus whatever sins are committed by me during day, I wash them the same evening and whatever sins I commit during night, I wash them immediately after I get up in morning. I see this very benefit in bathing day and night."

"Brahmin, only religion is that water-source which is clean and pure. Here when Shastra-learneds come to bathe, their every part is purified and they go to another edge."

"Shraman Gautama, this is strange. From today you know me as your fugitive devotee throughout my life.[144]

Thus, Gautama Buddha, addressing monks about the purity of life, has said, "*Bhikshus,* this pure life is not for cheating people or for getting something from them, or for achieving profit or fame, or for learning way of doing debates, or for making people know that this is certain individual. *Bhikshus,* by determination, this pure life is practised to keep body and speech restrained, to remove weapons, to release mind, and to achieve decline of desire."[145]

Thus, by above proofs, many-sided picture of thoughtful struggle managed by Buddhism comes to sight. Having denied *Vedic* religious ceremonies and *Brahamaneey* purity and superiority, Gautama Buddha and his pupils made unfatigued attempt to remove feeling of untouchability and high-low spreading in contemporary society. At that time other people of Vedic culture accompanied by Brahmins were making those people opposing their culture, inferior, low and untouchable. In protest of this inhuman act, Gautama Buddha gave not only logic but also called all-pervading bath, purity and oblation or religious ceremonies false duties and selfish acts. Thereby untouchable tribes got support by both, direct and indirect ways. In contemporary society, all Vedic religious ceremonies were performed by Brahmins for attaining benefit and name, cheating non-Brahmins and fulfilment of other interests and this was called unholy in Buddhism. By doing this, it cannot be denied that superiority and sacredness of other touchable tribes accompanied by Brahmins would have received a shock. It cannot be considered impossible too that it would have created a very good effect on the mentality of untouchable and inferior tribes.

(h) To Consider Religious Texts Sacred and Axiom is Wrong. Vedas had a great importance for people of contemporary Vedic religion. To be called Aryan without believing in Vedas was difficult. Brahmins had declared that Vedas are not only sacred texts but also axiom and that they have neither any sort of mistake nor possibly thereof.[146] Alongwith enchanting the *mantras* of Vedas, they performed oblations or religious ceremonies and had announced themselves superior. Buddhism rejected these announcements by Brahmins and managed thoughtful struggle against it. Gautama Buddha and his followers did not give any special importance to Vedas nor did they determine the talk of accepting them sacred and axiom right. They denied sacredness, self-reliability of Vedas and their being far from possibility of becoming wrong drastically. In *Tevijj Sutt,* Buddha has called Vedas waterless hole, pathless forest and destructive way and informed that men thirsty Buddhistically and morally, cannot quench their thirst even by going near the Vedas.[147]

Buddhism called self-reliability of Vedas and their being far from possibility of becoming wrong, incorrect. It did not put even knowledge and traditional talks separate from doubt. Protesting traditional sacredness and self-credibility of religious texts as *Vedas,* Gautama Buddha told Kalaam Kshatriyas:

"O Kalams! do not accept anything just because you have heard that. Do not accept anything just because many people support that. Do not accept anything just because this is written in (sacred) texts. Don't accept anything just because that is according to logic (*Shastras*). Do not accpet anything just because that is according to justice (*Shastras*). Do not accept anything just because that appears acceptable externally. Do not accept anything just because that is according to belief or vision. Do not accept anything just because that sounds true externally. Do not accept anything just because that is told by respected religious instructor."

"Then what should we do? What should be our touchstone?" Kalam Kshatriya asked.

"Kalams, the touchstone is that ask yourself whether is it well to hold a certain talk? Is certain talk condemnable? Is certain talk prohibited by wise people? Does holding certain talk provide pain and suffering?"

"Kalams, not only this, you should also see that point of view does not help in increasing the feelings of desire, hate, stupidity and malice."

"Kalams, not only this, you should also see that point of view does not make anyone the slave of his senses and incline him to perform violence. You should see that he motivates none to conduct theft, make him involved in false practice related to sensual enjoyment, instigate him to lie and encourage him to inspire others to commit same."

"And O Kalams! finally you should ask if it is not for suffering and evil?"

"O Kalams! what do you think now? In conducting these talks, is man's interest or disaster there?"

"Bhante, disaster."

"O Kalams! are these talks profitable or harmful?"

"Bhante, harmful."

"Are these talks condemnable."

"Bhante, condemnable."

"Are these prohibited or supported by wise males?"

"Prohibited by wise males."

"Does conducting these talks give pain and suffering?"

"Bhante, yes."

"Can any sacred text teaching all this, be acknowledged as axiom?" Can it be far from possibility of being wrong?"

"Bhante, no."

It becomes clear from the above conversation that Gautama Buddha has forbidden to believe all those talks and to change them in duties which are harmful, condemnable, prohibited by wise people and painful or distressing. He said clearly that those talks, traditional, *Vedas* or of religious scriptures, which increase desire, spread the feeling of hate, produce jealousy and malice and increase them, having spread superstitions among people produce stupidity and inconscience, should not be accepted. By acknowledging those talks there is increase in inclination of theft and violence, habit of telling lie and impatience, and if they are professed even by maximum people, approved by science of reasoning and logic and written in religious texts, should not be accepted. Buddha had noticed in contemporary society as to how people, closing their eyes, were accepting traditional talks and those of religious texts as a consequence of which feeling of caste-difference, high-low and touchable-untouchable were making society suffer. Brahmins, Kshatriyas, Vaisya, having called their superiority sanctioned by traditional religious writs, were proving Shudra and untouchable inferior, low and hateable while those touchable tribes did not possess such virtue. They, having become victims of greed, desire, hate and violence, were encouraging personal interest and property and breaking social fraternity.

Having not tested the talks described in tradition and religious texts on touchstone of good-bad, fraternity and malice, by accepting them superstitiously, feelings of caste-difference, touchable-untouchable, etc., were increasing in society, which were hurdles in way of social development as well as were oppugnants of equality and same feelings for all. In conjunction with this, these talks also create hurdles in opening new doors of origin and increase of new knowledge, new talks and new aspects of development. Gautama Buddha called maintenance of all those good talks proper, irrespective of their being not approved by tradition and sacred text, accepted by maximum people and said by some great person or religious instructor but acceptance of those ending sufferings helping in personal and social development, assisting in increase of morality and knowledge, are helpful in keeping good actions and bring equality and equal feeling. It is clear that Brahmins and touchable tribes, having called Chandal, Pulkas, etc. contemptible and untouchable on the base of Vedas and tradition, had dismissed them from society. Buddhism called it erroneous and constructed the path for people to come forward against it. Since Brahmins, called superior, preceptor and learned in four class society, were spreading the feeling of untouchability and people of all four classes accepted their talks without considering good-bad or proper-improper, Buddha called this practice incorrect and forbade people to accept anything, closing their eyes. All aforesaid talks of Buddha opened eyes of knowledge not only of many conscientious people of touchable tribes but they came in front of society against these inhuman traditional and religion approved talks.

Not only this, Buddhism called sheer reading of religious books irreligion. Calling enchanting mantras or reading religion related stories useless, Buddhism has called virtue and good actions of man important. Gautama Buddha found in contemporary society that Brahmins, by reading only Vedas, Upanishads etc. and *mantras,* call themselves high and superior and regard those, who having considered Vedas, etc., and *mantras* useless, protest same, inferior and contemptible calling them Sudra and untouchable. Buddha opposed Brahmins' this inhuman false viewpoint and work and called sheer reading of religious books wrong. In this connection conversation between king Prasenjit and Buddha is as follows:

"I hear that this Patisen (a new Buddhistic recluse) has no ability. He knows a single story only. Then how did he achieve enlightenment?" Prasenjit asked.

Buddha replied, "Knowledge be not much but virtue is important thing. This Patisen has understood the secret of this single story. His body, speech and thoughts have become calm completely. If a man possesses excessive knowledge but is devoid of practice accordingly, that entire knowledge cannot save him from decline.

"Whether a man reads one thousand stories, but if he unaware of the meaning, his reading is not equal to that of a single story by hearing which mind achieve peace. What objective of pronouncing thousands of words is there without understanding them? But hearing one word, understanding and practising accordingly, can get salvation.

"A man can read various scriptures but if he does not understand them, his reading is without objective. Understanding a single couplet of religion and working accordingly is the way of salvation."[149] Thus, Buddhism tried to end the feeling of untouchability and its institution prevalent in society by presenting various conjectures before society. Caste-difference, high-low and all talks were called wrong and useless, which take man and society towards hell. By presenting rectitude, morality and virtue before society, Gautama Buddha and his followers tried to free people from resolution and mental disease of high-low and touchable-untouchable. They not only denied resolutions of Brahmin and Vrishal based on tribe and lineage and proved them false but having based on god and bad acts, also presented a new explanation. Now people of so-called Brahmin tribe and lineage, committing wicked acts, could be Vrishal, inferior and untouchable, too as well as people of so-called Vrishal, Chandal, Pukkas tribes and lineage, too, committing good acts, could be called superior, Brahmins or Buddha's followers. Buddhism denied harmful actions and thoughts like oblations and religious ceremonies, and traditional prominence of Brahmins and stood many touchable Brahmins, Kshatriya and Vaisya against them. Buddhism tried to infuse new consciousness in society against harmful portions of Vedas and traditional talks. Calling all tribes as well as races equal, Gautama Buddha and his followers continued psychological battle against colour-difference, caste-variance and difference of touchable-untouchable for decades. In *Vasal Sutt,* it is stated, "By birth none is Vrishal or Chandal nor by birth anyone is Brahmin. By act only man is Chandal or Brahmin."[150]

Thus, on one side Buddha scorned all caste-difference and on the other hand, brought a psychological revolution in matter of high-low.[151]

Practical Attempts of Abolition of Untouchability

Against untouchability, caste-difference and high-low, Buddhism began not only philosophical and psychological battle but made various practical attempts which can be called a great revolutionary step of that time. Gautama Buddha believed in unity and equality of speech and action and he kept it throughout his life due to which he is called '*yathhakari tathavaadi*' (As he says, so he does).[152] Not only this, his followers kept unity and equality of speech and speech maintained for decades due to which Buddhist religion reached many countries, besides India. Therefore, Gautama Buddha and his followers, were unable to remove feeling of act of touching the untouchable and high-low, as well as complicated disease as untouchability, prevalent in contemporary society, by analysing sheer conversation, discussion and philosophical elements. For this, it was necessary to present such experiments and practices before society, which provide people healthy mentality and duty. Presenting practical examples was mandatory, which got redemption to people of contemporary society from distinction of high-low, caste-difference and untouchability. Having this understanding, Buddha and his followers put various practical codes before their religion supporters, which continued for decades constantly.

Practical attempts made by Buddhism against the social institution of untouchability and caste-difference, can be put in three categories, which are as follows:

(a) Providing Same Opportunity to Untouchable Tribes in Entry of Monasteries. Entry in Buddhistic monastery was open to all, irrespective of sub-divisions of a caste, sex and status. Buddhistic monastery had no space for racism nor was there any inquiry about social condition. All members inside the Buddhistic monastery were equal, and qualities and not birth decided big-small.[153] Buddhism, having opened its door for all four classes divided in high-low in contemporary society, had permitted them to participate in Buddhistic monastery as well as be Buddhistic recluses.[154] Same opportunities of achieving *nirvana* by entering Buddhistic monastery, were available also to people of Chandal and Pukkas tribe, considered so-called untouchable.[155] Gautama Buddha declared clearly that anyone belonging to any lineage or caste, can get education and be a teacher. Even if teacher is Chandal or Pukkas, he should be respected.[156] It is described in *Jatak* that a *bodhisatv,* coming from Chandal tribe, defeated a Brahmana in debate, but he was scorned due to his wrong behaviour with Brahmin.[157] In contemporary society Chandal tribe was considered contemptible and untouchable. Chandal son, Maatang, having got initiated in Buddhistic monastery, achieved great designations which many Kshatriyas and Buddhistic recluses coming from Brahmin tribes could not obtain.[158] Thus, Suneet came from a low tribe (untouchable) Pukkas, too which was created to include in *Ther Gatha.* In Suneet Thero of Ther Gatha, the story of his renunciation in Buddhism is described :

"A sweeper named Suneet lived in royal palace. Cleaning rubbish thrown on roads by householders was the only source of his livelihood. This was his traditional low profession. One morning, Buddha got up, wore tattered dress and accompanying many monks, left for alms. At that time, Suneet was arranging the heap after collecting rubblish, which he had to throw in vehicle through basket and to take away that vehicle by pulling. When he saw Buddha, accompanied by his disciples, approaching, his heart filled up with joy but at the same time he also got scared. Seeing no place of hiding on the road, he joined his vehicle with wall and himself stood to very close to wall with saluted hands.

When Buddha came a little close, he addressed Suneet by speech full of nectar, "Suneet, what is this source of your poor livelihood? Can you be admitted to Buddhistic monastery by leaving all this?" Suneet felt as if someone had showered down nectar on him. He replied, "How cannot I enter Buddhistic monastery where Lord Buddha lives? You please admit me in Buddhistic monastery." Then from Buddha's beautiful countenance, emerged, "*Bhikshu, aa* (come)." By this single phrase, Suneet got renunciation and *upsampada* and he became professor of tattered dress.

Buddha took him to Buddhistic monastery and educated him about religion and humility, "All creatures are purified by virtue, restrain and suppression." When asked as to how Suneet became so great, Buddha answered, "Just as a flavoured lotus can grow on heap of rubbish lying on the road, similarly, in this blind universe, this rubbish world, Buddha-son can be lighted too."[159]

Suneet himself has narrated the story of his renunciation, in *Ther Gatha* as follows:

"I have come from a small family. I was poor as well as needy. My occupation was of a very low kind. I used to clean withered flowers by broom. People used to see me with eye of hatred. I used to express respect for all very politely. Then I saw Buddha with his monks. They and that great hero, were visiting the most important city of Magadha. Then I threw my weight, taking it off and running, bent his head before them. Those superior men stopped, having mercy on me. I saluted in feet of *Prabhu* and going before him, requested him to admit me as monk. Then that kind *Prabhu,* who is treasure of mercy of all regions, told me, "O *bhikshu,* come here." Thus, I achieved initiation."[160]

Tribe and lineage had no significance in Buddhistic monastery and religion. In monastery-entry, Chandal, Pukkas, Sopak, etc. so-called inferior and untouchable had as much right as was obtainable to so-called Brahmins, Kshatriyas, Vaisyas, etc., called touchable and superior tribes. No difference, hurdle or restraint was there in getting initiated in Buddhism. To initiate two untouchables named Sopak and Supipya, in Buddhism, can be considered a strong example hereof. The story of their initiation in Buddhism described in *Ther Gatha—Chaturtho Vaggon,* is as follows:

"Sopak was an untouchable boy of Shravasti. His mother fell unconscious during pain of pregnancy. Her husband and relatives, thinking she is dead, took her to the graveyard and prepared a pyre for her. But at the same time it rained so heavily and such a storm came that it became impossible for the pyre to catch fire. Therefore, people left, leaving her as it is.

Sopak's mother did not die by that time. She died later. She begot a son before her death. That child was brought up by watchman of graveyard with his son Supipya. The child got the name, Sopak, in name of mother's tribe. One day Gautama Buddha was passing by graveyard. Sopak, seeing him, went to him. Having saluted him, he asked for Buddha's permission to get admitted in monastery.

At that time, Sopak was only seven years old. Lord Buddha asked him to bring his father's consent. Sopak brought his father. He saluted Buddha and requested him to admit his son in abbey. Having not cared for his being 'untouchable', Buddha admitted him in abbey and imparted him the education of religion and humility. Later, he became a Buddhistic monk.

Supipya and Sopak grew together and as Supipya's father brought up Sopak, Supipya, like his companion, got initiated in Buddhism. Supipya, whose traditional profession was keeping watch on graveyard, became a monk, too."[162]

Thus, in contemporary society, two children, coming from Sopak and Chandal, considered untouchable tribes, got initiation in monastery.

Thus, a Chandal girl, named Prakrati, was admitted in monastery by Buddha.[163] The story of her initiation in Buddhism is strange. Description of Prakrati's initiation of religion and humility, in *Shardool-karan Apdan,* is as follows:

"At that time Lord Buddha was wandering in Jetvan of Anath-pindak in Shravasti. His disciple, Anand, had been to Bhiksharth city. Having had his food, he was approaching river for drinking water. He saw a girl who was filling her pitcher in river. Anand asked for water.

She was Prakrati. She said, "I am a Chandal girl. I cannot give you water." Anand replied, "I want water and not your tribe." Then she gave him some water from her pot. Anand returned to Jetvan. She followed him and found out the address of his dwelling. She also found out that he was disciple of Buddha.

Having returned home, she narrated entire story to Matangi, her mother and started crying, lying on earth. Matangi asked her the reason therefore. She disclosed, "If you want to get me married, I shall marry none except Anand." Matangi inquired about. After returning, she told Prakrati, "Marriage is impossible as he has adopted celebacy." Having heard so, Prakrati became very sad. She left food. She was not prepared to accept his destiny. So she told her mother, "Mother, do you know witchery or not? why don't you perform magic for the fulfilment of this objective?" The mother answered, "I would see as to what can be done."

Matangi invited Anand for food. Prakrati was delighted. When Matangi informed Anand that Prakrati was very eaget to get married, he replied, "I have adopted celebacy. I cannot marry any woman." Matangi said, "If you do not marry her, she will commit suicide. She is deeply attached to you." Anand replied, "I am unable."

Matangi went home and conveyed truth to her daughter. Prakrati shouted, "Mother, where has gone your jugglery?" Matangi replied, "My witchcraft does not work against that of Buddha." Prakrati reshouted, "Close the gate. Don't let him be out. I shall see as to how he does not accept me as his wife tonight only." Matangi worked accordingly. During night, she arranged bed in room. Prakrati ornamented herself very well and came in. This did not influence Anand anyway. Finally, Matangi used her witchery. Consequently, fire got lit in room. Matangi held his clothes and said, "If you still don't want to marry Prakrati, I shall cast you into fire." Yet Anand did not submit. Matangi and Prakrati had to accept their defeat. They freed Anand.

Having returned, Anand narrated his story to Buddha. Second day, Prakrati, searching for him, reached Jetvan. Anand was leaving for alms. On seeing her, he tried to escape. But she followed Anand everywhere. On his returning, he found here awaiting him at the door of monastery. Anand informed Buddha that Prakrati does not abandon him anyhow. Buddha called her. When she appeared,

Buddha asked as to why she was following Anand. She replied to marry Anand at any cost. She said, "I have heard that he is bachelor. I am bachelor too." Lord Buddha said, "Anand is a monk and hairless. If you get your head shaved too like him, I shall see to it." She replied, "I am ready for herefor." Lord Buddha advised, "Before getting your head shaved, you should seek your mother's consent." She visited her mother and boasted, "Mother, what you could not do, I have done." Lord Buddha has promised that if I get my head shaved, he will get me married to Anand." Mother said furiously, "You should not do so. You are my daughter and so, should have hairs. Why do you flutter so much to marry Anand? I shall get you married to a good boy." Prakrati answered, "Either I shall marry Anand or die." Matangi asked, "Why are you insulting me?" Prakrati retorted, "If I am dear to you, let me do what I want" Matagi withdrew her objection and Prakrati got her head shaved.

Then Prakrati appeared before Buddha and said, "By your order, I have got my head shaved." Buddha asked, "After all what do you want? Which portion of his body you love? She answered, "I love his nose. I love his mouth. I love his ears. I love his voice." Then Buddha inquired, "Do you know that eyes are sheer halting place of tear, nose is the abode of mucus, mouth is full of spittle, in ears dirt and only dirt is there, and body is sheer storehouse of filth. Where birth exists, death exists too. Where deaths exist, suffering exists too. Girl, I don't know as to what you will achieve after marrying Anand?"

She thought seriously and finally found it useless to marry Anand she was dying for. She expressed her opinion to Buddha. Having saluted Buddha, she said "Because of having got succumbed under ignorance, I was after Anand. Now my eyes are opened. I am like that boatman whose boat, after meeting with an accident, reached another edge. I am equivalent to an unprotected old man who has got safety. I am equivalent to that blind man who has achieved eyes. Nectar of knowledge has dissolved my sleep." "O Prakrati, you are lucky. Although you are a Chandal girl, yet you will work as an ideal for supreme men and women. Even if you belong to 'low' tribe, Brahmins will receive education from you. Do not deviate from path of religion and justice. Your fame will be more than that of queens sitting on royal thrones," Buddha said. When the talk regarding marriage was dismissed, she had no choice except to get admitted in monastery. She expressed her desire for the same and got it fulfilled. Undoubtedly, she belonged to the 'lowest' tribe."[164]

When Buddha admitted her in monastery after imparting her education of religion and humility, this news spread all around. It is described in Mahayaan when Brahmins of Shravasti heard this news, they began to say mutually, "Chandal girl is renunciated in monastery. Let us see how she approaches the houses of Kshatriya-Brahmins to beg?" They also excited Prasenjit, the king of Kausal, against the incident. He, having got excited, himself ascended on chariot, visited Buddha to inquire about this incident and having saluated him, set aside. He discussed it.

Buddha said, "Highness, there was a king of Chandals, named Trishanku, in past. His sons name was Shardul. He was very beautiful as well as king-like. He got education of all Shastras duly. Trishanku required a girl for Shardul. He approached Pushkarsari, a Brahmin and asked for his daughter's hand for his son. Brahmin replied, "You are Chandal and myself a Brahmin. Chandals with Chandals and Brahmins with Brahmins establish relations. You have insulted me by saying so."

Trishanku replied, "O Pushkarsari, Brahmanas and Chandal are born of same vagina and former does not come from sky. Kshatriya, Brahmin, Vaisya and Sudra are sheer names formed by man. Just as children play on road and having made mud toys they themselves give them different names. They call some *kheer* (rice-milk), some curd and some ghee but those toys remain as it is and don't change according to fake names. Similarly, by taking different names, viz., Kshatriya, Brahmana, Vaisya or Sudra, no difference is created among them. Their features, viz., eyes, nose, ears, mouth, etc. all are of same kind. Just as difference among animal tribal as cow, horse, donkey, sheep, goat, etc., is found, similar difference does not appear in four human classes. Then to be proud of tribe is inappropriate."

Having heard Trishanku, Pushkarsari got delighted. Knowing that Shardul is master of Vedas, he got his daughter married to him.

Having heard Buddha's sermons, Prasenjit became greatly delighted. The doubt of conceit of his class was removed. He, having worshipped Buddha's feet, left for his city and pacified excitement created by discussion about aforesaid incident of Prakrati's renunciation in Buddhism.[165]

According to Buddhism, by birth or tribe, none is Vrishal or Chandal, and nor Brahmin. By action only, man becomes Chandal, vrishal inferior or low and by action only Brahmin, superior, high, etc.[166] Gautama Buddha has stated clearly that whoever kills creatures, has no mercy for them and robs villages and cities, and makes them deserted, is Chandal and Vrishal and can be called inferior, low and untouchable.[167] But such inferior and low, Vrishal and Chandal, has a right to get knowledge, too. Such Chandal and Vrishal, by rectitude, can achieve *Budhatv,* too. Low persons, murdering creatures and fulfilling their interests by robbing others, who can be called Chandal or Vrishal according to Buddhist religion, can also become Buddha's followers by keeping virtue and religion. According to qualities of Chandal described by Gautama Buddha, robber Angulimaal was Chandal, Vrishal, inferior, low and untouchable. Such man-killer, falling from rectitude, got admission in Buddhism too and was exempted from *Chandalatv.*[168] In Angulimaal Sutt of Majjim Nikaya, he himself has accepted his emancipation which is as follows:

"One day when Angulimaal, wearing tattered dress, was wandering for alms in Shravasti, a man threw a clodon on his head, second a stick and third a broken piece of clay. His head started bleeding. His begging-bowl was broken. His clothes were torn. In such condition, he reached Lord Buddha. When he came close, Buddha said, "Angulimaal, bear all this. Angulimaal, bear all this."

Thus, by accepting Lord Buddha's teachings, Angulimaal transformed into a saint. Enjoying the pleasure of freedom, he said,

"Who having been erring earlier, becomes unerring later, makes universe manifest like moon free from clouds. May my enemies also learn this lesson, profess this point of view and accept this path of learning. May they also adopt teachings of friendship, politeness and placability on time. May they practise accordingly. In form of Angulimaal, declining which was there, was my downfall and I was flowing in stream to downwards. Buddha, stood me on land by bringing me. In shape of Angulimaal, my hands were covered with blood. Now I am completely free."[169]

Thus, dacoit Angulimaal, becoming the Chandal by hateable of act of robbery and murder, was spending now holy life by getting united in Buddhistic abbey. About five hundred dacoits, in valley of mountain situated towards west, about seventy-five miles away from royal palace, also got initiation in Buddhism.[170]

According to Buddhism, these dacoits were Vrishal and Chandal by actions, too. It is described in Anguttar Nikaya as to how Gautama Buddha taught the lesson of religion and humility to about a group of 122 men and their wives by risking his life, in a region full of mountains, about 175 miles away from royal palace while this group made their livelihood by flesh of animals killed by them and they were attainable to low *Chandalatv.*[171] Thus, many people called Chandal or untouchable, on the basis of tribe and action, got admission in religion and Buddha's abbey and many people of inferior and small tribe were placed on important designations of monastery. In this connection, Ris Davids has given an interesting piece of information:

One of very important personalities of Buddhistic monastery was Upali who, according to rules of monastery, was seated on an important designation after Gautama. He was barber earlier. His profession was counted among hateable ones. Similarly, Suneet came from Pukkas, a low tribe, too while he was in category of those brothers whose creation was chosen for inclusion in Thergatha. Sati, proclaimer of strong atheism, came from Dheevar tribe. Dheevar was considered low tribe later on. In those days too, due to barbarism, people hated this profession. Nand was a shepherd. Two *panthhak* were born due to sexual relations of an unmarried girl of a noble family with a Das. ... A girl, named Chapa, was the daughter of a hunter. Punna and Punnika were Das, daughters. Mother Sumangal was daughter as well as wife of those people, working in forests of Saneethhe. Subha was the daughter of an ironsmith. Undoubtedly other examples can be provided too and when some more scriptures will be edited, similar examples will be found.[172]

(b) Taking Alms from All Tribes, Touchable-Untouchable. A man can not be called a Buddhistic recluse just because he eats by begging alms from others. When he adopts 'religion' completely, he can be called Buddhistic monk.[173] That monk who lives on alms, who does not err in maintenance of his duties, can end suffering in abundance of happiness of love.[174] These qualities are spoken of for Buddhistic recluse. Substantially, the monk who adopts religion completely, becomes devoid of feeling of enmity and malice, hate and praise and high-low the having become devoid of error, he increases happiness of love by man. For him as to who is touchable or who is untouchable finishes and feeling of equality and similar feelings develops in society. Buddhist religion, in contemporary society full of high-low and untouchability, kept door of its religion as well as monastery open not only to all for equality and similar feelings but also put this rule before his monks that in asking for alms, no practice having difference or variation be conducted. During begging, taking alms from every door was mandatory. To accept alms by leaving any door between two houses, was forbidden because by not doing so, possibilities of caste-difference, social status and getting importance by any category could have taken place. Gautama Buddha, calling this rule *Sapadnairiya,* permitted herefor.[175]

Gautama Buddha knew that society is inhabited by both kinds of people, rich and poor. People of Sudra and untouchable tribe are mainly poor. If monks do not have consciousness for *bhikshatan* (asking for alms), they will neglect Sudras and untouchables, and give more importance to houses of other classes and tribes. In conjunction with, possibility of poor people as Sudras, not having good or sufficient food was there. Therefore, it was necessary to throw light on talks relating to food, tattered dress and place of staying. Buddha has said in *Ariyavansutt:*

"monks, these four *Aryavansh* are chief and dynasty of many days. They are ancient and broad. They have never been, do not be and would not be narrow. They are never blamed by Buddhistic recluses and Brahmins. What four they are? Here monk is satisfied by tattered dress acquired easily. He praises such satisfaction. He does not conduct inappropriately for alms. He is not frightened if alms not obtained. If acquired, not becoming greedy, intoxicated and attached, and finally knowing fault in food, consumes grain only for emancipation. Then by such satisfaction, he does not praise himself or condemn others. Who is expert, careful, conscious and remembering in this sort of satisfaction, is called monk, keeping practice according to ancient, chief *Aryanvansh.*[176]. .."

It is clear from above Scott and Buddhistic monks used to accept food and tattered dresses obtained in alms as defective and consumed that only for redemption. They used to accept food acquired from touchable tribes with flaw as they did from untouchable and inferior tribes. Buddhistic recluses had neither any attachment for delicious food acquired for touchable tribes nor did they praise that. Similarly, they had neither dislikes for food obtained from untouchable tribes nor did they praise that. Similarly, they had neither dislike for food obtained from untouchable tribes nor did they criticise that. They respected alms collected from all tribes equally. It is described in Moneyaysutt that a saint should not converse much with families of village. If alms obtained, good but if not, it is good too. He should feel same in both conditions... he should not insult little alms as well as benefactor.

Buddhistic monks did not give any importance to whether benefactor is small or big, Brahmin or Vrishal and touchable or untouchable. They had their food, having collected alms from all people and tribe. They got cooked food in alms and carrying that outside the village, had that sitting under the tree. Alongwith this, sometime they accepted invitation by householders and had food in their houses but they never accepted same not more than one evening or one householder's food. But common routine was of alms. This was a speciality of Buddhistic monastery. Gautama Buddha himself maintained this rule. In a dialogue with Udayi, Buddha has said, "O Udayi, Buddhistic recluse Gautama remains satisfied by acquired alms and describes qualities of such satisfaction and therefore, if my mendicants, having respected me, had been living in my reclusory, out of them those depending on alms only and not talking of small house or big house, accept alms and live on that only, they, having respected me, would not have lived in my hermitage as sometimes I eat good food by accepting invitation by householders."[178]

This dialogue is big and aforesaid talks are referred to due to relevance. But it is found out hereby that all Buddhistic monks accompanied by Gautama Buddha, accepted alms from all tribes equally. Dharmanand Kosambi, discussing common routine, has written, "Lord Buddha gets up early in the morning and at that time, he either meditates or wanders near his dwelling. He would go to villages for alms in the morning. He would go outside the village, carrying his begging-alms which contained cooked food collected from all tribes and having had food there, would contemplate after some rest. He would wander again in night and stay in any temple or under a tree in any inn.[179]

All were equal in Buddha's eyes whether touchable or untouchable. If one day he would accept delicious food in royal palace of king Bimbisara, second day he would accept a piece in alms from the house of untouchable. By accepting alms from huts of untouchables, Buddha and his noble disciples felt honoured.[180] At the time of demanding water from aforesaid Prakrati, a Chandal girl, Anand, the Buddhistic recluse said clearly that he believed in no caste. Having accepted invitation of Matangi, Prakrati's mother, Anand had food there. Matangi belonged to untouchable Chandal tribe. Similarly, Gautama Buddha accepted his last food from Chund, a man of low tribe and thereafter only, he achieved final beatitude.

(c) Touchable and Untouchable Tribes publicised against caste-difference and untouchability unitedly. In contemporary society, Brahmins were spreading caste-difference and untouchability, presenting explanations on its justification and having placed that on religious and theoretical basis, providing firmness. When saint Buddha saw this inhuman act being conducted with maximum people, he blew bugle against it. Gautama Buddha knew that Brahmins and noble people, having become united due to their personal interest, were making social institutions strong based on caste-division and high-low and therefore, thoughtful and practical attack would have to be made collectively against it. It was necessary for Buddhism to emancipate society from complicated problems as untouchability and caste-difference that people of both classes, touchable and untouchable, participate in this widespread arduous task. But selfish and conservative people were objecting to Buddha's progressive thoughts because formation of tribeless and casteless social-system would have hurt their selfishness, provided a jolt to their superiority and self-conceit, and proved their thoughts and institutions false, especially livelihood and interest of Brahmin priests would have been hurt more.[181] But having got impressed by Buddha's argumentation and philosophy, thousands of touchable people as Brahmins, Kshatriyas and Vaisya entered Buddhism and favoured progressive thoughts of Buddha. People of Shudra and untouchable tribes also got admission in Buddhistic monastery and made this movement strong.

When in Uruvel, Gautama Buddha attracted Nagraj Muthlind, a distinctive oppugnant of those saints worshipping fire, towards himself by his personality, one thousand Brahmin disciples of Kashyap brothers, accompanied by them, having regarded it a miracle, accepted Buddha's disciplehood.[182] When Buddha, with more than one thousand monks, visited Rajgarh, the capital of Magadh, Senip Bimbisaar, king of Magadh, Brahmins of Magadh and twelve members of noble families, went for hearing Buddha's elucidation and became his followers.[183] In Rajgraj, Sariputt and Moggallayam, two youth Brahmins, who were spending religious life as followers of Pravrajak, participated in Buddhistic monastery, wearing red-brown clothes.[184] Thus, thousands of Brahmins, businessmen and noble people, became followers of Buddhism and operated a thoughtful and practical war against caste-difference and untouchability prevalent in Gautama Buddha's contemporary society. Youth Brahmins like Sariputt, Moggallayan and Kashyap brothers, noble boys like Anand, Rahul and Aniruddh and people like Yash, belonged to very decent families of contemporary society, who completed the task of conveying Buddha's progressive thoughts to people. Abreast these noble touchable people, untouchable and inferior people also like Suneet, Sopak, Supipya and Prakrati, became occupied with disclosing false vision of Brahmins and untouchables practising against untouchability and caste-difference. The stream of Buddhism continued for decades and performed the task of constructing society by washing the dirt of high-low and untouchability. Even after decades, Nagsen (150 BC), Ashoka, the emperor and Nagarjuna in spite of having been born in Brahmin and Kshatriya tribes, protested untouchability and caste-difference and performed the job of spreading Buddha's progressive thoughts to each and every individual. Till 200 BC, this flow continued thick and uninterrupted when we find that Nagarjuna (175 C), founder of nihilism, became a renowned Buddhistic philosopher. Despite of coming from Brahmin lineage, he developed Buddhistic conception. Thus, practical attempts made by Buddhism against untouchability were very original and significant. Untouchable tribes were deprived of seeking admission in any of the social, religious, political and educational institutions. Even their dwellings were separate from those of touchable tribes Brahmin, Kshatriya and Vaisya, etc. They could not stay with touchable tribes. Buddhism objected to this inhuman rule and system not only thoughtfully but also kept the door of his religion as well as Buddhistic monastery open for untouchable tribes. Unlike people of Vedic culture, he refused to accept system based on caste-difference and high-low and opened the door of monastery for mankind to achieve learning and knowledge and to maintain rectitude. In contemporary society, practice of act of touching or untouching was performed more in food and mode of eating and drinking. Buddhism understood this complicated entanglement of untouchability and to make a mince of all, applied the rule of collecting alms from all tribes and people. Whether small or big, poor or rich, Brahmin or Chandal, to have food after accepting invitation of all people, to accept alms from all people and to drink water by all hands, was chief duty of Buddhistic monks. Gautama Buddha and his followers behaved equally with all classes, all tribes and all people; considered all equal and none was smaller and bigger. Buddhism, having made people of so called Brahmin, Kshatriya and Vaisya, followers, engaged in publicity against caste-difference and untouchability. The followers of Buddhism, coming from touchable tribe, publicised not only Buddhist religion and philosophy but also performed dialogues and reasoning in protest of inhuman social disease as untouchability prevalent in contemporary society. Buddhism, having been made of people of untouchable tribes monks in Buddhistic monastery and religion, not only gifted a path of knowledge, spirituality and development of life of untouchables but also sent them by making touchable and superior among those very touchable tribes who considered former untouchable and called inferior and low. This would have definitely removed the delusion of people of Vedic culture as well as increased the morale of untouchable tribes.

Notes and References

1. *Buddhism,* p. 159: Ris. Davids.
2. Majjim Nikaya, pp. 107-13, binding-2, Nalanda, Devnagri Pali, *granthmala.*
3. Deegh Nikaya, 1/9 (Pottpaad-sutt), p. 71, Lucknow, 1979; Translation, monk Rahul Sankrityayan and monk Jagdish Kashyap.
4. Buddhahadev, pp. 5-9: Jaganmohan Sharma.
5. Majjim Nikaya, pp. 107-13, *op. cit.*

6. Sanyukt Nikaya, 4/1/4.
7. Anguttar Nikaya, Atthak Nipat: Udan 5/5.
8. *Dialogues of the Buddha,* p. 102, part 1, London, 1899: T.W.R. Ris Davids.
9. *Manual of Indian Buddhism,* p. 46, Starsburg, 1896: J.H.C. Karn.
10. Bauddh Darshan, p. 21, Allahabad, 1989: Rahul Sankrityayan.
11. *Majjim Nikaya,* 1/4/5.
12. Buddha-Charcha: translation, Rahul Sankrityayan.
13. Sanyukt Nikaya, 14.
14. Dhammpad, 213.
15. *Ibid,* 146.
16. *Ibid.*
17. Mahadukkanvarkhad Suttant.
18. *Ibid.*
19. *Buddha: His Life, His Teachings, His Order,* p. 64, Kolkata, 1927, H. Oldenburg.
20. Baudh Darshan, p. 23: *op. cit.* : *Majjim Nikaya,* 1/4/8.
21. *Majjim Nikaya,* 1/3/8.
22. *Sacred Books of the East,* 13, pp. 75-8: editor: F. Maxmuller.
23. *Origins of Buddhism,* pp. 428-29: Dr. Govind Chandra Pandey.
24. *Baudh Dharam ke Vikas ka Itihas,* p. 84, Hindi Samiti: Dr. Govind Chander Pandey.
25. Rigveda, Purush Sookt, 10/90/92.
26. *Origins of Buddhism,* p. 431: *op. cit.*
27. Sanyukt Nikaya, pp. 39–40, binding 2, Pali Text Society.
28. Origins of Buddhism, p. 429: *op. cit.*
29. Anguttar Nikaya, binding 1, p. 157.
30. Dhammpad, Brahmanvagg, 11-14.
31. Sutt Nipat: translation, Dharmanand Kaushambi.
32. Anguttar Nikaya, Suttak Nipat.
33. Majjim Nikaya, 41(Saleyyak Sutt).
34. *Ibid.*
35. *Ibid.*
36. Buddhcharya, Andeep Sutt: *op. cit.*
37. Majjim Nikaya, Basathh Suttant.
38. *Ibid.*
39. Dhampad, Brahman Vagg.
40. Sutt Nikaya, Vasal Sutt, *op. cit.*
41. *Ibid.*
42. Anguttar Nikaya, 3/1/34.
43. *Ibid.*
44. Deegh Nikaya, 2/2, Mahanidan Sutt, pp. 110–13, Lucknow, 1979: Bhikshu Rahul Sanskrityayan and Bhikshu Jagdish Kashyap: Buddhcharya, 133, *op. cit.*
45. Sanyukt Nikaya, 16.
46. *Ibid,* 12/7.
47. Dhammpad, Jaravaggo, 6.
48. Sutt Nipat, Vijay Sutt: *op. cit.*
49. Theri Apdan (Triteeya Bhanvar).
50. Dhammpad, Maggvaggo.

51. *Ibid.*
52. Deegh Nikaya, Brahmjal Sutt, pp. 12–13, described earlier.
53. *Ibid.*
54. Nidan-Sanyut, Vagg 2/5.
55. Sandh-Sanyut
56. Milind-Prashan, 2/1, pp. 30–34: 1937, translation: Bhikshu Jagdish Kashyap
57. Majjim Nikaya, 1/4/5.
58. *Ibid,* 1/12.
59. A History of Indian Philosophy, 1, p. 203, Cambridge, 1922-23: S.N. Dasgupta.
60. *Encyclopaedia of Religion of Ethics,* 2, p. 183, Edinbara, 1908–18: editor, J. Hastings.
61. *Ibid,* 6, pp. 269–70.
62. *Lokayat,* p. 392, Macmillan, 1973: D.P. Chattopadhyay.
63. *Indian Philosophy,* part 1, p. 455, London, 1923: S. Radhakrishnan.
64. Anguttar Nikaya, Tik Nipat, Sutt 6.
65. *Indian Philosophy,* part 1, p. 455, *op. cit.*
66. Deegh Nikaya, Savijjt Suttant 1/13, pp. 87–88: *op. cit.*
67. Rigveda, 10/90/12.
68. Deegh Nikaya, Savijj Suttant: *op. cit.*
69. Baudh Charya Paddhati, pp. 126–27, Lucknow: Bhad Ta Bodhayan Mahasthivir.
70. Milind–Prashan, p. 34: *op. cit.*, Sanyukt Nikaya 3/1/6.
71. *Baudh Charya Paddhati,* p. 129, *op. cit.*
72. *Ibid,* Mangal Sutt: *op. cit.*
73. Dhammpad 7/7.
74. *Ibid,* 7/1.
75. Deegh Nikaya, ¼, Sangeeti Suttant: *op. cit.*
76. Baudh Charya Paddhati, Ratan Sutt: *op. cit.*
77. *Ibid,* Sondranand.
78. *Ibid,* p. 135.
79. Dhammpad, 9, 202-203, Nibbaann Param Sukham.
80. Anguttar Nikava, 3/52.
81. Dhammpad, Magvaggo.
82. *Ibid.*
83. *Buddh Charcha: Dharamchakra Pravarttan Sutra: op. cit.*
84. Deegh Nikaya, 2/9, Maha Satipatthan Sutt, p. 197: *op. cit.*
85. *Bauddh Charcha Paddhati,* p. 126: *op. cit.*
86. *Ibid.,* p. 125.
87. *Bhagvan Buddh aur Unka Dharam,* p. 98: *op. cit.*
88. Deegh Nikaya, 2/9 Mahasati Patthan Sutt, p. 197: *op. cit.*
89. Baudh-Darshan, p. 96: *op. cit.*
90. Deegh Nikaya 2/9, *op. cit.*
91. Baudh Charcha Paddhati, p. 125: *op. cit.*
92. Anguttar Nikaya, Tik Nipat.
93. *Bhagvan Buddh aur Unka Dharam,* p. 98, *op. cit.*
94. *Baudh Charcha Paddhati,* p. 123: *op. cit.*
95. *Ibid,* 129.

96. Deegh Nikaya 2/9, *op. cit.*
97. *Ibid.*
98. *Ibid.*
99. Anguttar Nikaya, 5.
100. Deegh Nikaya 2/9: *op. cit.*
101. Dhammpad, Maggvaggo.
102. Majjim Nikaya, Saleyya Suttant, 1/5/1.
103. Dhammpad, Dandvaggo, 9–12.
104. Majjim Nikaya, Sadhurisdhamm Suttant.
105. *Baudh Charcha Paddhati,* p. 123: *op. cit.*
106. Majjim Nikaya, Satipatthhan Suttant.
107. *Ibid.*
108. *Ibid.*
109. *Bhagvan Buddh aur Unka Dharam,* p. 100: *op. cit.*
110. Deegh Nikaya, Mahasasipatthan Sutt: *op. cit.*
111. *Ibid.*
112. *Bhagvan Buddh aur Unka Dharam,* p. 100: *op. cit.*
113. Jativad: Samkaleen Srijan, pp. 39–40, Sanyuktank 5 7–8 July, 1989.
114. Baudh Charcha, Atideep Sutt: *op. cit.*
115. Baudha Charcha Paddhati, p. 143: *op. cit.*
116. Majjim Nikaya, Basetth Srettant.
117. Dhammpad, Brahman Vaggo.
118. Majjim Nikaya, Basetthh Suttant.
119. Sutt Nipat, Aggik-Bhardwaj Sutt.
120. *Ibid,* Vasal Sutt.
121. Majjim Nikaya, Basetthh Suttant.
122. *Ibid.*
123. *Ibid.*
124. Rigveda 10/90/12: Atharva Veda, 19/6/6: Yajurveda, 31/11.
125. Chhandogya Upanishad, 6.10.7.
126. Vajasneyi Sanhita, 30.17; Tetreeya Brahman, 3, 4.1–14.
127. Majjim Nikaya, Assalayn Suttant.
128. *Ibid.*
129. Deegh Nikaya, ¼, Sondand Sutt, p. 46: *op. cit.*
130. *Ibid.* 1/3, Ambatthh Sutt, p. 39: Buddha Charcha, Anbatthh Sutt: *op. cit.*
131. Majjim Nikaya, 2/5/6, Asukari Suttant.
132. *Ibid.*
133. *Ibid,* 2/5/3, Aashvalayan Suttant.
134. *Ibid.*
135. Deegh Nikaya, ¾, Aaggak Sutt, 241-45: *op. cit.*
136. *Ibid,* pp. 240-41.
137. Sutt Nipat, 2/7.
138. Anguttar Nikaya, 5/5/1.
139. *Ibid.*
140. Majjim Nikaya, 2/4/4, Madhur Surat.
141. *Bhagvan Buddha: Jeevan aur Darshan,* pp. 224-25: Dharmanand Koshambi.

142. Sutt Nipat, Aamgandh Sutt.
143. Sanyutt Nikaya, 1/7/1/9.
144. *Ibid.*, Sangarav Sutt.
145. Majjim Nikaya, 1/32, Mahasaropam Sutt.
146. *Bhagvan Buddha aur Unka Dharam*, p. 217: *op. cit.*
147. Deegh Nikaya, 1/13, Tevijj Sutt, p. 90: *op. cit.*
148. Anguttar Nikaya, Tik Nipat.
149. Dhammpad, Sahassvagg, 1/3.
150. Sutt Nipat.
151. *Buddha and Caste System*, p. 27: Bhikshu U. Dhammrj.
152. Deegh Nikaya 3/6, Prasadik Sutt, p. 268, *op. cit.*
153. Bhagvan Buddha aur Unka Dharam : pp. 331-32 : *op. cit.*
154. *Shudron ka Pracheen Itihas*, p. 117: *op. cit.*
155. Jatak, 3, p. 194: 4, p. 303: editor, V. Faasbaal, 7 binding, 1877–97, London, translation 6 binding, 1895, 1907 London.
156. *Ibid.*, 4, p. 200.
157. *Ibid.*, 3, p. 233.
158. *Shudron ka Pracheen Itihas*, pp. 118–19: *op. cit.*
159. *Bhagvan Buddha aur Unka Dharam*, p. 146: *op. cit.*
160. Buddha: His Life, His Teachings, His Order, p. 157: *op. cit.*
161. Supipya Thero, Sopak Thero Attakatha.
162. Bhagvan Buddha aur Unka Dharam, pp. 146–47: described earlier.
163. Shardul karan-Apdan.
164. Bhagvan Budhh aur Unka Dharam, pp. 153–56: described earlier.
165. Bhagvan Buddh aur Jati-Bhed, pp. 73-75, third edition, 1985 : Bhikshu Dharamrakshit.
166. Sutt Nipat, Vasal Sutt.
167. *Ibid.*
168. Majjim Nikaya, Angulimal Sutt.
169. Bhagvan Buddha aur Unka Dharam, p. 161: *op. cit.*
170. *Ibid.*, pp. 161–62.
171. *Ibid.*, p. 163.
172. Dialogues of the Buddha, p. 102: *op. cit.*
173. *Bhagvan Buddha aur Unka Dharam*, p. 338: *op. cit.*
174. *Ibid.*
175. *Buddha and Caste System*, p. 28: *op. cit.*
176. Anguttan Nikaya, Chatudak Nipat, Samrat Ashok ke Bhabru Shila-Lekh main Varnit (Bhagvan Buddha: Jeevan aur Darshan, p. 277: *op. cit.*).
177. Sutt Nipat, Nalak Sutt (It is described in *Bhabru Shila-Lekh* by name of *Moneyya Sutt.*).
178. Majjim Nikaya, Mahaskuludayi Sutt.
179. *Bhagvan Buddha: Jeevan aur Darshan*, p. 244: *op. cit.*
180. *Buddha and Caste System*, pp. 28–29: *op. cit.*
181. *Ibid*, p. 34.
182. Vinay Patak, Mahavagg, 9.
183. *Buddha: His Life, His Teachings*, His Order, p. 133: *op. cit.*
184. *Ibid.*

10

Evaluation and Conclusion

In the present work, the author has shown that the sphere of religion is to forbid to the Sudra the use of the most efficacious formulae and rites on the one hand, and to exhort him to perform most of the daily rites and the obligatory sacraments prescribed for the other castes. The doctrine of salvation through the conscientious discharge of the duties proper to caste is, indeed, mentioned here and there. But evidently the Brahmin law-givers of this period did not feel fully satisfied with that method of salvation. They had come to posses too much faith in the efficacy of the rites and sacraments to allow them to be neglected even by the Sudra. The liberalizing influence of the Buddhist revolt and of Vaishnava compassion led the Brahmins to devise ways and means of assuring spiritual betterment to the Sudra in the Brahminic way of rites and sacraments. It must also be mentioned that the performance of the Brahminic rites and sacraments by a large section of the people had a selfish interest for the Brahmin, which he could not have entirely lost sight off. Rites and sacraments require the services of a Brahmin. The Sudra caste—the largest section of the people—was the only one which was denied sacred knowledge. If the Sudras wanted to perform the Brahmanic rites and sacraments they would invariably have to requisition the services of a Brahmin. To allow the Sudra the privilege of these sacred performances was thus to ensure a large clientele for the Brahmin. Yet neither the genuine desire to widen the scope of his religious regulations so as to make it possible for the lowly Sudra to work for his spiritual uplift in the Brahmanic way, nor the selfish motive of procuring mass clientele was strong enough for the Brahmin to override completely his supreme faith in the sanctity of his lore or his high regard for ceremonial purity. He began to make a distinction between the Sudra who behaved properly according to the Brahmin's ideas, and the Sudra who was slovenly enough not to come up to this standard of conduct—the "Sat" and the "Asat" Sudra. Only the former class of Sudras was allowed the privilege of the practice of rites and sacraments though without the use of the Vedic formulae.

This study also reflects about the law-books, which shows that the Chandala should be dressed in the garments of the corpses he cremated, should eat his food from broken vessels, and should wear only iron ornaments. No man of higher class might have any but the most distant relations with a Chandala, on pain of losing his religious purity and falling to the Chandala's level. By Gupta times Candalas had become so strictly untouchable that like lepers in medieval Europe, they were forced to strike a wooden clapper on entering a town to warn the Aryans of their polluting approach.

This work has pointed out that the certain classes of out-castes or untouchables seem to have gained their unenviable position through the growth of the sentiment of non-violence, for instance the Nisada, who was a hunter, the fishing caste called Kaivarta, and the leather worker (karavara). The Pukkusa, who appears as a sweeper in Buddhist literature, may have fallen in status because members of his class made and sold alcoholic liquor. More difficult to account for are such base classes as basket-maker *(vena)* and the chariot-maker *(rathakara).* In early Vedic times the later were most respected craftsmen, but soon fell to the status of impure Sudra or outcastes.

With the context of his study, the beginning of the Christian era the outcastes themselves had developed a caste hierarchy and had their own outcastes. Manu mentions the *antyavasayin,* a cross between a Chandala and a Nisada, who was despised even by the Candalas themselves. In later India every untouchable group imagined that some other group was lower than itself and this stratification evidently began quite early.

The present work clarifies that the untouchable was not altogether without hope. Though he was denied access to the temples and the comforts of orthodox religion, Buddhist monks preached to him, and the more enlightened wandering ascetics would give him instructions. The untouchable dying in defence of Brahmins, cows, women, and children secured a place in heaven. Orthodox texts contain frequent warnings on the evils which arise when Sudras and outcastes grow too powerful, and this would seem to show that a Chandala might occasionally become influential.

The present study also shows another class of untouchable (mleccha), the word commonly used for outer barbarians of whatever race or colour. As an invader he was loathed, but once he had come into contact with Indian ways and was less strange and forbidding his status might improve. In fact, it was not blood which made a group untouchable, but conduct. Generally there was no chance of an individual rising in the social scale, but for a group this was possible, over a number of generations, by adopting more orthodox practices and following the rules of the Smritis. Thus, the Indian class system was always somewhat fluid.

This study considers that the Sudras were burdened by a very marked social and religious inferiority. Their caste, in Vedic times, seems to have included the dark-skinned aborigines conquered by the Aryans, to whom were added later some of the poorer Aryans themselves and certain other people who had forfeited their rights for one reason or another. They were therefore not only despised from the earliest times, but also considered impure. They nevertheless took part in the dharma: but their benefits therefrom were limited to seeking redress under the law, and, under certain conditions, the opportunity to study the sacred texts of Hinduism, namely the Puranas and the Scriptures known as the Tantras, to take part in private but not public rites. This was the limit of their rights.

This study shows the Shudra's rights, for they had no possibility of freeing themselves from the servitude which was their by reason of birth. This is where the theory of Karma assumed its full significance: since being born into a particular caste was considered the fruit of acts accomplished in previous existences, it was quite clear that the Shudras had to their debit a heavy load of evil deeds from their past lives. Since this debt ruled the condition of the individual throughout his present life and could only be modified at the next rebirth, the clear implication was that there was no hope of their improving this situation during their lifetime. They had one single means of achieving rebirth in a superior class, and that was to perform their allocated duties conscientiously. This idea was responsible for an under-standable feeling of inferiority on the part of this underprivileged caste, more especially as the whole concept was carefully maintained by the ruling classes, and showed itself in the behaviour of everyone throughout India. We lack much information about the composition of this caste, but it appears to have included servants of all sorts. Wage-earners, workmen, labourers and minor functionaries. To these were added small clerks, tradesmen and craftsmen; some of the latter, however, were able to exercise relatively lucrative trades and crafts, and even practise husbandry. On the whole they were too conscious of their despicable situation to make any attempt to escape from it, but it must not be assumed that therefore led an unbearable existence. Many of them worked for wealthy tradesmen and landlords, were paid a regular wage, fed lodged (sometimes on the employer's premises, sometimes outside) and received further benefits in kind: agricultural workers, for example, were paid a fifth of their wages in goods and produce if they were fed and lodged, or a third if not. They remained attached to the same family, from father to son. Their low status compelled them to eat only the remnants from the master's table, to wear his cast-off clothing and to make use only of discarded objects. The employer was supposed to treat them decently, and they were in fact protected, to some extent, by the law; he was obliged to make a contract with them, a document enumerating the names of all the employee's dependents. While the Shudra was expected to give proof of zeal and professional competence, his master was in his turn obliged to furnish him with the instruments necessary for his work and to replace those which were out or defective. The contract laid down the number of hours to be worked and the wages to be paid, and specified the goods and produce which would normally be provided over and above the wages. If the wages were not paid or if the contract was unjustifiably terminated, the employer was liable to prosecution.

The present study reflects that the Shudras were subjected to what seems a relatively light taxation. On the other hand, they were subject throughout the year to perform forced labour consisting of one or two days work a month. Those particularly affected by this law were the workers who processed rice, flour, oil or sugar, and those who worked in spinning or weaving mills, and in factories making arms and military supplies. This forced labour could sometimes be avoided by paying a sum of money.

This work reveals with the servile class which was not homogeneous since, even here, distinctions were made between the 'pure' or 'unexcluded' and the excluded'. The latter were practically identical with the 'outcastes' (untouchables).

This study reflects that segment of the population was only sketchily described in the sacerdotal texts, which referred to its members as 'last-born, low-born or those who may not approach the (sacred) vessels.' These are the people whom we designate, in modern times, by the term 'pariah' or 'untouchable'. They comprised a series a sub-castes among which that of the candalas is the one most frequently mentioned. The outcastes all had trades or crafts which were despised, or even condemned, by religious orthodoxy, either because their work involved the taking of human or animal life, or because their functions involved some ritual defilement. Included in these two categories were hunters, fishermen, butchers, curriers, executioners, gravediggers, undertakers, those who sold liquor, sweepers, and, during certain historical periods.

In 200 C., it appears by seeing social, economical, political and cultural condition of untouchable species that the movement operated by Buddhism for eight hundred years against caste-difference and untouchability caused no special change. Instead of ending or reducing untouchability, it increased. From 600 BC to 200 C., this social institution adopted more solid shape and even, many other tribes were united in this group, which were not untouchable earlier. Now it is natural for this question to arise as to why constant attempt of Buddhism for decades did not succeed in achieving its objective.

In connection of caste-difference and untouchability, historical role and success-failure of Buddhism has been the subject of debate. On this subject, learned investigators are divided in two clear tenets, out of which according to one, the attempt of Buddhism was a successful socio-cultural movement while the other considers it to be an unsuccessful attempt. Dr Sarvpalli Radhakrishnan, a renowned Indian philosophical scholar, has written, "When any fanciful man will see that in 600 BC there was a prince in India, whose spiritual strength, grand theory of feelings, excellent life and attachment for mankind, none either before or after him, could match, he will be surprised."[1] Although T.W.R. Ris Davids is reluctant to connect himself to any of the tenets, but he, portraying Gautama Buddha as a sympathiser of trampled people, says, "First thing is that as long as own religion and monastery are concerned, and on which he had complete control, he neglected special profits and conveniences or inconveniences produced by birth, profession and social renown, and finished all hurdles and inabilities produced due to religious or social pollution related agreeable rules."[2]

But H. Oldvarg, the reputed scholar, challenging this success and historical role of Buddhism, has penned, "In today's era, those investigating about history, having provided importance to social effect of religious movements or having found out their effect, enjoy in increasing their knowledge in connection of these movements. We can understand very well how this inclination of historians had made Buddha a social reformer who broke chains of caste and having estabiished religious monastery, offered place to poor and ruined people therein. But whoever, will try to describe Buddha's attempts and if he is loyal to truth, then this consideration will have to be denied strongly that Buddha got fame due to his social reforms. If according to someone, Buddhism had democracy, he should remember that talks like reconstruction of national life, establishment of a golden rule or operating some ideal religion, were completely external for Buddhistic monastery. At that time there was nothing in India like social topsyturvy. Buddha's nature was totally devoid of that excitement and attachment as is found in those in accepting the challenge of protecting afflicted ones from torturers. Let the state and society be as it is. No relation should exist between their management and activities as well as such religious man. One who having become recluse, has deserted world, caste-difference is nothing for him because now he is unaffected by worldly talks. But he has never any idea to attempt to end that class system for welfare or to break the strictness of its rules for those who are entangled in worldly circumstances, and are lagging behind.[3]

Similarly, the great saint Rahul Sankrityayan has written, "Buddha's philosophy is excessive momentary, he does not believe anything staying for more than a moment but he was not willing to apply his vision on economical condition of society. It was natural for a talented philosopher like him to achieve more respect in high class society on establishing piece with rich ruler-exploiting society thus. Rich and great Brahmins like Sondand, strong supporters of priest class, became his followers. Kings appeared curious for his reception. More than that, multi-millionaire business class of that time, kept its bags opened for his hospitality as today's Indian for Mahatma Gandhi will. Multi-millionaire Sudatt (Anathpindak) of Shravasti, having covered by coin, bought a heavy garden (Jetvan) and gifted for stay of Buddha and his monks. Another wealthy woman, Vishakha of that very city, got another monastery constructed spending a large amount of money. Three wealthy persons of Koshambi, a great centre of business with South and South-West India competed mutually in getting monastery constructed. The truth is that businessmen helped more than kings in spreading the religion of Buddha. Had Buddha gone against contemporary economical system, where could this comfort come from?"[4]

H. Oldandvarg, accusing Buddha of getting influenced by nobles, and neglecting poor and helpless people, has written:

"....here are Brahmin youths like Sariputt, Moggallayan, members of noble birth like Anand, Rahul, Anirudhh, sons of big businessmen and distinguished men of town-assembly like Yash, essentially all these people and youths belonged to very noble classes of contemporary society and their qualification was according to their social standard, too."[5] ... "In those people who sought shelter of Buddha *dhamm* and monastery, princes and noble persons, Brahmins and businessmen also appear to us. It seems that here also the people of prosperous and big houses were included. Probably, it was not so in Buddhism that poor, unfortunate and miserable people be given any support. Buddha had two friends in category of important people, one of them being Bimbisar, king of Magadh and the other, Prasendi, king of Kausal. They were almost equal to Buddha in age and throughout their lives, remained true saviours of Buddhism."[6]

Thus, by evaluation of aforesaid scholars, in reality it appears that the scholars of both tenets have put strong arguments in support of their views but their analysis and conclusions are partial and exaggerated. Both these viewpoints have been unsuccessful in testing historical role of Buddhism by balanced eye. This is the truth that Buddhism had been achieving protection and assistance of Kings and businessmen since its inception. The powerful followers of Buddha, included people of prosperous and noble classes. This is true also that if any recluse gave *pabbajja* to any debtor or running Das, he was criminal of *dukkat* (A minor crime). In this connection, following example from Vinay Patak is worthy of mention:

"At that time, who was indebted, ran away and took initiation from Buddhistic monks. When lenders saw him, they said, "He is our debtor, let us take him (towards prison)." But some answered, "Sir, do not do so. Soniy Bimbisar has issued the royal mandate, "Those who are initiated by Sakyaputitya Samno, none will cause them harm; their philosophy is good, let them spend sacred life for complete prevention of suffering." People murmured due to acrimony and anger. "In fact, these Sakyaputitya Saman are free from everything, there is no permission to do anything against them. But how can they admit any debtor in Buddhistic monastery?"

They conveyed this thing to Buddha.

"O monks! no debtor should get *pabbajja.* Whoever gives *pabbajja* to any debtor, is accused of *dukkat* (a minor crime)."[7] This is true also that generally the entry of Das was banned. It becomes clear from description of Vinay Patak that no running Das was admitted in monastery because Buddha has written, "O monks! No *pabbhajja* should be given to any Das. Whoever gives *pabbajja* to any Das, is criminal *dukkat* (a minor crime)."[8] But if any Das or debtor got admission somehow in monastery, that monk admitting might be accused but that Das achieved same respect and protection as did a monk coming from common people. Once Buddha asked Ajatshatru, king of Magadh, "If any slave of royal palace, after leaving palace and wearing red-brown clothes, enters monastery and committing no mental, verbal and bodily mistake, spends a monk's life, then also will you say that he must come back and again be a slave?" Then, Ajatshatru replied, "No *prabhu,* we will respect him, stand for him leaving our seat and request him to be seated. And, we will request him to accept clothes, bowls, rest-place and medicines for patients (these things are for use of hermits and ascetics) and then we will also arrange for his safety according to rules." Similarly, renunciation of royal employees and soldiers in monastery was banned. It is known by account of Vinay Patak's Mahavagg that on complaint of king Bimbisar, Gautama Buddha after delivering religious sermons, addressing monks, said, "O monks! who is in government service, should not be given *pabbajja.* Whoever, gives *pabbajja* to such man, is accused of *dukkat* (a minor crime)."[7]

It is clear from aforesaid proofs that the entry of debtor, slaves and royal employees in monastery was banned but no such ban was imposed on admission of untouchables. We have seen that Buddhism operated a movement against untouchability and high-low by its philosophical, psychological and practical attempts. This is true too that against difference of birth and clan as well as untouchability, the battle of Buddhism continued for decades. Not only this, in contemporary monastery of Buddha, many untouchables like Sopak, Supipya, Suneet, Prakrati got admission, who became renowned monks in future. In list of authors of Thers and Therigathas, ten[11] out of two sixty nine Thers and eight out of sixty nine Therees, were actors, Chandal, basket manufacturers, hunters, prostitutes and maids.[12] Having seen these proofs probably, D.P. Chattopadhyay has written, "Protection of kings and businessmen was not so much as it would have become an original base of its remarkable success. As in sacred texts of Buddhism, the number of common people in followers of this religion, might be exaggerated, yet this proof will have to be accepted that class-difference, that is, due to presence of system of caste-tribe, against injustice or uselessness of religious ceremonies of Brahmins, common people might be attracted towards it because of Buddha's thoughts."[13]

Substantially, common people and even untouchables, were attracted towards Buddhism while king and businessmen, rich and great merchants, participated in this arduous task too and it is absolutely surprising. Then it is certain that this religion had some qualities by which touchable and untouchable, poor and rich, king and subordinates, having got attracted, had participated in it. These qualities were: incorporation of morality and values of tribal society in Buddhism, which were being broken by royal system very cruelly and greedily at that time. D.D. Koshambi has written, "In Ganga valley, in 600 BC, many social groups, having different identities, were in different phases of development."[14] D.P. Chattopadhyay, throwing light on social, economical and political circumstances produced by this irregular development phase, has written, "For the rise of Buddhism, to understand importance of this disproportional development, we have also to remember that the rulers of primary period in movement of defeating others and expanding their kingdom, were making a mince of contemporary free tribes by in a very planned way. Wherever they had established their supremacy, talks like "there trivial inclination of greed, cruelty, sexuality, mutual hatred, robbing public property for personal interest" were taking place, missing in latest tribal life. In this revolutionary period of history, Buddha came forward and said to have searched real solution of all problems. He asked people to enter his Buddhistic monastery. These monasteries had democratic system of tribes. Thus, monasteries were the supreme option for vanished life system."[15] K.P. Jayasval has stated that, "Buddha regarded his contemporary parties or monasteries an ideal of his recluse monastery".[16]

Substantially, the talks of aforesaid scholars are affirmed by different aspects of Buddhism. If we consider the process of admission in Buddhistic monastery, internal administration thereof and personal property therein, it appears clearly that these talks consisted of tribal ideal, system and morality. Entry in Buddhistic monastry was followed by *pabbajja* and *up sampada* functions and activities. To be a complete member of Buddhistic monastery, these two phases were there, first phase, that is, *pabbajja* was held as a preparation for second phase, that is, *upsampada.*[17] The light is thrown hereon in E.R.E.: "*Pabbajja'* (*pravajya*) means going out. By this function, one goes out of state of his previous birth—*'Upsampada'* means 'reaching', and enters the circle of completely recognised members of monastery."[18] Unlike tribal society, Buddhistic monastery was not originally an assembly of relatives and so, the fixation of its membership did not depend on blood-relation, or lineage or clan. Membership of Buddhistic monastery was achieved after closing of that democratic system of acceptance which was an arrangement like adoption function by people-assembly in tribal society where it was asked to give membership to a man of different lineage or any outsider. This democratic system of Buddhistic monastery appears to resemble that religious activity of Iroki aboriginal about whom L.H. Morgan has informed: "In assembly hall, after gathering of people, a chief, getting up, provided some information about the man and then the information of the reason of his adoption, his name, lineage and the name given to newcomer. Then, two chiefs, holding that newcomer's arms, revolved on foot, accompanying him and in conjunction with, sang adoption song. In the end of every stanza, all people answered in similar voice. Unless all stanzas were finished, revolving continued. It completed in three rounds. With this only, the function ended."[19]

Fundamental nature of aforesaid description of Morgan and *upsampada* initiation activity, explained in Mahavagg (1.28) of Vinay Patak, resembles each other.

"Then Buddha has addressed monks thus: "O monks! I direct that you adopt *upsampada* initiation by traditional process of monastery, under which after announcement (*natti*) three questions are there."

"And O monks! you should give this *upsampada* initiation thus: some scholarly monk should conduct this *natti* (announcement of proposal) before monastery:

"O respectful people of monastery, listen to me. This man wants to get *upsampada* initiation from this man utmost respected n.n. (that is fully respected n.n. will be his *upjajhya*). If monastery is ready, monastery provide *upsampada* initiation to monastery n.n. in which n.n. be his *upjajhya,* this is announcement." "Respected *mahanubhav*, monastery, listen to me. This man n.n. wants to get *upsampada* initiation from utmost respected n.n. Monastery provides *upsampada* initiation to n.n. and n.n. is his *upjajhya.* Out of venerable men, who is in favour of giving *upsampada* initiation to n.n. as well as n.n.'s becoming his *upjajhya,* be silent and who is opposed to it, speak out.

And now second time, I tell you the same thing: monastery, listen to me ... (as earlier).

n.n. has achieved *upsampada* initiation by monastery and n.n. is his *upjajhya*. Monastery is in its favour and so silent. I understand the same."[20]

Maxmullar has written, "Later as monasteries were developed, some new problems essentially originated, due to which it became necessary to maintain some new rules during *upsampada* function.[21] But its original identity of following tribal adoption system never disappeared.[22]

Ordination of internal administration of Buddhistic monastery was absolutely democratic. R.C. Majumdar, the renowned historian, has provided important information in this connection, "Great conference of monks had achieved supreme power and the process of its session was completely decisive... In the very beginning, completely initiated all monks of some sect were members of this committee. Out of them, only one having been punished for some crime, had no right to vote. Otherwise all had right to vote. Any conference was not regarded regular unless all members having right to vote be not present or if absent, at least they had to declare their vote duly. To accept any rule, the minimum number of members was fixed or to say, this rule was fixed in Mahavagg as to what minimum number should be there.... On gathering of all, the proposer, first of all, had to announce that proposal before present monks, which was to be presented there and this declaration was called *natti.* After *natti,* questions were put before monks whether they approved that proposal or not. Question was asked once or three times.... After presenting proposal duly, if present members remained silent, this proposal was regarded approved voluntarily. If some spoke against that or some sort of difference happened, then the decision of majority was accepted. According to rule, votes were taken and for this, a man, who collected votes, was appointed duly."[23]

Substantially, the constitution of Buddhistic monasteries was very democratic. But this democratic system was not Buddha's invention but a mere imitation of tribal democracy or tribal democratic process.[24] It is also affirmed by interpretation of K.P. Jayasval when he tells that Buddha adopted that very method for counting his members as that of tribal corporations or parties:

When people asked monks coming for alms:

"Venerable *mahanubhavon,* how many monks are there?

They replied, "Friends, we do not know."

People got irritated, they murmured and became furious: "*Shakyaputtiya Samans* know nothing about one another, what other good talks they will be knowing?"

They conveyed this to Buddha.

"Monks, I order that you count all monks." Now they thought: "When should we count monks?" They conveyed this to Buddha. Buddha told, "I direct that you count according to the method of parties on fast day or take them to *matshakha*". (Mahavagg—2.18)

Jayasval has said clearly that Buddha might be born among democratic people. There were groups only in his neighbourhood among whom he grew. The community he established, was named by him *Bhikshu Sangh* or *Bhikshuon ka Loktantra.* At the time of establishing his religious monastery, he possibly followed his contemporary teachers and adopted the names of political groups as well as preamble."[25] When Kausal king besieged the capital of Shakya and it was to be decided in connection of surrendering or not, they gathered for majority described by W. Rakhil as follows:

"When king sent his ambassador to Shakyas and gave the message, "O *Mahanubhavon,* although you are not dear to me and yet there is no hatred for you in my mind, everything is finished, therefore, open the city-gate soon." Then Shakya said, "Let us consider whether we should open gate or not." When they gathered, some Shakyas said, "Open the gate" and other Shakyas denied it. Some said, "Since different ideas are expressed, we will find out the majority." And then they started to take votes on this subject."[26] If we see those seven rules prescribed by Gautama Buddha called by him not only necessary for safety and prosperity of Vajji people but also regarded mandatory for prosperity of Buddhistic monastery, it will be clarified to a great extent that tribal democratic system was an ideal for him. King Ajatshatru, by attacking on Vajji people, wanted to merge in his kingdom. He sent Brahmin Vassakar, his prime minister, to seek Buddha's blessings. Although Buddha himself explained seven rules of prosperity and safety of Vajji people to him, prevalent among them, but did not bless. After his departure, Buddha collected all monks of royal palace through Anand and repeated those very seven rules for the prosperity of Buddhistic monastery. Ris Davids has put the example of description of Deegh Nikaya's Mahaparinirvan Sutt as follows:

"O monks, ! as long as all friends keep meeting one another often and remain present in formal conferences of their monastery and community; as long as they stay with complete consent and maintain all duties of monastery with full consent; as long as they donot commit any thing or task not interpreted in provisions earlier nor do they desert any duty directed earlier and work according to rules described by monastery; as long as all friends respect, worship and support their experienced elders and give respect to religious instructors and leaders of monastery and consider it their duty to listen to their talks and to understand them; as long as all friends are not affected by their internal desire which creates longing for new existence; as long as all people experience happiness in retired life; as long as they do not prepare themselves mentally for self-restraint so that virtuous people approach them and experience comfort; it should be expected that their decline would not happen and they will grow prosperous. As long as these seven talks will be present in these friends, as long as they understand them very well, it will be expected that their prosperity and not decline, will be there."[27]

It is well known that in primary tribal society personal property was absent. This society was not only democratic but there was also collective ownership on entire property that is, equal right. In tradition of Buddha's period, the memory of that vanished collective life always remained firm which was regarded the golden era of past. Discussing Aggann Sutt of Deeghnikaya, D.D. Koshabi has written, "Memory of a society devoid of class as well as difference, remained a story of a golden era when that auspicious land without any labour, easily generated sufficient grain because in this period man had neither any personal property nor did he have any feeling of greed."[28]

In Buddhistic text 'Mahavastu Avdaan', the story described in connection of advent of monarchy, also contains similar memory of peaceful era before divided society completely devoid of personal property.[29] In Buddhistic monastery also, like initial tribal society no monk had personal property on commodity. R.C. Majumdar has written: "... In Buddhistic monastery, the man was merged in whole monastery. In religious order of Buddha that every commodity is the property of monastery and not of any particular monk, and that monk can get that very item fixed certainly for him, only this thing is reflected as to how sort of relation was there between man and group. And this rule is exactly according to this doctrine that the property of any monk poshthumously was received by monastery."[30] It is affirmed by comments of Ris Davids and Olderburg also: "Following rule, in which most of them were not prevalent now, maximum are based on similar customs of community. There was the tradition of giving all clothes to any single monk or community on ending of raining season in monastery or monk community on any place. Here attention should be paid to this thing that no monk had his personal clothes; although generally these were for his personal use. Substantially, these were for him only but if seen on the base of rule, all these were the property of the monastery. The monk above mentioned, put all clothes for drying up and later fulfilled the needs of those monks whose clothes got spoilt due to wetting or any other reason."[31]

No member of Buddhistic monastery could accept any gold-silver nor did he ever use that. Buddhistic scriptures contain long stories on *pachchiteeya* crimes related to requisition, the complete series of which is based on property related viewpoint of equilibrium. The example related to requisition described in *'Sacred Books of the East'* is worthy of quotation: "Whoever monk will receive gold or silver or for receiving for his own sake, ask any other man or deposit with someone, he will be accused of *pachhiteeya* crime and that gold-silver will be confiscated. Whoever monk will conduct similar practice having the use of silver, he will be accused of *pachchiteeya* crime and that silver will be forfeited. Sinner monk will have to hand over gold or silver to his monastery....then here also any *anmik* or devotee will come, he will be given this gold or silver to buy ghee or oil for monastery and whatever will be bought, will be joint property of monastery but faulty monk will have no share in that."[32]

Thus, it is clear from aforesaid proofs that Gautama Buddha constructed his monastery according to tribal system and values and offered it a solid identity. With the Buddhistic monastery, disappearing "the system of admission, its internal administration and collective ownership in place of joint property', were reconstructed, having accepted tribal society as an ideal, which was a separate world from sufferings and problems prevalent in contemporary society. In contemporary society, monarchy system was being developed by breaking government of people and tribal societies per force but Buddha did not regard monarchy system an ideal nor did he provide any importance to personal property based on personal interest or libido. D.P. Chattopadhyay has written correctly, "In Buddhistic monastery there were strict oppugnants of personal property. This was logical. The suffering they wanted to escape, and in whose connection they said repeatedly, was the consequence of greed which they were noticing on their all sides. Buddha knew that the root of this greed is the power of personal property. He was unable in matter of reforming society but inside monastery his power was supreme. He never wanted to be influenced by power of gold."[33]

In this condition the only alternative for Gautama Buddha and his followers was to free themselves at least from those things which were the reason of misery in contemporary society and they did exactly the same. In this condition, Karl Marx's comment made on religion can be kept in mind: "Man makes religion and not vice-versa. But man is not a formless commodity sitting outside world. Man is this universe, kingdom and society. This kingdom, this society produces an 'opposite world consciousness' of religion because they are king opposite world. Religion, for pacification and justification of this opposite world, is a common principle; is extensive base of its universal duties, modish logic, its spiritual height, its zeal, its moral encouragement, and its completeness; is expression of religious calamity, real agony, and feeling of opposition against itself. Religion is the belief of afflicted and tortured people. It is the mind of heartless world as exactly as it is reasoning of irrational condition. It is opium for people. It is necessary for real comfort of people that this religion creating delusion of comfort, be ended. The meaning of demand of leaving the delusion of situation is demanding the desertion of that condition which requires delusion. Therefore, the fundamental target of criticising religion is criticising that feeling of accepting suffering and pain, which has been decorated by halo of light of religion."[34]

Substantially, Buddhism pacified wretched and afflicted folk as well as was able to provide a new ray of hope to contemptible and backward tribes. Although this ray did not prevent crisis and suffering of their real lives nor was it possible because original reasons of their problems and suffering remaind as it is; they received no attack. The demand of prevention of real suffering of untouchable people was to stop their oppugnants from committing robbery, to dismiss them from that socio-political power and to keep them separate from possession they had made on economical resources since decades lest they should regard themselves supreme as well as backward labour tribes deprived of power and property, inferior and hateable. Then only the culture of wretched and afflicted tribes could have been saved and reach new phase after developing. But this was not done nor was it possible on this turn of history. Therefore, Gautama Buddha, possessing talent, founded a world as well as religion which became a centre of attraction as well as a shelter for exploited and helpless people. Reality of statement of Chattopadhyay is exactly this: "Period of Buddha was such period in which cruel royal dignity on wreckage of tribal society was rising as a result of development of production power in Indian Northern area. Common life had been so pitiable by merchandise and war as cannot be imagined. There was no limit of greed of accumulating personal property. Yet production powers had not developed so much as to fulfill the needs of all. Instead, where finally, real comfort by further development was possible, it was also certain that exploitation would have been done more cruelly and in conjunction with, the plight of people will have been more miserable. In this condition, demand of leaving 'that condition' for which deception be required, was very ridiculous from historical viewpoint. Substantially according to that era, second alternative, only a single possible one, was to produce the delusion of correct type for that period, which might be universal base of zeal, moral approval and completeness for its pacification and justification. And Buddha produced similar delusion, created reasoning for that irrational situation."[35]

Opposite to this painful world, Gautama Buddha, having created opposite world, devoid of suffering, that is Buddhistic monastery and religion, put deceptive hope before tortured and untouchable people, having got which, untouchable boys like Suneet, Supipya and Sopak, became emotional. They were untouchable and contemptible in real universe and society but were achieving equality and similar feelings in its opposite universe or Buddhistic monastery and that is why untouchable Suneet appreciated his emancipation in *Thergatha,* "I have come from a small family. I was poor as well as needy. My occupation was of a very low kind. I used to clean withered flowers by broom. People used to see me with eye of hatred. I used to express respect for all very politely. Then I saw Buddha with his monks. They and that great protagonist, were visiting the most important city of Magadha. Then I threw my weight, taking it off and running, bent my head before them. Those superior men stopped, having mercy on me. I saluted in feet of *Prabhu* and going before him, requested him to admit me as monk. Then that kind *Prabhu,* who is treasure of mercy of all regions, told me, "O *bhikshu,* come here." Thus, I achieved initiation."[36]

Not only Suneet of Pukkas tribe, but Sati, the man, Chapa, the hunter daughter and Punna and Punnika the slave daughters of even Dheevar tribe, regarded cruel and contemptible, which was declared untouchable in Parvarti period and Sumangalmata of low tribe working in Saneethha forest, sang the song of their freedom by happy throat. The song of Sumangalmata's emancipation explained in *Thergatha* is worthy to be seen: "...O woman! I am good after emancipation. How independent I am today. How completely free I have become today from fire-place. My hands and feet, all were stained by blackness of pots. My cruel husband could not provide even that sort of shadow under which he, sitting, kept weaving cloth.

But today I have been exempted from libido and hate. I am thinking, sitting under the shadow of branches at tree spread all over that I am very happy today. I am free today.[37]

If Prakrati, a Chandal girl, could not achieve Anand, a learned monk, as husband, no care, at least she got comfort in dream by taking initiation of religion and humility in Buddhistic monastery and thus suffering of not getting him was prevented. Similarly, Mukta, the daughter of a poor Brahmin of Kosal, was emancipated from hunch-backed husband and having got admission in Buddhistic monastery, became sentimental and hummed in *Thergatha*:

"Oh! Today I am really independent and have been emancipated from three distortions: quern, mortar and hunch-backed husband. Truly I have become free from rebirth and death. I have thrown that ploughshare that pulled me."[38]

It is clear from aforesaid data that Buddhism gifted conscience in this heartless universe for untouchable and tortured people to a very deep level, created comfort of deception in painful society and installed the feeling of similarity and equality among those people with new excitement and logic. In real society and life, the morality, equality, similarity and fraternity being crushed cruelly, Buddhism made them the base of this doctrine and philosophy and provided them the greatest importance in collective doctrines of his monastery. The comfort of Buddhism got established as a last goal of deception *nibbaanam paramam sukham.*[39] Not only this, Gautama Buddha transformed the real suffering of man in a universal ideal and considering suffering and pain a disease, suggested the rules for their prevention. J.H.S. Karn has written about these rules that "it is not difficult to see that these four Arya truths are nothing but four fundamental rules of Indian medical science, which were used for spiritual awakening of mankind. Similarly, there is the same sort of relationship between "Prateetya Samutpad" and four "Arya truths" as is of entire medical science system with anatomy science."[40] Although in Buddhism for suffering-prevention, these rules were made the base but the reasons of suffering quoted, were possibly very far from reality. To search real causes of as to why several types of disabilities were being loaded on untouchables and Sudras, why tribal communities were being broken and why a claim of imposing different types of bans on them continued for decades, was a riddle for Buddha and his followers. For this it was necessary to evaluate the physical environment of that period.

Discussing the physical environment of Buddha's time, Dr. Ramsharan Sharma has written, "Grounds of Ganga were made fit for agriculture as iron was used on a large scale and initially, big farms were constructed due to use of ploughshare. Division of agricultural land became easy and some people happened to occupy so much land as they could not plough by the help of their families. Therefore, they required labour which could be slaves and ironsmiths... In agriculture not only big farmers and householders required labour but common householders required few slaves or ironsmiths too. Due to giving tax by farmers, money-dealers and big states originated, whose officer class lived on tax and was free from production work. For their service and domestic work also, slaves and ironsmiths were required. Such priests and Brahmins, who became rich by donation of kings and peasants, needed attendants too. Workers were required on a large scale for manufacturing weapons and instruments for kings and farmers, respectively. Thus, agricultural workers and artisans began to be engaged for operating agriculture and workmanship. A good portion of their labour was acquired by high class people. Different types of disabilities were loaded on them so that they might serve high class people constantly, give sufficient part of their labour for their comforts and not perform any sort of opposition against them."[41] We have seen the account of Kautilya's *Arthasastra* in last chapter as to how new monarchies were wrecking tribal community and resettling them separately in number of ten-twenty each so that they might not rebel unitedly and be engaged in agriculture and arts.

Although till recently, those people who were spending the life of democratic rights and fraternity in tribal society and in *parvarti* period also socio-economical life of tribes in whose neighbourhood remained firm, how they were exploited by new kings and ruined their society. R. Fik, having analysed *Jatak* stories, has described thus: "Common orthodox Buddha walks on which ideal, the practice of king will not always be according to that ideal. We mostly see that he has become independent and cruel and works according to his whims and prejudice. He suppresses his subjects, punishes them, tortures them, recovers tax from them and robs them exactly as sugar is beaten in sugar factory. His subjects appear to him as contemptible as a particle of sand piercing in eye, pebble in rice or nail causing pain to hand piercing in it." According to virtuous people quoted in 'Ten Rajdhamm', "a king has many flaws, and these flaws, as if, present another side of any currency, in which real character of king is exhibited, that is, intoxication and cruelty (in Khantivadi Jatak and Chool Dhamm Paal Jatak), corruption (in Bharu Jatak), falsehood and infidelity (in Chaiteey Jatak) .....In spiritual and worldly subjects, rectitude of their advisers can be helpful in stopping their choice and independence. Where this obstructing power was not present and his ministers or priests became helpful in fulfilment of his desires, mostly such circumstances originated where single passage available to people, that is, they had to be bound to adopt the passage of open revolt."[42] It is clear from aforesaid information that due to development entered in production technique, how various socio-political institutions originated and simultaneously, deterioration in moral values and how cruelty, libido and personal interest sank the common folk in ocean of suffering. Consequently, inhuman institutions like caste-difference, class-difference and untouchability came into existence and developed subsequently. It was inevitable from historical viewpoint and it happened. Gautama Buddha and his followers could not identify the root of this great historical change and contrary to this, they could notice disease of thoughts and feelings like cruelty, libido, selfishness, caste-difference, high-low and untouchability only. Consequently, against these feelings and thoughts, they created opposite thoughts and rules like way of suffering prevention and *nirvana,* and called them the way of emancipation from suffering. It was natural as Karl Marx and Fredrick Angels have written:

"This is true that thinking is that process which so called meditative completes consciously. But this consciousness is false. He remains ignorant about instigator powers and if it would not be so, this can never be the process of theoretical notion. Therefore, those instigator powers false or appearing from outside, are imagined by him. Since this is a contemplation process, he designs it also by thoughts which belong either to his ancestors or to himself. He functions only by thought-material, which he accepts, without testing, as the result of thoughts and does not discover any other source apart from thought. In fact, this is common thing of his routine life because when all activities are managed by the power of thinking only, on seeing that it seems that finally, this depends on thoughts."[43]

In fact, we have seen how Buddhism regarded preceding tribal society an ideal in his community and contemplation and worked accordingly. In philosophical and theoretical area, he made previous society and its wreckage the base. Although he did not accept Lokayat, present worldly, atheist, witchery, etc. of tribal society clearly but kept maintained a series of thoughtful and cultural movement against heaven, god and oblation or religious ceremonies. We have seen in last chapter how Gautama Buddha and his *parvarti* followers opposed Vedic and Brahmneeya thoughts and religious ceremonies strongly. Since these thoughts were supporters of interests of contemporary ruler classes that is high classes and oppugnants of those Sudra, untouchable and other backward contemptible people. Thus, Buddhism definitely managed a thoughtful battle against these thoughts, in which he got the support of maximum people. Gautama Buddha put a religion devoid of god and heaven before society and objected to oblation, religious ceremonies, etc. In fact, these thoughts impressed defeated and tortured people a lot because in tribal society also, along with god and heaven, religious ceremonies such as oblation and austerity never took place. Hereby a ray of thoughtful hope certainly took birth inside those so called untouchable people because they were descendents of Asuras, Rakshas, Das, Nag, etc., who had been living having made their culture unbroken since decades. Work of breaking and ruining tribal society of people believing Lokayat, atheist, presentworldly culture had become fast because without breaking them neither new empires could develop nor could slaves, workers and artisans be available to ruler classes of Vedic or Brahmneeya culture, viz., Kshatriya, Brahmin, businessmen, big farmers and householder. Therefore, despite the thought movement of equality and similarity of Buddhism, society of so called contemptible and backward classes of this non-Vedic and non-Brahmneeya culture, has been breaking and destroying for decades and they have been used as house servants performing physical labour, workers, slaves and artisans by ruler class and high class people. Despite the struggle of Buddhism, the walls of difference of high-low and touchable-untouchable kept developing because having separated themselves from labour, the hatred against labour originated in ruler classes. This feeling of hatred of rulers classes against labour, as well as Lokayatik, atheist and presentworldly culture which were oppugnants of Vedic or Brahmneeya culture, not only produced untouchability and difference of high-low but developed it subsequently, which after 200 C. appeared in more solid and developed shape in Gupta period.

The demand of abolition of caste-difference based on untouchability and high-low was that those physical circumstances be changed in which ruler class of Vedic or Brahmneeya culture itself, and controlled on power and property and having separated itself from labour and hard work, were exploiting laborious class, and called itself supreme and high but regarded people of this non-Vedic or non-Brahmneeya culture, who performed labour, low and contemptible. But to fulfill such demand from historical viewpoint was impossible and on this historical turn, we come across that very drawback in attempts of Buddhism. D.P. Chattopadhyay has written correctly: "Buddha considered sufferings and pains of his period a sort of disease. Even he wanted to prevent it according to principles of medical science of his time. Although he declared himself *tathagat* yet we do not expect from him that he had found out real social root of this disease. That is, we do not hope that he had analysed those great historical changes taking place at that time nor he would have understood as to why at the time of such a vast progress of production technique, so much human suffering and moral decline were taking place. If seen from historical viewpoint, the only thing remained for him to do that real problem be changed into an ideal one and external incidents be seen from external viewpoint; in brief, his duty was to create 'an opposite world consciousness'. Consequently, the sorry plight of public of that time was converted into one to be investigated thoroughly. Thus, initial Buddhist religion transformed into complete delusion of that era."[44]

Thus, it appears from investigation of all aforesaid facts that in reality, Buddhism, having universalised suffering and pain of untouchable tribes and common people, converted it into a problem fit for thorough investigation. Having achieved this as well as the way of suffering-prevention, people of all classes and species got attracted towards Buddhism. Untouchable and touchable, low and high, people of all tribes, in large number, participated in movement of Buddhism and Buddhistic monastery protesting high-low and untouchability. But since root of untouchability and high-low could not be attacked, it could not be abolished. In fact, for elimination of this institution, it was necessary to get the people suffering from curse of caste-difference and untouchability back to their socio-political power as well as to remove the hurdles of natural development of economic resources. Then only these tribes made backward unnaturally, progressing economically and passing from unequal development phases, were able to reach development level of Vedic or Brahmneeya people. For it, Buddhism had required to operate an economical-cultural movement which had to be managed against Brahmin system, accompanying crushed and afflicted people. But in historical era, similar collective movement did not have to stand and same happened. But Buddhism performed remarkable task against untouchability and high-low socio-cultural system, and its remote consequence appeared in

Indian history. First of all, Buddhism, firstly classified inhuman institution like caste-difference and untouchable the chief base of his movement. This movement, by its philosophy and arguments, flung a hard challenge by raising a question on the justification of social system based on untouchability and high-low. Secondly, by putting philosophical and theoretical argumentation in front against superiority-inferiority of tribe and lineage publicised by Vedic or Brahmneeya culture, Buddhism moved all classes and tribes to consider proper-improper, good-bad actions, etc. Having presented wise reasoning against useless imagination as god, immortality, soul, heaven as well as superstitions, Buddha and his followers put uselessness of oblations, religious ceremonies, etc., before public. Hereby the Brahminhood and the fast speed of superstitions definitely was stopped and people of all classes and species, untouchable and touchable participated in this movement managed against high-low and blind-faiths. Hereby Brahminhood received a deep shock and they could be stopped from adopting inhuman way. And lastly, Buddhism, having annexed untouchables in its religion and monastery and accepted victuals from all people equally against untouchability, not only denied wrong resolutions of Brahmins relating to inability and disability of untouchables but also established several untouchable people as important monks among all classes. Thus, the background of *Bhakti* movement coming in *parvarti* period, got prepared in which Indian society made saints of lower tribes its spiritual guides and teachers, separate from tribe and lineage. Therefore, it can be said implicitly that the attempt of Buddhism relating to untouchability-elimination was a progressive step of that era.

Notes and References

1. Indian Philosophy, Part 1, p. 347, London, 923.
2. *Dialogues of the Buddha,* Part 1, p. 102, London, 1899.
3. *Buddha: His life, His Teachings, His Order,* pp. 153-54, Calcutta, 1927.
4. *Buddha-Darshan,* p. 21, Allahabad, 1989.
5. *Op. cit.*, p. 156.
6. *Ibid,* p. 163.
7. *Sacred Books of the East,* 13, p. 199, Oxford, 1979; (S.) F. Maxmuller.
8. *Ibid*
9. Ris Davids, *op. cit.,* p. 77.
10. Max Muller, *op. cit.,* 13, p. 196.

11. Ateendranath Bose, *Social and Rural Economy of Northern India,* 2, p. 285, Calcutta, 1945.
12. *History of Pali Literature,* 2, pp. 501–16, London, 1933: B.C. La.
13. Lokayat, pp. 367–68, Calcutta, 1973.
14. *An Introduction to the Study of Indian History,* p. 140, Bombay, 1956.
15. *Op. cit.,* p. 368.
16. *Hindu Polity,* 1, 45–55, Calcutta, 1924.
17. Chattopadhyay, *op. cit.,* p. 384.
18. J. Hastings (S.): E.R.E., 7, p. 319, Edinbura, 1908–1918.
19. *Ancient Society,* p. 61, Calcutta.
20. Max Muller, *op. cit,* pp. 169–70.
21. *Ibid.,* pp. 151-238.
22. Chattopadhyay, *op. cit.,* 385.
23. *Corporate Life in Ancient India,* pp. 310–12, Calcutta, 1919.
24. Chattopadhyay, *op. cit.* p. 386.
25. *Op. cit.,* 1, p. 45.
26. *Life of Buddha and Early History of His Order,* pp. 118–19, London, 1884.
27. *Op. cit.,* 2, pp. 81–82, London, 1910.
28. *Op. cit.,* p. 162.
29. Chattopadhyay, *op. cit.,* p. 380.
30. *Op. cit,* pp. 316–18.
31. Max Muller, *op. cit.,* 13, p. 18 comment.
32. *Ibid,* p. 26.
33. *Op. cit.,* p. 390.
34. On Religion, pp. 41–42, Moscow, 1957: Karl Marx and Fredrick Angels.
35. *Op. cit.,* p. 394.
36. Olderburg, *op. cit.,* p. 157.
37. Ris Davids: *Some of Early Buddhism,* 1, p. 25.
38. *Ibid*
39. Dhammpad, 9, 202–203.
40. *Manual of Indian Buddhism,* pp. 46–47, Strawsburg, 1896.
41. *Shudras ka Pracheen Itihas,* pp. 123–24, Delhi, 1979.
42. *Op. cit.,* pp. 101–03.
43. Selected Correspondence, p. 541, Mowcow, 1946.
44. *Op. cit,* p. 396.

LIST OF SCRIPTURES

Original Scriptures

1. *Rigveda Sanhita,* accompanied by Sayan's comentary, Vedic Sanshodan Mandal, Pune 1933–51, translation of first six Mandals, H.H. Wilson, London, 1850-57.
2. *Atharva Veda Sanhita* (of Shonak followers), editor, C.R. Lanman, translation W.D. Hiwtone.
   Harward Oriental Series, 7 and 8, Harward University, 1905. Accompanied by Sayan's commentary, Editor, S. Pandurang, Pandit, Bombay, 1895–1898.
3. *Chhandogya Upanishad,* original, translation, and commentary Emil Senort,

Paris, 1930.
4. *The Thirteen Principle Upanishad,* translation, R.R. Hume, Oxford, 1931.
5. *Vajasneyi Sanhita,* accompanied by commentaries of Uvat and Maheedhar, editor, Vasudev Lakshman Shastri Pansikar, Bombay, 1912.
6. *Tantreeya Sanhita,* editor A. Vebar, translator A.B. Keeth, Harward Oriental Series, 18 and 19, Harward, 1914.
7. *Apstamb Dharamsutra,* editor G. Buhler, Bombay, 1932.
8. *Gautama Dharamsutra,* editor A.S. Stengler, London, 1876, accompanied by commentary of Maskarin, editor L. Shrinivasacharya, Mysore, 1917.
9. *Bodhayan Dharamsutra,* editor E. Hulsh, Lipjig, 1884.
10. *Vashishta Dharamsutra,* editor A.A. Fuhrer, Bombay, 1912.
11. *Apstamb,* translation of sacred text of Gautama, Vashishta and Bodhayan, G. Buhler, Sacred Book of the East, 2 and 14, Oxford, 1879–1882.
12. *Manusmriti,* editor B.N. Mandlik, Bombay, 1886, translator G. Buhler, Sacred Books in the East, 25, Oxford, 1886.
13. *Kautilya's Arthasastra,* editor R. Shama Shastri, Mysore, 1924, translator R. Shama Shastri, Mysore, 1929.
14. *Narad Smriti,* editor-translator, J. Jali, Oxford, 1889.
15. *Yagyavalakya Smriti,* Chaukhamba series, Benaras, 1986.

Buddhistic Scriptures

1. *Anguttar Nikaya,* editor R. Mauris and E. Hardy, Pali Text Society, London, 1885–1900, translation of binding 1, 2 and 5 by F.L. Udvard and 3 and 4 by E.M. Hanar, Pali Text Society London, 1932–1936
2. *Deegh Nikaya,* translator monk Rahul Sankrityayan and monk Jagdish Kashyap, Lucknow, 1979., editor D.W. Rees Davids and J.E. Carpenter, Pali Text Society, London, 1890–1911.
3. *Majjhim Nikaya,* editor V. Trancnor and R. Chamars, Pali Text Society, London, 1888–1896, translation Lord Chamars, Sacred Books of the Buddhists, 1926–1927.
4. *Vinay Patak,* editor H. Olderburg, London, 1879–1883, translation I.B. Harnar 5 part, *Sacred books of the Buddhists,* London, 1938–1952, *Sacred Books of the East,* 13, Oxford, 1879: Sn.F. Max Muller.
5. Jatak accompanied by commentary, editor V. Fasbal, London, 1877–1897, London, 1895–1907.
6. *Buddhcharya,* translator Rahul Sankrityayan.
7. *Sutt Nipat,* translation Dharmanand Koshambi.
8. *Milind Panho,* editor V. Tranknor, London, 1928; translator E.W. Rees Davids, Sacred Books of the East, Oxford, 1890–1894, Hindi translation, monk Jagdish Kashyap.
9. *Saddharampundrik,* editor N. Das, Calcutta, 1952, translator H. Karn, *Sacred Books of the East,* 1, Oxford.
10. *Thergatha Atathhkatha,* accompanied by commentary of Dharampal, editor F.L. Woodward, 2 binding, Pali Text Society, London, 1940–1952.

English Scriptures

1. Angels, F.: *The Origin of the Family, Private Property and the State,* Moscow, 1952.
2. Bose, Ateendra Nath: *Social and Rural Economy of Northern India,* Part 2,

Calcutta, 1945.
3. Dutt, N.K.: *Origin of Growth of Caste in India,* London, 1931.
4. Dasgupta, S.N.: The History of Indian Philosophy, Cambridge, 1922–1955.
5. Dhammratan, monk U.: *Buddha and Caste System,* Lucknow, 1982–1983.
6. Fik, R.: *The Social Organisation in North-East India in Buddha's Time,* Calcutta, 1920.
7. Ghurya, G.S.: *Caste and Class in India,* Bombay, 1930.
8. Hunter, W.W.: *The Imperial Gazetteer of India,* first edition, London, 1881.
9. Hastings, J.: *Encyclopaedia of Religion and Ethics,* Edinbera, 1908–1918.
10. Jha, Vivekanand: *Stages in the History of Untouchables,* I.H.R. 11.
11. Jayasval, K.P.: *Hindu Policy,* Calcutta, 1924, first edition.
12. Kane, P.P.: *History of Dharamshastra,* Part 1, Pune, 1930, part 2, 1941.
13. Keeth, A.V.: *Rigveda Brahmanas,* H.O.S. 25, Cambridge, 1920.
14. Karn, J.H.C.: *Manual of Indian Buddhism,* Stasburg, 1896.
15. Koshambi, D.D.: *An Introduction to the Study of Indian History,* Bombay, 1956.
16. K.P. Jayasval. *Manu and Yagvalakya,* Calcutta, 1930.
17. Karn, H.: *Sacred Books of the East,* Oxford, 1884.
18. Kulluk of Manu.
19. La, B.S.: *A History of Pali Literature,*London, 1933.
20. Majumdar, R.C.: (1) *Corporate Life in Ancient India,* Calcutta, 19; (2) *Vedic Age,* London, 1951.
21. Marx, K. and Angels, F.: (1) *On Religion,* Moscow, 1957; (2) *Selected Correspondence,* Moscow, 1946.
22. Max Muller, F.: *Sacred Books of the East,* Oxford, 1879.
23. Morgan, L.H.: *Ancient Society,* Calcutta.
24. Oldenburg, H.: *Buddha: His Life, His Teachings, His Order,* Calcutta, 1927.
25. Pandeya, G.C.: *Origin of Buddhism.*
26. Rasel, R.V. and Heeralal Raibahadur: *The Tribes and Castes of the Central Provinces of India,* London, 1916.
27. Rockhill, W.: *Life of Buddha and Early History of His Order,* London, 1884.
28. Radhakrishnan, S.: *Indian Philosophy,* Part 1, London, 1920, Part 2, 1948.
29. Ris Davids, T.W.R.: *Dialogues of the Buddha,* London, Part 1, 1899, Part 2, 1910, Part 3, 1921; (2) *Milind Panho,* translation, *Sacred Books of the East,* Oxford, 1890–1894.
30. Ris Davids, Mrs.: (1) *Some of Early Buddhism,* (2) *Buddhism.*
31. Thomson, G.: *Ascillus and Athens,* London, second edition.
32. Wheeler, M.: *The Indus Civilisation,* complete part of Cambridge History of India, Cambridge, 1953.
33. Wheum, I.E.: *Thirteen Principle Upanishad,* Oxford, 1921.

Hindi Scriptures

1. Ambedkar, B.R.: (1) *The Untouchables (Who Were They and How They Became Untouchables),* Delhi, 1948. *Translation Achhoot Kaun or Kaise?* Lucknow, 1989; (2) *Bhagvan Buddha aur Unka Dharam,* Bombay, 1986, translator Bhadant Anand Kosalyayan.
2. Dharamrakshit, Bhikshu: *Bhagvan Budh aur Jati-Bhed,* Lucknow, 1985.
3. Koshambi, Dharmanand: *Bhagvan Buddha: Jeevan aur Darshan,* Allahabad, 1982.

4. Mahasthavir, Bhadant Bodhayan: *Baudh-Charcha Paddhati,* Lucknow, 1979.
5. Pandey, Govindchandra: *Baudh-Dharam ke Vikas ka Itihas,* Hindi Society, Lucknow, 1976.
6. Sharma, Ramsharan: *Shudron ka Pracheen Itihas,* Delhi, 1979.
7. Verma, Jaganmohan: *Buddhdev.*
8. Sankrityayan, Rahul: *Baudh-Darshan,* Allahabad, 1989.
9. *Samkaleen Srajan,* Sanyuktank 7–8 July, Calcutta.
10. *Sanyukt Nikaya,* Pali Text Society.

Bibliography

Adikāram *Early History of Buddhism in Ceylon,* Migoda (Puswella], 1946.

Akanuma : The Comparative Catalogue of Chinese Āgamas and Pāli Nikāyas, Nagoya (Hazinkaku), 1929. Bukkyō-kyotenshiron, Nagoya (Hajinkaku), 1939.

Bāṇa Harṣacarita ed. Parab, 1946 and the TSS edition, ed. Pillai, 1958: translated by Cowell and Thomas, London (RAS), 1897.

Bareau: 'La date du Nirvāṇá JA 1953 27ff. Les premiers conciles bouddhiques, Paris, 1955.

Basham: *History and Doctrines of the Ājīvikas,* London (Luzac), 1951.

Bhartṛhan: Vākyapadīya, kāṇḍa I ed. Cārudeva Śāstrī, Lahore (Ramlal Kapur Trust Soc.) 1934 Raghunātha Sharma, Varanasi (Sarasvatī Bhavana Granthamālā) 1963, II ed. Gaṅgādhara Śāstrī, Benares (Sanskrit Series) 1887, III ed. (1-7) Subramania Iyer, Poona (Deccan College Monograph Series) 1963, and (8-14) ed. Sāmbaśiva Śāstrī and Ravi Varma, TSS 1935 1942 12 2 Vols); I and II trs. Pillal, Delhi, 1971.

Bhāsa. Bhāsanāṭakacakra - Plays Ascribed to Bhāsa ed. Devadhar, Poona (Oriental Series) 1951, translated by Woolner and Sarup. Panjab University Oriental Publications, London, 1930-1 (2 vols.).

Bibliogrophie Bouddhique Paris, Geuthner, later Maisonneuve, in the series Buddhica, 1930 in progress (annual bibliographies beginning with 1928).

Bloch: *Les inscriptions d'Aśoka, Paris,* Institut de Civilisation Indienne (Collection Émile Senart), 1950.

Brāhmaṇas: Śatapatha translated by Eggeling SBE (5 Vols.) reprint Delhi (Motilal Banarsidass), 1963.

Coedès: Les Élats Hindouisés d'Indochine et d'indonésie, Paris, Boccard (Historic du Monde VIII.2), 1948.

Cordier and Lalou: *Catalogue du Fonds Tibétain de la Bibliothèque Nationale,* Paris, 1909-31.

Dasgupta: *Obscure Religious Cults,* Calcutta, Mukhopadhyaya, 2nd ed., 1962.

Edgerton; *Buddhist Hybrid Sanskrit Dictionary,* New Haven, Yale University Press, 1953.

Eggermont: *The Chronology of the Reign of Asoka* Moriya, Leiden (Brill), 1956.

Eliot: *Hinduism and Buddhism,* London, Edward Arnold. 1921(3 vols.) reprinted 1954 (Routledge and Kegan Paul).

Elliot: *The History of India as told by its own Historians,* 2nd ed. Calcutta, 1952 ff.

Frauwallner: *On the Dole... of... Vasubandhu,* SOR, 1951.

Gaurinath Sastri: *The Philosophy of Word and Meaning,* alcutta (Sanskrit College Research Series), 1959.

Guérinot: *La religion Djaīna,* Paris, Geuthner, 926.

Hemacandra: *Pariśiṣṭaparvan in Trisaṣṭiśalakāpuru-ṣacarita,* ed. Jacobi BI 1883-91, 2nd ed. 1932; extracts translated by Hertel, Leipzig, 1908.

Hirakawa; Ritsuzo no Kenkyū, Tokyo (Sankibō Busshorin) 1960 (A Study of the Vinaya- Pitaka).

Hōbōgirin, *Fascicule Annexe, 'Tables du Taishō Issaikyō',* ed. Demiéville, Tokyo, Maison Franco-Japonaise, 1931 (Index to Taishō ed. of Chinese Tripiṭaka).

Jaimin: *Mīmāṃ sa Sūtra,* Kolhāpūra, Śrīmajjagadguru-śaṅkarācāryakaravīrapīṭha, Dhārmikagranthāvali No. 10, 1951.

Kalhana: *Rājataraṅgiṇī* ed. Stein 1892 (reprinted Delhi, Munshi Ram Manohar Lal, 1960) and translated by him in 2 vols., Westminster 1900 (reprinted Delhi, Motilal Banarsidas, 1961).

Kant: *Critique of Pure Reason,* English translation by Meiklejohn, London, Bell, 1890.

Kauṭilya: *Arthaśāstra* ed. Gaṇapati TSS 1924-5 (3 vols.) and Kangle, University of Bombay, 1960, translated by Kangle, University of Bombay, 1963.

Koūhala: *Līlāvaī* ed. Upadhye Bombay, Ṣinghi Jain Series, 1949.

Kunst: *Kamalaśila's Commentary on Śāntarakṣita's Anumanāparīkṣā* . . . . MCB 1947 (Introduction on the bibliography of Tibetan).

Lalou: *Rēpertoire du Tanjur d'après le Catalogue* de P. Cordier, Paris, 1933.

Lamotte: *Histoire du Bouddhisme Indien* Vol. I, Louvain, Muséon, 1958.

Lin Li-kouang: *L'Aide-mémoire de la Vraie Loi*, Paris, AMG, 1949.

Mahābhārata ed. Sukthankar and others, Poona, Bhandarkar Oriental Research Institute, 1933-66; translated by P.C. Roy, Calcutta, 1884.

Mahāvyutpatti ed. Minaev and Mironov BB 1911: Ogiwara, Tokyo 1951; Sakaki, Kyoto, 1916-25.

Majumdar, R.C. : *The Classical Accounts of India,* Calcutta, Mukhopadhyay, 1960. (editor) *The History and Culture of the Indian People,* Bombay, Bhāratīya Vidyā-Bhavan, 1951-77.

Malalasekra: *Dictionary of Pāli Proper Names,* London, Murray, Indian Texts Series, 1937-1938 (2vols.), since reprinted by the PTS, Pāli Literature of Ceylon, London, RAS, 1928.

Matsumoto : Butten no Kenkyū, Tokyo (Heigo Shuppansha), 1914.

Mayeda : A History of the Formation of Original Buddhist Texts, Tokyo (Sankibō Busshorin), 1964.

Nanjio : *A Catalogue of the Buddhist Tripiṭaka* Chinese, Oxford, 1883.

Narain : *The Indo-Greeks,* Oxford, 1957.

Nilakanta : *A History of South India,* London, Oxford University Press, 2nd, ed. 1958. (editor) *A Comprehensive History of India,* Calcutta, Orient Longmans, 1957.

Nyanatiloka : *Guide through the Abhidhamma-Piṭaka,* Colombo, 1938 (since reprinted).

Nyāyasūtra of Akṣapāda ed. And translated by Nanda Lal Ṣinha, Allahabad, Sacred Books of the Hindus, 1930.

Obermiller : *The Doctrine of Prajñā-pāramitā,* Acta O, 1932-33.

Pa-chow : *A Comparative study of the Prātimokṣa,* Santiniketan, Sino-Indian Cultural Society, 1955.

Pargiter : *Ancient Indian Historical Tradition,* reprinted by Motilal Banarsidass, Delhi, 1962.
The Purāṇa Texts of the Dynasties of the Kali Age, Oxford, 1913.

Purāṇa: Viṣṇu ed. Vāsudevācārya, Bombay. Gopāla Nārāyaṇa, 1902; translated by H.H. Wilson, London, 1840,

reprinted Calcụtta, Punthi Pustak, 1961.
Vāyu ed. R. Mitra BI 1888.
Matsya, Ānandāśrama ed. Poona, 1907 (see also Ramacandra Dikshitar, *The Matsya Purāṇa,* a study. Madras, 1925)
Mārkaṇḍeya ed. Banerjea BI 1862, translated by Pargiter BI 1904.
'yugapurāṇa (from gārgisaṃhita) ed. Mankad, vallabhvidyanogar (Charutor Prakashan), 1951.
Purātanaprobandhasmgraha ed. Jina Vijaya Muni, Singhi Jain Series, Calcutta, 1936.
Przyluski : *La légende de pempereur Aṣoka,* Paris AMS 1923. LE CONCILE DE Rājagṛha Paris (Geuthner), 1926.
Rāhula : *History of Buddhism in Ceylon,* Colombo (Gunasena),1956.
Rājaśekhara : *Kāvyamimāṃsā* ed. Dalal and R.A. Sastry GOS 3rd ed., 1934.
Ray : *History of Chemistry in Ancient and Medieval India,* Calcutta 1956 (includes text of Rasaratnākara).
N. Ray : *Theravāda Buddhism in Burma,* Calcutta (University), 1946.
Ṛgvedasaṃhitā ed. Anfrecht, Bonn, 2nd ed. 1877 (2 vols., recently reprinted) also ed. Max Müller, London, W.H. Allen 1849-74 (6 Vols.) with Sāyaṇa's commentary and Rajwade, Poona, Tilak University, 1933-51 (5 vols.), translated by Griffith, Benaras 1889-92 (4 vols.), reprinted in 2 vols. Chowkhamba Sanskrit Studies, 1963 (this appears to be the most accurate translation, surpassing Geldner's more recent version).
Roerich : *Biography at Dharmasvāṃin,* Patna, Jayaswal Research Institute Historical Research Series, 1959.
Rosenberg : *Diie Problemder buddhistischen Philosophie* MKB 1924 (translated from the Russian ed. df 1918, Petrograd). An introduction to the study of Buddhism from Chinese and Japanese Sources Tokyo, 1917.
Śabara : *Bhāṣya on Mimāṃsā Sūtra,* BI 1873 ff. translated by Ganganattha Jha Gos 1933-6 (3 vols).
Sāṅkṛtyāyana: 'Sanskrit Palm-Leaf MSS. In Tibet' *JBORS* Vol. XXI, 1935. 'Second Search of Sanskrit Palm-Leaf MSS. in Tibet' *JBORS* Vol. XXIII, 1937. 'Search for Sanskrit MSS. in Tibet *JBORS* Vol. XXIV, 1938

Sarvadarśanasaṃgraha (Mādhava) ed. Iśvaracandr Bl 1858, translated by Cowell and Gough, London, Trübne, 4th Ed. 1904 (repr. 1914).

Schubring Die Lehra der Fainas, Berlin and Leipzing, 1935; English version, the Doctrine of the Fains, Delhi, Motilal Banarsidass, 1962.

R.S. Sharma : *Aspects of Political Ideas and Institutions in Ancient India,* Delhi, Motilal Banarsidass, 1959. Indian Feidalism, Calcutta (University), 1965.

Soothill and Hodous : *Dictionary of Chinese Buddhist Terms,* London, Kegan Paul, 1937.

Stcherbatsky : `*The Central Conception of Buddhism London* RAS 1923. *Conception of Buddhist Nirvāṇa* Leningrad Academy of Sciences of the U.S.S.R., 1927. *Buddhist Logic* (2 vols.) BB Vol. I, 1932. Vol. II, 1930, reprinted I-IR 1958. 'Die drei Richtungen in der Philosophie des Buddhismus' RO, 1934. 'Erkenntnistheorie und Logik nach der spateren Buddhisten' zeitschrift für Buddhismus (München-Neubiberg) 1922 ff. (translated from Teoriya poznaniya I logika..., St. Petersburg, 1909, by O. Strauss; there is also a French version, Paris, Geuthner, 1926, AMG; the versions all differ slightly).

Sūryasiddhānta translated by Burgess, reprinted with additions, Calcutta University, 1935.

Takakusu : *The Essentials of Buddhist Philosophy,* 3rd ed., Honolulu, 1956.

'The Sarvāstivādin Abhidharma Books' JPTS, 1905.

Tatsuyama : *Indo Bukyō-shi,* 8th Impression, revised, 1961.

Upaniṣads : Chāndagya ed. Kāsīnātha, Ānandāśrama Series, Punya, 1890.

The Principal Upaniṣads ed. and translated by Radhakrishnan, London, Allen and Unwin, 1953.

Die Philosophen der Upanishaden ruben, Bern Francke, 1947.

Vācaspatimiśra : Nyāyavārttikatātparyaṭikā ed. Rājeśvara Benares, Chowkhamba (Kāśisāmskrtasīrij = Haridāsa saṃskṛtagranthamālā) 1925-26.

Vālmīki: Rāmāyaṇa ed Mudholkara, Gujarati Printing Press, Bombay 1912-20 (7 Vols.).

Waldschmidt, Claviter and Sander-Holzmann : *Sanskrithand-schriften aus den Turfanfunden,* Wiesbaden (Steiner) 1965 in progress.

Warder, A.K.: *Introduction to Pali* PTS 2nd edn. 1974. Pali metre pts 1967.

Outline of Indian Philosophy, Delhi (Motilal Banarsidass), 1971.

An Introduction to Indian Historiography Bombay/New York (Popular Prakashan/ Humanities Press) 1972.

Indian Kāvya Literature Delhi (Motilal Banarsidass) Vol. I, 1972, Vol. II, 1974, Vol. III, 1977; Vol. IV in press, other volumes in preparation.

'On the Relationships between Early Buddhism and other Early Contemporary Systems, BSOAS, 1956.

'The Date of Bhamaha', *Journal of Oriental Research,* Madras 1958.

'Desiderata in Indian Historiography', *Journal of the Economic and Social History of the Orient,* Leiden, 1959.

The Mātikā, in Mohavichedani PTS 1961.

'The Pali Canon and its Commentaries as a Historical Record', in *Historions of India, Pakistan and Ceylon* (ed. Philips), London (Oxford University Press) 1961. "The Earliest Indian Logic', in *Trudi Dvadsat Pyatogo Mejdunarodnogo Kongressa Vostokovedov,* Moscow (Izdatelstvo Vostochnio Literaturi), 1963, Vol. IV.

"The possible Dates of Pārśva, Vasumitra (ii), Caraka and Mātṛceṭa', in *The Date of Kaniṣka* (ed. A.L. Bassham), Leiden (Brill), 1968.

'The Concept', *Journal of Indian Philosophy,* Dordrecht (Raide), 1971.

'Dharmas and Data', *Journal of Indian Philosophy,* Dordrecht (Reide), 1971.

'Is Nāgārjuna a Mahāyānist?', in *Two Truth in Buddhism and Vedānta* (ed. Sprrung), Dordrecht (Reide), 1973.

'Feudalism and Mahāyāna Buddhism', in *India Societ: Historical Probings* (ed. R.S. Sharma), New Delhi (Peoples Publishing House, 1974.

'Objects', *Journal of Indian Philosophy,* Dordrecht, 1975.

'The Ghosts at Nirvāṇa', *Buddhist Studies,* Vol VIII, Hamamatsu (International Buddhist Association), 1979.

Willetts, William Chinese Art, London (Penguin Books) 2 Vols., 1958 (the new edition as Foundations of Chinese Art is inferior, being abridged and eliminating much of the discussions most important for art history, though it is more richly illustrated, Thames and Hudson, 1965).

Woodward and others (ed. Hare, Norman and Warder) : Pāli Tipiṭaka Concordance PTS 1952.

Zaehner *Hinduism,* London (Oxford University Press 1962.

Zurcher : *The Buddhist Conquest of China,* Leiden (Brill), 2 vols., 1959.

Miscellaneous Bibliography (In Order to Non-alphabetical)

Mc Crindle, *Ancient India as Described by Ptolemy,* Calcutta, 1927.

Cunnfngham (A), *The Ancient Geography of India,* London, 1871; Calcutta, 1924

Dey, N.L., *The Geographical Dictionary of Ancient and Mediaeval India,* Calcutta, 1899, 2nd ed., Cal. Orient. Series, 21,1927.

Przyluski, J., *Noms de villes indiennes dans la Géographie de Ptolémée, Soc. Ling.,* Paris, 27, fasc. 3, No. 83.

Sion, J., *Asie des Moussons,* Paris.

Baines, A., *Ethnography,* VIII, 1912.

Census of India, 1901 and 1911.

Grierson, G.A., *Linguistic Survey of India,* Calcutta, 1903, etc.

Meillet, A., and others. *Les Langues du monde, Paris,* 1924.

Risley, H.H., The People of India, 2nd Ed., London, 1915.

Ruggeri, G., *Outline of a Systematic Anthropology of Asia,* Calcutta,1921.

Konow, S., Munda, XXXVII.

Lèvi, S., Préaryen et prédravidien July, 1923, XV.

Przyluski, J., Les Udumbara, 1926, XV - in XXXVIII.

Rivet, P., *Le Groupe océanien, Soc. Ling., Paris,* 27, fasc. 3, No. 83.

Schmidt, W., *Les Peuples mōn-khmers,* 1907, X.

Skeat and Blagden *Pagan Races of Malay Peninsula,* 1906.

Uxbond, F.A., *Wanderings. The Munda Peoples,* a Link between Maori and Magyar, London.

Bloch, J., XXXVIII.

Brown, G.W., *The Possibility of a Connection between Mitanni and the Dravidian Languages,* 1930, XVI.

Caldwell, R., *A Comparative Grammar of the Dravidian or South-Indian Family of Languages,* 3rd ed., London, 1913.

Kennedy, J, *The Early Commerce of Babylon with India,* 1898, XXI.

Konow, S., Dravidian, XXXVII.

Brunnhofer, H., Urgeschichte der Arier in Vrder-und Centralasien, Leipzig, 1893. - Arische Urzeit, Berne, 1910.

Carnoy, A., Les Indo-Européens, Brussels and Louvain, 1921.

Dutt, N.K., The Aryanisation of India, Calcutta, 1925.

Feist, S., Indogermanen und Germanen, Halle, 1914.

Gauthiot, R., Essai de grammaire sogdienne, Paris, 1914-23.

Grierson, G., and Konow, S., *Indo-Aryan Family,* XXXVII.

Keith, A.B., *Early History of the Indo-Iranians,* Poona, 1917.

Konow, S., *The Aryan Gods of the Mitani People.* Oslo, 1921.

La Vallèe-Poussin, L. De, Indo-Européens et Indo-Iraniens, Paris, 1924.

Lèvi, S., Le Tokharien B, langue de Koutcha, 1913, XV.

Meillet, A., Introduction a l'étude comparée des langues indo-européennes, 5th ed., Paris, 1922.

-Les Dialectes indo-européennes, 1908. "Le Tokharien," in Indogermanisches Jahrb., 1914.

Courtillier, G., *Les Anciennes civilisations de l'Inde,* Paris, 1930.

Grousset, R., *Hist. De* l'Extrème-Orient, Paris, 1929.

Pargiter, F.E., *Ancient Indian Historical Tradition,* Oxford, 1922.

Rapșon, E.J., *Ancient India,* Cambridge, 1914.

— and others, *The Cambridge History of India,* Vol. I, Ancient India, Cambridge, 1922.

Smith, V.A., *The Early History of India,* 3rd ed., Oxford, 1914; 4th ed. 1924. The Oxford History of India, Oxford 1919.

Banerji, A., *Asura India,* Patna, 1926.

Maitra, P., *Prehistoric India,* Calcutta, 1923.

Oldenberg, H., *Zur Geschichte des indischen kastenwesens,* XXIX, Vol II, 267.

Senart, E., *Les Castes dans l'Inde,* new ed, Paris, 1927.

Shama Shastri, *Evolution of Caste,* Madras, 1916.

Kautplya, Arthacatra translated into English by Shama Shastri, i-iv, Mysore, 1908; v-xv, 1909-1910, XIII.

Alteker, A.S., *A History of Village Communities in Western India,* Oxford, 1927.
Bandyopadhyaya, N.C., *Development of Hindu Polity and Political Theories,* Calcutta, 1927.
Dumont, P.E., *L'Acvamedha,* Paris, 1927.
Foy, W., *Die konigliche Gewalt nacch den Dharmastûtren,* Leipzip, 1895.
Jacobi, J., "Unber die Echtheit des Kautilya," in *Sitz.* d.k.preuss. Ak.d.Wis., 1912.
Keith, A.B., The Authenticity of the Kautiliya, 1916, XXI.
Sarkar, B.K., *The Political Institutions and Theories of the Hindus,* Leipzig, 1922.
Mackenzie, J., Hindu Ethics, Oxford, 1922.
Viassom-Oursel, P., Esquisse d'une histoire de to philosophie indienne, Paris, 1923.
- La philosophie comparee, Paris, 1923. (Comparative philosophy, London, 1923).
Oltramare, P., Hist. Des idées théosophiques dans l'Inde. i. Brahmanisms. ii. Bouddhisme, Paris, 1906 and 1923 (Musee Guimet).
Radhakrishnan, S., *Indian Philosophy,* i, 1923; ii, 1927; London.
Satrauss, O., *Indische philosophie,* Munich, 1925.
Bergaigne, A., La Religion védique, Paris, 1878-1883.
Geldner, K., Glossar, 1907-9.
Grassmann, H., *Wörterbuch zum Rigveda,* 1872.
Hillebrandt, A., *Vedische Mythologic,* Breslau, 1891-1902.
Keith, A.B., *Indian Mythology,* Boston, 1917.
MacDonell, A., *Vedic Mythology,* 1897, VIII.
Oldenbrerg, H., *Die Religion des Veda,* Berlin, 1894.
Renou, L., *Les Máitres de la philosophie vêdique,* Paris, 1928.
Lèvi, S., *La Doctrine du sacrifice dans les Bráhmanas,* Paris, 1898.
Dldenberg, H., *Die Weltanschauung der Bráhmana*-Texte, Göttingen, 1919.
Deussen, P., *Allgemeine Geschte der Philosophic,* Leipzig, 1899.
— *Sechzig Upannishads des Veda,* 3rd ed., Leipzig, 1921.
Gouch, A., *Philosophy of the Upanishads,* London, 1882-4.
Hume, R.E., *The Thirteen Principal Upanishads,* trans., Oxford, 1921 (2nd ed., 1931).

Keith, A.B., The Religion and Philosophy of the Veda and Upanishads, Cambridge, Mass, 1925.

Oldenberg, H., *Die Lehre der Upanishaden und die Anfange des Buddhismus,* Göttingen, 1915.

Senar, E., *Chándogya Up.,* French trans., Paris, 1930.

Winternitz, M., CCLXXVIII, II. B. 2. Hälfte, die heiligen Texte der Jains, Leipzip, 1920.

Guèrinot, A., *La Religion djaīna* Paris, 1926.

Jacobi, H., *Jaina-sutras* (Sac. Books of the East, Vols. xxi, xiv), Oxford, 1884-1895.

Winternitz, M., CCLXXVIII, J. Halifte, Die Buddhistische Litt., Leipzing, 1913 (Index and suppl. In 2. Halfte).

Burnouf, E., *Introd. a l'hist. Du Bouddhisme indien,* Paris, 1844,1876.

Keith, A.B., Buddhist philosophy in India and Ceyon, Oxford, 1923.

Kern, H., *Manual of Indian Buddhism,* 1896, VIII.

La Vallèe-Poussin, L. de, *Bouddhisme,* Paris, 1909.

— La Morale bouddhique, Paris, 1927.

— *The Way to Nirvána,* Cambridge, 1917.

— *Nirvána Paris,* 1925.

— *Le Dogme et la philosophie du bouddhisme,* Paris, 1930.

Lèvi, S., *Asanga, le Máhaydána-sútrálamkára,* ed. and trans. Paris (Bibl. De l' Ec. Des H. Et.)

- Matériaux pour l'étude du systéme vijńaptimátra, *ibid.,* 1932.

Ober, Miller E., *Abhissamayálamkára-prajńappāramitá, upaddeca-cdstra,* trans. (with T. Scherbatski) (Bibl. Buddhica, 23, Fasc. 1), Leningrad, 1929.

— *The Jexelry of Scripture,* by Bu-ston tran. From the Tibetan, with introd., by T. Scherbatski, Heidelberg, 1931.

— *The Sublime Science of Great Vehicle to Salvation* (Maháyánottaratantra), Acta Orientalia, Vol. IX, 1931.

— *The Doctrine of Prajńa -pára mitá as exposed in the Abhisamayālamkara of Maitreya, ibid.* Vol. IX, 1932.

Przyluski, J., *La Légende de Vempereur Asoka,* Paris, 1923.

— *Le Concile de Rájagrha,* Paris, 1926-1928.

— *La Bouddhisme,* Paris, 1932.

Rosenberg, O., *Die Probleme der Buddhistischen Philosophic,* German trans., Heidelberg, 1924.

Scherbatski, T., *L'Épistémologie et la logique chez les Bouddhistes taridfs,* French trans. by I. De Manziarly and P. Masson-Oursel, Paris, 1926.

— *The Central Conception of Buddhism* (Dharma), London, Roy. As. Soc., 1923.

— *The Conception of Buddhist Nirvāṇa* Leningrad. Acad of Sci., 1927.

— *Buddhist Logic* Leningrad, 1932.

Tucci, G, *Buddhist Logicbefore Dinnâga,* xxi, 1929, 651.

— *Pre-Dinnâga Buddhist Texts on Logic from Chinese Sources,* Baroda, 1929.

Tuneld, E., *Recherches sur la valeur des traditions boddhiques palie et non pâlie,* Lund, 1915.

UI, H., *Studies in Indian Philosophy* (in Japanese).

Yamakami, *Systems of Buddhistic Thought,* Calcutta, 1912.

Pali Text Society (many publications), London, 1882.

Abegg, E., *Der Messiasglaube in Indian and Iran,* Berlin, 1928.

Avalon, A., Sir John Woodroffe, *Tantrik Texts,* Calcutta and London, various dates. *The World as Power,* Madras, 1922-9.

Bhandarkar, R.G., *Vaisnavism, Caivism and Minor Religious Systems,* 1913, viii.

Glasenapp, H., Von, *Der Hinduismus,* Munich, 1922.

— Madhva's philosophie des Vishnu—Glaubens, Bonn. 1923.

Jacobi, H., *Die Entwicklung der Gottesidee bei den Indern,* Bonn, 1923.

Kirfel, W., *Das Purana Pañcalaksāna,* 1927.

Macnidol, N., *Psalms of Māratha Saints,* Oxford, 1919.

Otto, R., Vishnu-Náráyana

— *Siddhánta des Rámánuja,* Jena, 1917.

— *Dipiká des Nivaśa,* Tübingen, 1916.

Radhakrishnan, S., *L'Hindouisme et la vie,* French trans. By P. Masson-Oursel, Paris, 1930.

Schomerus, H.W., *Der Caiva-Siddhánṭa, Leipzig,* 1912.

- Sivaitische Heiligenlegenden, Jena.

Schrader, O., *Introd. to the Páñcarátra and the Ahirbudhnya* Samhita, Adyar, 1916.

Index